PLURALISING ACTORS AND NORMS IN HUMAN RIGHTS TREATIES

This book seeks to challenge the classical yet still-dominant paradigm of international law, where 'states', as unitary and monolithic entities, are treated as the sole subjects of legal observation and regulation. It proposes the 'separation of powers in a globalised democratic society' model as a novel theoretical framework, where both actors and norms are pluralised beyond a unitary and monolithic 'state' and international law as norms of, by, and for 'states'.

Under this model, each type of state organ – national courts, parliaments, administrative organs, and national human rights institutions – bears distinct 'duties', independently from the obligations owed by the 'state' as a whole, and interacts with human rights treaty organs – the European Court of Human Rights, the Inter-American Court of Human Rights, and UN human rights treaty bodies – in a principled manner. The 'duties' of state organs and their autonomous status in human rights treaties are anchored in the cooperative interactions between 'inter-state organ norms' and human rights treaties under global legal pluralism.

Applying this model, this book analyses and evaluates the current practices of human rights treaty organs and proposes reforms where necessary.

Volume 101 in the series Studies in International Law

Studies in International Law

Recent titles in this series

Judicial Decisions in International Law Argumentation:
Between Entrapment and Creativity
Letizia Lo Giacco

South-South Migrations and the Law from Below:
Case Studies on China and Nigeria
Oreva Olakpe

Territorial Status in International Law
Jure Vidmar

Marine Bioprospecting, Biodiversity and Novel Uses of Ocean Resources:
New Approaches in International Law
Edited by Niels Krabbe and David Langlet

The Standard of Review Before the International Court of Justice:
Between Principle and Pragmatism
Felix Fouchard

Global Lawmaking and Social Change: The Varieties of Customary
International Law
Gregor Novak

The Effectiveness of the Inter-American Court of Human Rights:
The Case of Indigenous Territorial Rights
Gabriela CB Navarro

Individuals in International Humanitarian Law: A Historical Analysis
Sarina Landefeld

The Pathology of Plenty: Natural Resources in International Law
Lys Kulamadayil

The United Nations Security Council and the Authorisation of Force:
Form, Character and Nature
Marko Svicevic

Protecting the Right to Leave in an Era of Externalised Migration Control
Emilie McDonnell

Pluralising Actors and Norms in Human Rights Treaties:
Beyond Monolithic States
Hinako Takata

For a complete list of titles in this series
see www.bloomsbury.com/uk/series/studies-in-international-law/

Pluralising Actors and Norms in Human Rights Treaties

Beyond Monolithic States

Hinako Takata

• HART •
OXFORD • LONDON • NEW YORK • NEW DELHI • SYDNEY

HART PUBLISHING

Bloomsbury Publishing Plc

Kemp House, Chawley Park, Cumnor Hill, Oxford, OX2 9PH, UK

1385 Broadway, New York, NY 10018, USA

Bloomsbury Publishing Ireland Limited, 29 Earlsfort Terrace, Dublin 2, D02 AY28, Ireland

HART PUBLISHING, the Hart/Stag logo, BLOOMSBURY and the Diana logo are trademarks of Bloomsbury Publishing Plc

First published in Great Britain 2026

A catalogue record for this book is available from the British Library.

A catalogue record for this book is available from the Library of Congress.

ISBN: HB: 978-1-50998-407-7
ePDF: 978-1-50998-409-1
ePub: 978-1-50998-408-4

Typeset by Compuscript Ltd, Shannon

To my family

Preface

My journey that led to this book began when I enrolled in the Graduate School of Law at Kyoto University, Japan, in 2014. I am deeply grateful for the exceptionally supportive and stimulating environment I experienced during my time at Kyoto University. I am especially grateful to my supervisor, Professor Shotaro Hamamoto, for providing me with invaluable opportunities and guidance. I am also grateful to Professors Masahiko Asada and Hironobu Sakai for their insightful courses on international law. My time at Kyoto University was further enriched by my colleagues, especially Tomoko Yamashita, Shiho Sugiki, Megumi Ochi, Yohei Okada, Minghao Yang, Miharu Hirano, Rieko Kitamura, Kento Nisugi, Haruka Ito, Kie Abe, Oumou Salamata Bah, Nico Buitendag, Lina Shen, Zhongyu Li, Manaka Murakado, Gensaku Maeda and Keiichiro Kawai. Conversations over coffee breaks and meals with them allowed me to reflect critically on my research and helped shape my identity as a researcher.

The Kyoto Study Group on International Law, which holds weekly meetings at Kyoto University, played a vital role in my intellectual development. Here, I benefited from presenting my research regularly and being continually exposed to cutting-edge discussions on a wide range of international law topics. In these meetings, I was able to interact with esteemed researchers and practitioners, including Professors Shigeru Kozai, Nisuke Ando, Takane Sugihara, Shigeki Sakamoto, Yasuhiro Shigeta, Akiho Shibata, Mari Takeuchi, Takuhei Yamada, Dai Tamada, Kentaro Wani and Machiko Kanetake. Their scholarship and feedback have significantly enriched my work.

Since 2022, I have been serving as an Associate Professor at the Osaka School of International Public Policy, Osaka University, where I am fortunate to be surrounded by dedicated and thoughtful colleagues, supportive staff and motivated students. I also extend my gratitude to colleagues from various research communities in Japan, particularly those focused on international human rights law, constitutional law and global constitutionalism, especially Professors Kaoru Obata, Takao Suami, Akiko Ejima, Hajime Yamamoto, Koji Teraya, Masaaki Saito, Tamitomo Saito, Hiromichi Matsuda, Yota Negishi, Yusuke Kaide, Kanaho Imaoka, Yin-Wen Wang and Akinaga Yoshida. I am also thankful to Professors Kimio Yakushiji, Yuji Iwasawa, Shuichi Furuya, Hiroko Akizuki, Mikiko Otani, Keiko Ko and Naoko Maeda, who are former or current members of UN human rights treaty bodies and whose insights helped me develop a concrete understanding of the actual practices of these bodies. Needless to say, any errors remain my own.

I have been fortunate to present parts of this research at various seminars and workshops, from which I received invaluable feedback. These included weekly meetings of the Kyoto Study Group on International Law; the Seoul-Kyoto Joint Student Seminar in International Law (2014 and 2016); the PKUSTL-Kyoto Joint Seminar on International Law (2015); the CUHK-Kyoto Joint Workshop in International Law (2016, 2017 and 2018); the Seminar on Domestic Compliance with International Human Rights and Criminal Tribunals with Professor Courtney Hillbrecht (2016); the NCCU-Kyoto Joint Seminar in International Law (2017 and 2019); the Kyoto Seminar Series on International Law with Professors David Kretzmer and Ruth Halperin-Kaddari (2019); the 12th Annual Conference of the Japan Chapter of Asian Society of International Law (2021); Symposium: The Principle of Equality/Non-discrimination: Seeking for Resilience and Sustainability of Human Rights in an Unstable World (2024); French-Japanese Seminar: Contemporary Limitations to the Development of Human Rights Law (2025); and the Japan-Korea Young International Lawyers' Workshop (2025). I extend my heartfelt thanks to the organisers and participants of each of these events.

Lastly, I would like to express my deepest gratitude to my family. My father, mother and brother have always been pillars of support, encouraging my aspirations and dreams. I have the utmost respect for and trust in my husband, Takuma Naka – not only as my life partner but also as a researcher. My son, Amane, fills my world with light and wonder, reminds me of the joys of discovery and strengthens my resolve to contribute to a better world for future generations. I eagerly look forward to welcoming the birth of a new family member, Haruse, very soon.

Hinako Takata
April 2025

Acknowledgements

THIS BOOK IS partly based on my previously published articles. I am grateful to the reviewers and editors of the journals in which these articles appeared:

- 'NHRIs as Autonomous Human Rights Treaty Actors: Normative Analysis of the Increasing Roles of NHRIs in UN Human Rights Treaties' (2021) 24 *Max Planck Yearbook of United Nations Law* 170.
- 'Reconstructing the Roles of Human Rights Treaty Organs under the "Two-Tiered Bounded Deliberative Democracy" Theory' (2022) 22 *Human Rights Law Review* 1.
- 'How are the Paris Principles on NHRIs Interpreted? Towards a Clear, Transparent, and Consistent Interpretative Framework' (2022) 40 *Nordic Journal of Human Rights* 285.
- 'Human Rights, Treaty Bodies, General Comments/Recommendations' (2023) in A Peters (ed), *Max Planck Encyclopedias of International Law* (Oxford University Press online edition) (co-authored with S Hamamoto).
- 'Separation of Powers in a Globalized Democratic Society: Theorizing the Human Rights Treaty Organs' Interactions with Various State Organs' (2024) 13 *Global Constitutionalism* 458.
- 'Dissecting Stakeholder Participation in UN Human Rights Treaty Body Activities with Normative and Empirical Approaches: A Comparison of NGO and NHRI Participation' (2024) 25 *German Law Journal* 237.
- 'Jinken jouyaku niokeru kobetsu no kokka kikan no ichizuke (1) [The Autonomous Status of State Organs in International Human Rights Treaties (1)]' (2020) 188(2) *Kyoto Law Review* 37 (in Japanese).
- 'Jinken jouyaku niokeru kobetsu no kokka kikan no ichizuke (2)' (2020) 188(3) *Kyoto Law Review* 123 (in Japanese).
- 'Jinken jouyaku niokeru kobetsu no kokka kikan no ichizuke (3)' (2021) 189(2) *Kyoto Law Review* 53 (in Japanese).
- 'Jinken jouyaku niokeru kobetsu no kokka kikan no ichizuke (4)' (2021) 189(5) *Kyoto Law Review* 60 (in Japanese).
- 'Jinken jouyaku niokeru kobetsu no kokka kikan no ichizuke (5)' (2021) 189(6) *Kyoto Law Review* 56 (in Japanese).
- 'Jinken jouyaku niokeru kobetsu no kokka kikan no ichizuke (6)' (2021) 190(1) *Kyoto Law Review* 67 (in Japanese).

- 'Jinken jouyaku no jitsugen ni okeru gikai no yakuwari [The Roles of Parliaments in the Realisation of Human Rights Treaties]' (2022) 94(4) *Houritsu jihou* 58 (in Japanese).
- 'Jinken jouyaku niokeru jouyaku toujikoku no touchirinen-taisei no tayousei toiu nandai [Challenges Faced by Human Rights Treaties in Addressing the Diversity of Political Systems among Member States]' (2023) 13 *Kenpou kenkyu* 55 (in Japanese).

I would also like to acknowledge that this work was supported by JSPS KAKENHI Grant Numbers 22K13291, 23H00035, 23H00037, 25K00580 and 25K00583, and the Sumisei Woman Researcher Encouragement Prize grant programme.

This book is substantially based on research conducted up to March 2023, with literature and materials updated through March 2025. All online sources cited in this book were last accessed on 31 March 2025.

Contents

List of Abbreviations

These terms are defined in full and abbreviated only in their first appearance in the book, following which only the abbreviations are used. However, relatively less well-known terms among these are defined again in full and abbreviated the first time these appear in each new chapter, following which only the abbreviations are used.

ACHR	American Convention on Human Rights
AfCtHPR	African Court on Human and Peoples' Rights
AJIL	*American Journal of International Law*
CDDH	Steering Committee on Human Rights of the Committee of Ministers
CEDAW	Committee on the Elimination of Discrimination against Women
CERD	Committee on the Elimination of Racial Discrimination
CESCR	Committee on Economic, Social and Cultural Rights
CIJC	Conferencia Iberoamericana de Justicia Constitucional
CoM	Committee of Ministers
CRPD	Committee on the Rights of Persons with Disabilities
CRC	Committee on the Rights of the Child
DIHR	Danish Institute for Human Rights
ECHR	European Convention on Human Rights
ECtHR	European Court of Human Rights
EJIL	*European Journal of International Law*
ENNHRI	European Network of National Human Rights Institutions
EU	European Union
GANHRI	Global Alliance of National Human Rights Institutions
GIHR	German Institute for Human Rights
HRC	United Nations Human Rights Committee
HRLJ	*Human Rights Law Journal*
HRLR	*Human Rights Law Review*
IACmHR	Inter-American Commission on Human Rights

IACtHR	Inter-American Court of Human Rights
ICC	International Coordinating Committee of National Institutions for the Promotion and Protection of Human Rights
ICCPR	International Covenant on Civil and Political Rights
ICESCR	International Covenant on Economic, Social, and Cultural Rights
ICJ	International Court of Justice
ICLQ	*International and Comparative Law Quarterly*
I-CON	*International Journal of Constitutional Law*
IHROBH	Institution of Human Rights Ombudsmen of Bosnia and Herzegovina
IJHR	*International Journal of Human Rights*
ILA	International Law Association
ILC	International Law Commission
ILO	International Labour Organization
IPU	Inter-Parliamentary Union
NHRI	National human rights institution
NGO	Non-governmental organisation
NJHR	*Nordic Journal of Human Rights*
OAS	Organization of American States
OHCHR	Office of the United Nations High Commissioner for Human Rights
PACE	Parliamentary Assembly of the Council of Europe
PAM	Parliamentary Assembly of the Mediterranean
SCA	Sub-Committee on Accreditation
SUHAKAM	National Human Rights Commission of Malaysia
UDHR	Universal Declaration of Human Rights
UN	United Nations
VCLT	Vienna Convention on the Law of Treaties (1969)
WCCJ	World Conference on Constitutional Justice

Table of Cases, Treaties, Legislation and Other Official Documents

Cases

Permanent Court of International Justice

International Court of Justice

UN Human Rights Committee

Other UN Human Rights Treaty Bodies

European Court of Human Rights

Judgments

Advisory Opinions

Inter-American Court of Human Rights

Judgments

Orders and Resolutions

Advisory Opinions

Inter-American Commission on Human Rights

National Courts

Argentina

Australia

Chile

Costa Rica

Dominican Republic

Ecuador

Germany

Guatemala

Kyrgyzstan

Mexico

Peru

Spain

Switzerland

UK

US

Treaties

Legislation

Argentina

Cameroon

Colombia

Czech Republic

Former Yugoslav Republic of Macedonia

France

Italy

Lithuania

Peru

Ukraine

UK

Other Official Documents

United Nations

General Assembly

Commission on Human Rights

Human Rights Council

Office of the UN High Commissioner for Human Rights

UN Human Rights Committee

General Comments

Reports on Sessions

Concluding Observations

Papers and Guidelines

Others

Other UN Human Rights Treaty Bodies

CEDAW

CERD

CRC

International Law Commission

Other UN Documents

Council of Europe

Committee of Ministers

Parliamentary Assembly

PACE Resolutions

Other PACE Documents

European Court of Human Rights

Steering Committee for Human Rights

High Level Conferences

Other Council of Europe Documents

Organization of American States

Global Alliance of National Human Rights Institutions

SCA Reports

Other GANHRI Documents

Inter-Parliamentary Union

National Documents

Australia

Japan

New Zealand

Switzerland

UK

Others

1

Introduction

THIS BOOK SEEKS to challenge the classical yet still-dominant paradigm of international law, where 'states', as unitary and monolithic entities, are treated as the sole subjects of legal observation and regulation. It aims to offer a new paradigm for understanding and guiding recent human rights law practices, where both actors and norms are pluralised beyond a unitary and monolithic 'state' and international law as norms of, by and for 'states'. It argues that each type of state organ – national courts, parliaments, administrative organs and national human rights institutions (NHRIs) – bears different 'duties', independently from the obligations owed by the 'state' as a whole, and interacts with regional human rights courts and United Nations (UN) human rights treaty bodies[1] (both hereinafter referred to as 'human rights treaty organs' or 'treaty organs') in a principled manner under the 'separation of powers in a globalised democratic society' model. In this model, the 'duties' of state organs and their autonomous status in human rights treaties are anchored in the cooperative interactions between 'inter-state organ norms' on human rights and human rights treaties under global legal pluralism. This book uses the model to analyse and evaluate the current practices of human rights treaty organs and propose reforms where necessary.

To present this argument systematically, the introductory chapter undertakes several tasks. First, it outlines the background leading to the research question (section 1.1), addressing: how and why the traditional paradigm of international law conceptualises 'states' as unitary and monolithic legal entities (section 1.1.1); how and why human rights treaty organs and scholarship have increasingly promoted the roles of individual state organs and their interactions with treaty organs – phenomena this book comprehensively labels as 'disaggregation of a state' (section 1.1.2); and how earlier studies have engaged in the theorisation of the 'disaggregation of a state' and where

[1] The phrase 'UN human rights treaties' in this book refers to the nine core international human rights treaties, and the phrase 'UN human rights treaty bodies' refers to the monitoring bodies established under those treaties: the Committee on the Elimination of Racial Discrimination (CERD), the Committee on Economic, Social and Cultural Rights (CESCR), the Human Rights Committee (HRC), the Committee on the Elimination of Discrimination against Women (CEDAW), the Committee against Torture (CAT), the Committee on the Rights of the Child (CRC), the Committee on Migrant Workers (CMW), the Committee on the Rights of Persons with Disabilities (CRPD) and the Committee on Enforced Disappearances (CED).

gaps remain (section 1.1.3). Second, it presents the objectives and structure of the book, and explains its intended theoretical and practical contributions (section 1.2). Third, it sets out the methodology and scope of the study (section 1.3). Finally, it introduces the book's comparative approach, which examines the UN human rights treaty systems (especially the International Covenant on Civil and Political Rights (ICCPR)),[2] the European Convention on Human Rights (ECHR)[3] and the American Convention on Human Rights (ACHR).[4] To support this comparative method, the chapter offers a preliminary discussion of the comparability of these three systems (section 1.4).

1.1. FRAMING THE QUESTION

1.1.1. 'States' as Unitary and Monolithic Legal Entitles in Classical International Law

International law has traditionally been defined as comprising rules of law that govern relationships between states.[5] There, 'states' were considered unitary and monolithic legal entities represented by the executive, typically heads of state or government and ministers for foreign affairs[6] on the international plane.[7] Individual state organs comprising the state, such as domestic courts, parliaments, various administrative organs and NHRIs,[8] were given no autonomous status in international law scholarship. While their important roles in the implementation of international law were widely recognised, such roles were overlooked, from a legal perspective, as merely *factual*. Accordingly, international human rights law studies have focused on identifying the contents and nature of the obligations of states as unitary and monolithic entities under human rights treaties and the relationship between human rights treaty organs and states. On the opposite side of the same coin, respective state organs remained invisible from the perspective of international law: they did not bear international legal obligations or establish direct

[2] International Covenant on Civil and Political Rights (adopted 19 December 1966, entered into force 23 March 1976) 999 UNTS 171.

[3] Convention for the Protection of Human Rights and Fundamental Freedoms (signed 4 November 1950, entered into force 3 September 1953) 213 UNTS 222 (as amended by Protocols Nos 11, 14 and 15).

[4] American Convention on Human Rights (signed 22 November 1969, entered into force 18 July 1978) 1144 UNTS 123.

[5] *Affaire du 'Lotus' (France c Turquie)* [1927] CPJI série A No 10, 18.

[6] See art 7(2) of the Vienna Convention on the Law of Treaties (signed 23 May 1969, entered into force 27 January 1980) 1155 UNTS 331.

[7] For the general principle that the executive represents the 'state' on the international plane, see *Application of the International Convention on the Elimination of All Forms of Racial Discrimination (Georgia v Russian Federation) (Preliminary Objections)* [2011] ICJ Rep 70, para 37.

[8] For the definition of NHRIs and their competences and responsibilities, see ch 2, section 2.4.1.

relations with human rights treaty organs without the mediation of national laws.[9]

Few previous studies ever expressly discussed or questioned the perception of a 'state' as a unitary and monolithic legal entity, thereby (perhaps unconsciously) reinforcing and reproducing such a perception. This situation has its basis in the following three premises, which derive from the traditional assumptions of state sovereignty, sometimes described as 'positivist', 'statist' or 'Westphalian'.[10] The first premise is that international and national laws are separate legal orders. The question of whether state organs have any status in international law has been primarily discussed within the framework of the dualist-monist debate. Advocates of dualism, such as Paul Laband,[11] Heinrich Triepel[12] and Dionisio Anzilotti,[13] have observed that international law regulates the relationship between states as unitary and monolithic entities, and that the rights and obligations of state organs and individuals are solely a matter of respective national laws. In contrast, authors who supported the monist understanding of international and national laws, such as Hans Kelsen, have argued that international law could create competence and obligations for individual state organs directly, without the mediation of national laws.[14] Georges Scelle's theory of 'dédoublement fonctionnel', where state organs are given the authority to act as an agent of international law, is the most prominent example.[15] Nevertheless, as dualism has long remained in the mainstream under the dominance of positivism,[16] individual state organs were invisible from the point of view of international law.

There have indeed been attempts to restructure the relationship between international and domestic laws. Some authors, such as Sir Gerald Fitzmaurice, have advanced the so-called coordination approach, shifting the focus from the doctrinal dichotomy between dualism and monism to the regulation of actual interactions between international and national laws.[17] Other

[9] See, eg, P Gonzalez-Dominguez, *The Doctrine of Conventionality Control: Between Uniformity and Legal Pluralism in the Inter-American Human Rights System* (Intersentia 2018) 175.

[10] For the traditional assumptions of sovereignty, see L Henkin, 'Human Rights and State "Sovereignty"' (1996) 25 *Georgia Journal of International & Comparative Law* 31, 32.

[11] P Laband, *Das Staatsrecht des Deutschen Reiches, Vol 2*, 5th edn (Mohr 1911) 126–28.

[12] H Triepel, *Völkerrecht und Landesrecht* (CL Hirschfeld 1899) 121.

[13] D Anzilotti, *Cours de droit international* (translated by G Gidel) (Librairie du Recueil Sirey 1929) paras 60–61 (the original text is: D Anzilotti, *Corso di diritto internazionale: Volume 1: Introduzione: teorie generali* (Athenaum 1927)).

[14] H Kelsen, 'La transformation du droit international en droit interne' [1936] *Revue Générale du Droit International Public* 5, 11.

[15] G Scelle, 'Règles générales du droit de la paix' (1934) 46 *Recueil des Cours de l'Académie de La Haye* 327, 358.

[16] P Gragl, *Legal Monism: Law, Philosophy, and Politics* (Oxford University Press 2018) 10–11.

[17] G Fitzmaurice, 'The General Principles of International Law Considered from the Standpoint of the Rule of Law' (1957) 92 *Recueil des Cours de l'Académie de La Haye* 1, 79–80. For a summary of the coordination approach, see H Owada, 'Problems of Interaction between the International and Domestic Legal Orders' (2015) 5 *Asian Journal of International Law* 246, 252–54.

theories have been proposed, such as 'cosmopolitan constitutionalism' by Mattias Kumm,[18] 'pluralism' by Nico Krisch,[19] 'reflexive authority of international law' by Başak Çalı,[20] 'ius constitutionale commune' by Armin von Bogdandy et al,[21] the 'trapezium model' by Yota Negishi,[22] the 'discordant parity paradigm' by Eyal Benvenisti and Alon Harel,[23] a revival of 'moderate monism' proposed by Antonio Cassese,[24] and Paul Gragl's advocacy of a rejuvenation of monism under the primacy of international law.[25] However, such theories have not focused on the roles of various state organs and have only considered the relationship between legal orders as such. Moreover, when discussing such relationships, the relevant scholars have unconsciously assumed that international law is interpreted and applied by international judicial bodies, and national laws are interpreted and applied by the respective domestic courts:[26] they have overlooked the relevance of state organs beyond the judiciary, despite the fact that multiple state organs participate in the interpretation and application of human rights treaties, often adopting conflicting attitudes towards the interpretation of human rights treaties (see Chapter 4, section 4.4).[27] They have also not fully considered the possibility that international judicial bodies and state organs bridge international and national laws to concurrently interpret and apply them.

[18] M Kumm, 'The Cosmopolitan Turn in Constitutionalism: On the Relationship between Constitutionalism in and beyond the State' in JL Dunoff and JP Trachtman (eds), *Ruling the World? Constitutionalism, International Law, and Global Governance* (Cambridge University Press 2009) 258.

[19] N Krisch, *Beyond Constitutionalism: The Pluralist Structure of Postnational Law* (Oxford University Press 2010).

[20] B Çalı, *The Authority of International Law: Obedience, Respect, and Rebuttal* (Oxford University Press 2015) ch 4.

[21] A von Bogdandy, '*Ius Constitutionale Commune in América Latina*: Observations on Transformative Constitutionalism' in A von Bogdandy et al (eds), *Transformative Constitutionalism in Latin America: The Emergence of a New Ius Commune* (Oxford University Press 2017) 27.

[22] Y Negishi, *Conventionality Control of Domestic Law: Constitutionalised International Adjudication and Internationalised Constitutional Adjudication* (Nomos 2022).

[23] E Benvenisti and A Harel, 'Embracing the Tension between National and International Human Rights Law: The Case for Discordant Parity' (2017) 15 *International Journal of Constitutional Law (I-CON)* 36.

[24] A Cassese, 'Towards a "Moderate Monism": Could International Rules Eventually Acquire the Force to Invalidate Inconsistent National Laws?' in A Cassese (ed), *Realizing Utopia: The Future of International Law* (Oxford University Press 2012) 187. See also T Kleinlein, 'Alfred Verdross as a Founding Father of International Constitutionalism?' (2012) 4 *Goettingen Journal of International Law* 385.

[25] Gragl (n 16).

[26] M Forteau, 'Repenser la logique de traitement des rapports entre ordres juridiques: Changer de regard: Tout ne serait-il pas affaire de droit applicable, plutôt que d'ordres juridiques ?' in B Bonnet (ed), *Traité des rapports entre ordres juridiques* (LGDJ 2016) 633, 635.

[27] For example, in the execution of *Artavia Murillo et al v Costa Rica* judgment of the Inter-American Court of Human Rights in 2012, the measure for compliance taken by the executive branch in 2015 was invalidated by the Supreme Court in 2016. See Constitutional Chamber of the Supreme Court, Judgment no 2016-001692, File no 15-013929-0007-CO (3 February 2016) (Costa Rica).

The second premise that has made state organs invisible under international law is the dominance of the concept of 'subject of international law/international legal personality' in international law scholarship. This concept has distinguished between social entities relevant to the international legal system and those excluded from it,[28] thereby leading the international law scholarship to focus solely on the rights and obligations of 'states'.[29] 'Subjects of international law' are those who (have the capacity to) bear rights and obligations under international law directly, without the need for the intervention of national laws.[30] Under this conceptual framework, state organs, which are not subjects of international law in the noted sense, were considered to be relevant only under respective national laws, not international law.[31] There have been attempts to offer alternative conceptual frameworks to 'subjects of international law', the most successful of these being Rosalyn Higgins' 'participants' conception.[32] Nevertheless, whereas the status of entities other than states, such as individuals, has been increasingly conceptualised,[33] that of state organs remains underdeveloped.

The final premise that has supported the unitary and monolithic nature of 'states' is the 'equality between political regimes'.[34] Emer de Vattel stated that 'as human beings are naturally equal … the Nations … are naturally equal and essentially possess the same obligations and the same rights'.[35] Regardless of the political models adopted at the national level, states are recognised as sovereign as long as they exercise effective control over their territory and people.[36] As a consequence of the combination of the principles of state sovereignty and non-intervention in the internal affairs of states,[37]

[28] R Portmann, *Legal Personality in International Law* (Cambridge University Press 2010) 1.

[29] See, eg, JT Abdy, *Kent's Commentary on International Law*, 2nd edn (Bell and Co 1878) 5; TE Holland, *Lectures on International Law* (Sweet & Maxwell 1933) 53. For a critical observation on the 'widespread and uncritical acceptance' of the binary distinction between subjects and objects of international law, see R Higgins, *Problems and Process. International Law and How We Use it* (Clarendon Press 1994) 49.

[30] See generally J Crawford, *Brownlie's Principles of Public International Law*, 9th edn (Oxford University Press 2019) ch 4.

[31] Anzilotti (n 13) paras 125–26.

[32] Higgins (n 29) ch 3. Higgins emphasised 'the need to look behind the monolithic face of the state' (R Higgins, 'The Concept of "The State": Variable Geometry and Dualist Perceptions' in LB de Chazournes and V Gowlland-Debbas (eds), *The International Legal System in Quest of Equity and Universality* (Martinus Nijhoff 2002) 547, 561) and addressed, albeit very briefly, the issue of which specific state organs are the addressees of the margin of appreciation of the European Court of Human Rights (R Higgins, 'Derogations under Human Rights Treaties' (1976) 48 *British Year book of International Law* 281, 315).

[33] For early discussions, see M Bourquin, 'Règles générales du droit de la paix' (1931) 35 *Recueil des Cours de l'Académie de La Haye* 1, 40–47.

[34] LA Sicilianos, *L'ONU et la démocratisation de l'état: systèmes régionaux et ordre juridique universel* (Pedone 2000) ch 1.

[35] E de Vattel, *Le droit des gens, ou Principes de la loi naturelle, appliqués à la conduite et aux affaires des Nations et des Souverains, Vol 1* (London 1758) 11.

[36] LFL Oppenheim, *International Law, Vol 1* (Longman 1905) 403–05.

[37] Sicilianos (n 34) 27.

every state has the inalienable right to choose its political systems without interference.[38] This 'equality between political models' principle, which has its origin in the Peace of Westphalia, was an essential condition for the coexistence of states with diverse political systems and ideologies.[39] Thus, the drafters of the UN Charter[40] have set out 'peace-loving states' as the only criterion for UN membership, deliberately avoiding criteria connected with a particular political system.[41] The first preambular paragraph of the 1969 Vienna Convention on the Law of Treaties (VCLT) refers to 'peaceful cooperation among nations, whatever their constitutional and social systems', and the International Court of Justice (ICJ) has stated in *Western Sahara* (1975) that '[n]o rule of international law ... requires the structure of a State to follow any particular pattern'[42] and in *Nicaragua* (1986) that 'adherence by a State to any particular doctrine does not constitute a violation of customary international law; to hold otherwise would make nonsense of the fundamental principle of State sovereignty, on which the whole of international law rests'.[43] Given this 'equality between political models' principle, it is unacceptable that international law imposes certain duties on individual state organs, such as regulating how parliaments must be composed or how they must function, which would inevitably favour one political system over another.

Indeed, classical international law was already familiar with the idea that international legal obligations must be implemented by a specific state organ. The concept of 'obligation of conduct', which is contrasted with 'obligation of result', introduced by Roberto Ago, the Special Rapporteur of the International Law Commission (ILC) on state responsibility, is most typical. According to Ago, in the former case, 'the obligations are laid upon the State, requiring it to take or to refrain from taking some specific action: for example, to adopt or to refrain from adopting a specific legislative, administrative or judicial act'.[44] Nevertheless, such obligations are still owed by 'states', and it is the national laws of respective states that directly address state organs.

[38] UNGA Res 2625 (XXV), 'Declaration on Principles of International Law concerning Friendly Relations and Co-operation among States in accordance with the Charter of the United Nations' (24 October 1970).

[39] This explanation applied even among the relatively homogeneous European states. See C Schmitt, *Der Nomos der Erde im Völkerrecht des Jus Publicum Europaeum* (Greven 1950) pt III, ch 1.

[40] The Charter of the United Nations (signed 26 June 1945, entered into force 24 October 1945) XV UNCIO 335 (amendments in 557 UNTS 143, 638 UNTS 308 and 892 UNTS 119).

[41] U Fastenrath, 'Membership: Article 4' in B Simma et al (eds), *The Charter of the United Nations: A Commentary Vol I*, 3rd edn (Oxford University Press 2012) 341, 348.

[42] *Sahara occidental (avis consultative)* [1975] CIJ Recueil 12, para 94.

[43] *Military and Paramilitary Activities in and against Nicaragua (Nicaragua v United States of America) (Merits)* [1986] ICJ Rep 14, para 263.

[44] Special Rapporteur Robert Ago, 'Sixth Report on State Responsibility' (1977) UN Doc A/CN.4/302 and Add.1-3, III-5, para 3.

1.1.2. Towards the 'Disaggregation of a State': Increasing Roles of Individual State Organs as Autonomous Human Rights Treaty Actors

However, in recent years, it has become questionable whether the above-mentioned perception of 'states' as unitary and monolithic legal entities remains tenable, both from the descriptive and normative perspectives.

From the descriptive perspective, we have witnessed a new tendency, which this book comprehensively labels as 'disaggregation of a state'.[45] As this book will closely analyse in Chapters 2 and 4, human rights treaty organs have increasingly fostered a direct relationship with various state organs beyond the executive, which has traditionally represented the state on the international plane. First, treaty organs have developed procedural channels to permit and encourage the participation of individual state organs in their proceedings and activities. The European Court of Human Rights (ECtHR), the Inter-American Court of Human Rights (IACtHR) and UN human rights treaty bodies all recognise the important roles of NHRIs as amicus curiae or third-party intervenors in their proceedings. The ECtHR has interacted with national courts through the advisory opinion procedure under Protocol No 16 of the ECHR.[46] UN human rights treaty bodies have encouraged the participation of parliaments and parliamentarians in various stages of their activities. Second, treaty organs order remedies or reparations that are substantially addressed to specific state organs, such as the amendment of legislation and the re-opening of judicial proceedings. The IACtHR has invented the doctrine of 'conventionality control' to directly oblige national courts. Third, in reviewing a measure's necessity and proportionality and ordering remedial/reparation measures, treaty organs tend to require national courts, parliaments and administrative organs to adhere to different procedural standards, and change their level of scrutiny depending on the level of adherence of the particular state organ to those standards.

Moreover, as this book will examine in Chapter 5, the roles of individual state organs as human rights treaty actors are increasingly acknowledged in international and transnational fora. Some of the prominent examples include the 'Principles Relating to the Status of National Institutions' (hereinafter 'Paris Principles') adopted at an international workshop on NHRIs in 1991[47]

[45] The term 'disaggregation of a state' originates from LR Helfer and AM Slaughter, 'Toward a Theory of Effective Supranational Adjudication' (1997) 107 *Yale Law Journal* 273. Note, however, that this book uses the term to cover a wider range of phenomena than those introduced in Helfer and Slaughter's article.

[46] Protocol No 16 to the Convention on the Protection of Human Rights and Fundamental Freedoms (signed 2 October 2013, entered into force 1 August 2018) CETS No 214.

[47] UN Commission on Human Rights, 'Further Promotion and Encouragement of Human Rights and Fundamental Freedoms, Including the Question of the Programme and Methods of Work of the Commission: Report of the International Workshop on National Institutions for the Promotion and Protection of Human Rights' (1991) UN Doc E/CN.4/1992/43, 45–49 (V-A: Recommendations).

and subsequently endorsed by the UN Commission on Human Rights[48] and the UN General Assembly,[49] the 'Basic Principles for Parliamentary Supervision of International Human Rights Standards' (2011) adopted by the Parliamentary Assembly of the Council of Europe (PACE),[50] and the 'Draft Principles on Parliaments and Human Rights' (2018) drafted under the auspices of the UN Human Rights Council.[51] They provide the roles of NHRIs and parliaments respectively instead of those of 'states'. These emerging practices as a whole call for a reconstruction of the conception of the 'state' as a unitary and monolithic legal entity.

From the normative perspective too, theorising the roles of individual state organs in human rights treaties is a matter of priority. It first contributes to the effectiveness of human rights treaty systems. Developments in (human rights) compliance theories through the interdisciplinary interactions between international law, political science and international relations scholarships[52] have greatly contributed to the increased attention to the roles of individual state organs for the effective implementation of international (human rights) law.[53] In their 1997 article, Laurence R Helfer and Anne-Marie Slaughter argued that 'direct relationships' shall be constructed 'between the [supranational] tribunals and different governmental institutions such as courts, administrative agencies, and legislative committees'.[54] This can improve the effectiveness of the human rights treaty bodies because:

> [E]ven in a political system that is otherwise corrupt or oppressive, it is possible that a particular government institution – a court or administrative agency or even a legislative body – will choose to forge a relationship with a supranational tribunal as an ally in a domestic political battle against corruption or oppression.[55]

Some have empirically demonstrated the importance of the roles of individual state organs for the effectiveness of human rights treaties. For example, Alexandra

[48] UN Commission on Human Rights Res 1992/54, 'National Institutions for the Promotion and Protection of Human Rights' (3 March 1992).

[49] UNGA Res 48/134, 'National Institutions for the Promotion and Protection of Human Rights' (20 December 1993).

[50] PACE Res 1823, 'National Parliaments: Guarantors of Human Rights in Europe' (23 June 2011), Appendix.

[51] Report of the Office of the United Nations High Commissioner for Human Rights (OHCHR), 'Contribution of Parliaments to the Work of the Human Rights Council and Its Universal Periodic Review' (2018) UN Doc A/HRC/38/25, Annex I.

[52] See generally ES Bates, 'Sophisticated Constructivism in Human Rights Compliance Theory' (2014) 25 *European Journal of International Law (EJIL)* 1169.

[53] See, eg, R Murray and C de Vos, 'Behind the State: Domestic Mechanisms and Procedures for the Implementation of Human Rights Judgments and Decisions' (2020) 12 *Journal of Human Rights Practice* 22.

[54] Helfer and Slaughter (n 45) 277.

[55] ibid 335. Similarly, Tamitomo Saito observed that the real obstacle to the effective implementation of human rights treaties is the fact that 'the international law scholarship is not yet equipped with the foundational theory that enables it to view international law from "inside" of the state'. T Saito, 'Kokusaihougaku niokeru mouhitotsuno shutaisei [Another Legal Subjectivity in International Law Scholarship]' (2019) 64 (7) *Hougaku Seminar* 28, 30.

Huneeus has shown that the compliance rate with the reparation orders of the IACtHR is low when substantially addressed to state organs other than the executive.[56] She thus suggested that international human rights courts must directly engage state organs beyond the foreign ministry in order to cultivate them as compliance partners.[57] Based on quantitative analysis and case studies, Courtney Hillebrecht argued that:

> [C]ompliance with international human rights tribunals' rulings is an inherently domestic affair. Pro-compliance partnerships, comprising executives, judges, legislatures, and civil society actors, facilitate compliance on the domestic level.[58]

Thus, theorising state organs as human rights treaty actors with duties of their own, independent of the obligations of states under human rights treaties, will greatly contribute to the effectiveness of human rights treaty systems. It can raise awareness among state organs[59] and provide a basis to develop the mechanisms for state organs' implementation of their duties.

Second, as this book will discuss in Chapter 2, the increasing impact of human rights treaties and treaty organs on domestic legal orders has highlighted the democratic legitimacy challenge of human rights treaty systems. Previous studies have emphasised the roles of parliaments in this regard. Murray Hunt argued that 'as the bodies elected to represent the sovereign people, [parliaments] are the institutions best placed to confer democratic legitimacy' in human rights law and discourse.[60] Moreover, drawing an analogy from national constitutional law scholarship, some authors proposed that treaty organs should treat state organs differently, as per their characteristics and competence under domestic law.[61] For example, Geir Ulfstein argued that because there is no representative organ at the international level:

> [The ECtHR should] pay due respect to the fact that the democratic legitimacy of policy choices between different values and interests lies primarily with the national legislatures. This means that national legislatures should be allowed more discretion in such choices than what is allowed for both the executive and national courts.[62]

[56] A Huneeus, 'Courts Resisting Courts: Lessons from the Inter-American Court's Struggle to Enforce Human Rights' (2011) 44 *Cornell International Law Journal* 493, 509.

[57] ibid 496–97.

[58] C Hillebrecht, *Domestic Politics and International Human Rights Tribunals: The Problem of Compliance* (Cambridge University Press 2014) 3.

[59] Huneeus (n 56) 522–24; W Ferdinandusse, 'Out of the Black-Box? The International Obligation of State Organs' (2003) 29 *Brooklyn Journal of International Law* 45, 47.

[60] M Hunt, 'Introduction' in M Hunt, H Hooper and P Yowell (eds), *Parliaments and Human Rights: Redressing the Democratic Deficit* (Hart Publishing 2015) 1, 14. See also PACE, *Handbook for Parliamentarians: National Parliaments as Guarantors of Human Rights in Europe* (Council of Europe 2018) 18.

[61] M Saul, 'Structuring of Parliamentary Processes by the European Court of Human Rights' (2016) 20 *International Journal of Human Rights (IJHR)* 1077, 1078.

[62] G Ulfstein, 'The European Court of Human Rights and National Courts: A Constitutional Relationship?' in OM Arnardóttir and A Buyse (eds), *Shifting Centres of Gravity in Human Rights Protection: Rethinking Relations between the ECHR, EU, and National Legal Orders* (Routledge 2016)

Previous studies have also highlighted the essential roles of NHRIs in addressing criticisms that human rights treaties and treaty organs' decisions are 'foreign' to local contexts,[63] and in mitigating the confrontation between the international and national levels in the implementation of human rights treaties,[64] based on their 'home-made' human rights expertise.[65] Hence, theorising the roles of state organs is also necessary from the perspective of the democratic legitimacy of human rights treaties.

1.1.3. Previous Studies and What they Fail to Address

1.1.3.1. Studies that Focus on Specific State Organs

Given the current developments briefly mentioned above, the roles of individual state organs in human rights treaties and their relationship with treaty organs are drawing increasing academic attention. Many works examine national courts, especially under the concepts of 'domestic application', '(vertical) judicial dialogue' and 'shared judicial responsibility'.[66] Some have described the role of the domestic judiciary as that of 'agents' or 'trustees' of human rights treaties,[67] and others have presented original theories such as Başak Çalı's 'responsible domestic courts doctrine'.[68]

Regarding national parliaments, the publication of two edited volumes – *Parliaments and Human Rights*[69] and *The International Human Rights Judiciary*

46, 55. See also, J Callewaert, 'Quel avenir pour la marge d'appréciation?' in P Mahoney et al (eds), *Protection des droits de l'homme: la perspective européenne* (C Heymanns 2000) 147, 151.

[63] J Jarab, 'Perspectives on the Need for National Human Rights Institutions in Europe and the World' in J Wouters and K Meuwissen (eds), *National Human Rights Institutions in Europe* (Intersentia 2013) 287, 294–95.

[64] MN Poblete, 'In Hoc Signo Vinces: Identity, Mission and Authority of National Human Rights Institutions in Latin America' in S Lopez Escarcena et al (eds), *National Human Rights Institutions in Europe and Latin America: International and Comparative Perspectives* (Intersentia 2024) 95, 111.

[65] MM Qafisheh, 'The International Status of National Human Rights Institutions: A Comparison with NGOs' (2013) 31 *Nordic Journal of Human Rights (NJHR)* 55, 73.

[66] See, eg, A Caligiuri and N Napoletano, 'Application of the ECHR in the Domestic Systems' (2010) 20 *Italian Yearbook of International Law* 125; J Gerards and J Fleuren (eds), *Implementation of the European Convention on Human Rights and of the Judgments of the ECtHR in National Case Law* (Intersentia 2014); ECtHR, *Proceedings of the Seminar: Dialogue between Judges 2014: Implementation of the Judgments of the* www.echr.coe.int/documents/d/echr/dialogue_2014_eng; E Ferrer Mac-Grego, 'What Do We Mean When We Talk about Judicial Dialogue?' (2017) 30 *Harvard Human Rights Journal* 89; R Kunz, 'Judging International Judgments Anew? The Human Rights Courts before Domestic Courts' (2019) 30 *EJIL* 1129; C Giannopoulos, 'The Reception by Domestic Courts of the *Res Interpretata* Effect of Jurisprudence of the European Court of Human Rights' (2019) 19 *Human Rights Law Review (HRLR)* 537; AM Maués et al, 'Judicial Dialogue between National Courts and the Inter-American Court of Human Rights' (2021) 21 *HRLR* 108; M Loja, 'Recent Engagement with International Human Rights Norms by the Courts of Singapore, Malaysia, and Philippines' (2021) 19 *I-CON* 98.

[67] See, eg, E Bjorge, *Domestic Application of the ECHR: Courts as Faithful Trustees* (Oxford University Press 2015).

[68] B Çalı, 'From Flexible to Variable Standards of Judicial Review' in Arnardóttir and Buyse (n 62) 144.

[69] Hunt, Hooper and Yowell (n 60).

and National Parliaments[70] – and a monograph by Donald and Leach in 2016[71] is emblematic of this trend. Parliaments are therein described as treaty organs' 'compliance partners'[72] and 'human rights actors',[73] and theories such as 'parliamentary civil disobedience'[74] are introduced. While a large part of these works concerns the ECHR, relevant practices at the universal level or in other regions have also drawn attention.[75]

As for NHRIs, the edited works by Meuwissen and Wouters (2013),[76] and Lopez Escarcena et al (2024)[77] provide the most comprehensive account of recent developments. Richard Carver suggested that the role of NHRIs must be discussed in a triangular framework of 'treaty body-state-NHRI'.[78] Gérard Fellous describes NHRIs as 'acteurs de troisième type' located between states and civil society.[79] Rachael Murray argued that beyond the dichotomous distinction between states and non-state actors, and between subjects and objects of international law, NHRIs must be perceived as 'participants' that exercise functions along with various actors in a multi-layered reality of the global sphere.[80] Katrien Meuwissen argued that the unique status of NHRIs should be explained by the idea of the 'disaggregated state'.[81] Yin-Wen Wang observed that the recent practice of treaty bodies has transformed the roles of NHRIs from the 'implementation' of human rights treaties as part of the state to the 'monitoring' of their implementation as actors independent of the state.[82]

These studies, as a whole, attest to the increasing importance of the roles of individual state organs and their relationship with human rights treaty organs. However, they have treated the relationship in a fragmented manner by focusing

[70] M Saul et al (eds), *The International Human Rights Judiciary and National Parliaments* (Cambridge University Press 2017).

[71] A Donald and P Leach, *Parliaments and the European Court of Human Rights* (Oxford University Press 2016).

[72] A Donald, 'Parliaments as Compliance Partners in the European Convention on Human Rights System' in Saul et al (n 70) 75.

[73] K Roberts Lyer, 'Parliaments as Human Rights Actors: The Potential for International Principles on Parliamentary Human Rights Committees' (2019) 37 *NJHR* 195.

[74] A Føllesdal, 'Law Making by Law Breaking? A Theory of Parliamentary Civil Disobedience against International Human Rights Courts' in Saul et al (n 70) 329.

[75] See J Krommendijk, 'National Parliaments: Obstacles or Aid to the Impact of International Human Rights Bodies?' in M Wind (ed), *International Courts and Domestic Politics* (Cambridge University Press 2018) 227; Roberts Lyer (n 73); L Marsteintredet, 'The Inter-American Court of Human Rights and the Mobilisation of Parliaments' in Saul et al (n 70) 248.

[76] Wouters and Meuwissen (n 63).

[77] Lopez Escarcena et al (n 64).

[78] R Carver, 'A New Answer to an Old Question: National Human Rights Institutions and the Domestication of International Law' (2010) 10 *HRLR* 1, 20.

[79] G Fellous, *Les institutions nationales des droits de l'homme: Acteurs de troisième type* (La Documentation Française 2006) 11.

[80] R Murray, *The Role of National Human Rights Institutions at the International and Regional Levels: The Experience of Africa* (Hart Publishing 2007) 61–64.

[81] K Meuwissen, 'NHRIs and the State: New and Independent Actors in the Multi-layered Human Rights System?' (2015) 15 *HRLR* 441, 481.

[82] Y Wang, 'Kokusaijinkenhou niokeru Kokunaijinkenkikan: Shitekikeisei to Gendaitekiyakuwari [National Human Rights Institutions in International Human Rights Law: Historical Development and Contemporary Roles]' (2018) 131 *Kokka Gakkai Zasshi* 163, 214–15.

on just one type of state organ, one treaty organ or one aspect of the treaty organs' activities. Consequently, existing studies have not fully explored the possibility that the relationship is governed by a set of common principles as a totality, nor have they exploited the opportunity that the experiences of one treaty organ can provide beneficial implications for others. Therefore, it is necessary to comprehensively cover those phenomena, which have previously been covered only as a patchwork, as a single movement, to ascertain the common principles that underlie them. Only with such an inquiry does it become possible to show that the recent developments regarding the individual state organs are not sporadic, haphazard or opportunistic, but rather are systemic and consistent, and that they therefore bear significance that may shake the foundational assumptions of traditional international law.

1.1.3.2. Studies that Construct Theories on Disaggregation of a State

As was introduced in the previous subsection, Helfer and Slaughter have advocated for the need to depart from the 'bedrock assumption of traditional public international law: that states, functioning as unitary entities, are the only subjects of international rules and institutions and hence the only recognised actors in the international realm' and promoted the 'disaggregation of the state'.[83] Following this article, Slaughter presented the concept of 'disaggregated sovereignty', where respective state organs 'exercise at least some independent rights and [are] subject to some independent, or at least distinct, obligations'.[84] Such obligations of state organs, she argues, can be understood in parallel to their obligations under the domestic constitutional law.[85] Helfer later proposed the concept of the 'embeddedness' of the ECtHR in national systems and argued that it significantly improves the prospects for compliance with the ECHR.[86] Ward Ferdinandusse suggested that the dominant view in international law, which envisages the state as a 'black-box', is no longer valid; today, not only states as monolithic entities but also their organs are bound by international legal obligations.[87] Amrei Müller has similarly observed that state organs have 'obligations' under the ECHR to 'secure convention rights in light of present-day conditions',[88] and parliaments and domestic courts are

[83] Helfer and Slaughter (n 45) 288.

[84] AM Slaughter, 'Disaggregated Sovereignty: Towards the Public Accountability of Global Government Networks' (2004) 39 *Government and Opposition* 159, 188.

[85] ibid.

[86] LR Helfer, 'Redesigning the European Court of Human Rights: Embeddedness as a Deep Structural Principle of the European Human Rights Regime' (2008) 19 *EJIL* 125, 133.

[87] Ferdinandusse (n 59). See also Y Negishi, 'The Subsidiarity Principle's Role in Allocating Competences between Human Rights Courts and States Parties' in A von Bogdandy et al (eds), *Ius Constitutionale Commune en América Latina, Vol III* (Juruá Editora 2016) 125, 146.

[88] A Müller, 'Domestic Authorities' Obligations to Co-develop the Rights of the European Convention on Human Rights' (2016) 20 *IJHR* 1058, 1060.

obliged 'to interact for co-developing convention rights'.[89] Steven LB Jensen and others discussed the roles played by NHRIs and parliaments under the umbrella concept of 'domestic institutionalisation of human rights'.[90]

Nevertheless, these studies leave the following problems unresolved. First, except for Müller, they have not fully clarified the contents of the 'obligations' imposed on respective state organs and how they differ from those of states. Even Müller focused only on one aspect – that is, updating human rights protection in light of present-day conditions – leaving other aspects of state organs' obligations unexplored. Second, they have not provided a concrete account of the specific principles that regulate the relationship between human rights treaty organs and various state organs, and how they (should) operate in different circumstances. Third, they have not fully explored the legal and theoretical foundations of the new concepts such as 'disaggregation of the state' and 'obligation' of state organs. Thus, the legal consequences incurred by the violation of such 'obligations' and the mechanisms to ensure their implementation remain unclear. Without solving these problems, such new concepts cannot theoretically stand as autonomous theoretical concepts or provide concrete guidance to relevant actors, despite their intuitive appeal.

1.2. THE OBJECTIVES AND OVERALL STRUCTURE OF THIS BOOK

Against this background, this book aims to present an original theoretical framework – that is, the 'separation of powers in a globalised democratic society' model – for the comprehensive understanding of the 'disaggregation of a state' in human rights law. In this model, each type of state organ bears different 'duties' and interacts with human rights treaty organs in a principled manner. The 'duties' of state organs and their autonomous status in human rights treaties are anchored in the cooperative interactions between 'inter-state organ norms' on human rights and human rights treaties under global legal pluralism. This book uses the model to analyse and evaluate the current practices of treaty organs and propose reforms where necessary.

To this end, in Chapter 2, this book integrates the increasing attempts of human rights treaty organs to disaggregate a state into its component organs in various forms into a broader context – that is, the blurring of the boundaries between international and national laws, and between the spheres where treaty and state organs respectively operate. This chapter introduces three types of disaggregation. In the first type, as part of their efforts to increase their effectiveness and impact on national legal orders, treaty organs penetrate the surface of the state, imposing definitive demands on individual state organs.

[89] ibid 1063.

[90] SLB Jensen, S Lagoutte and S Lorion, 'The Domestic Institutionalisation of Human Rights: An Introduction' (2019) 37 *NJHR* 165.

In this top-down and intrusive approach, state organs are treated as compliance partners for treaty organs. The second type of disaggregation involves treaty organs' responses to challenges concerning the democratic legitimacy of human rights treaty systems – challenges that arise from their growing impact on national legal orders. In contrast to the first type, treaty organs respect the decision-making authority of different types of state organs under their respective national constitutions by granting them deference. In this bottom-up and deferential approach, state organs are regarded as the primary decision-makers on human rights matters. In the third type of disaggregation, primarily applicable to NHRIs, treaty organs increasingly recognise state organs as autonomous interlocutors in their proceedings and activities. This form of disaggregation provides institutional support and serves as the foundation for both the top-down and bottom-up approaches to the disaggregation of a state.

In Chapter 3, this book establishes an original normative framework through which to prescribe the authorities and duties of treaty organs and individual state organs, and regulate their relationship in a principled manner. Traditionally, international law concerned the division of authority between treaty organs and 'states' as unitary and monolithic entities based on the standard of state consent. Today, however, given the growing intrusion of human rights treaties and treaty organs into national legal orders, it is essential to establish a new legitimacy framework for 'globalised democratic societies', where respective national societies are greatly affected by international human rights standards and have become spaces where treaty and state organs closely intersect regardless of their formal origins. Thus, drawing lessons from the intellectual heritage of national constitutional law scholarship, this chapter relies on the principle of the separation of powers and embodies it within the original theory of 'two-tiered bounded deliberative democracy'. In this framework, which this book refers to as the 'separation of powers in a globalised democratic society' model, each type of state organ bears a duty to take part in national 'bounded' deliberations in their respective ways. Treaty organs, for their part, must ensure the basis of such deliberations; respect, regulate and promote them; and review and contribute to international deliberations on human rights, which will then serve as 'bounds' on national deliberations. The relationships between state and treaty organs should be governed by the 'principled and continuous dialogue' and 'subsidiarity' principles.

In Chapter 4, this book analyses the actual practices of treaty organs under the 'separation of powers in a globalised democratic society' model, with reforms proposed where necessary. To this end, it first examines treaty organs' practices of allocating authority to state organs and analyses how treaty organs treat each type of state organ differently. Specifically, it covers the following two areas where the decision-making authority is fiercely contested between treaty and state organs: the treaty organs' approach to deference when reviewing the necessity and proportionality of the measure in question, and their practice in ordering/recommending remedial measures after finding a violation of the treaty. Second, it examines how treaty organs treat the information and views submitted by NHRIs, and how these submissions have contributed to fostering 'bounded' national deliberations. Third, it analyses how treaty organs address 'triangular relationships' among a treaty organ and two state organs – cases where two or more state organs within one state take different positions regarding the application of the treaty. Finally, it conducts a comparative analysis of the three treaty organs' practices and finds that although they tend to support the 'separation of powers in a globalised democratic society' model, they differ substantially in terms of the extent and mode of adopting it.

In Chapter 5, this book addresses the questions regarding the nature of 'duties' of state organs under the 'separation of powers in a globalised democratic society' model, and the status of state organs in human rights treaties. It introduces the original concept of 'inter-state organ norms' – autonomous normative orders of, by and for individual state organs and not states – and shows that such norms are emerging for NHRIs, parliaments and national courts in the field of human rights, albeit with variations in terms of degree and mode. The duties of state organs are founded on the cooperative interactions between the inter-state organ norms on human rights and human rights treaties under global legal pluralism. Such cooperative interactions facilitate state organs to possess triple identities and duties – not only identities and duties under their respective national laws, but also those under inter-state organ norms and under human rights treaties, thereby transforming state organs into autonomous actors of human rights treaties. Efforts by state organs to fulfil these duties simultaneously will contribute to the gradual permeation of the separation of powers in a globalised democratic society model into national legal systems and practices.

These findings provide three strands of theoretical and practical contributions to international law, especially international human rights law (for a detailed analysis, see Chapter 6, section 6.2). First, although the human rights law community has long strived to promote the effectiveness and the democratic legitimacy of human rights treaty systems, these two aims are not easily reconcilable, as effectiveness requires larger intrusion on domestic legal orders, whereas democratic legitimacy demands respect for national decisions.[91] Paolo G Carozza and Pablo González have called this situation 'one of the central challenges inscribed in the structural design of human rights law'.[92] This book contributes to solving this challenge by conceptualising the intrusive and

[91] See G Ulfstein, 'The Human Rights Treaty Bodies and Legitimacy Challenges' in N Grossman et al (eds), *Legitimacy and International Courts* (Cambridge University Press 2018) 284, 286; JK Schaffer, A Føllesdal and G Ulfstein, 'International Human Rights and the Challenge of Legitimacy' in A Føllesdal, JK Schaffer and G Ulfstein (eds), *The Legitimacy of International Human Rights Regimes: Legal, Political and Philosophical Perspectives* (Cambridge University Press 2013) 1, 19.

[92] PG Carozza and P González, 'The Final Word? Constitutional Dialogue and the Inter-American Court of Human Rights: A Reply to Jorge Contesse' (2017) 15 *I-CON* 436, 441–42.

deferential approaches of treaty organs as two sides of the same coin under the 'subsidiarity' principle.

Second, this book supplements the classical paradigm of international law, where monolithic states are the only relevant legal entities, by offering a new theoretical framework of the 'separation of powers in a globalised democratic society' to accommodate a more complex reality. The increasing penetration of domestic legal spheres by international and transnational norms and institutions, and the consequent blurring of the boundaries between international, transnational and national laws, and between law and non-binding norms, has led to many theoretical attempts to restructure the global legal system, such as 'global administrative law',[93] 'global constitutionalism/constitutionalisation of international law',[94] 'informal international law-making'[95] and 'global legal pluralism'.[96] This book is situated within this context.

Third, it builds on long-standing theoretical debates addressing the interactions between international and national laws from a new angle by considering the relationship between actors instead of legal orders as such, and by offering the concept of 'inter-state organ norms' to add a new dimension to the binary structure of international versus national laws.

1.3. THE METHODOLOGY AND SCOPE OF THIS BOOK

This book employs both normative and descriptive approaches. Chapter 2 is largely descriptive in that it aims to describe and classify the increasing attempts by human rights treaty organs to disaggregate the state into its component organs. Chapter 3 highlights the normative contributions. It argues that the original model of 'separation of powers in a globalised democratic society' governs how human rights treaty organs *should* interact with state organs. The primary function of the model is not to describe the existing reality accurately and neutrally, but to critically evaluate and guide the existing systems and practices of relevant actors. The approach taken by Chapter 3 may not be purely normative in the sense that it does not derive the model from pure ideology and philosophy that are completely detached from social facts. Nevertheless, it does not merely reflect and endorse the immediate reality and short-sighted trends either. Instead, it relies on broader normative assumptions shared in the global human rights law community in a more stable

[93] B Kingsbury, N Krisch and RB Stewart, 'The Emergence of Global Administrative Law' (2005) 68 *Law and Contemporary Problems* 15.

[94] J Klabbers, A Peters and G Ulfstein, *The Constitutionalization of International Law* (Oxford University Press 2009).

[95] J Pauwelyn, R Wessel and J Wouters (eds), *Informal International Lawmaking* (Oxford University Press 2012).

[96] PS Berman (ed), *The Oxford Handbook of Global Legal Pluralism* (Oxford University Press 2020).

and profound manner, as well as the heritage of national constitutional law scholarship. Chapter 3 refers to positive materials, such as international and transnational documents, to ascertain such normative assumptions (for the relationship between social and normative legitimacies, see Chapter 3, section 3.1.1). In contrast, Chapter 4 primarily takes a descriptive approach, closely analysing the practices of treaty organs. Nevertheless, Chapter 4 goes beyond neutral descriptions: the 'separation of powers in a globalised democratic society' model is used to critically evaluate whether and for what reasons current practices are (not) consistent with the model, and propose reforms and improvements. Chapter 5 contains both descriptive and normative dimensions. It argues that human rights treaties should – and in fact do, to some extent – cooperatively interact with inter-state organ norms under the shared values in 'globalised democratic societies'.

Finally, certain clarifications are necessary concerning this book's scope. First, in Chapter 4, this book primarily confines its examination to the practice of human rights treaty organs, leaving the comprehensive analysis of the state organs' practice to future research. Second, it focuses on the allocation of powers between treaty organs and each type of state organ, while that between state organs within the same state under human rights treaties[97] must be integrated into the model in future studies. Finally, under the generic term 'human rights treaty organs' or 'treaty organs', this study focuses on the ECtHR, the IACtHR and UN human rights treaty bodies. Given the limited space for covering all nine UN human rights treaty bodies, this book will primarily address the practice of the UN Human Rights Committee (HRC), which has the richest experiences[98] and monitors the ICCPR, which has a general catalogue of rights similar to those of the ECHR and the ACHR, even though other bodies are mentioned when they demonstrate leading practices. Among the functions of UN human rights treaty bodies, the study mostly focuses on the individual communication procedure, which closely resembles judicial adjudication and thus has the sharpest intrusion into domestic legal orders. Nevertheless, it will touch on other functions such as producing General Comments and consideration of state reports wherever they contribute to the creation of the general jurisprudence and exert considerable influence on domestic legal orders. The African Court on Human and Peoples' Rights (AfCtHPR), a relatively new regional court that began its operations in 2006, is excluded from the scope of this study: only six states accept the competence of the AfCtHPR

[97] See, eg, AS Tsampi, *Le principe de séparation des pouvoirs dans la jurisprudence de la cour européenne des droits de l'homme* (Pedone 2019).

[98] The HRC possesses the longest record of receiving individual communications and has addressed, by a significant margin, the highest number of such communications among the UN human rights treaty bodies. For detailed data on the volume of individual communications and the resulting Views issued by these bodies, see AJ Ullmann and A von Staden, 'A Room Full of "Views": Introducing a New Dataset to Explore Compliance with the Decisions of the UN Human Rights Treaty Bodies' Individual Complaints Procedures' (2024) 68 *Journal of Conflict Resolution* 534, 538.

to receive individuals' complaints,[99] and there have been relatively few judgments rendered on the merit and reparations.[100] As a result, the impact of the AfCtHPR on domestic legal orders – the rationale of the treaty organs' interaction with individual state organs – remains uncertain, and its jurisprudence is in the process of consolidation.[101]

1.4. COMPARABILITY OF THE THREE HUMAN RIGHTS TREATY SYSTEMS

In Chapter 3, this book establishes the 'separation of powers in a globalised democratic society' model to normatively evaluate and regulate the phenomenon of disaggregation of a state in all of the three human rights treaty systems: the ECHR, the ACHR and the ICCPR systems. However, the extent to which the model properly describes the current treaty systems and treaty organs' practices differ per system. Therefore, in Chapter 4, this book conducts a comparative study of the three systems under the model, thereby identifying and analysing their commonalities and differences, and drawing lessons and implications from one system for another. Comparative study is beneficial only when the objects of comparison are 'simultaneously and without contradiction, unified and plural'.[102] Thus, as a preliminary observation, it is convenient to briefly examine the main factors of unity (section 1.4.1) and plurality (section 1.4.2) among the three systems that may affect the application of the 'separation of powers in a globalised democratic society' model, such as the operation of deference.

1.4.1. Unity Among the Three Human Rights Treaty Systems

The three human rights treaty systems are unified, in that they all form part of the international law system and are aimed at human rights protection. Moreover, they are rooted in the Universal Declaration of Human Rights

[99] See 'Declarations' at the AfCtHPR's website at: https://www.african-court.org/wpafc/declarations/.

[100] See the statistics of cases provided in the AfCtHPR's website at: https://www.african-court.org/cpmt/statistic.

[101] Nevertheless, the AfCtHPR undoubtedly merits a closer review in the near future, as it faces similar legitimacy challenges to those of the three treaty organs within the scope of this study. See generally N de Silva, 'A Court in Crisis: African States' Increasing Resistance to Africa's Human Rights Court' *OpinioJuris* (19 May 2020), http://opiniojuris.org/2020/05/19/a-court-in-crisis-african-states-increasing-resistance-to-africas-human-rights-court.

[102] C Valcke, 'Comparative Law as Comparative Jurisprudence: The Comparability of Legal Systems' (2004) 52 *American Journal of Comparative Law* 713, 720–21.

(UDHR),[103] and thus share similar catalogues of rights.[104] Therefore, the members of the HRC, the ECtHR and the IACtHR have actively interacted to exchange information and views,[105] and these treaty organs have often referred to one another's jurisprudence.[106] The increasing mutual reference of jurisprudence among the treaty organs, which Sandrine Turgis calls 'fécondation croisée',[107] is a phenomenon that goes beyond what the systemic integration principle enshrined in Article 31(3)(c) VCLT formally requires, as the scope of the states parties to these treaties do not fully overlap.[108] Even though treaty organs may have been somewhat motivated by strategic and opportunistic reasons, the universality of human rights and the perception that treaty organs are trustees of the larger global human rights system normatively underlie the mutual reference.[109] The IACtHR is most explicit to this effect; in the very first advisory opinion in 1982, it stated that 'it would be improper to make distinctions based on the regional or non-regional character of the international obligations assumed by States, and thus deny the existence of the common core of basic human rights standards'.[110] Further, in the 1999 Advisory Opinion OC-16/99 concerning the right to information on consular assistance, it justified the reference to external human rights law sources by introducing the concept of 'corpus juris of international human rights law', which 'comprises a set of international instruments of varied content and juridical effects (treaties, conventions, resolutions and declarations)'.[111]

[103] UNGA Res 217A (III), 'Universal Declaration of Human Rights' (10 December 1948). The preambles to all three treaties expressly refer to the UDHR.

[104] See, eg, Crawford (n 30) 618.

[105] For example, the HRC has appointed focal points for interacting with the ECtHR and the IACtHR, and held meetings with their judges to share views and experiences on common human rights issues, achievements and challenges. See, eg, HRC Report on its Work on its 126th–128th Sessions (2020) UN Doc A/75/40, paras 49–50. See also AfCtHPR, ECtHR and IACtHR, '2020 Joint Law Report' (2020), www.echr.coe.int/documents/d/echr/Joint_Report_2020_AfCHPR_ECHR_IACHR_ENG.

[106] See generally S Turgis, *Les interactions entre les normes internationales relatives aux droits de la personne* (Pedone 2012); E Abrusci, *Judicial Convergence and Fragmentation in International Human Rights Law: The Regional Systems and the United Nations Human Rights Committee* (Cambridge University Press 2022).

[107] Turgis (n 106).

[108] 'Rules of international law applicable in the relations between the parties' under art 31(3)(c) only indicate rules that bind all Member States when integral, interdependent or *erga omnes partes* treaties are concerned. See Study Group of the ILC (Mr Martti Koskenniemi), 'Fragmentation of International Law: Difficulties Arising from the Diversification and Expansion of International Law' (2006) UN Doc A/CN.4/L.682, para 472.

[109] W Sandholtz, 'The ECtHR, Transregional Dialogues and Global Constitutionalism' (2020) 9 *Global Constitutionalism* 543, 547.

[110] *'Other Treaties' Subject to the Consultative Jurisdiction of the Court*, IACtHR, Series A No 1, Advisory Opinion OC-1 (24 September 1982) para 40.

[111] *The Right to Information on Consular Assistance in the Framework of the Guarantees of Due Process of Law*, IACtHR, Series A No 16, Advisory Opinion OC-16/99 (1 October 1999) para 115.

1.4.2. The Main Elements of Plurality Among the Three Human Rights Treaty Systems

1.4.2.1. The Composition of States Parties

As a universal human rights treaty adopted within the framework of the UN in 1966, the ICCPR has 174 Member States from all regions, of which 116 are also parties to the Optional Protocol to the ICCPR[112] on the individual communication procedure (as of March 2025). As there is a high level of diversity among them regarding culture, religion, social and economic systems, and the level of economic development, the HRC has often faced claims based on economic, social and cultural particularities.[113] The quality of democratic governance and human rights records also vary greatly.[114]

The ECHR was originally adopted in the Council of Europe in 1950, which was then known as a 'club of democracies'[115] of Western Europe and Nordic countries with a high level of homogeneity. In the drafting process of the ECHR, a firm commitment to European values, such as democracy, the rule of law and human rights, was expressed.[116] Consequently, its preamble explicitly describes the states parties as 'like-minded' and possessing 'a common heritage of political traditions, ideals, freedom and the rule of law'. Building on this ideological homogeneity and the fact that Member States generally possessed stable democratic institutions and high human rights records,[117] the ECtHR has developed unique jurisprudence, such as the living instrument approach, the European consensus approach and the margin of appreciation doctrine. However, after the end of the Cold War, the Council of Europe expanded its membership to the East, thereby transforming into a 'training-centre of democracy'.[118] Its membership has extended to 47 countries at the most: there are members with authoritarian features, especially Russia (it ceased to be a member of the Council of Europe in

[112] Optional Protocol to the International Covenant on Civil and Political Rights (adopted 16 December 1966, entered into force 23 March 1976) 999 UNTS 302.

[113] E Brems, *Human Rights: Universality and Diversity* (Martinus Nijhoff 2001) 346–52.

[114] According to the Economist Intelligence Unit's 2024 Democracy Index, which rated countries based on electoral process and pluralism, functioning of government, political participation, political culture and civil liberties, Norway, New Zealand, Sweden, Iceland and Switzerland are the top five ranked countries, and Syria, the Central African Republic, North Korea, Myanmar and Afghanistan are the bottom five (Economist Intelligence Unit, *Democracy Index 2024: What's Wrong with Representative Democracy?* (2024), www.eiu.com/n/campaigns/democracy-index-2024, 15–21). All of them, except Myanmar, are parties to the ICCPR.

[115] JL Burban, *Le Conseil de l'Europe* (Presses Universitaires de France 1985) 13.

[116] E Bates, *The Evolution of the European Convention on Human Rights: From its Inception to the Creation of a Permanent Court of Human Rights* (Oxford University Press 2010) pt I.

[117] Although Turkey, which has distinct historical and religious backgrounds from the West, has been a member since 1954, it did not recognise the compulsory jurisdiction of the ECtHR until 1990.

[118] F Sudre, 'La Communauté européenne et les droits fondamentaux après le traité d'Amsterdam: vers un nouveau système européen de protection des droits de l'homme?' [1998] *La Semaine Juridique* 9, 9. See generally R Harmsen, 'The European Convention on Human Rights after Enlargement' (2001) 4 *IJHR* 18.

March 2022 and a party to the ECHR in September 2022) and Azerbaijan. Some members from Eastern Europe and the former Soviet Union continue to struggle with the heritage of their communist past and the rise of populism.

The ACHR was adopted in 1969 within the framework of the Organization of American States (OAS) and has 23 Member States from Latin America, 20 of which have recognised the jurisdiction of the IACtHR. The great legal, historical, religious and cultural affinities among these members, and the fact that they have largely encountered common problems such as inequality, exclusion, poverty and authoritarian legacies must have encouraged the IACtHR to generate 'a remarkable case law tailored to Latin American problems', including the doctrine of conventionality control and the 'pro homine/persona' principle.[119] When the ACHR entered into force in 1978, the majority of Latin American countries were controlled by military dictatorships and authoritarian regimes. Although they largely retain democracy in terms of free and fair elections today, some struggle with rising authoritarianism and democratic fragility.[120] Moreover, many still struggle with the negative legacy of the past, of which the issue of granting amnesty to perpetrators of serious human rights violations during the dictatorship/authoritarian era[121] is symbolic.

Previous studies have related this difference in the composition of states parties among the three systems to the different approaches to deference by treaty organs to national decisions for two reasons. First, previous studies observe that it has yielded different types of cases before the treaty organs. The ECtHR's main task was the 'fine-tuning [of] sophisticated national democratic engines that were, on the whole, working well':[122] a large part of the cases before it concerned a rather 'nuanced' type of human rights violations stemming from good-faith restriction of rights for public interests and others' rights, which allows room for reasonable disagreement and thus justifies deference to national decisions. On the contrary, Paolo G Carozza, a former President of the Inter-American Commission on Human Rights (IACmHR), observed that the type of cases before the IACtHR compelled it to take a non-deferential approach, as the typical cases before it have been the systematic abuses of non-derogable rights, which 'do not reasonably allow for the tolerance of divergent understandings and applications'.[123] Similarly, Andrew

[119] A von Bogdandy, '*Ius Constitutionale Commune en América Latina*: Observations on Transformative Constitutionalism' (2015) 109 *AJIL Unbound* 109, 113.

[120] See, eg, S Levitsky and J Loxton, 'Populism and Competitive Authoritarianism in the Andes' (2013) 20 *Democratization* 107; E Gómez Ramírez, 'Democracy and Human Rights in Latin America: Is Democratic Erosion Gathering Pace?' (2022), https://www.europarl.europa.eu/thinktank/it/document/EPRS_BRI(2022)698868.

[121] See generally N Roht-Arriaza and L Gibson, 'The Developing Jurisprudence on Amnesty' (1998) 20 *Human Rights Quarterly* 843.

[122] P Mahoney, 'New Challenges for the European Court of Human Rights Resulting from Expanding Case Load and Membership' (2002) 21 *Penn State International Law Review* 101, 104.

[123] PG Carozza, 'The Anglo-Latin Divide and the Future of the Inter-American System of Human Rights' (2015) 5 *Notre Dame Journal of International & Comparative Law* 153, 168. See also P Contreras, 'National Discretion and International Deference in the Restriction of Human Rights: A Comparison between the Jurisprudence of the European and the Inter-American Court of Human Rights' (2012) 11 *Northwestern Journal of International Human Rights* 28, 56.

Legg analysed that the fact that the majority of the cases before the HRC concerned torture, disappearance and arbitrary detention by the Uruguayan military government initially,[124] and then Caribbean death penalty trials and detention, deprived the HRC of an opportunity to develop a jurisprudence on deference.[125]

Second, previous studies associated the deference by treaty organs to national decisions with the democratic quality of the states parties. Therefore, the reluctance of the IACtHR and the HRC against deference, as opposed to the ECtHR, has been explained by the lack of democratic institutions in many of their Member States. Antônio Augusto Cançado Trindade, a former President of the IACtHR, has stated:

> How could we apply [the margin of appreciation doctrine] in the context of a regional human rights system where many countries' judges are subject to intimidation and pressure? How could we apply it in a region where the judicial function does not distinguish between military jurisdiction and ordinary jurisdiction? ... We have no alternative but to strengthen the international mechanisms for protection.[126]

Legg also observed that because the ICCPR and its Optional Protocol 'encompass a broader range of governments', 'there is less scope for the [HRC] to give deference on the basis of democratic legitimacy'.[127]

However, the two factors of plurality, namely the type of cases and the maturity of democratic institutions, have recently shown a gradual tendency of convergence among the three systems. Indeed, after the ECHR's expansion to the East, the ECtHR has increasingly encountered cases of massive and serious human rights violations. For example, the increasing cases of arrest and detention of political opponents in bad faith compelled the ECtHR to develop 'Article 18 jurisprudence'.[128] Moreover, the democratic quality of domestic institutions of ECHR Member States has become much more heterogeneous. Thus, in 1993, Judge Martens questioned the continued validity of the margin of appreciation doctrine in the face of the expansion of the ECHR.[129] Paul Mahoney, a former registrar and judge at the ECtHR also wondered:

> [W]hether the standards carefully constructed over the last 40 years for a community of likeminded Western European States can be carried over into the much larger

[124] Indeed, out of the 31 cases in which the HRC has examined the merits from 1979 to 1984, 21 cases are raised against Uruguay. See HRC, 'Selected Decisions under the Optional Protocol' (1985) UN Doc CCPR/C/OP/1.

[125] A Legg, *The Margin of Appreciation in International Human Rights Law: Deference and Proportionality* (Oxford University Press 2012) 5.

[126] AA Cançado Trindade, *El derecho internacional de los derechos humanos en el siglo XXI*, 2nd edn (Editorial Jurídica de Chile 2006) 389–90.

[127] Legg (n 125) 73–74. See also Ulfstein (n 91) 292.

[128] C Heri, 'Loyalty, Subsidiarity, and Article 18 ECHR: How the ECtHR Deals with Mala Fide Limitations of Rights' (2020) 1 *European Convention on Human Rights Law Review* 25.

[129] *Brannigan and McBride v UK*, ECtHR, App Nos 14553/89; 14554/89, Merits and Just Satisfaction (25 May 1993) Concurring Opinion of Judge Martens, para 3.

> community created by the influx of former Soviet bloc States from Central and Eastern Europe, many of whom have little or no democratic tradition.[130]

In contrast, arguments grew in favour of the deference in the ACHR and ICCPR systems, given the progress of democratisation in their Member States. For example, Jorge Contesse notes the increase in 'less "obvious"' cases[131] – cases in which human rights are restricted for the general welfare or protection of the rights of others – in the IACtHR's caseloads and argues that as 'democratic regimes are now the norm in Latin America', 'the relationship between these governments and the organs of regional rights protection warrants revision'.[132] Medes Malaihollo and Lottie Lane argue that 'the "democratic quality" between the state parties to the ECHR and those to the [ACHR] is not so different', and thus the ECtHR's experiences in using the margin of appreciation doctrine could be useful for the IACtHR.[133] Dominic McGoldrick has also observed that because '[m]any States within the ICCPR system are now broadly democratic', the HRC should move 'towards respecting the decisions of and the balances struck by national legislatures, executives and courts'.[134]

1.4.2.2. The Conception of Democratic Society/Democracy

The ECHR was adopted within the framework of the Council of Europe as a safeguard to protect liberal democracy in Europe[135] against the potential risks from the Nazism/fascism legacy[136] and the growing threat of communism in the context of the Cold War.[137] In contrast, the American states had no firm

[130] P Mahoney, 'Universality versus Subsidiarity in the Strasbourg Case Law on Free Speech: Explaining Some Recent Judgment' [1997] *European Human Rights Law Review* 364, 370–71.

[131] J Contesse, 'Inter-American Constitutionalism: The Interaction between Human Rights and Progressive Constitutional Law in Latin America' in CA Rodríguez Garavito (ed), *Law and Society in Latin America: A New Map* (Routledge 2015) 220, 227.

[132] J Contesse, 'The Final Word? Constitutional Dialogue and the Inter-American Court of Human Rights' (2017) 15 *I-CON* 414, 415. For similar observations, see, eg, ML Deftou, 'Fostering the Rule of Law in the Americas: Is There Any Room for Judicial Dialogue between the IACtHR and National Courts?' (2020) 38 *NJHR* 78, 94; JP Perez-Leon-Acevedo and J Pablo, 'The Control of the Inter-American Court of Human Rights over Amnesty Laws and Other Exemption Measures: Legitimacy Assessment' (2020) 33 *Leiden Journal of International Law* 667, 682.

[133] M Malaihollo and L Lane, 'Mapping out Due Diligence in Regional Human Rights Law: Comparing Case Law of the European Court of Human Rights and the Inter-American Court of Human Rights' (2024) 37 *Leiden Journal of International Law* 462, 470.

[134] D McGoldrick, 'A Defence of the Margin of Appreciation and an Argument for its Application by the Human Rights Committee' (2016) 65 *International and Comparative Law Quarterly (ICLQ)* 21, 43.

[135] Council of Europe (ed), *Collected Edition of the Travaux Préparatoires of the European Convention on Human Rights* (hereinafter 'ECHR Travaux'), vol 2 (Martinus Nijhoff 1975) 60.

[136] ECHR Travaux (n 135) vol 1, 38–44.

[137] European Movement, *European Convention on Human Rights*, INF/5/E/R (1949), 'Examination of Criticisms' para 5, reproduced in the European Movement, *European Movement and the Council of Europe* (Hutchinson & Co Ltd 1949) 125.

and common determinations to create a regional human rights instrument,[138] and the aims of drafting the ACHR were not clear-cut:[139] the IACmHR's expansive activities[140] have paved the way for OAS Member States to adopt the ACHR.[141] The ACHR was a product of compromise between the region's strong commitment to the principles of non-intervention[142] and the desires to protect human rights and democracy for regional peace and security,[143] and to promote regional economic development and integration.[144] As for the ICCPR, the sharp East-West divide under the intensifying Cold War notably affected multiple aspects of its drafting process.[145] Moreover, the decolonisation movement resulted in an increased influence of developing states.[146]

Based on these different backgrounds, while all three human rights treaties incorporate the concept of 'democratic society',[147] which is key to building the 'separation of powers in a globalised democratic society' model and the 'two-tiered bounded deliberative democracy' theory that underlies it, the extent to which such a concept has attained shared understanding differs between treaties. The ECHR has had the clearest vision of democracy since its inception.[148] During the drafting process of the ECHR, a so-called 'democracy protection

[138] A Schreiber, *The Inter-American Commission on Human Rights* (AW Sijthoff 1970) 16–22.

[139] See generally RK Goldman, 'History and Action: The Inter-American Human Rights System and the Role of the Inter-American Commission on Human Rights' (2009) 31 *Human Rights Quarterly* 856, 863–65.

[140] See generally DV Sandifer, 'Human Rights in the Inter-American System' (1965) 11 *Howard Law Journal* 508.

[141] Y Ouchi, 'Beishu jinken hoshou seido no hatten ni okeru Beishu jinken iinkai no yakuwari [The Role of the Inter-American Commission on Human Rights in the Development of the Inter-American Human Rights Institution]' (2011) 164 *International Relations* 86.

[142] It was noted that '[i]nternational protection of essential rights of man would eliminate the misuse of diplomatic protection of citizens abroad, the exercise of which has more than once led to the violation of the principles of non-intervention and of equality between nationals and aliens' (OAS Res XL, 'International Protection of the Essential Rights of Man' (7 March 1945) reproduced in US Department of State, *Report of the Delegation of the United States of America to the Inter-American Conference on Problems of War and Peace, Mexico, February 21–March 8, 1945* (1946) 108).

[143] J Cabranes, 'Human Rights and Non-intervention in the Inter-American System' (1967) 65 *Michigan Law Review* 1147, 1164.

[144] IACmHR, 'Comparative Study of the United Nations Covenants on Civil and Political Rights and on Economic, Social and Cultural Rights and the Draft' (1968) OAS Doc OEA/Ser.L/II.19, Doc 26, 3, cited in Goldman (n 139) 865.

[145] For example, for the decision to split an initially single instrument into the ICCPR and the International Covenant on Economic, Social and Cultural Rights ((adopted 16 December 1966, entered into force 3 January 1976) 993 UNTS 3: ICESCR), see WA Schabas, *Nowak's CCPR Commentary: UN International Covenant on Civil and Political Rights*, 3rd edn (NP Engel Verlag 2019) lxiii.

[146] Symbolically, the right to self-determination was inserted into art 1 ICCPR, despite the vehement opposition by Western states. See ibid 12–15.

[147] Articles 6(1), 8(2), 9(2), 10(2), and 11(2) ECHR and art 2(3) and (4) of its Protocol No 4; arts 15, 16(2), 22(3) and 32(2) ACHR; arts 14(1), 21 and 22(2) ICCPR.

[148] See generally S Marks, 'The European Convention on Human Rights and Its "Democratic Society"' (1996) 66 *British Year Book of International Law* 209.

clause' was initially included[149] and provided that '[e]very State a party to this Convention undertakes faithfully to respect the fundamental principles of political democracy, and in particular', '[t]o hold … free elections' and '[t]o take no action which will interfere with the right of political criticism and the right to organize a political opposition'.[150] Although this clause was eventually deleted, its legacy remains in the preamble to the ECHR, which refers to 'effective political democracy' as a foundation of the fundamental freedoms. The preamble also mentions the 'common heritage of political traditions' among 'like-minded' states parties, strongly implying that the concept of democracy/the democratic society in the ECHR is defined in accordance with Western liberal democracy.[151] The ECtHR was initially relatively careful in developing the content of the concept of democracy.[152] However, after the enlargement of the Council of Europe to the East, the ECtHR has not hesitated to state that '[d]emocracy is without doubt a fundamental feature of the European public order' and '[d]emocracy … appears to be the only political model contemplated by the Convention and, accordingly, the only one compatible with it',[153] directly deriving substantive interpretations from such a conception[154] (see also Chapter 3, section 3.3.5.1).

Given that the ACHR was adopted under the fragility of democracy in the Latin American region, it underscores the importance of democratic institutions in the preamble[155] and provides the interpretative principle that no provision shall be interpreted to preclude 'other rights or guarantees … derived from representative democracy as a form of government' under Article 29(c). It also includes Article 23 (right to participate in government) into a list of

[149] Although this clause was eventually deleted, part of it was retained in art 3 of Protocol No 1 to the ECHR (right to free elections) (Protocol to the Convention for the Protection of Human Rights and Fundamental Freedoms (signed 20 March 1952, entered into force 18 May 1954) 213 UNTS 262). Because of its origin as a clause to protect democracy as a political system, it employs collective and general terms. Nevertheless, the ECtHR has interpreted it as containing individuals' subjective rights to free elections. See WA Schabas, *The European Convention on Human Rights: A Commentary* (Oxford University Press 2015) 1019.

[150] See art 2 of the draft European Convention on Human Rights prepared by the European Movement in 1949, reproduced in ECHR Travaux (n 135) vol 1, 296–302.

[151] In fact, in the drafting process of the ECHR, several drafters stressed that the Western conception of democracy underlies the Convention. See, eg, ECHR Travaux (n 135) vol 5, 290.

[152] R O'Connell, *Law, Democracy and the European Court of Human Rights* (Cambridge University Press 2020) 1. However, the ECtHR also referred to the concept of 'a democratic society' and identified its elements, such as freedom of political debate, in some earlier cases (*Lingens v Austria*, ECtHR, App No 9815/82, Merits and Just Satisfaction (8 July 1986) para 42). See generally Marks (n 148).

[153] *United Communist Party of Turkey and Others v Turkey*, ECtHR, App No 133/1996/752/951, Merits and Just Satisfaction (30 January 1998) para 45.

[154] See, eg, ibid para 46; *Bladet Tromsø and Stensaas v Norway*, ECtHR, App No 21980/93, Merits and Just Satisfaction (20 May 1999) paras 59 and 64.

[155] Human rights and representative democracy have been closely associated in the history of the development of regional human rights protection within the OAS. See NT Zúñiga, *The Inter-American Court of Human Rights: The Legitimacy of International Courts and Tribunals* (Routledge 2022) 67.

non-derogable rights under Article 27(2).[156] Nevertheless, the drafting process of the ACHR and its provisions are less clear on the concrete meaning of the concepts of 'democratic society' and 'democracy'.[157]

In the ICCPR, the concept of 'democratic society' had long been understood in a politically neutral manner.[158] In the drafting process of the UDHR, which first introduced the concept of 'democratic society', drafters initially assumed that a 'democratic society' should be defined according to a certain political model. However, there was a lack of consensus on a single conception of 'democracy', as Eastern[159] and Western Bloc[160] delegations blamed each other's political model, while defending their own to the extent that 'there existed two strongly divergent views as regards the meaning of the word "democracy"'.[161] Thus, drafters could not agree on a politically rich meaning of the term 'democratic society',[162] and a rather logically circular definition that 'the criterion of democracy in any nation was the extent to which human rights were really respected' remained.[163] The ICCPR's drafting process followed a similar pattern.[164] Considerations for diverse political systems were also prominent in the discussions on Article 25 (right to free elections).[165] Against this background, the HRC has long refrained from adopting interpretations based on a particular conception of democracy.[166]

[156] See also *The Word 'Laws' in Article 30 of the American Convention on Human Rights*, IACtHR, Series A No 6, Advisory Opinion OC-6/86 (9 May 1986) para 34.

[157] Those concepts were never the subject of real discussions in the ACHR's *travaux préparatoires*. See OEA, 'Conferencia Especializada Interamericana sobre Derechos Humanos, San José, Costa Rica' (1969) OEA/Ser.K/XVI/1.2. For the argument that the ACHR shares with the ECHR a commitment to liberal democracy and a fear of communism, see A Huneeus, 'When Illiberals Embrace Human Rights' (2019) 113 *AJIL Unbound* 380, 380–81.

[158] AL Svensson-McCarthy, *The International Law of Human Rights and States of Exception* (Martinus Nijhoff 1998) 101. In contrast, Garibaldi argued that 'some Western concept(s) of democracy' was adopted. However, such an argument is only based on the fact that the Soviet proposals were rejected and is not supported by positive evidence. See OM Garibaldi, 'On the Ideological Content of Human Rights Instruments' in T Buergenthal (ed), *Contemporary Issues in International Law: Essays in Honor of Louis B Sohn* (NP Engel 1984) 23, 65.

[159] See, eg, Statement by Mr Pavlov (USSR) in UN Commission on Human Rights, 51st mtg (28 May 1948) UN Doc E/CN.4/SR.51, 7–9.

[160] See, eg, Statement by Mr Mayhew (UK) in UNGA, Third Committee, 103rd mtg (15 October 1948) UN Doc A/C.3/SR.103, 160.

[161] Statement by Mr Baroody (Saudi Arabia) in UNGA, Third Committee, 152nd mtg (22 November 1948) UN Doc A/C.3/SR.152, 637.

[162] Svensson-McCarthy (n 158) 101.

[163] See, eg, Statement by Mr Cassin (France) in UN Commission on Human Rights, 51st mtg (28 May 1948) UN Doc E/CN.4/SR.51, 10.

[164] Garibaldi (n 158) 59–63.

[165] GH Fox, 'The Right to Political Participation in International Law' (1992) 17 *Yale Journal of International Law* 539, 555–60.

[166] See, eg, J Vidmar, 'Judicial Interpretations of Democracy in Human Rights Treaties' (2014) 3 *Cambridge Journal of International and Comparative Law* 532, 535–36.

1.4.2.3. The Competence of Treaty Organs

The most decisive difference between the two regional human rights courts and the HRC regarding their competence is that the former are judicial bodies and render *binding* judgments, while the latter is not a judicial body and issues *non-binding* 'Views' in the individual communications procedure. Nevertheless, the HRC's Views 'exhibit some of the principal characteristics of a judicial decision'[167] and it is 'the closest institution to an international adjudicatory body for human rights'.[168] The HRC applies procedural rules similar to those of (international) courts, such as: dividing the consideration of communication into the admissibility and merits phases; receiving statements, replies, rejoinders and additional submissions from the respondent states and victims in turn;[169] adopting interim measures;[170] applying judicial concepts such as burden of proof[171] and mootness;[172] adopting the structure of Views similar to judgments; and appending separate opinions of individual members.[173] The HRC interprets the ICCPR in accordance with the law of treaties under general international law[174] and its consolidated jurisprudence, and the Views are accompanied by legal reasoning, which has become increasingly elaborate in recent years. Thus, authors have recognised that '"Views" have a judgment-like quality'.[175] Moreover, the HRC has recently established formal procedures to hold oral hearings[176] and receive third-party intervention[177] (for a detailed examination of these procedures, see Chapter 3, section 3.3.5.2). Thus, the HRC's individual communication procedure and the regional courts' individual complaint procedure have comparable functions.

Furthermore, as far as the specific purpose of this study is concerned, the bindingness of treaty organs' decisions under international law per se does not make a decisive and qualitative difference. As this book will argue in Chapter 2, the disaggregation of a state in human rights treaties is interrelated to the blurring of the boundary between international and national

[167] HRC, 'General Comment No 33: Obligations of States Parties under the Optional Protocol to the International Covenant on Civil and Political Rights' (2008) UN Doc CCPR/C/GC/33, para 11.

[168] L Hennebel, 'The Human Rights Committee' in F Mégret and P Alston (eds), *The United Nations and Human Rights: A Critical Appraisal,* 2nd edn (Oxford University Press 2020) 339, 355.

[169] Rule 92 of the Rules of Procedure of the HRC (2021) UN Doc CCPR/C/3/Rev.12.

[170] ibid Rule 94.

[171] See D McGoldrick, *The Human Rights Committee: Its Role in the Development of the International Covenant on Civil and Political Rights* (Clarendon Press 1994) 145–50.

[172] Rules of Procedure of the HRC (n 169) Rule 104.

[173] ibid Rule 103.

[174] For the HRC's interpretive approach, see generally B Schlütter, 'Aspects of Human Rights Interpretation by the UN Treaty Bodies' in H Keller and G Ulfstein (eds), *UN Human Rights Treaty Bodies: Law and Legitimacy* (Cambridge University Press 2012) 261.

[175] ibid 266.

[176] HRC, 'Guidelines on Making Oral Comments concerning Communications' (2017) UN Doc CCPR/C/159.

[177] HRC, 'Guidelines on Information and Documentation Submitted by Third Parties' (2019) UN Doc CCPR/C/160.

legal orders, driven by the increasing embeddedness of human rights treaties and treaty organs in national legal orders. From this perspective, and given that international law does not have coercive enforcement mechanisms equivalent to those under national law even when a judgment is binding, a more important question than bindingness is the actual influence of treaties and treaty organs in the national legal orders of the states parties, which may depend on other factors such as the effectiveness of the international and national mechanisms for implementation of judgments/Views (see Chapter 2, section 2.1).

This book does not aim to provide a precise comparison of the compliance rates among the three human rights treaty organs. Nevertheless, Courtney Hillebrecht's study reports that, as of 2009, the compliance rate with ECtHR judgments stood at 48 per cent, while the rate for the IACtHR was 34 per cent as of 2008.[178] A study by Andreas J Ullmann and Andreas von Staden found that the overall compliance rate with UN human rights treaty bodies' Views between 1979 and 2019 ranged from 19 per cent to 39 per cent.[179] Although the methodology for calculating compliance rates is widely debated and varies across studies,[180] these studies suggest that the difference between the regional human rights courts and the HRC is quantitative, not qualitative: the former is more deeply embedded in national legal orders than the latter, thereby generating a higher chance of compliance. The same quantitative difference may apply between the ECtHR and the IACtHR, even though both have binding jurisdiction. It should be examined whether there is a trade-off between the impact of treaties and treaty organs on national legal orders and the intrusiveness of the treaty organs' approach in substance (see Chapter 4, section 4.5.2).[181]

This subsection has revealed the main, though not comprehensive, factors of plurality among the three systems that potentially influence the treaty organs' approaches to the disaggregation of a state and the operation of the 'separation of powers in a globalised democratic society' model. Given this plurality, one may wonder whether this book should treat the three systems separately and establish three different models that are most appropriate for the respective systems. Indeed, such an approach would have its merits, and the model

[178] Hillebrecht (n 58) 48–49.
[179] Ullmann and von Staden (n 98) 543.
[180] D Hawkins and W Jacoby, 'Partial Compliance: A Comparison of the European and Inter-American American Courts for Human Rights' (2010) 6 *Journal of International Law and International Relations* 35; G Stafford, 'The Implementation of Judgments of the European Court of Human Rights: Worse Than You Think – Part 1: Grade Inflation' *EJIL Talk!* (7 October 2019), https://www.ejiltalk.org/the-implementation-of-judgments-of-the-european-court-of-human-rights-worse-than-you-think-part-1-grade-inflation.
[181] Ulfstein (n 91) 300; Y Shany, 'Can Strasbourg Be Replicated at a Global Level? A View from Geneva' in H Aust and E Demir-Gürsel (eds), *The European Court of Human Rights: Current Challenges in Historical Perspective* (Edward Elgar 2021) 71, 81.

this book eventually proposes may truly be more suitable, either normatively or descriptively, to one system than another. Nevertheless, we cannot ignore the important elements of unity that underlie the three systems and signs of conversion among them in certain important aspects. Together with the elements of plurality, they make comparison beneficial and mutual learning possible under common frameworks.

2

Situating the Disaggregation of the State in a Broader Context

State Organs as Compliance Partners, Primary Decision-Makers and Autonomous Interlocutors

This chapter aims to integrate different strands of phenomena that constitute the disaggregation of the state in human rights treaties under a broader context – namely, the blurring of boundaries between international and national laws, and between the respective spheres in which treaty organs and state organs operate. After presenting an overview of human rights treaty organs' efforts to enhance the effectiveness of human rights treaty systems, which form the background of the disaggregation of the state in human rights treaties (section 2.1), the chapter introduces three types of disaggregation. In the first type, as part of their efforts to increase their effectiveness and impact on national legal orders, human rights treaty organs penetrate the surface of the state, imposing definitive demands on individual state organs. In this top-down and intrusive approach, state organs are treated as compliance partners for treaty organs (section 2.2). The second type of disaggregation involves treaty organs' responses to challenges concerning the democratic legitimacy of human rights treaty systems – challenges that arise from their growing impact on national legal orders. In contrast to the first type, treaty organs respect the decision-making authority of different types of state organs under their respective national constitutions. In this bottom-up and deferential approach, state organs are regarded as the primary decision-makers on human rights matters (section 2.3). In the third type of disaggregation, treaty organs increasingly recognise state organs as autonomous interlocutors in their proceedings and activities. This approach primarily applies to NHRIs, but it may also extend to other state organs, such as courts and parliaments. This form of disaggregation provides institutional support and serves as the foundation for both the top-down and bottom-up approaches to the disaggregation of the state (section 2.4).

2.1. EFFORTS OF HUMAN RIGHTS TREATY ORGANS AND STATES PARTIES TO ENHANCE THE EFFECTIVENESS OF HUMAN RIGHTS TREATIES

Unlike traditional fields of international law, which regulate relationships between states horizontally, human rights treaties govern the vertical relationship between a state and the individuals under its jurisdiction, a domain previously regulated solely by national public law.[1] Furthermore, compared with other fields of international law that focus on specific sectors, human rights treaties engage with the wide-ranging aspects of states' exercise of public authority.[2] As a result, non-compliance with human rights treaties, particularly with treaty organs' decisions,[3] often occurs when states lack appropriate national mechanisms for implementation.[4] Such states are not equipped to manage the need for legislative reform, annulment of administrative acts, interministerial coordination, payment of compensation or re-examination of domestic judgments.[5] Traditionally, the execution of international judgments was understood as 'executive or political in nature',[6] with international law largely indifferent to the mode of execution of international obligations and judgments.[7] However, effective implementation of human rights treaties and treaty organs' decisions requires 'embeddedness' within domestic legal

[1] G Ulfstein, 'A Transnational Separation of Powers?' in M Saul, A Follesdal and G Ulfstein (eds), *The International Human Rights Judiciary and National Parliaments: Europe and Beyond* (Cambridge University Press 2017) 21, 22.

[2] JH Fahner, *Judicial Deference in International Adjudication: A Comparative Analysis* (Hart Publishing 2020) 208–09.

[3] When discussing effective compliance with treaties, a distinction is often made between 'first-order compliance' (ie, compliance with the rules of the treaty itself) and 'second-order compliance' (ie, compliance with judgments and recommendations by authoritative bodies that interpret and apply the rules of the treaty): R Fischer, *Improving Compliance with International Law* (University Press of Virginia 1981) 25. Nevertheless, the distinction between first- and second-order compliance is not clear-cut and remains relative (see at 29). The precise meaning of typically vague and abstract treaty terms cannot be determined in isolation, and the jurisprudence of human rights treaty organs significantly influences this determination. Thus, this chapter refers to the effectiveness of human rights treaties as encompassing the effectiveness of human rights treaty organs.

[4] MG Schmidt, 'Follow-up Mechanisms Before UN Human Rights Treaty Bodies and the UN Mechanisms Beyond' in A Bayefsky (ed), *The UN Human Rights Treaty System in the 21st Century* (Kluwer Law International 2000) 233, 236–37. See also International Law Association (ILA), International Human Rights Law Committee, 'Final Report on the Domestic Implementation of Judgments/Decisions of Courts and Other International Bodies That Involve International Human Rights Law' (2016), www.ila-hq.org/en/documents/conference-report-johannesburg-2016-5, para 23.

[5] R Murray and C de Vos, 'Behind the State: Domestic Mechanisms and Procedures for the Implementation of Human Rights Judgments and Decisions' (2020) 12 *Journal of Human Rights Practice* 22, 23. Some states refrain from accepting treaty organs' jurisdiction precisely for this reason. See, eg, Toshiro Iijima (Counsellor, Minister's Secretariat, Ministry of Foreign Affairs), Committee of Judicial Affairs of the House of Representatives, 193rd Session of the National Diet, No 19 (2 June 2017) 17 (Japan).

[6] RF Oppong and AM Barreto, 'Enforcement' in WA Schabas and S Murphy (eds), *Research Handbook on International Courts and Tribunals* (Edward Elgar 2017) 273, 276.

[7] A Schaus, '1969 Vienna Convention: Article 27 Internal Law and Observance of Treaties' in O Corten and P Klein (eds), *The Vienna Conventions on the Law of Treaties: A Commentary* (Oxford University Press 2011) 688, 689.

orders.[8] 'Embeddedness' is a broader concept than the mere 'incorporation' of human rights treaties;[9] it aims to transform state organs into 'first-line defenders' of human rights treaties[10] and to realise human rights treaties and treaty organs' decisions 'at home'.[11] Since the 1990s and 2000s, when treaty organs established the basic frameworks of their procedures and jurisprudence, and gained solid support from states parties and other stakeholders, they have worked in cooperation with states parties to develop both international supervisory mechanisms and national mechanisms for increasing embeddedness of human rights treaties within national legal orders.

2.1.1. The European Convention on Human Rights

In addition to the obligation to provide financial compensation to victims by way of 'just satisfaction' under Article 41 ECHR, the obligation to abide by the ECtHR's judgments under Article 46(1) has been interpreted as requiring individual measures to ensure *restitutio in integrum* for the applicant and general measures to prevent similar and repetitive violations.[12] Multiple mechanisms within the Council of Europe support the supervision of the execution of ECtHR judgments.

Under Article 46(2) ECHR, the Committee of Ministers (CoM) – the Council of Europe's statutory decision-making body, composed of the foreign ministers of Member States – bears the primary responsibility for supervising the execution of ECtHR judgments. Supervision mainly takes place at the CoM's human rights meetings. Since the entry into force of Protocol No 11 to the ECHR[13] in 1998, which established a single, full-time court with compulsory jurisdiction, the CoM has made various efforts to improve the effectiveness and efficiency of supervision. First, it created the Department for the Execution of Judgments of the European Court of Human Rights,[14] which assists it in assessing the state of execution, proposing resolutions for adoption, engaging in ongoing dialogue with national authorities,[15] and providing

[8] LR Helfer, 'Redesigning the European Court of Human Rights: Embeddedness as a Deep Structural Principle of the European Human Rights Regime' (2008) 19 *EJIL* 125.

[9] ibid 137.

[10] ibid 156.

[11] ibid 159.

[12] CoM, 'Rules of the Committee of Ministers for the Supervision of the Execution of Judgments and of the Terms of Friendly Settlements' (2006) Rule 6 (2).

[13] Protocol No 11 to the Convention for the Protection of Human Rights and Fundamental Freedoms, restructuring the control machinery established thereby (signed 11 May 1994, entered into force 1 November 1998) CETS No 155.

[14] See generally 'Mandate of the Department for the Execution of Judgments of the European Court of Human Rights' *Council of Europe*, https://rm.coe.int/16805a997c.

[15] For the effectiveness of such dialogues, see C Sandoval, P Leach and R Murray, 'Monitoring, Cajoling and Promoting Dialogue: What Role for Supranational Human Rights Bodies in the Implementation of Individual Decisions?' (2020) 12 *Journal of Human Rights Practice* 71, 79.

technical advice and support.[16] Second, the CoM has required states which have been the subject of violation judgments to submit 'action plans' outlining the measures they intend to take to implement judgments,[17] and 'action reports' on the measures taken.[18] The CoM has also received communications from non-governmental organisations (NGOs) and NHRIs regarding the execution of judgments,[19] thereby preventing the premature closure of case supervision.[20] Third, since 2011, the Committee has applied a twin-track supervision procedure, dividing cases into standard and enhanced procedures, with the latter prioritised to allocate more time and resources for supervision.[21]

Since the 2000s, the Parliamentary Assembly (PACE), the statutory organ of the Council of Europe composed of 306 parliamentarians from the national parliaments of 46 Member States, has become increasingly involved in supervising the execution of ECtHR judgments (see also Chapter 5, section 5.3).[22] It has recommended that the CoM, the ECtHR, states parties and state organs, including national parliaments, take steps to ensure more rapid and effective execution.[23] Since 2006, the PACE's Committee on Legal Affairs and Human Rights has appointed rapporteurs on the execution of ECtHR judgments, who conduct in situ visits to countries with serious non-execution issues to discuss solutions with the relevant national authorities.[24]

In addition, Protocol No 14 of the ECHR,[25] which came into force in 2010, introduced an infringement procedure by inserting Article 46(4) into the ECHR.[26] The procedure aims to add 'further possibilities of bringing pressure to bear [on existing procedures]' as its 'mere existence, and the threat of using

[16] B Çali and A Koch, 'Foxes Guarding the Foxes? The Peer Review of Human Rights Judgments by the Committee of Ministers of the Council of Europe' (2014) 14 *HRLR* 301, 313–19.

[17] CoM, 'Information Documents, Human Rights Working Methods: Improved Effectiveness of the Committee of Ministers' Supervision of Execution of Judgments' (2004) CM/Inf (2004) 8-final.

[18] CoM, 'Decisions Adopted at the 1059th (DH) Meeting' (2009) CM/Del/Dec (2009) 1059-immediat.

[19] CoM (n 12) Rule 9.

[20] A Küçüksu, 'Enforcing Rights beyond Litigation: Mapping NGO Strategies in Monitoring ECtHR Judgement Implementation' (2022) 22 *HRLR* 1.

[21] CoM, 'Information Documents, Supervision of the Execution of Judgments and Decisions of the European Court of Human Rights: Implementation of the Interlaken Action Plan – Modalities for a Twin-Track Supervision System' (2010) CM/Inf/DH(2010)37.

[22] See generally A Drzemczewski, 'The Parliamentary Assembly's Involvement in the Supervision of the Judgments of the Strasbourg Court' (2010) 28 *Netherlands Quarterly of Human Rights* 164.

[23] See, eg, PACE Res 1226, 'Execution of Judgments of the European Court of Human Rights' (28 September 2000).

[24] PACE's Committee on Legal Affairs and Human Rights, Mr Erik Jurgens (Rapporteur), 'Implementation of judgments of the European Court of Human Rights' (2006) PACE Doc 11020, A-5.

[25] Protocol No 14 to the Convention for the Protection of Human Rights and Fundamental Freedoms, amending the control system of the Convention (signed 13 May 2004, entered into force 1 June 2010) CETS No 194.

[26] See generally F de Londras and K Dzehtsiarou, 'Mission Impossible? Addressing Non-execution through Infringement Proceedings in the European Court of Human Rights' (2017) 66 *ICLQ* 467.

it, should act as an effective new incentive to execute the Court's judgments'.[27] The ECtHR's 2019 judgment, applying this procedure for the first time, and confirming Azerbaijan's failure to implement the *Ilgar Mammadov* judgment, ultimately led to Azerbaijan's compliance.[28]

In tandem with these developments concerning the supervision mechanism, the impact of the ECHR and the ECtHR within national legal orders has rapidly increased. In 1990, the ECHR lacked legal effect in the national legal orders of many states.[29] However, soon after Protocol No 11 entered into force in 1998, all states parties incorporated the ECHR.[30] According to a 2008 survey by Helen Keller and Alec Stone Sweet, in the legal orders of many Member States, the ECHR: (i) binds all national officials in the exercise of public authority; (ii) holds at least supra-legislative status; and (iii) can be directly invoked by individuals before judges.[31] As such, the ECHR enjoys the status of 'a kind of surrogate, or shadow, Constitution'.[32] In a few states, such as Belgium[33] and Luxembourg,[34] national courts have held that treaties, especially the ECHR,[35] prevail over national constitutions. When national courts interpret the ECHR, they are required to[36] – and most do[37] – consider the ECtHR's jurisprudence,

[27] Council of Europe, 'Explanatory Report to Protocol No 14 to the Convention for the Protection of Human Rights and Fundamental Freedoms, Amending the Control System of the Convention' (2004) para 100.

[28] CoM, 'H46-3 Ilgar Mammadov Group v. Azerbaijan (Application No 15172/13): Supervision of the Execution of the European Court's Judgments, Decisions' (2020) CM/Del/Dec(2020)1377bis/H46-3, para 2.

[29] Such states included Denmark, Iceland, Ireland, Norway, Sweden and the UK.

[30] J Polakiewicz, 'The Status of the Convention in National Law' in R Blackburn and J Polakiewicz (eds), *Fundamental Rights in Europe: The European Convention on Human Rights and its Member States 1950–2000* (Oxford University Press 2001) 31, 36. See generally H Keller and AS Sweet (eds), *A Europe of Rights: The Impact of the ECHR on National Legal Systems* (Oxford University Press 2008).

[31] H Keller and AS Sweet, 'Assessing the Impact of the ECHR on National Legal Systems' in Keller and Sweet (n 30) 677, 683.

[32] ibid 686.

[33] See generally Y Lejeune, 'Les rapports normatifs entre la Constitution belge et le droit international ou européen dans l'ordre interne à l'aune des relations entre ordres juridiques primaires' (2012) 45 *Revue Belge de Droit International* 372.

[34] See generally K Patrick, 'Le rôle du droit international dans l'ordre juridique luxembourgeois' (2010) 34 *Pasicrisie luxembourgeoise* 399, 413–15.

[35] Even though national courts in these states have declared the primacy of treaties over the constitution in general terms, such cases mostly concerned the ECHR. See S Hamamoto, 'Naze jouyaku ga kenpou ni yui suru no ka: Berugi to Rukusenburuku no jissen [Why Treaties Prevail over Constitutions: The Practices of Belgium and Luxembourg]' (2018) 1131 *Houritsu jihou* 66, 70.

[36] High-Level Conference on the Future of the European Court of Human Rights, 'Interlaken Declaration' (19 February 2010) Action Plan: B-4-(c); Steering Committee for Human Rights, 'CDDH Report on the Longer-Term Future of the System of the European Convention on Human Rights' (2015) Doc CDDH(2015)R84 Addendum I, para 37.

[37] PACE's Committee on Legal Affairs and Human Rights, 'Contribution to the Conference on the Principle of Subsidiarity, Skopje, 1–2 October 2010' (2010) AS/Jur/Inf (2010) 04, 17–44; J Gerards and J Fleuren, 'Comparative Analysis' in J Gerards and J Fleuren (eds), *Implementation of the European Convention on Human Rights and of the Judgments of the ECtHR in National Case Law* (Intersentia 2014) 333, 357–63.

including its judgments directed towards other states parties, under the principle of *res interpretata*.[38] Prominent examples include the UK's Human Rights Act 1998, which provides that UK courts 'must take into account any judgment, decision, declaration or advisory opinion' of the ECtHR,[39] and Ukrainian Law No 3477–IV of 2006, which stipulates that '[national] courts shall apply the Convention and the case law of the Court as a source of law'.[40]

In 2000, the CoM adopted Recommendation No R (2000) 2, which states that in certain circumstances, the re-examination or re-opening of proceedings is the most efficient way to achieve *restitutio in integrum*, which is necessary for the implementation of the ECtHR's judgments.[41] The CoM then encouraged states parties to examine their national legal systems to ensure adequate possibilities for the re-examination of cases based on ECtHR judgments.[42] Member States responded swiftly and, by 2006, more than 80 per cent of them had established the possibility of re-opening criminal proceedings.[43] Although only half of the states had admitted this possibility in civil and administrative proceedings at the time,[44] the number has since increased. For example, the Czech Republic introduced retrial procedures for criminal cases in 2004 and extended them to civil and administrative cases in 2013.[45] Similarly, France created procedures for re-examining criminal decisions in 2000[46] and civil decisions in 2016.[47]

Some states parties have implementation legislation that defines the competences and responsibilities of the relevant actors, along with mechanisms to coordinate their efforts in implementing ECtHR judgments.[48] Italy's 2006 Azzolini Law coordinates the relationship between the main domestic organs

[38] See generally A Bodnar, 'Res Interpretata: Legal Effect of the European Court of Human Rights' Judgments for Other States Than Those Which were Party to the Proceedings' in Y Haeck and E Brems (eds), *Human Rights and Civil Liberties in the 21st Century* (Springer 2014) 223.

[39] Human Rights Act 1998 (9 November 1998) (UK) s 2(1)(a).

[40] Law No 3477–IV of 2006 on the Implementation of Decisions and Application of the Practice of the European Court of Human Rights (23 February 2006) (Ukraine) art 17 (1).

[41] CoM Recommendation No R (2000) 2 (19 January 2000) Preamble.

[42] ibid para II.

[43] CoM, 'Ensuring the Continued Effectiveness of the European Convention on Human Rights: The Implementation of the Reform Measures Adopted by the Committee of Ministers at its 114th Session' (2006) CM(2006)39-final, IV.2.

[44] ibid.

[45] I Pospíšil (Secretary General of the Constitutional Court of the Czech Republic), 'Comments on Reopening Trials in the Civil Matters after the ECtHR Judgments: Experience from the Czech Republic' *Round Table on Reopening of Proceedings Following a Judgment of the European Court of Human Rights* (5–6 October 2015), www.coe.int/cs/web/execution/reopening-of-proceedings ?desktop=true.

[46] Code de procédure pénale, as originally introduced by Act No 2000-516 (15 June 2000) (France) art 622-1.

[47] Code de l'organisation judiciaire, as amended by Act No 2016-1547 (18 November 2016) (France) art L452-1.

[48] PACE's Parliamentary Project Support Division, 'The Role of Parliaments in Implementing ECHR Standards: Overview of Existing Structures and Mechanisms' (2016) PPSD (2016)19, Section 4: National Implementation Laws.

involved in implementing ECtHR judgments.[49] Ukraine also introduced a law in 2006, imposing specific duties on state organs for supervision.[50] The former Yugoslav Republic of Macedonia (now the Republic of North Macedonia) adopted the Law on Enforcement of ECtHR Judgments in 2009, amending it in 2014, under which an Inter-Departmental Commission initiates the implementation of ECtHR judgments.[51] In 2015, the Office of the Czech Government Agent established a Committee of Experts on the Execution of Judgments of the European Court of Human Rights, which discusses and recommends measures for the implementation of ECtHR judgments.[52]

2.1.2. The American Convention on Human Rights

Unlike the ECHR, the ACHR does not designate a body or procedure for supervising the execution of IACtHR judgments.[53] Left in a position to create its own supervisory function,[54] the IACtHR has assumed this role on its own since 1996,[55] relying on its *compétence de la compétence* and Articles 33, 62(1), 62(3) and 65 ACHR, as well as the general acceptance of the IACtHR's monitoring function by states parties and other actors.[56]

According to Article 69(1) of the Rules of Procedure of the IACtHR, the IACtHR requires states with violation judgments to submit reports on the implementation measures, which are followed by the observations of the victim and the IACmHR. Since 2007, the IACtHR has held hearings whenever necessary.[57] Through this monitoring procedure, the IACtHR determines whether a judgment has been complied with – if not, it issues orders on the necessary measures.[58] This

[49] Law No 12/2006 (10 January 2006) (Italy).

[50] Law No 3477–IV of 2006 (Ukraine) (n 40).

[51] Law on the Enforcement of the Decisions of the European Court of Human Rights, No 07–2328/1 (21 May 2009) (Former Yugoslav Republic of Macedonia).

[52] PACE, *Handbook for Parliamentarians: National Parliaments as Guarantors of Human Rights in Europe* (Council of Europe 2018) 46.

[53] Article 65 of the ACHR refers to the supervision of the execution of IACtHR's judgments only indirectly: 'the Court shall submit, for the [General Assembly of the Organization of American States]' consideration, a report on its work during the previous year. It shall specify, in particular, the cases in which a state has not complied with its judgments, making any pertinent recommendations'.

[54] CM Bailliet, 'Procedure for Monitoring Compliance with Judgments and Other Decisions: Inter-American Court of Human Rights (IACtHR)' (last updated 2021) in A Peters (ed), *Max Planck Encyclopedias of International Law* (Oxford University Press online edition) para 3.

[55] *Velásquez Rodríguez v Honduras*, IACtHR, Order on Monitoring Compliance with Judgment (10 September 1996); *Godínez Cruz v Honduras*, IACtHR, Order on Monitoring Compliance with Judgment (10 September 1996).

[56] *Baena Ricardo et al v Panama*, IACtHR, Series C No 104, Competence (28 November 2003) paras 68 and 84–104.

[57] JM Pasqualucci, *The Practice and Procedure of the Inter-American Court of Human Rights*, 2nd edn (Cambridge University Press 2013) 304. See art 69 (3) of the Rules of Procedure of the IACtHR.

[58] Article 69(4) of the Rules of Procedure of the IACtHR.

procedure is repeated until the state fully complies with the judgment. For example, since the IACtHR delivered its judgment on merit in *Barrios Altos v Peru* in 2001, it has issued 12 orders on compliance with this judgment as of March 2025. In addition, the IACtHR conducts on-site visits, during which its delegation directly communicates with relevant authorities to facilitate compliance.[59]

Like their European counterparts, the ACHR and the IACtHR have had an increasingly significant impact on national legal orders. Manuel Góngora Mera noted that since around 2000, the ACHR has acquired a status equivalent to that of national constitutions as part of the 'constitutional block'[60] in most Member States, either through a decision of *pouvoir constituant* (political constitutionalisation) or through judicial rulings (judicial constitutionalisation).[61] The former case includes Argentina, where the Constitution provides that human rights treaties, including the ACHR, 'have constitutional hierarchy'.[62] The latter case includes Panama, where the Supreme Court relied on Article 4 of the 1972 Constitution, which merely states that Panama complies with international law, to recognise the constitutional status of certain human rights treaties, including the ACHR.[63] When national courts interpret the ACHR as part of the 'constitutional block', they normally take into account the IACtHR's jurisprudence, including judgments directed towards other states parties.[64] For instance, the Supreme Court of the Dominican Republic held that the IACtHR's interpretations are binding on the Dominican Republic and its judiciary.[65] Similarly, the Constitutional Court of Peru accepted that the IACtHR's judgments and interpretations, even when addressed to other states, are binding on all domestic institutions, including the Constitutional Court.[66] The Supreme Court of Argentina recognised that the IACtHR's jurisprudence constitutes 'an ineludible guide' for state organs in interpreting the ACHR.[67]

Certain states have adopted implementation laws. As early as 1981, Costa Rica signed an agreement with the IACtHR granting its judgments the same effect as those handed down by Costa Rica's national courts once transmitted to

[59] Bailliet (n 54) para 14.

[60] For this concept and its adaptation in Latin American countries, see M Góngora-Mera, 'The Block of Constitutionality as the Doctrinal Pivot of a *Ius Commune*' in A von Bogdandy et al, *Transformative Constitutionalism in Latin America: The Emergence of a New Ius Commune* (Oxford University Press 2017) 235.

[61] M Góngora-Mera, *Inter-American Judicial Constitutionalism: On the Constitutional Rank of Human Rights Treaties in Latin America through National and Inter-American Adjudication* (Inter-American Institute of Human Rights 2011) 66.

[62] 1994 Constitution (Argentina) s 75(22).

[63] Góngora-Mera (n 61) 85–87.

[64] See *Cabrera García and Montiel Flores v Mexico*, IACtHR, Series C No 220, Preliminary Objection, Merits, Reparations, and Costs (26 November 2010) paras 226–32.

[65] Supreme Court, Res No 1920-2003 (13 November 2003) (Dominican Republic).

[66] Constitutional Court, No 2730-2006-PA/TC (21 July 2006) (Peru) Ground 12.

[67] Supreme Court, *Mazzeo, Julio Lilo et al*, Appeal for Annulment and Constitutional Motion, M. 2333. XLII (13 July 2007) (Argentina) para 20.

domestic administrative or judicial authorities.[68] After the fall of the Fujimori regime, Peru first adopted presidential decrees and later enacted a law[69] regulating the coordination procedure among relevant state organs for implementing judgments and recommendations from international human rights organs.

Unlike ECHR Member States, few ACHR Member States have procedures for re-opening proceedings based on IACtHR judgments.[70] Nevertheless, in certain states, national courts have relied on an IACtHR judgment to re-open criminal proceedings. For example, following the IACtHR's *Barrios Altos v Peru* judgment in 2001, the Constitutional Court of Peru permitted the re-opening of criminal proceedings, even in cases not directly involved in the judgment.[71] After the IACtHR's ruling in *Fermín Ramírez v Guatemala* in 2005, the Supreme Court of Justice of Guatemala decided to conduct a new trial for the applicant, ensuring due process of law.[72] In 2019, the Supreme Court of Chile annulled criminal convictions against indigenous leaders after the IACtHR's judgment in *Norin Catrimán et al (Leaders, Members and Activists of the Mapuche Indigenous People) v Chile* (2014).[73]

2.1.3. UN Human Rights Treaties

In contrast to the judgments of the ECtHR and the IACtHR, the Views of the HRC in the individual communications procedure are not binding under international law. Nevertheless, the gradual development of follow-up procedures for these Views has made it increasingly difficult for states parties to persist in non-implementation.[74] In the early days of its work, due to the absence of express provisions concerning the monitoring of the implementation of Views

[68] Cited in Thomas Buergenthal, 'The Inter-American Court of Human Rights' (1982) 76 *American Journal of International Law (AJIL)* 231, 240.

[69] Law No 27.775, Regulating the Procedure for the Execution of Judgments Issued by Supranational Tribunals (27 June 2002) (Peru).

[70] Pasqualucci (n 57) 312.

[71] Constitutional Court, *Martín Rivas*, No 4587-2004-PA/TC-AA/TC (29 November 2005) (Peru). These cases of voluntary re-opening of proceedings are positively valued as the bottom-up conventionality control. See J Contesse, 'The International Authority of the Inter-American Court of Human Rights: A Critique of the Conventionality Control Doctrine' (2018) 22 *IJHR* 1168, 1179–83.

[72] Supreme Court, Agreement No 96–2006 (23 January 2006) (Guatemala), cited in J Martínez Ventura, 'Jurisprudencia de los órganos de protección de derechos humanos y derecho penal internacional: Casos de Guatemala, Costa Rica y El Salvador' in K Ambos, E Malarino, and G Elsner (eds), *Sistema Interamericano de protección de los derechos humanos y derecho penal internacional* (Konrad-Adenauer Stiftung 2010) 103, 105–06.

[73] Supreme Court, Decision AD 1386-2014 (16 May 2019) (Chile). The attitude of the Supreme Court in this case is described as 'an inter-American tribunal'. See J Contesse, 'The Supreme Court of Chile as an Inter-American Tribunal' *I-CONnect* (31 May 2019), www.iconnectblog.com/the-supreme-court-of-chile-as-an-inter-american-tribunal.

[74] However, for the criticisms against the lack of transparency and effectiveness of the HRC's follow-up procedure, see ILA (n 4) paras 21–23.

in the Optional Protocol to the ICCPR and the principle of non-intervention in domestic affairs under Article 2(7) of the UN Charter,[75] the HRC refrained from taking an active role.[76] However, as the HRC gained the trust of states parties and the East–West tensions within the Committee were alleviated following the end of the Cold War,[77] the idea that monitoring the implementation of its Views is inherent in the tasks of the HRC 'to achieve the purposes of the [ICCPR] and the implementation of its provisions' (Preamble to the Optional Protocol to the ICCPR) gradually became prevalent.[78] Thus, in 1990, the HRC began appointing a Special Rapporteur to follow up on its Views.[79] Since 1995, the HRC has published information on its follow-up activities in its annual reports.[80] In 2005, the HRC started to publish a list of cases and categorised the recommendations issued in Views as 'satisfactory response', 'unsatisfactory response' and 'no follow-up response', based on states' follow-up responses.[81] Since 2013, the HRC has rated the measures indicated in states' follow-up reports on a scale from A (reply/action largely satisfactory) to E (the measures taken go against the recommendations).[82] In 2022, the HRC adopted the Guidelines for the Follow-up Reports on Views aimed at improving the efficiency, effectiveness and consistency of the follow-up procedure. For example, when a state party has one or more cases pending implementation, the List of Issues or the List of Issues Prior to Reporting for the state reporting procedure will automatically include questions concerning the case(s).[83] The guidelines also introduced the category of 'focused cases', which require prioritised attention and treatment.[84]

[75] For the opinions of Committee members opposing the follow-up function, see HRC Report (1983) UN Doc A/38/40, para 392.

[76] For the history of the development of the HRC's follow-up roles, see Schmidt (n 4) 234–44.

[77] T Buergenthal, 'The U.N. Human Rights Committee' (2001) 5 *Max Planck Yearbook of United Nations Law* 341, 368.

[78] AM de Zayas, 'Follow-up Procedure of the UN Human Rights Committee: The Commentary' (1991) 47 *Review: International Commission of Jurists* 28, 31. Nevertheless, a couple of states still resist the HRC's competence to conduct follow up to its Views. See Views of the Chinese Government Regarding the Human Rights Treaty Body Strengthening Process (2011) UN Doc HRC/NONE/2011/184, para 2.8; Comments of the Russian Federation on the List of Issues Identified during the Treaty Body Strengthening Consultations (2012) UN Doc HRC/NONE/2012/1, 6, available at: www.ohchr.org/EN/HRBodies/HRTD/Pages/StatesPartiesSubmissions.aspx.

[79] HRC Report (1990) UN Doc A/45/40 (Vol. II) Appendix XI. For the HRC's effort on follow-up before 1990, see N Ando, 'The Follow-up Procedure of the Human Rights Committee's Views' in N Ando et al (eds), *Liber Amicorum Judge Shigeru Oda*, vol 2 (Kluwer Law International 2002) 1437, 1442–44.

[80] HRC Report (1995) UN Doc A/50/40, paras 544–65.

[81] HRC Report on its Work on its 82nd-84th Sessions (2005) UN Doc A/60/40 (vol. I) 120–38.

[82] HRC Report on its Work on its 108th-110th Sessions (2014) UN Doc A/69/40 (vol. I) para 262. Some authors have pointed out the risks and flaws in such categorisation. See A Donald, D Long and AK Speck, 'Identifying and Assessing the Implementation of Human Rights Decisions' (2020) 12 *Journal of Human Rights Practice* 125, 142.

[83] HRC, 'Guidelines for the Follow-up Reports on Views' (2022) UN Doc CCPR/C/162, para 32.

[84] ibid para 19.

Although the HRC's Views are not binding, they form, along with its General Comments (and to a limited extent, concluding observations), 'jurisprudence' and 'interpretative case law'.[85] Such jurisprudence is given 'great weight' not only as a matter of international law – as the ICJ stated in *Diallo* (2010)[86] – but also, in many states, as a matter of national law, although its impact is far more modest compared to the influence of regional human rights courts.[87] Kate Fox Principi's study in 2017 indicated that, in at least 27 cases, the Views of UN human rights treaty bodies (mostly the HRC) led to the enactment, amendment, repeal, or development of legislation.[88] Moreover, a survey conducted by the International Law Association (ILA) in 2004 concluded that UN human rights treaty bodies' jurisprudence is given 'considerable weight' before most national courts.[89] Machiko Kanetake observed that national courts felt 'normative expectations' to consider the jurisprudence of UN human rights treaty bodies, including the HRC.[90] Even when arriving at conclusions different from those of the UN human rights treaty bodies' jurisprudence, national courts tend to provide thorough explanations and/or try to distinguish their cases from the jurisprudence of the treaty bodies.[91] The Spanish Supreme Court's judgment in 2018 went so far as to affirm that the Views of the Committee on the Elimination of Discrimination against Women (CEDAW) were binding at the national level.[92] Although the Spanish Supreme Court 'retrace[d] its steps'[93] in 2020 by distinguishing the HRC's Views from binding ECtHR judgments and permitting only the latter as grounds for retrial,[94] it reaffirmed the binding/compulsory character of UN human rights treaty bodies' Views in 2023.[95]

[85] *Affaire Ahmadou Sadio Diallo (République de Guinée c République démocratique du Congo) (fond)* [2010] CIJ Recueil 639, para 66.

[86] ibid.

[87] ILA (n 4) paras 85 and 88.

[88] KF Principi, 'United Nations Individual Complaint Procedures: How Do States Comply?' (2017) 37 *Human Rights Law Journal (HRLJ)* 1, 7.

[89] ILA, Committee on International Human Rights Law and Practice, 'Final Report on the Impact of Findings of the United Nations Human Rights Treaty Bodies' (2004), www.ila-hq.org/en/documents/conference-report-berlin-2004-9, para 175. For a more recent study, see M Kanetake, 'UN Human Rights Treaty Monitoring Bodies before Domestic Courts' (2018) 67 *ICLQ* 201.

[90] M Kanetake, 'Giving Due Consideration: A Normative Pathway between UN Human Rights Treaty-Monitoring Bodies and Domestic Courts' in N Krisch (ed), *Entangled Legalities beyond the State* (Cambridge University Press 2021) 133, 148.

[91] See, eg, Federal Constitutional Court, 1 BvL 8/15 (26 July 2016) (Germany) para 90.

[92] Supreme Court, ROJ: STS 2747/2018 (17 July 2018) (Spain) 12.

[93] K Casla, 'Spain's Supreme Court is at it Again: UN Treaty Body Decisions are Binding' *EJIL: Talk!* (22 January 2024), www.ejiltalk.org/spains-supreme-court-is-at-it-again-un-treaty-body-decisions-are-binding.

[94] Supreme Court, ROJ: STS 1/2020 (12 February 2020) (Spain) Sixth legal basis.

[95] Supreme Court, ROJ: STS 1597/2023 (29 November 2023) (Spain) Seventh legal basis. For an analysis of the series of judgments by the Supreme Court of Spain on the nature of Views of UN human rights treaty bodies, see E Jiménez Pineda, 'The Legal Value of the Decisions Given by the United Nations Human Rights Treaty Bodies in Light of the Judgments of the Spanish Supreme Court of 13 June 2023 (STS 786/2023) and of 29 November 2023 (STS 1597/2023): End of Story?' (2023) 27 *Spanish Yearbook of International Law* 191.

A dozen states provide for the re-opening of criminal and/or civil proceedings based on decisions made by UN human rights treaty bodies.[96] In 2001, Norway amended its criminal and civil procedures to allow for the re-opening of cases based on decisions made by an international body, including the HRC.[97] Some national courts have treated treaty bodies' decisions as newly discovered evidence that permits the re-opening of proceedings.[98] Additionally, several states have established constitutional and legislative procedures to provide compensation to victims following treaty bodies' decisions.[99] In 1996, Colombia adopted Law 288, which provides for a mechanism to compensate victims in accordance with the HRC's decisions.[100] Lithuania passed the Law on the Compensation of Damage Caused by the Unlawful Actions of Public Authorities in 2002, which is also applicable to the implementation of the HRC's Views.[101] Some states have established laws and procedures to facilitate coordination among relevant authorities for implementation. In Czechia, the Ministry of Justice is responsible for coordinating the implementation of the HRC's Views under Act No 517/2002 Coll.[102] The Republic of Korea created the 'Task Force in Individual Communications' in 2006, involving pertinent ministries, courts, and the NHRI,[103] while in 2011, Cameroon set up the Inter-ministerial Committee responsible for monitoring the implementation of decisions by international and regional human rights mechanisms.[104]

2.2. STATE ORGANS AS HUMAN RIGHTS TREATY ORGANS' COMPLIANCE PARTNERS: A TOP-DOWN AND INTRUSIVE APPROACH

As part of the broader trend and effort to enhance the impact of human rights treaties and human rights treaty organs on national legal orders, as discussed in

[96] KF Principi, 'Internal Mechanisms to Implement U.N. Human Rights Decisions, Notably of the U.N. Human Rights Committee' (2017) 37 *HRLJ* 237, 241–44.

[97] Fifth Periodic Report of Norway to the HRC (2004) UN Doc CCPR/C/NOR/2004/5, para 157.

[98] See, eg, Supreme Court, No 4-0743/16 Criminal Case (12 June 2016) (Kyrgyzstan) cited in Principi (n 96) 243.

[99] Principi (n 96) 244–46.

[100] Law 288 (5 July 1996) (Colombia). For a detailed analysis of this law, see J Acosta-López and G Vega-Barbosa, 'Compliance with International Human Rights Obligations in Colombia: Assessing the Normative Evolution and Practical Challenges' in R Grote, M Morales Antoniazzi and D Paris (eds), *Research Handbook on Compliance in International Human Rights Law* (Edward Elgar 2021) 313, 323–25.

[101] Law on Reparation of Damage Caused by Unlawful Acts of Public Authorities, No IX-895 (21 May 2002) (Republic of Lithuania) arts 1(1) and 2(5).

[102] Act No 517/2002 Coll of Laws on Some Measures in the System of Central State Organs (14 November 2002) (Czechia).

[103] Fourth Periodic Report of the Republic of Korea to the HRC (2013) UN Doc CCPR/C/KOR/4, para 29.

[104] Order No 81/CAB/PM (15 April 2011) (Cameroon). See the Fifth Periodic Report of Cameroon to the HRC (2016) UN Doc CCPR/C/CMR/5, paras 11–16.

the previous section, treaty organs have sought to pierce the veil of the state to transform individual state organs into compliance partners. To this end, they began imposing specific orders and requests on individual state organs in a top-down, intrusive manner. This practice aligns with the findings of so-called 'compliance theories', which empirically showed that compliance with human rights treaties requires cooperation not only from the executive branch, which has traditionally represented the state on the international plane, but also from other state organs, including courts and parliaments (see Chapter 1, section 1.1.2).[105]

2.2.1. The European Court of Human Rights

Article 41 ECHR, the only express provision concerning the ECtHR's competence to order remedial measures, refers solely to 'just satisfaction' for the injured party. The *travaux préparatoires* of this provision indicate that the ECHR's drafters intentionally avoided granting the ECtHR the authority to amend national legislation or judgments.[106] In line with this intention, the ECtHR has long denied its competence to order specific measures beyond monetary compensation. The content of remedial measures and the allocation of roles among state organs are left to the discretion of the state. In *Marckx v Belgium* (1979), concerning the unequal treatment of legitimate and illegitimate children under Belgium's Civil Code, the ECtHR stated that 'the Court's judgment is essentially declaratory and leaves to the State the choice of the means [for the implementation of a judgment]'.[107] Although the ECtHR acknowledged the possibility that 'a judgment finding a breach of the Convention … might render desirable or necessary a reform of the law', it emphasised that '[i]t is for the respondent State, and the respondent State alone, to take the measures it considers appropriate to ensure that its domestic law is coherent and consistent'.[108] In *La Compte, Van Leuven and De Meyere v Belgium* (1982), the ECtHR maintained that 'it is not empowered under the Convention' to order states to annul sanctions and sentences.[109] The ECtHR consistently upheld this interpretation of Article 41 in subsequent

[105] For the list of studies to this effect, see Murray and de Vos (n 5) 22–23. See also presentations by D Kosar, J Petrov, D Paris and Ø Stiansen in the *Informal Dialogue on the Execution of Judgments of the European Court of Human Rights Seen through the Lens of Compliance Research* (Strasbourg, 30 November 2020) DH-DD(2020)1138.

[106] JL Sharpe, 'Article 50' in LE Pettiti et al (eds), *La convention européenne des droits de l'homme; commentaire article par article* (Economica 1999) 809, 809–10.

[107] *Marckx v Belgium*, ECtHR, App No 6833/74, Merits and Just Satisfaction (13 June 1979) para 58.

[108] ibid para 42.

[109] *Le Compte, van Leuven and de Meyere v Belgium*, ECtHR, App No 6878/75; 7238/75, Just Satisfaction (18 October 1982) para 13.

cases.[110] This modest approach likely stems from the ECtHR's respect for state sovereignty.[111]

The ECHR system underwent significant change in the 2000s. First, to address so-called 'clone cases' arising from structural issues and flaws in national legal systems, the concept of the pilot judgment procedure gradually emerged during the drafting of Protocol No 14. Although the ECtHR suggested that such a procedure should be expressly provided for in Protocol No 14,[112] the Steering Committee on Human Rights of the Committee of Ministers (CDDH) indicated that 'the pilot judgment procedure could be followed without there being a need to amend the ECHR'.[113] Consequently, in 2004, the CoM invited the ECtHR 'to identify, in its judgments finding a violation of the Convention, what it considers to be an underlying systemic problem and the source of this problem'.[114] The CoM further recommended that Member States 'review, following Court judgments which point to structural or general deficiencies in national law or practice, the effectiveness of the existing domestic remedies and, where necessary, set up effective remedies'.[115] Given this political initiative, the ECtHR introduced the pilot judgment procedure in 2004.[116] Although the CoM only asked the ECtHR to identify structural problems and their sources, the ECtHR voluntarily went further by often indicating specific remedial measures in the operative part of its judgments. Some have criticised this practice, arguing that it undermines 'the principle that States [are] free to choose the means of executing judgments' and lacks a clear legal basis.[117] However, since the first pilot judgment in *Broniowski v Poland* (2004), the ECtHR has maintained that this competence derives from Article 46 ECHR.[118]

As structural problems are often caused by flawed or inadequate legislation, the ECtHR has frequently ordered measures that substantially address national

[110] See, eg, *Campbell and Cosans v UK*, ECtHR, App No 7511/76; 7743/76, Just Satisfaction (23 March 1983) para 16; *Gillow v UK*, ECtHR, App No 9063/80, Just Satisfaction (14 September 1987) para 9.

[111] B Dickson, 'The Council of Europe and the European Convention' in B Dickson (ed), *Human Rights and the European Convention: The Effects of the Convention on the United Kingdom and Ireland* (Sweet & Maxwell 1997) 1, 19; E Steiner, '"Just Satisfaction" under Art 41 ECHR: A Compromise in 1950 – Problematic Now' in A Fenyves at al (eds), *Tort Law in the Jurisprudence of the European Court of Human Rights* (De Gruyter 2011) 3, 9 (citing A von Staden's statement).

[112] ECtHR, 'Position Paper of the European Court of Human Rights on Proposals for Reform of the European Convention on Human Rights and Other Measures as Set out in the Report of the Steering Committee of Human Rights of 4 April 2003' (2003) CDDH(2003)006 final, para 46.

[113] CDDH, 'Interim Activity Report: Guaranteeing the Long-term Effectiveness of the ECtHR – Implementation of the Declaration Adopted by the Committee of Ministers at its 112 Session (14–15 May 2003)' (2004) CM(2003)165-Add I, para 21.

[114] CoM Res Res(2004)3 (12 May 2004) para I.

[115] CoM Recommendation Rec(2004)6 (12 May 2004) para II.

[116] For the pilot judgment procedure, see generally D Haider, *The Pilot-Judgement Procedure of the European Court of Human Rights* (Brill 2013).

[117] *Sejdovic v Italy*, ECtHR [GC], App No 56581/00, Merits and Just Satisfaction (1 March 2006) paras 115–17.

[118] *Broniowski v Poland*, ECtHR, App No 31443/96, Merits (22 June 2004) para 194.

parliaments, such as legislative amendments.[119] For example, in *Ürper and Others v Turkey* (2009), after finding that the suspension of the publication and distribution of newspapers concerned under anti-terrorist legislation violated Article 10 ECHR, the Court stated that 'the respondent Government should revise section 6(5) of Law No 3713 to take account of the principles enunciated in the present judgment'.[120] In *Manushaqe Puto and Others v Albania* (2012), the Court required the respondent state to 'avoid frequent changes of the legislation and carefully examine all legal and financial implications before introducing further modifications'.[121] Markus Fyrnys described this new practice as 'judicially decreed cooperation of an international court with domestic legislation' and 'an innovative judicial strategy of imposing the Court's legal arguments on domestic legal and political systems' to secure more effective compliance.[122]

Second, following the CoM' initiative to encourage national systems for re-opening proceedings based on ECtHR judgments (see section 2.1.1), the ECtHR began indicating the re-opening of domestic proceedings in the context of Article 41.[123] In several judgments against Turkey on 23 October 2003, after finding that the applicants were sentenced by a court that was not independent and impartial, in violation of Article 6 (1) of the ECHR, the ECtHR held that 'in principle, the most appropriate remedy would be to have the applicant retried in good time by an independent and impartial tribunal'.[124] Initially, the ECtHR limited itself to suggesting retrial as an appropriate remedy and refrained from including such measures in the operative part of the judgment. However, some judges proposed that the re-opening of proceedings should be ordered in the operative part of the judgment to ensure effective implementation.[125] Thus, in *Maksimov v Azerbaijan* (2009), the ECtHR ordered the re-opening of proceedings in the operative paragraph.[126] While most cases of this nature concern

[119] See generally KM Larsen, 'Compliance with Judgments from the European Court of Human Rights: The Court's Call for Legislative Reforms' (2013) 31 *NJHR* 496, 504–07.

[120] *Ürper and Others v Turkey*, ECtHR, App Nos 14526/07, 14747/07, 15022/07, 15737/07, 36137/07, 47245/07, 50371/07, 50372/07 and 54637/07, Merits and Just Satisfaction (20 October 2009) para 52.

[121] *Manushaqe Puto v Albania*, ECtHR, App Nos 604/07, 43628/07, 46684/07 and 34770/09, Merits and Just Satisfaction (31 July 2012) para 110.

[122] M Fyrnys, 'Expanding Competences by Judicial Lawmaking: The Pilot Judgment Procedure of the European Court of Human Rights' (2011) 12 *German Law Journal* 1231, 1244.

[123] See generally P Leach, 'No Longer Offering Fine Mantras to a Parched Child? The European Court's Developing Approach to Remedies' in A Føllesdal, B Peters and G Ulfstein (eds), *Constituting Europe: The European Court of Human Rights in a National, European and Global Context* (Cambridge University Press 2013) 142, 152–57.

[124] *Gençel v Turkey*, ECtHR, App No 53431/99, Merits and Just Satisfaction (23 October 2003) para 27, and other similar judgments against Turkey rendered on the same date.

[125] *Vladimir Romanov v Russia*, ECtHR, App No 41461/02, ECtHR, Merits and Just Satisfaction (24 July 2008) Joint Concurring Opinion of Judges Spielmann and Malinverni, para 6; *Salduz v Turkey*, ECtHR, App No 36391/02, ECtHR, Merits and Just Satisfaction (27 November 2008) Joint Concurring Opinion of Judges Rozakis, Spielmann, Ziemele and Lazarova Trajkovska, para 13.

[126] *Maksimov v Azerbaijan*, ECtHR, App No 38228/05, Merits and Just Satisfaction (8 October 2009) operative para 3.

criminal matters, the ECtHR has issued similar orders in a few civil cases.[127] Moreover, in *Scoppola v Italy (No 2)* in 2009, the ECtHR went a step further.[128] Beyond ordering a retrial, it prescribed the specific outcome to be achieved by the national court, ordering that 'the sentence of life imprisonment imposed on the applicant is replaced by a penalty consistent with the principles set out in the present judgment'.[129] Although these recommendations and orders are formally addressed to states, they are substantially addressed to national courts, as only national courts can implement them.

Beyond the context of re-opening of proceedings, the ECtHR has also emphasised the role and responsibility of national courts and the need to establish a partnership with them to ensure the implementation of the ECHR and ECtHR judgments. In *Fabris v France* (2013), which concerned the application by national courts of transitional provisions in legislation enacted to comply with a previous ECtHR judgment on similar facts, the ECtHR reiterated the principle:

> The adoption of general measures requires the State concerned to prevent, with diligence, further violations similar to those found in the Court's judgments ... This imposes an obligation on the domestic courts to ensure, in conformity with their constitutional order and having regard to the principle of legal certainty, the full effect of the Convention standards, as interpreted by the Court.[130]

Raffaela Kunz analysed that this 'brave formulation' is likely due to facts unique to the *Fabris* judgment, in that it reinforces an earlier ruling and reflects the fact that the ordinary judiciary in France now reviews national legislation in light of the ECtHR's jurisprudence.[131] Although this case has been rather isolated in affirming the 'obligation' of domestic courts, it supports the ECtHR's general approach of piercing the veil of the unitary state.[132]

2.2.2. The Inter-American Court of Human Rights

Article 63 (1) ACHR authorises the IACtHR to order three types of reparation measures when it finds a violation: the court shall rule that (i) the injured party be ensured the enjoyment of the right or freedom that was violated; (ii) the consequences of the measure or situation that constituted the breach of

[127] *Lungoci v Romania*, ECtHR, App No 62710/00, Merits and Just Satisfaction (26 January 2006) operative para 3.

[128] Some authors felt that the ECtHR went 'too far'. See Leach (n 123) 157.

[129] *Scoppola v Italy (No 2)*, ECtHR, App No 10249/03, Merits and Just Satisfaction (17 September 2009) operative para 6(a).

[130] *Fabris v France*, ECtHR [GC], App No 16574/08, Merits (7 February 2013) para 75.

[131] R Kunz, 'Judging International Judgments Anew? The Human Rights Courts before Domestic Courts' (2019) 30 *EJIL* 1129, 1138.

[132] ibid.

such right or freedom be remedied; and (iii) fair compensation be paid to the injured party. In contrast to Article 41 ECHR, which only mentions the ECtHR's competence to grant 'just satisfaction', this provision, especially elements (i) and (ii) above, provides a solid basis for the IACtHR to exercise its competence more broadly.[133] Beyond ordering monetary compensation, it is authorised to order measures for *restitutio in integrum* and non-repetition. In the *travaux préparatoires* of the ACHR, the original draft of this provision, which stated that 'the Court shall be competent to determine the amount of compensation to be paid to the injured party', was changed to the current version,[134] to grant the IACtHR more comprehensive competence.[135]

In its early days, the IACtHR exercised this competence in a limited manner, principally confining its orders to monetary compensation.[136] For example, in *Velásquez-Rodríguez v Honduras* (1989), concerning the breach of obligations to prevent and investigate the forced disappearances, the IACtHR refrained from ordering measures beyond monetary compensation such as investigation and punishment of the perpetrators in the operative part of the judgment, despite the IACmHR's request to that effect.[137] Scholars have criticised the IACtHR's modest approach, arguing that it succumbed to state sovereignty and failed to exploit its potential to promote the effective enforcement of human rights.[138]

However, since around 2000, the IACtHR has rapidly expanded its jurisprudence on ordering concrete reparation measures, which are often described as 'innovative' and 'far-reaching'.[139] Some of these orders are substantially addressed to individual state organs. In *Olmedo-Bustos et al v Chile (The Last Temptation of Christ)* (2001), the IACtHR ordered that 'the State must amend its domestic law, within a reasonable period, in order to eliminate prior censorship to allow exhibition of the film "The Last Temptation

[133] J Schneider, *Reparation and Enforcement of Judgments: A Comparative Analysis of the European and Inter-American Human Rights Systems* (epubli GmbH 2015) 98.

[134] 'Observations by the Governments of the Member States on the Draft Inter-American Convention on Protection of Human Rights: Guatemala' (8 November 1969) OEA/Ser.K/XVI/1.1 doc. 24, reprinted in T Buergenthal and RR Norris (eds), *Human Rights: The Inter-American System: Booklet 13, Vol. 2* (Oceana Publications 1982) 119, 132.

[135] L Hennebel and H Tigroudja, *The American Convention on Human Rights: A Commentary* (Oxford University Press 2022) 1302–03.

[136] See generally D Cassel, 'The Expanding Scope and Impact of Reparations Awarded by the Inter-American Court of Human Rights' in M Bossuyt et al (eds), *Out of the Ashes: Reparations for Gross Violations of Human Rights* (Intersentia 2006) 91.

[137] *Velásquez-Rodríguez v Honduras*, IACtHR, Series C No 7, Reparations and Costs (21 July 1989) para 32.

[138] JM Pasqualucci, 'Victim Reparations in the Inter-American Human Rights System: A Critical Assessment of Current Practice and Procedure' (1996) 18 *Michigan Journal of International* 1, 12 and 57; D Shelton, 'Reparations in the Inter-American System' in DJ Harris and S Livingstone (eds), *The Inter-American System of Human Rights* (Oxford University Press 1998) 151, 169; LJ Laplante, 'Bringing Effective Remedies Home: The Inter-American Human Rights System, Reparations, and the Duty of Prevention' (2004) 22 *Netherlands Quarterly of Human Rights* 347, 388.

[139] D Shelton, *Remedies in International Human Rights Law*, 3rd edn (Oxford University Press 2015) 229–30.

of Christ"'.[140] In *Hilaire, Constantine and Benjamin et al v Trinidad and Tobago* (2002), the IACtHR ordered the state to modify the Offences against the Person Act of 1925[141] and even specified the elements to be included in the new legislation.[142] In *Molina-Theissen v Guatemala* (2009), the IACtHR ordered the respondent state to appoint officers for specific administrative institutions and tasks, including coordinating with public prosecutors and courts to establish a schedule to advance investigations and legal proceedings concerning serious human rights violations.[143] Where the IACtHR finds a violation of the obligation to investigate, prosecute and punish serious human rights violations, it orders the respondent state, as a reparation measure, to investigate, prosecute and punish the perpetrators.[144] The IACtHR also orders the annulment of national judgments when they involve violations of the ACHR.[145] These orders are formally directed at states. Nevertheless, in normal constitutional democracies, including ACHR Member States, only a parliament can amend legislation, and only domestic courts can issue sentences. Thus, these orders are, in effect, directed towards parliaments, administrative organs and domestic courts.[146]

The increased intrusion of the IACtHR into the allocation of national authority also appears in the form of determining the legal effect of national laws. Initially, the Court followed the traditional model where international courts interpreted and applied international law, and national courts interpreted and applied national law.[147] In Advisory Opinion OC-14/94 (1994), in response to the question of the 'legal effects of a law that manifestly violates [the ACHR]', the IACtHR stated that: 'It is not appropriate for the Court to rule on its domestic legal effect within the state concerned. That determination is within the exclusive jurisdiction of the national courts and should be decided in accordance with their laws.'[148] However, with the growing national

[140] *Olmedo-Bustos et al ('The Last Temptation of Christ') v Chile*, IACtHR, Series C No 73, Merits, Reparations and Costs (5 February 2001) operative para 4.

[141] *Hilaire, Constantine and Benjamin et al v Trinidad and Tobago*, IACtHR, Series C No 94, Merits, Reparations and Costs (21 June 2002) operative paras 8–9.

[142] ibid para 212.

[143] *Molina-Theissen v Guatemala*, IACtHR, Order on Monitoring Compliance with Judgment (16 November 2009) para 32.

[144] *Bámaca-Velásquez v Guatemala*, IACtHR, Series C No 70, Merits (25 November 2000) operative para 8.

[145] See, eg, *Gustavo Adolfo Cesti Hurtado v Peru*, IACtHR, Series C No 56, Merits (29 September 1999) operative para 8.

[146] Y Negishi, 'The Subsidiarity Principle's Role in Allocating Competences between Human Rights Courts and States Parties' in A von Bogdandy, MM Antoniazzi and F Piovesan (eds), *Ius constitutionale commune na America latina*, vol III (Juruá Editora 2016) 125, 144–45. See also R Murray and C Sandoval, 'Balancing Specificity of Reparation Measures and States' Discretion to Enhance Implementation' (2020) 12 *Journal of Human Rights Practice* 101, 108–09.

[147] Ximena Fuentes Torrijo, 'La evolución de la relación normativa entre el Sistema Interamericano de Derechos Humanos y los sistemas jurídicos nacionales' (2021) 19 *I-CON* 1207, 1209–10.

[148] *International Responsibility for the Promulgation and Enforcement of Laws in Violation of the Convention (Arts. 1 and 2 of the American Convention on Human Rights)*, IACtHR, Series A No 14, Advisory Opinion OC-14/94 (9 December 1994) paras 31 and 34.

trend towards expanding the 'constitutional block' to include the ACHR,[149] the IACtHR took a bold step in *Barrios Altos v Peru* (2001) by stating in the operative paragraph that 'Amnesty Laws No. 26479 and No. 26492 are incompatible with the American Convention on Human Rights and, consequently, lack legal effect'.[150] This judgment has attracted academic attention for adopting a monist approach to the relationship between international and national legal orders.[151] However, from the perspective of the relationship between actors, this judgment is notable for the IACtHR's assertion of authority to decide the validity of national legislation, traditionally the sole competence of the national parliament and/or national courts.[152]

Furthermore, in *Almonacid Arellano v Chile* (2006), a case concerning the application of an amnesty law, the IACtHR introduced the doctrine of 'conventionality control' (*control de convencionalidad*).[153] This doctrine primarily governs the relationship between the IACtHR and national courts,[154] directly addressing national courts to transform them into the IACtHR's 'objective allies'.[155] It posits that the ACHR directly obliges not only the state as a whole but also 'the Judiciary [to] exercise a sort of "conventionality control" between the domestic legal provisions which are applied to specific cases and the [ACHR]'.[156] Moreover: 'To perform this task, the Judiciary has to take into account not only the [ACHR], but also the interpretation thereof made by the [IACtHR], which is the ultimate interpreter of the [ACHR].'[157] The IACtHR has used this doctrine to emphasise the obligation of national courts under the ACHR not to enforce laws, particularly amnesty laws, that contradict the ACHR and the IACtHR's judgments, thereby 'transfer[ring] authority to domestic judges, bypassing domestic legislatures'.[158] The highest courts of some states have accepted this obligation, albeit sometimes with nuance,[159] contributing to the effective implementation of the ACHR and the

[149] Fuentes Torrijo (n 147) 1210.

[150] *Barrios Altos v Peru*, IACtHR, Series C No 75, Merits (14 March 2001) operative para 4.

[151] See, eg, Schneider (n 133) 110.

[152] See A Cassese, 'Y-a-t-il un conflit insurmountable entre souveraineté des États et justice pénale internationale?' in A Cassese and M Delmas-Marty (eds), *Crimes Internationaux et juridictions internationals* (Presses universitaires de France 2002) 13, 16.

[153] See generally P Gonzalez-Dominguez, *The Doctrine of Conventionality Control: Between Uniformity and Legal Pluralism in the Inter-American Human Rights System* (Intersentia 2018).

[154] Note that the scope of this doctrine was later extended to all state organs. See *Cabrera García and Montiel Flores v Mexico* (n 64) para 225. Nevertheless, the IACtHR has invoked this doctrine mostly with regard to national courts.

[155] L Burgorgue-Larsen, 'Chronique d'une théorie en vogue en Amérique latine Décryptage du discours doctrinal sur le contrôle de conventionalité' (2014) 100 *Revue française de droit constitutionnel* 831, 836.

[156] *Almonacid-Arellano et al v Chile*, IACtHR, Series C No 154, Preliminary Objections, Merits, Reparations and Costs (26 September 2006) para 124.

[157] ibid.

[158] J Contesse, 'The International Authority of the Inter-American Court of Human Rights' (2018) 22 *IJHR* 1168, 1170.

[159] See generally L Burgorgue-Larsen, 'Conventionality Control: Inter-American Court of Human Rights (IACtHR)' (last updated 2018) in H Ruiz Fabri (ed), *Max Planck Encyclopedias of*

IACtHR's judgments. For example, in 2011, following the IACtHR's judgment in *Radilla Pacheco v Mexico*, the Mexican Supreme Court recognised the obligation of all Mexican judges to exercise conventionality control and thus refrained from applying a norm that provided for military courts' jurisdiction over cases involving civilians.[160]

2.2.3. The UN Human Rights Committee

Article 5(4) of the Optional Protocol to the ICCPR simply states that '[t]he Committee shall forward its views to the State Party concerned and to the individual' and does not specify the scope of the HRC's competence to recommend remedial measures. In its earliest cases, the HRC confined itself to declaring in general terms that the state party concerned was obliged to 'take immediate steps to ensure strict observance of the provisions of the Covenant and to provide effective remedies to the victims'.[161] However, the HRC soon began to rely on Article 2(3) ICCPR – a provision concerning states parties' obligations to ensure remedies for victims of violations of Covenant rights – to recommend specific remedial measures.[162] Previous studies have noted that the HRC's jurisprudence on reparation is more similar to that of the IACtHR than the ECtHR, as the HRC typically recommends concrete measures beyond monetary compensation, whereas the ECtHR considers such indications to be an exception.[163] The reparation measures indicated by the HRC aim to provide full reparations to victims (restitution, compensation, rehabilitation and measures of satisfaction), and to ensure guarantees of non-repetition.[164] They encompass wide-ranging measures.[165]

Some of these recommendations are specifically directed towards particular state organs such as parliaments and courts. For example, in *Shirin*

International Procedural Law (Oxford University Press online edition) paras 34–42; ML Deftou, 'Fostering the Rule of Law in the Americas' (2020) 38 *NJHR* 78, 90–92. See also the various articles published in (2016) 64 *Revista del Instituto Interamericano de Derechos Humanos* on the acceptance of the conventionality control doctrine in ACHR Member States. National courts consider not only judgments rendered in contentious cases but also advisory opinions. See W Arévalo Ramírez and A Rousset Siri, 'Compliance with Advisory Opinions in the Inter-American Human Rights System' (2023) 117 *AJIL Unbound* 298, 301–02.

[160] Supreme Court, No 912/2010, Resolution (14 July 2011) (Mexico).

[161] *Bazzano/Valentini/Massera v Uruguay*, HRC, Communication No 5/1977 (15 August 1979) UN Doc CCPR/C/OP/1, 40, para 10.

[162] See, eg, *Delia Saldias de Lopez v Uruguay*, HRC, Communication No 52/1979 (29 July 1981) UN Doc CCPR/C/13/D/52/1979, para 14. See generally E Klein, 'Individual Reparation Claims under the International Covenant on Civil and Political Rights: The Practice of the Human Rights Committee' in A Randelzhofer and C Tomuschat (eds), *State Responsibility and the Individual Reparation in Instances of Grave Violations of Human Rights* (Nijhoff 1999) 27.

[163] V David, 'Reparations at the Human Rights Committee: Legal Basis, Practice and Challenges' (2014) 32 *Netherlands Quarterly of Human Rights* 8, 39.

[164] HRC, 'Guidelines on Measures of Reparation under the Optional Protocol to the International Covenant on Civil and Political Rights' (2016) UN Doc CCPR/C/158, para 2.

[165] Shelton (n 139) 198–99.

Aumeeruddy-Cziffra and 19 Other Mauritian Women v Mauritius (1981), after finding that the Immigration (Amendment) Act 1977 and the Deportation (Amendment) Act 1977 resulted in discrimination against the authors on the grounds of sex, the HRC recommended that 'the State party should adjust the provisions of the [abovementioned acts] in order to implement its obligations under the Covenant'.[166] In *Jeong-Eun Lee v Republic of Korea* (2005), after finding a violation of Article 22 on freedom of association, the HRC identified a specific provision within the law that needed amending.[167] In *Violeta Setelich v Uruguay* (1981), where Article 14 on the right to a fair trial was violated, the HRC recommended that the state party 'give [the author] a fresh trial with all the procedural guarantees prescribed by article 14 of the Covenant'.[168] In some cases, the HRC went even further, suggesting the outcome that such a trial should achieve, such as the annulment of a conviction[169] or the commutation of a sentence.[170] The HRC also recommended investigating the disappearance of the victim and punishing those responsible.[171]

The HRC has supplemented this approach of addressing specific state organs with its General Comments and concluding observations. It consistently recommended that states parties consider incorporating the ICCPR[172] and has urged domestic courts to apply and take it into account.[173] In recent years, the HRC has also encouraged states parties to strengthen their legislative scrutiny of laws affecting human rights.[174]

2.3. STATE ORGANS AS PRIMARY DECISION-MAKERS: A BOTTOM-UP AND DEFERENTIAL APPROACH

Given developments at both the international and national levels, as well as the human rights treaty organs' efforts described in the previous subsections, human rights treaties and treaty organs are now significantly embedded in domestic legal orders. Human rights treaty organs, particularly regional courts, often play roles

[166] *Shirin Aumeeruddy-Cziffra and 19 Other Mauritian Women v Mauritius*, HRC, Communication No 35/1978 (9 April 1981) UN Doc CCPR/C/OP/1, 67, para 11.

[167] *Jeong-Eun Lee v Republic of Korea*, HRC, Communication No 1119/2002 (20 July 2005) UN Doc CCPR/C/84/D/1119/2002, para 9.

[168] *Violeta Setelich v Uruguay*, HRC, Communication No 63/1979 (28 October 1981) UN Doc CCPR/C/OP/1, 101, para 21.

[169] See, eg, *Hak-Chul Shin v Republic of Korea*, HRC, Communication No 926/2000 (16 March 2004) UN Doc CCPR/C/80/D/926/2000, para 9.

[170] See, eg, *Bernard Lubuto v Zambia*, HRC, Communication No 390/1990 (31 October 1995) UN Doc CCPR/C/55/D/390/1990, para 9.

[171] See, eg, *Barbarin Mojica v Dominican Republic*, HRC, Communication No 449/1991 (15 July 1994) UN Doc CCPR/C/51/D/449/1991, para 7.

[172] HRC, 'General Comment No 31: The Nature of the General Legal Obligation Imposed on States Parties to the Covenant' (2004) UN Doc CCPR/C/21/Rev.1/Add.13, para 13.

[173] See, eg, HRC, 'Concluding Observations on the Fourth Periodic Report of Paraguay' (2019) UN Doc CCPR/C/PRY/CO/4, paras 4–5.

[174] See, eg, HRC, 'Concluding Observations on the Sixth Periodic Report of Australia' (2017) UN Doc CCPR/C/AUS/CO/6, paras 11 and 12.

similar to those of 'constitutional courts',[175] substantially overturning constitutions, statutory laws, and judgments of supreme or constitutional courts, thereby significantly interfering in the competences of state organs under national constitutions.[176] The ECtHR has shaped key national policies across a wide range of areas, including LGBTIQ+ rights, reproductive rights, the rights of immigrants and asylum seekers, the rights of Roma and Travellers, environmental rights, hate crime and hate speech issues, personal data protection, anti-terrorism, and judicial systems.[177] Similarly, the IACtHR's impact on national amnesty laws[178] and LGBTIQ+ rights[179] is well known.[180] In the edited volume *The Impact of the Inter-American Human Rights System: Transformations on the Ground* (2024), the authors demonstrate that the IACtHR's judgments and advisory opinions have fostered structural 'transformations' that go beyond 'compliance', throughout Latin America, in various fields.[181] The edited book *The Impact of the United Nations Human Rights Treaties on the Domestic Level: Twenty Years on* (2024) examines the impact of UN human rights treaties on 20 selected countries across all regions.[182] Owing to the non-binding nature of its Views and recommendations, the HRC exerts the least influence among the three treaty organs.[183] Nevertheless, it has often affected national policies in areas such as minority rights, LGBTIQ+ rights, the rights of asylum seekers and migrants, and social legislation,[184] albeit typically not as the sole factor, but as one of the reasons.[185] To cite a couple of

[175] AS Sweet, 'Sur la constitutionnalisation de la Convention européenne des droits de l'homme' (2009) 80 *Revue trimestrielle des droits de l'homme* 923.

[176] G Ulfstein, 'The European Court of Human Rights and National Courts: A Constitutional Relationship?' in OM Arnardóttir and A Buyse (eds), *Shifting Centres of Gravity in Human Rights Protection: Rethinking Relations between the ECHR, EU, and National Legal Orders* (Routledge 2016) 46, 47; A von Bogdandy, 'Ius Constitutionale Commune en América Latina: Observations on Transformative Constitutionalism' (2015) 110 *AJIL Unbound* 109, 109.

[177] For the most comprehensive review on the ECtHR's impact on national policies in various fields, see the thematic factsheets published by the Department for the Execution of Judgments of the European Court of Human Rights, available at: www.coe.int/en/web/execution/thematic-factsheets.

[178] L Mallinder, 'The End of Amnesty or Regional Overreach? Interpreting the Erosion of South America's Amnesty Laws' (2016) 65 *ICLQ* 645.

[179] Constitutional Chamber of the Supreme Court, Res No 12782–2018 (8 August 2018) (Costa Rica); Constitutional Court, 10-18-CN/19 Case No 10-18-CN (Marriage between Same-sex Persons) (12 June 2019) (Ecuador); Constitutional Court, 11-18-CN/19 Case No 11-18-CN (Equal Marriage) (12 June 2019) (Ecuador).

[180] For its impact in other policy areas, see MM Antoniazzi, and P Saavedra Alessandri, 'Inter-Americanization: Its Legal Bases and Political Impact' in von Bogdandy et al (n 60) 255, 269–75.

[181] A von Bogdandy et al (eds), *The Impact of the Inter-American Human Rights System: Transformations on the Ground* (Oxford University Press 2024).

[182] C Heyns, FJ Viljoen and R Murray (eds), *The Impact of the United Nations Human Rights Treaties on the Domestic Level: Twenty Years on*, 2nd edn (Brill 2024).

[183] ILA (n 4) paras 85 and 88.

[184] For a list of such cases, see KF Principi, 'Implementation of Decisions under Treaty Body Complaints Procedures: Do States Comply? How Do They Do it?' (January 2017), https://hr.un.org/sites/hr.un.org/files/editors/u4492/Implementation%20of%20decisions%20under%20treaty%20body%20complaints%20procedures%20-%20Do%20states%20comply%20-%202015%20Sabbatical%20-%20Kate%20Fox.pdf, Annex I.

[185] See generally Heyns, Viljoen and Murray (n 182).

well-known examples,[186] given the HRC's Views in *Toonen v Australia* (1994), concerning the criminalisation of homosexual contact between consenting adults in private spaces, the Australian Parliament passed the Human Rights (Sexual Conduct) Act 1994 to override the Tasmanian law in question. In 2018, the Irish government decided to hold a referendum on liberalising its strict abortion laws, a decision strongly influenced by the HRC's Views in *Amanda Mellet v Ireland* (2016) and *Siobhán Whelan v Ireland* (2017).[187]

The growing influence of treaty organs on national legal orders has raised concerns about democratic legitimacy. Richard Bellamy argued that treaty organs are 'not only less democratically legitimate than domestic legislative and judicial mechanisms for the promotion and protection of rights but [they] also risk undermining these domestic [mechanisms]'.[188] Andreas Føllesdal highlighted that 'the treaty bodies surely "make law" when they interpret dynamically – yet they carry out this legislative task without democratic accountability'.[189] Domestic authorities have invoked this democratic legitimacy challenge, particularly when human rights treaty organs substantially overturned constitutions, statutory laws, and judgments of supreme or constitutional courts. In some cases, the challenge is exacerbated by regional courts' efforts to disaggregate the state and target specific state organs directly – efforts that this book described in section 2.2 as a top-down and intrusive approach.[190] Furthermore, populist politicians have often exploited the discourse surrounding the democratic legitimacy of human rights treaty organs, with the tabloid media sensationalising the issue and spreading it widely among the public.[191] Consequently, the backlash based on democratic legitimacy challenges has intensified, especially against the ECtHR (section 2.3.1) and the IACtHR (section 2.3.2), undermining the stability of these regimes. Although the HRC and other UN human rights treaty bodies are not affected to the same extent, they have not been entirely immune (section 2.3.3). In this context, treaty organs have introduced a bottom-up and deferential approach, recognising the distinct competences of individual state organs in national decision-making

[186] In addition to the cases cited below, for Nordic and Baltic cases of amending laws based on HRC Views, see M Scheinin, 'Domestic Implementation of International Human Rights Treaties: Nordic and Baltic Experiences' in P Alston and J Crawford (eds), *The Future of UN Human Rights Treaty Monitoring* (Cambridge University Press 2000) 229, 241–42.

[187] See KF Principi, 'Implementation of UN Treaty Body Decisions: A Brief Insight for Practitioners' (2020) 12 *Journal of Human Rights Practice* 185, 190.

[188] R Bellamy, 'The Democratic Legitimacy of International Human Rights Conventions: Political Constitutionalism and the European Convention on Human Rights' (2014) 25 *EJIL* 1019, 1020.

[189] A Føllesdal, 'The Legitimacy Deficits of the Human Rights Judiciary: Elements and Implications of a Normative Theory' (2013) 14 *Theoretical Inquiries in Law* 339, 344.

[190] See the UK's reaction to the ECtHR's judgment in *Greens and MT v UK* (2010) in section 2.3.1, and Guatemala's reaction to the IACtHR's 2019 order on provisional measures and supervision of compliance regarding the *Chichupac* judgment in section 2.3.2.

[191] J Petrov, 'The Populist Challenge to the European Court of Human Rights' (2020) 18 *I-CON* 476, 494–505.

affecting human rights and showing a degree of deference when these organs act within their competence (section 2.3.4).

2.3.1. Democratic Legitimacy Challenges against the European Court of Human Rights

The criticism surrounding democratic legitimacy has been most pronounced in the UK. Given its strong confidence in the long history of stable democracy, the UK's primary motivation for joining the ECHR was not to protect democracy or human rights domestically, but to prevent the resurgence of totalitarianism abroad.[192] Consequently, the UK has long viewed the ECHR as a foreign matter. When it incorporated the ECHR via the Human Rights Act 1998, it was emphasised that this would 'allow British judges … to make their own distinctive contribution to the development of human rights in Europe'[193] and reinstate the UK as 'an international standard bearer of liberty and justice' and 'the world's teacher, not its pupil'.[194] Furthermore, the UK upholds 'parliamentary sovereignty' as a core constitutional principle[195] and follows a system of political constitutionalism.[196] Given these factors, it is unsurprising that the UK has become the centre of democratic legitimacy criticisms against the ECtHR.[197]

The UK's hostility towards the ECtHR became evident in the issue of prisoner voting. In *Hirst (No 2) v UK* (2005), the ECtHR ruled that prohibiting convicted prisoners from voting in elections under the Representation of the People Act 1983 violated Article 3 of Protocol No 1.[198] Following the UK's ongoing failure to implement this judgment, the ECtHR employed the pilot judgment procedure in *Greens and MT v UK* (2010), ordering the UK to 'bring forward … legislative proposals intended to amend the 1983 Act … in a manner which is Convention-compliant'.[199] The fact that the ECtHR not only criticised the 1983 Act, enacted by a democratically elected parliament, but also ordered its amendment

[192] A Moravcsik, 'The Origins of Human Rights Regimes. Democratic Delegation in Postwar Europe' (2000) 54 *International Organization* 217, 242.

[193] The Lord Chancellor (Lord Irvine of Lairg), HL Deb, vol 582, col 1227 (3 November 1997) (UK).

[194] Lord Chief Justice, Lord Bingham, 'The European Convention on Human Rights: Time to Incorporate', *Denning Lecture, Bar Association of Commerce, Finance and Industry* (1993), reproduced in R Blackburn, *Towards a Constitutional Bill of Rights for the United Kingdom: Commentary and Documents* (Pinter 1999) 1019, 1022–23.

[195] AV Dicey, *Lectures Introductory to the Study of The Law of Constitution* (MacMillan & Co. 1885) Lecture II: The Sovereignty of Parliament.

[196] R Bellamy, 'Political Constitutionalism' in P Cane and H Kumarasingham (eds), *The Cambridge Constitutional History of the United Kingdom* (Cambridge University Press 2023) 59.

[197] Therefore, in the drafting process of the ECHR, participants from the UK were reluctant to create the ECtHR for its allegedly 'anti-democratic' character. See Council of Europe, *Collected Edition of the "Travaux préparatoires" of the European Convention on Human Rights*, vol 2 (Martinus Nijhoff 1975) 168.

[198] *Hirst v UK (No 2)*, ECtHR [GC], App No 74025/01, Merits and Just Satisfaction (6 October 2005).

[199] *Greens and MT v UK*, ECtHR, App Nos 60041/08 and 60054/08, Merits and Just Satisfaction (23 November 2010) operative para 6.

sparked significant controversy about the relationship between the ECtHR and the UK Parliament. A backbench debate was held in the House of Commons in 2011, where MP David Davis, a leading sponsor of the debate, raised a fundamental question: 'Who should decide? Should it be the European Court of Human Rights, or this House on behalf of the British people?'[200] Eventually, a motion was passed by 234 to 22 votes, emphasising that 'legislative decisions of this nature [ie, prisoner voting] should be a matter for democratically-elected lawmakers'.[201] Parliament is not the sole source of criticism. Lord Hoffmann, who served as a Lord of Appeal in Ordinary, expressed concern that:

> [The ECtHR] lacks constitutional legitimacy. … [D]etailed decisions about how [UK's legal system] could be improved should be made in London, either by our democratic institutions or by judicial bodies which, like the Supreme Court of the United States, are integral with our own society and respected as such.[202]

Then-Prime Minister David Cameron also opposed the ECtHR's prisoner voting judgments, saying: 'It makes me physically ill even to contemplate having to give the vote to anyone who is in prison.'[203] Since then, there have been intense debates about whether to withdraw from the ECHR[204] and amend the 1998 Human Rights Act;[205] these debates resurface regularly whenever the ECtHR delivers politically significant judgments, even when the UK is not directly involved.[206]

The ECtHR's democratic legitimacy has also been increasingly disputed in other Member States.[207] Although criticism of the ECtHR is not new, as Mikael Rask Madsen observed, the generalisation of the democratic legitimacy discourse across Europe and its application to very different human rights situations – including established democracies and countries with comparatively

[200] Mr David Davis, HC Deb, vol 523, col 493 (10 February 2011) (UK).

[201] HC Deb, vol 523, cols 585–586 (10 February 2011) (UK).

[202] Lord Hoffmann, 'The Universality of Human Rights' *Judicial Studies Board Annual Lecture* (19 March 2009) paras 38–39.

[203] Prime Minister D Cameron, HC Deb, vol 517, col 921 (3 November 2010) (UK).

[204] C Hope, 'Theresa May to Fight 2020 Election on Plans to Take Britain out of European Convention on Human Rights after Brexit is Completed' *The Telegraph* (28 December 2016), www.telegraph.co.uk/news/2016/12/28/theresa-may-fight-2020-election-plans-take-britain-european.

[205] Bill of Rights Bill, Bill 117 2022-23 (Commons) (22 June 2022) (UK). According to s 1(1) of the Bill, it aims at 'clarif[ying] and re-balances the relationship between courts in the United Kingdom, the European Court of Human Rights and Parliament' by stressing that 'it is the Supreme Court (and not the European Court of Human Rights) that determines the meaning and effect of Convention rights for the purposes of domestic law' and that 'decisions about the balance between different policy aims, different Convention rights and Convention rights of different persons are properly made by Parliament'.

[206] For the reaction of the Conservative politicians in the UK against the ECtHR's judgment in *KlimaSeniorinnen Schweiz and Others v Switzerland* in 2024, see C Hymas et al, 'Tory Backlash against European Court of Human Rights Climate Ruling' *The Telegraph* (9 April 2024), www.telegraph.co.uk/politics/2024/04/09/tory-backlash-european-court-human-rights-climate-echr/.

[207] See generally P Popelier, S Lambrecht and K Lemmens (eds), *Criticism of the European Court of Human Rights: Shifting the Convention System: Counter-dynamics at the National and EU Level* (Intersentia 2016); M Breuer (ed), *Principled Resistance to ECtHR Judgments: A New Paradigm?* (Springer 2019).

few cases in Strasbourg – is a novel development that poses a serious threat to the ECHR system.[208] In Switzerland, the controversy over the democratic legitimacy of the ECtHR[209] intensified following the Federal Supreme Court's 2012 judgment on the legality of the deportation of a Macedonian drug dealer, where it implied, in an obiter dictum, that the ECHR would prevail even over a directly applicable constitutional provision enacted by referendum.[210] To re-establish popular sovereignty, the Swiss People's Party launched a constitutional initiative titled 'Swiss law instead of foreign judges' in 2015 to reduce the impact of the ECHR and the ECtHR's judgments on the Swiss legal system.[211] According to Helen Keller and Reto Walther, '[i]t was the most concerted, large-scale attack [against the ECtHR] that Switzerland has seen',[212] although the initiative was ultimately rejected by 66.3 per cent to 33.7 per cent in 2018.[213] More recently, the ECtHR's judgment in *Verein KlimaSeniorinnen Schweiz and Others v Switzerland* (2024),[214] holding that the state failed to comply with its positive obligations to address climate change under Article 8 ECHR, re-ignited the criticism against the ECtHR.[215] The National Council (the lower house of the Parliament) of Switzerland issued a declaration in response to this judgment, blaming the ECtHR's 'inadmissible and inappropriate judicial activism' and refusing to take measures for compliance.[216]

In the Netherlands, Thierry Baudet, leader of the political party Forum voor Democratie, wrote a newspaper article in 2010 criticising the ECtHR as 'an all-consuming monster that, without any legitimacy, renders numerous national laws and regulations inoperative'.[217] This sparked a widespread public debate on

[208] MR Madsen, 'The Challenging Authority of the European Court of Human Rights: From Cold War Legal Diplomacy to the Brighton Declaration and Backlash' (2016) 79 *Law and Contemporary Problems* 141, 174.

[209] See, eg, S Bradley, 'ECHR under Pressure on Swiss Anniversary' *Swissinfo* (27 November 2014), www.swissinfo.ch/eng/echr-under-pressure-on-swiss-anniversary/41132266.

[210] Federal Supreme Court, Entscheidungen des Schweizerischen Bundesgerichts [BGE] 139 I 16 (12 October 2012) (Switzerland) consid 5.

[211] 'Initiative populaire fédérale, 'Le droit suisse au lieu de juges étrangers (initiative pour l'autodétermination)' *Chancellerie fédérale ChF*, www.admin.ch/ch/f/pore/vi/vis460.html.

[212] H Keller and R Walther, 'Resistance in Switzerland: Populist Rather Than Principled' in Breuer (n 207) 161, 186.

[213] 'Votation No 624: Tableau récapitulatif: Initiative populaire du 12.08.2016 "Le droit suisse au lieu de juges étrangers (initiative pour l'autodétermination)"' *Chancellerie fédérale ChF*, www.bk.admin.ch/ch/f/pore/va/20181125/det624.html.

[214] *Verein KlimaSeniorinnen Schweiz and Others v Switzerland*, ECtHR, App No 53600/20, Merits and Satisfaction (9 April 2024).

[215] A Niranjan, 'Swiss Lawmakers Reject Climate Ruling in Favour of Female Climate Elders' *The Guardian* (12 June 2024), www.theguardian.com/world/article/2024/jun/12/swiss-lawmakers-reject-climate-ruling-in-favour-of-female-climate-elders.

[216] Déclaration du Conseil national, 'Arrêt de la Cour EDH "Verein Klimaseniorinnen Schweiz et autres c. Suisse"' BO 2024 N 1179 (12 June 2024) (Switzerland).

[217] T Baudet, 'Het Europees Hof voor de Rechten van de Mens vormt een ernstige inbreuk op de democratie [The European Court of Human Rights is a Serious Violation of Democracy]' *NRC Handelsblad* (13 November 2010), www.nrc.nl/nieuws/2010/11/13/het-europees-hof-voor-de-rechten-van-de-mens-vormt-11969294-a512137.

the ECtHR's democratic legitimacy.[218] In France, Marine Le Pen, leader of the political party Rassemblement National and who came second in the first round of the French presidential elections in 2017 and 2022 (winning respectively 33.9 per cent and 41.46 per cent of the vote in the second round), has advocated France's withdrawal from the ECHR, accusing the ECtHR of imposing 'visions that the people reject'.[219]

2.3.2. Democratic Legitimacy Challenges against the Inter-American Court of Human Rights

In some Latin American countries, the atmosphere surrounding the IACtHR is increasingly hostile.[220] In Costa Rica, where the IACtHR is located, Fabricio Alvarado – who consistently criticised the IACtHR for its undemocratic nature and whose primary manifesto included withdrawing from the ACHR and the IACtHR's jurisdiction – won the most votes in the first round of the 2018 presidential election.[221] Additionally, there have been cross-national initiatives against the IACtHR. In 2017, approximately 700 parliamentarians from 18 ACHR Member States adopted the 'Declaration of Mexico', warning that the IACtHR 'constitute[s] an attack against representative democracy in the region [by seeking] to impose on member states so-called "rights" that have not been validated by them'.[222] Furthermore, in 2019, the governments of Argentina, Brazil, Chile, Colombia and Paraguay jointly issued a declaration on the inter-American human rights system, emphasising that 'the legitimate space of autonomy available to states must be respected' and that human rights must be ensured 'through their own democratic processes … in accordance with their constitutional provisions'.[223]

In certain cases, the IACtHR's attempts to disaggregate the state in a top-down manner have provoked a backlash. In its 2019 order on provisional

[218] BM Oomen, 'A Serious Case of Strasbourg-Bashing? An Evaluation of the Debates on the Legitimacy of the European Court of Human Rights in the Netherlands' (2016) 20 *IJHR* 407.

[219] 'GPA: Marine Le Pen souhaite que la France quitte la CEDH' *Le Pont Politique* (5 October 2014), www.lepoint.fr/politique/gpa-marine-le-pen-souhaite-que-la-france-quitte-la-cedh-05-10-2014-1869602_20.php. Nevertheless, her position is not consistent. See C Sapin, 'Marine Le Pen ne juge plus "utile" de quitter la CEDH' *Le Figaro* (25 May 2021), www.lefigaro.fr/politique/marine-le-pen-ne-juge-plus-utile-de-quitter-la-cedh-20210525.

[220] See generally J Contesse, 'Resisting the Inter-American Human Rights System' (2019) 44 *Yale Journal of International Law* 179.

[221] 'Latin America's Human-Rights Court Moves into Touchy Territory' *The Economist* (1 February 2018), www.economist.com/the-americas/2018/02/01/latin-americas-human-rights-court-moves-into-touchy-territory.

[222] El Congreso Hemisférico de Parlamentarios, 'Declaración de México' (15 June 2017).

[223] Governments of Argentina, Brasil, Chile, Colombia and Paraguay, 'Declaración sobre el Sistema Interamericano de Derechos Humanos' (23 April 2019), www.mre.gov.py/index.php/noticias-de-embajadas-y-consulados/gobiernos-de-argentina-brasil-chile-colombia-y-paraguay-se-manifiestan-sobre-el-sistema-interamericano-de-derechos-humanos, para 2.

measures and supervision of compliance regarding the *Chichupac* judgment, the IACtHR found that bill 5377 under consideration in the Guatemalan Congress, which aimed to reform the Law of National Reconciliation 1996 to ensure blanket amnesty, would impede Guatemala's compliance with the judgment. The IACtHR ordered Guatemala to 'interrupt the legislative process of bill 5377'.[224] Although the Guatemalan Constitutional Court granted a provisional injunction to suspend the processing of bill 5377 in July 2019,[225] many parliamentarians, including the President of the Congress, harshly criticised the IACtHR's legitimacy.[226]

The Supreme Court of Argentina, which has long 'served as an example to its peers in its commitment to the inter-American human rights system', displayed a 'judicial backlash' against the IACtHR.[227] In *Fontevecchia and D'Amico v Argentina* (2011), the IACtHR found that the Supreme Court's judgment, which had ordered the applicants to pay compensation for their publications, violated Article 13 ACHR (freedom of expression). The IACtHR consequently ordered the state to 'set aside' (*dejar sin efecto*) the Supreme Court's judgment.[228] However, in 2017, the Supreme Court refused to implement this judgment and criticised the IACtHR for disregarding the principles of the fourth instance and subsidiarity.[229]

2.3.3. Democratic Legitimacy Challenges against UN Human Rights Treaty Bodies

The UN human rights treaty bodies are not exempt from democratic legitimacy challenges, particularly in countries that take pride in their own democratic institutions,[230] even though these challenges tend to be less serious and more sporadic compared to those directed at the two regional human rights courts. In Australia, during discussions on the Human Rights (Sexual Conduct) Bill 1994, tabled in response to the HRC's Views in *Toonen v Australia* (1994), some

[224] *The Members of the Village of Chichupac and Neighboring Communities of the Municipality of Rabinal, Case of Molina Theissen and 12 Other Guatemalan's Cases v Guatemala*, IACtHR, Order on Provisional Measures and Monitoring Compliance with Judgment (12 March 2019) operative para 2.

[225] Constitutional Court, Case File No 682-2019 (18 July 2019) (Guatemala).

[226] Statement by Alvaro Arzú (President of the Congress of Guatemala) at his personal Twitter (X) account (23 August 2019), https://twitter.com/AlvaroArzuE/status/1164878332737011715.

[227] J Contesse, 'Judicial Backlash in Inter-American Human Rights Law?' *I-CONnect* (2 March 2017), www.iconnectblog.com/judicial-backlash-interamerican/.

[228] *Fontevecchia and D'Amico v Argentina*, IACtHR, Series C No 238, Merits, Reparations, and Costs (29 November 2011) operative para 2 (reparation).

[229] Supreme Court, *Ministerio de Relaciones Exteriores y Culto s/ informe sentencia dictada en el caso 'Fontevecchia y D'Amico vs Argentina' por la Corte Interamericana de Derechos Humanos*, CSJ 368/1998 (34-M)/CS1 (14 February 2017) (Argentina).

[230] J Krommendijk, 'National Parliaments: Obstacles or Aid to the Impact of International Human Rights Bodies?' in M Wind (ed), *International Courts and Domestic Politics* (Cambridge University Press 2018) 227, 242–45.

parliamentarians criticised the HRC, stating that '[a] state government in Australia is more likely to protect people's rights than an unelected, unaccountable UN committee would ever do'.[231] Similarly, in response to repeated concerns and criticisms from the Committee on the Elimination of Racial Discrimination (CERD) regarding amendments to the Native Title Act 1993, Australia's Prime Minister Howard remarked in 2000:

> It isn't really the business of a UN committee when we clearly have a democratic system in this Government and everybody's given an opportunity to put their view … That might be appropriate if you were dealing with a country that didn't have a robust democracy, didn't have a free press and didn't have an incorruptible judicial system, but it's not appropriate for a country like Australia.[232]

In New Zealand too, critical views towards the HRC and other UN human rights treaty bodies are frequently voiced in Parliament. For example, given the CERD's criticism against the Foreshore and Seabed Act 2004,[233] a parliamentarian stated:

> [T]hat overseas committee considered that important matter for simply 35 minutes, and … it was not a committee made up of countries that we could say have a better race relations record than New Zealand does … Government members travelled for 18 months around this country, holding public meetings and hui, trying to engage with all New Zealanders from all cultural backgrounds in order to raise awareness on [the foreshore and seabed] issue.[234]

New Zealand's Prime Minister Helen Clark also criticised the CERD's decision-making process.[235]

In Canada, in response to the CERD's recommendation to suspend large-scale development projects affecting indigenous people,[236] Alberta's Minister of Energy asserted that 'Canada's duly elected representatives – not unaccountable international committees – are responsible for governing decisions in this country'.[237]

[231] Christopher Gordon Miles, Parliamentary Debates, House of Representatives Official Hansard, No 197 (12 October 1994) 1841 (Australia).

[232] Interview with the Prime Minister Howard, *ABC Television* (21 August 2000), reproduced in S Joseph, 'The Howard Government's Record of Engagement with the International Human Rights System' (2008) 27 *Australian Year Book of International Law* 45, 56. Other similar statements are cited in D Hovell, 'The Sovereignty Stratagem: Australia's Response to UN Human Rights Treaty Bodies' (2003) 28 *Alternative Law Journal* 297, 288–99.

[233] CERD, 'Decision 1 (66): New Zealand Foreshore and Seabed Act 2004' (11 March 2005) UN Doc CERD/C/66/NZL/Dec.1, paras 7 and 8.

[234] Darren Hughes, Hansard, vol 624 (16 March 2005) 19250 (New Zealand).

[235] 'Prime Minister Critical of UN Committee's Process' *New Zealand Herald* (14 March 2005), www.nzherald.co.nz/kahu/prime-minister-critical-of-un-committees-process/DFDY7OLHMXI5AKZPRY6PAG3NTM.

[236] CERD, 'Prevention of Racial Discrimination, Including Early Warning and Urgent Action Procedure: Decision 1 (100)' (13 December 2019).

[237] 'Alberta Fires Back at UN Committee for Criticism of Energy Megaprojects' *CBC* (7 January 2020), www.cbc.ca/news/canada/edmonton/alberta-fires-back-at-un-committee-for-criticism-of-energy-megaprojects-1.5418338.

In some states, the issue of democratic legitimacy has been invoked as a reason for not ratifying a UN human rights treaty or refusing to accept a treaty body's competence to receive individual communications. For example, when the US Senate failed to approve the ratification of the Convention on the Rights of Persons with Disabilities[238] in 2012, former senator and Republican presidential candidate Rick Santorum criticised the Committee on the Rights of Persons with Disabilities as an 'unelected, unaccountable committee' which 'tak[es] power and responsibility away from our elected representatives'.[239]

2.3.4. Human Rights Treaty Organs' Response: The Bottom-up Disaggregation of a State

The democratic legitimacy challenges described thus far have underscored the need for treaty organs to be mindful of their role within national legal orders and their relationships with respective state organs. This necessitates treating different state organs in different ways – considering their composition, capacity and functions, and giving due respect to their mandates under national constitutions. In this context, treaty organs have increasingly begun to recognise the specific competences of individual state organs, affording a degree of deference to their decisions when they act properly within their competences.

To cite representative examples of such a practice (which will be explored in detail in Chapter 4), in *Maurice v France* (2005), the ECtHR acknowledged that due to 'direct democratic legitimation' that the domestic policy-maker enjoys, '[i]n matters of general policy, on which opinions within a democratic society may reasonably differ widely, the role of the domestic policy-maker should be given special weight'.[240] In *Von Hannover v Germany (No 2)* (2012), the ECtHR established the principle that 'where the balancing exercise has been undertaken by the national authorities in conformity with the criteria laid down in the Court's case-law, the Court would require strong reasons to substitute its view for that of the domestic courts'.[241] In *Mémoli v Argentina* (2013), the IACtHR recognised that 'domestic judicial authorities were in a better position to assess which right suffered most harm'.[242] The HRC has also

[238] Convention on the Rights of Persons with Disabilities (adopted 13 December 2006, entered into force 3 May 2008) 2515 UNTS 3.

[239] R Santorum, 'UN Disabilities Treaty Would've Had Bureaucrats Unseat Parents' *Daily Beast* (5 December 2012), www.thedailybeast.com/santorum-un-disabilities-treaty-wouldve-had-bureaucrats-unseat-parents.

[240] *Maurice v France*, ECtHR, App No 11810/03, Merits and Just Satisfaction (6 October 2005) para 117.

[241] *Von Hannover v Germany (No 2)*, ECtHR, App Nos 40660/08 and 60641/08, Merits and Just Satisfaction (7 February 2012) para 107.

[242] *Mémoli v Argentina*, IACtHR, Series C No 265, Preliminary Objections, Merits, Reparations and Costs (22 August 2013) para 143.

frequently emphasised that 'it is generally for the courts of the States parties to the Covenant to evaluate facts and evidence of a particular case, unless it is found that the evaluation was clearly arbitrary or amounted to a denial of justice'.[243]

2.4. STATE ORGANS AS AUTONOMOUS INTERLOCUTORS

The executive branch, represented by the ministry of foreign affairs, has been the primary body responsible for making pleadings before treaty organs and receiving their judgments and recommendations.[244] For instance, when the Legislative Assembly of Costa Rica sought an advisory opinion from the IACtHR on proposed constitutional amendments to naturalisation, the IACtHR declined to admit the request. It stated that the Legislative Assembly was 'not one of the governmental entities empowered to speak for Costa Rica on the international plane'.[245] The IACtHR then clarified that 'only when the Minister of Foreign Affairs formally filed the request … did the Court become seized of the matter now before it'.[246]

However, in recent years, treaty organs have interacted with state organs beyond the executive branch in their proceedings. They have allowed and encouraged NHRIs to act as autonomous interlocutors, providing insights and perspectives in proceedings (section 2.4.1). Additionally, they have been equipped with certain mechanisms, especially the ECtHR's advisory opinion procedure under Protocol No 16, to directly engage with the national highest courts (section 2.4.2) (for a discussion of national parliaments as interlocutors, see Chapter 5). These developments have the potential to enhance both the effectiveness and democratic legitimacy of human rights treaties. On the one hand, treaty organs foster direct partnerships with state organs, ensuring the efficient and effective communication of their messages to national legal systems, thus promoting top-down disaggregation. On the other hand, these avenues provide state organs with opportunities to directly convey local values, needs and specificities to treaty organs, enabling the latter to issue judgments and recommendations that properly incorporate such elements, thereby supporting bottom-up disaggregation.

[243] See, eg, *Mehrez Ben Abde Hamida v Canada*, HRC, Communication No 1544/2007 (18 March 2010) UN Doc CCPR/C/98/D/1544/2007, para 8.4.

[244] Murray and de Vos (n 5) 25.

[245] *Proposed Amendments to the Naturalization Provisions of the Constitution of Costa Rica*, IACtHR, Series A No 4, Advisory Opinion OC-4/84 (19 January 1984) para 11.

[246] ibid.

2.4.1. The Participation of National Human Rights Institutions in Human Rights Treaty Organs' Proceedings and Activities

NHRIs are generally defined as state organs with constitutional and/or legislative mandates to protect and promote human rights.[247] Their competences, responsibilities, composition and methods of operation are governed by the Paris Principles (for a detailed examination of the Paris Principles, see Chapter 5, section 5.2). The Paris Principles stipulate that NHRIs must be independent of the government and that their composition should ensure a pluralist representation of the social forces of civil society. The competences and responsibilities of NHRIs must include, among other functions, advising the government, parliament and other competent bodies on human rights issues, promoting the effective implementation of human rights treaties and contributing to the activities of international human rights bodies. The Global Alliance of National Human Rights Institutions (GANHRI), a global organisation comprising NHRIs, operates an accreditation system for NHRIs. It awards 'A-status' to NHRIs that fully comply with the Paris Principles and 'B-status' to those that do so partially (see Chapter 5, section 5.2.2 for a detailed examination of the accreditation system).

Since the 2000s, human rights treaty organs have increasingly allowed and encouraged NHRIs to participate in their proceedings and activities. Treaty organs acknowledge NHRIs not as representatives of the state, but as independent actors, which contribute to the national implementation of the treaty, and provide human rights treaty organs with valuable information and insights – the broader context of the issue at hand, relevant domestic legislation and practices, and the diversity of positions and views in the society concerned.

2.4.1.1. National Human Rights Institutions before the European Court of Human Rights

Following the adoption of the Paris Principles and the creation of the International Coordinating Committee of National Institutions for the Promotion and Protection of Human Rights (ICC, now GANHRI) in 1993, interactions and networking among NHRIs have become increasingly active at the European level.[248] The Council of Europe has facilitated meetings of European NHRIs since 1994, leading to the formation of the European Group of NHRIs in 1997. That same year, the CoM adopted Recommendation No R (97) 14, encouraging Member States to consider establishing NHRIs and promoting cooperation between NHRIs and the Council of Europe.[249] Since 2001, the European Group

[247] 'National Human Rights Institutions: What are NHRIs?' *GANHRI*, https://ganhri.org/nhri.

[248] See generally G de Beco, 'National Human Rights Institutions in Europe' (2007) 7 *HRLR* 331, 336–38.

[249] CoM Recommendation No 9 (97) on the Establishment of Independent National Institutions for the Promotion and Protection of Human Rights (30 September 1997) paras (a) and (c).

of NHRIs has attended meetings of the CDDH[250] and promoted initiatives to strengthen NHRIs.[251] In 2013, the European Group evolved into a more formal institution known as the European Network of National Human Rights Institutions (ENNHRI), comprising over 40 NHRIs in Europe, and recognised as a regional branch of the GANHRI.[252] ENNHRI (and former European Group of NHRIs) has participated in high-level conferences on reforming the ECHR system, emphasising the crucial and unique roles NHRIs play within the system.[253] Consequently, the Brighton and Brussels Declarations endorsed the importance of establishing NHRIs and cooperating with them to ensure the effective implementation of the ECHR.[254] In the 2018 Copenhagen Declaration, the 'significant role' of NHRIs in the implementation of the ECHR was explicitly recognised.[255]

In tandem with these developments, the role of NHRIs as interlocutors with the ECtHR was facilitated. Although the ECHR does not explicitly mention NHRIs, Article 36(2) allows the President to invite third-party submissions 'in the interest of the proper administration of justice'. The ECtHR has admitted third-party interventions from NHRIs in numerous cases (for a detailed analysis, see Chapter 4, section 4.3.1).[256] While the Northern Ireland Human Rights Commission (formerly the Standing Advisory Commission on Human Rights) has frequently intervened since the 1990s, other European NHRIs have generally begun making use of such procedures only since the 2010s.[257] In the first such case, *Brannigan and McBride v UK* (1993), the President permitted the Standing Advisory Commission on Human Rights to submit comments on the existence

[250] Bureau of the CDDH, 57th mtg (8–9 February 2001) CDDH-BU (2001) Appendix IV.

[251] See, eg, CDDH's Report, 99th mtg (28 November–1 December 2023) CDDH (2023)R99, para 14. See generally CT Antoniazzi, 'Promoting the Execution of Judgments of the European Court of Human Rights: The (Potential) Role of National Human Rights Institutions', PhD thesis, University of Trento (2019) 130–32.

[252] For the history leading to the establishment of the ENNHRI, see C Lacatus, 'Regulatory Networks and Regional Human Rights Governance: A Study of the European Network of National Human Rights Institutions' (2022) 36 *International Relations* 192, 200–01.

[253] See B Adamson, 'NHRIs and Their European Counterparts: Scope for Strengthened Cooperation and Performance towards European Human Rights Institutions' in K Meuwissen and J Wouters (eds), *National Human Rights Institutions in Europe: Comparative, European and International Perspectives* (Intersentia 2013) 127, 142–45.

[254] High-Level Conference on the Future of the European Court of Human Rights, 'Brighton Declaration' (20 April 2012) paras 4, 9(c)(i) and 20(g); High-Level Conference on the Implementation of the European Convention on Human Rights, Our Shared Responsibility, 'Brussels Declaration' (27 March 2015) Preamble, B.1(g), B.2(a), (f), (j) and 'Implementation of the Action Plan' (5).

[255] High-Level Conference on the Reform of the European Convention on Human Rights System, 'Copenhagen Declaration' (13 April 2018) para 18.

[256] See generally A Buyse, 'The Court's Ears and Arms: National Human Rights Institutions and the European Court of Human Rights' in Meuwissen and Wouters (n 253) 173, 177–84. In addition, NHRIs have occasionally participated indirectly by supplying information and views to the Council of Europe Commissioner for Human Rights. See G de Beco, 'La contribution des institutions nationales des droits de l'homme au renforcement de l'efficacité de la Cour européenne des droits de l'homme' (2009) 77 *Revue Trimestrielle des Droits de L'homme* 165, 174–79.

[257] Antoniazzi (n 251) 140–142.

of a public emergency in Northern Ireland and on the operation of national courts in relation to submissions based on confidential information.[258] NHRIs often provide the ECtHR with information that directly challenges governments' submissions or addresses issues 'not addressed by either party'.[259]

2.4.1.2. National Human Rights Institutions before the Inter-American Court of Human Rights

The OAS and its organ IACmHR have actively promoted the establishment of NHRIs and cooperation with them. In Resolution 2132 (XXXV-O/05) of 2005, the OAS's General Assembly referred to the Paris Principles[260] and recommended that OAS Member States 'consider the possibility of establishing and operating [NHRIs] within the framework of their legal order'.[261] Moreover, the resolution encouraged 'the establishment of forums for dialogue between [NHRIs] and the pertinent organs of the inter-American system'.[262] Similar resolutions have been adopted regularly.[263] In a resolution in 2009, the OAS decided to grant NHRIs accredited with A-status by the ICC the right to participate and speak in their own capacity at human rights-related meetings of the OAS.[264] Since 2018, the IACmHR and 12 NHRIs have signed the Declaration of Commitment on Technical Cooperation and other bilateral agreements to establish coordinated processes for information exchange and broaden the channels of independent participation of NHRIs in IACmHR activities.[265] The IACmHR and NHRIs have held annual discussions[266] and other meetings to share best practices and discuss the role of NHRIs in strengthening human rights and contributing to IACmHR's activities.[267]

[258] *Brannigan and McBride v UK*, ECtHR, App Nos 14553/89 and 14554/89, Merits and Just Satisfaction (25 May 1993) paras 45 and 55.

[259] *McCaughey and Others v UK*, ECtHR, App No 43098/09, Merits and Just Satisfaction (16 July 2013) para 119.

[260] OAS General Assembly Res, 'Strengthening of The National Human Rights Systems of The Member States and Support for The Work of Defenders of The People, Defenders of The Population, and Human Rights Attorneys or Commissioners (Ombudsmen)' (7 June 2005) AG/RES. 2132 (XXXV-O/05) preambular para 4.

[261] ibid para 3.

[262] ibid para 4.

[263] See the OAS General Assembly's resolutions with the same title as cited in n 260. AG/RES. 2221 (XXXVI-O/06) (6 June 2006); AG/RES. 2345 (XXXVII-O/07) (5 June 2007).

[264] OAS General Assembly Res, 'Strengthening the Role of National Institutions for the Promotion and Protection of Human Rights in the Organization of American States' (4 June 2009) AG/RES. 2448 (XXXIX-O/09) para 2.

[265] 'IACHR and National Human Rights Institutions (NHRIs) Sign Declaration of Commitment for Technical Cooperation' *IACmHR* (19 November 2018), www.oas.org/en/iachr/media_center/PReleases/2018/246.asp.

[266] See, eg, 'IACHR Holds Fifth Dialogue with National Human Rights Institutions from the Americas' *IACtHR* (17 October 2023), www.oas.org/en/iachr/jsForm/?File=/en/iachr/media_center/preleases/2023/247.asp.

[267] IACmHR, 'Annual Report 2023' (2023) ch 1, paras 66–70.

Although the ACHR does not refer to NHRIs, the IACtHR has advanced the practice of allowing NHRIs to participate in its proceedings in several ways.[268] First, as Article 44 ACHR does not restrict the right to petition to victims themselves, the IACmHR has permitted NHRIs to act as petitioners or represent victims.[269] When such cases are referred to the IACtHR, the IACtHR has allowed NHRIs to act as representatives of the alleged victims[270] and has 'positively value[d]' such participation, noting that 'it strengthens the general protection of human rights and, consequently, the Inter-American system for the protection of Human Rights'.[271]

Second, under Article 44 of the Rules of Procedure, the IACtHR has admitted amicus curiae briefs from NHRIs,[272] even when the respondent state opposed them. In *YATAMA v Nicaragua* (2005), the Ombudsman of Nicaragua submitted amicus curiae briefs that provided evidence and perspectives opposing the position taken by the state.[273] Although the respondent state objected to these submissions, arguing that 'it is inconceivable that State institutions, such as the Office of the Ombudsman … can intervene at their own discretion, against the interests of the State at the international level', the IACtHR admitted them based on the reason that they '[relate] to the facts of the instant case'.[274] In *Xucuru Indigenous People and Its Members v Brazil* (2017), the IACtHR again rejected the government's argument that the ombudsman 'did not have a different legal personality to that of the Brazilian State' and therefore could not 'testify against the State before an international court.[275] Since 2010, the IACtHR has signed agreements with the Ibero-American Federation of Ombudsmen to encourage the participation of NHRIs as amicus curiae.[276]

Third, the IACtHR summons NHRIs (and their members) as expert witnesses. For instance, in *Ivcher-Bronstein v Peru* (2001), where the petitioner

[268] See generally T Pegram and N Herrera Rodriguez, 'Bridging the Gap: National Human Rights Institutions and the Inter-American Human Rights System' in P Engstrom (ed), *The Inter-American Human Rights System* (Palgrave Macmillan 2019) 167.

[269] *Janet Espinoza Feria, et al v Peru*, IACmHR, Report no 51/02, Petition 12.404, Admissibility (10 October 2002) para 35.

[270] See generally E Vio Grossi, '(Notes on) the Inter-American Court of Human Rights, Non-Governmental Organisations and National Human Rights Institutions' in S Lopez Escarcena et al (eds), *National Human Rights Institutions in Europe and Latin America: International and Comparative Perspectives* (Intersentia 2024) 113, 126–27.

[271] *Ticona Estrada et al v Bolivia*, IACtHR, Series C No 191, Merits, Reparations and Costs (27 November 2008) para 181. See also Concurring Vote of Judges García-Sayán and García Ramírez, para 3 (calling NHRIs an 'emerging actor').

[272] See generally Vio Grossi (n 270) 126.

[273] *YATAMA v Nicaragua*, IACtHR, Series C No 127, Preliminary Objections, Merits, Reparations and Costs (23 June 2005) para 42.

[274] ibid para 114.

[275] *Xucuru Indigenous People and its Members v Brazil*, IACtHR, Series C No 346, Preliminary Objections, Merits, Reparations and Costs (5 February 2018) para 12.

[276] M Solano Carboni, 'The Role of National Human Rights Institutions in Implementing Decisions of the Inter-American System: Three Recent Examples from Costa Rica' (2020) 12 *Journal of Human Rights Practice* 217, 219.

was deprived of his nationality allegedly in an arbitrary manner, the IACtHR invited the Defence Counsel of the Peruvian Office of the Ombudsman to serve as an expert witness.[277] He assisted the IACtHR in understanding the detailed contents of relevant national legislation and its actual application.[278]

In recent years, NHRIs have also been involved in monitoring compliance with IACtHR judgments.[279] In monitoring the judgment in *Artavia Murillo et al (In Vitro Fertilization) v Costa Rica*, in which Costa Rica's Defensoría de los Habitantes participated as amicus curiae during the merits stage, the Defensoría submitted reports detailing the measures it had taken and the reluctance of the relevant national authorities to comply.[280] The Defensoría also requested the IACtHR to hold public hearings.[281] The IACtHR accepted the request and invited the Defensoría to testify.[282] Since then, the IACtHR has frequently sought information from NHRIs concerning compliance, relying on Article 69(2) of the Rules of Procedure, which authorises the IACtHR to consult 'other sources' in its monitoring compliance procedures.[283]

The IACtHR has strengthened its ties with NHRIs beyond formal proceedings by signing cooperation agreements with them, facilitating collaborative endeavours.[284] For instance, in 2018, Colombia's Defensoría del Pueblo organised a high-level meeting with IACtHR judges and other stakeholders to discuss compliance with IACtHR judgments addressed to Colombia.[285]

2.4.1.3. National Human Rights Institutions before UN Human Rights Treaty Bodies

As Anne Gallagher observed, until the 1990s, '[NHRIs] and the [UN] human rights treaty system … had very little direct contact with each other', and NHRIs were 'not yet recognised as separate players in the international human rights arena'.[286] In fact, the CERD's General Recommendation in 1993 did not acknowledge the independent status of NHRIs and treated them as part of a government delegation.[287]

[277] *Ivcher-Bronstein v Peru*, IACtHR, Series C No 74, Merits, Reparations and Costs (6 February 2001) para 44.

[278] ibid para 62 (at pp 25–27).

[279] See generally Sandoval, Leach and Murray (n 15) 92–94.

[280] *Artavia Murillo et al (In Vitro Fertilization) v Costa Rica*, IACtHR, Order on Monitoring Compliance with Judgments (26 February 2016) para 7 and fn 10.

[281] ibid fn 10. See also M Solano Carboni, 'The Role of National Human Rights Institutions in Implementing Decisions of the Inter-American System: Three Recent Examples from Costa Rica' (2020) 12 *Journal of Human Rights Practice* (2020) 217, 220.

[282] Solano Carboni (n 281) 220.

[283] See, eg, IACtHR, 'Annual Report 2022' (2022) 97–99.

[284] Pegram and Herrera Rodriguez (n 268) 177.

[285] Sandoval, Leach and Murray (n 15) 93.

[286] A Gallagher, 'Making Human Rights Treaty Obligations a Reality: Working with New Actors and Partners' in Alston and Crawford (n 186) 201, 208.

[287] CERD, 'General Recommendation XVII on the Establishment of National Institutions to Facilitate the Implementation of the Convention' (1993) GAOR 48th Session Supp 18, 117, para 2.

However, since the 2000s, UN human rights treaty bodies have begun to recognise the autonomous status of NHRIs as distinct from that of states in UN human rights treaties.

At the fourth Inter-Committee Meeting of Human Rights Treaty Bodies in 2005, representatives of NHRIs were invited for the first time to discuss interactions between treaty bodies and NHRIs,[288] and the participants agreed on the need to develop 'harmonized criteria for the participation of [NHRIs] in treaty body sessions'.[289] At the International Roundtable in Berlin in 2006, participants from NHRIs, treaty bodies and civil society adopted the 'Draft Harmonized Approach to National Human Rights Institutions (NHRIs) Engagement with Treaty Body Processes'.[290] This emphasised that treaty bodies should recognise the independent standing of NHRIs as distinct from the government and civil society in their procedures.[291] Owing to these initiatives, today, the vast majority of UN human rights treaty bodies formally recognise the right of NHRIs to participate in the activities of treaty bodies in their own capacity. In 2012, the HRC issued the 'Paper on the Relationship of the Human Rights Committee with National Human Rights Institutions'.[292]

NHRIs' participation is most advanced in state reporting procedures. To facilitate their participation, some UN human rights treaty bodies, including the HRC, issue formal invitation letters and information notes to NHRIs whose states are subject to review, providing practical information.[293] The participation of NHRIs is further encouraged because treaty bodies have welcomed the use of new technologies, such as video or telephone conferencing and webcasting, and have allowed Geneva-based representatives of the GANHRI to represent A-status NHRIs which cannot travel to Geneva.[294] The aforementioned HRC's 2012 Paper states that NHRIs may directly engage with the HRC by submitting written contributions, holding meetings with HRC members to develop a List of Issues, submitting alternative reports, providing oral presentations during the examination of the state party's report, and addressing the HRC in formal, private and closed meetings.[295] Out of the 20 states parties reviewed

[288] Note by the UN Secretary-General, 'Report of the Chairpersons of the Human Rights Treaty Bodies on Their Seventeenth Meeting' (2005) UN Doc A/60/278, Annex: Report of the Fourth Inter-Committee Meeting of Human Rights Treaty Bodies, para 28.

[289] ibid para 35-XIV.

[290] Sixth Inter-Committee Meeting of the Human Rights Treaty Bodies, 'Conclusions of the International Roundtable on the Role of National Human Rights Institutions and Treaty Bodies (Berlin, 23 and 24 November 2006)' (2007) UN Doc HRI/MC/2007/3, Annex.

[291] ibid para 1.

[292] HRC, 'Paper on the Relationship of the Human Rights Committee with National Human Rights Institutions' (2012) UN Doc CCPR/C/106/3.

[293] GANHRI, 'Background Paper: National Human Rights Institutions and United Nations Treaty Bodies' (May 2016) 14.

[294] OHCHR, 'Informal Background Paper by the Secretariat: Engagement of NHRIs with the UN Human Rights Treaty Bodies: An Overview of Procedures and Practices' (May 2016) paras 4 and 18.

[295] HRC (n 292) paras 12, 14 and 15.

by the HRC during the 136th–138th sessions (2022–2023), NHRIs from eight states parties submitted reports; seven of them also attended the briefing.[296]

In the individual communication procedure, NHRIs can participate as representatives of victims. In *Marcia Cecilia Trujillo Calero v Ecuador* in 2018, the Committee on Economic, Social and Cultural Rights (CESCR) held that the submission by Ecuador's Office of the Ombudsman on behalf of the alleged victims was admissible.[297] Furthermore, several treaty bodies, including the HRC, have recently established procedures for receiving amicus curiae or third-party interventions in individual communication procedures[298] from stakeholders, including NHRIs.[299] Although the HRC has never had the opportunity to receive submissions from NHRIs, the CERD did receive an amicus curiae brief from the German Institute for Human Rights, which was submitted not independently but through the petitioner in *TBB-Turkish Union in Berlin/Brandenburg v Germany* in 2013.[300]

2.4.2. The Participation of National Courts in Human Rights Treaty Organs' Proceedings and Activities

2.4.2.1. National Courts in the Advisory Opinion Procedure of the European Court of Human Rights

Protocol No 16 of the ECHR was adopted in 2013 and entered into force in 2018 as a 'package of subsidiarity'[301] together with Protocol No 15,[302] which introduced in the ECHR's preamble the concepts of 'subsidiarity' and the idea that states parties 'have the primary responsibility' for implementing the Convention. Protocol No 16 conferred on the ECtHR the jurisdiction to give advisory opinions on questions of principle relating to the interpretation or application of the ECHR when requested by the highest court of a state party. First proposed in the report of the Group of Wise Persons to the CoM

[296] Report of the UN Secretary-General, 'National Institutions for the Promotion and Protection of Human Rights' (2023) UN Doc A/78/182, Annex III: Engagement of National Human Rights Institutions in the Work of the Treaty Bodies (August 2022–July 2023).

[297] *Marcia Cecilia Trujillo Calero v Ecuador*, CESCR, Communication No 10/2015 (26 March 2018) UN Doc E/C.12/63/D/10/2015, para 9.2.

[298] Rules of Procedure of the HRC (2019) UN Doc CCPR/C/3/Rev.11, Rule 96 (1).

[299] Note by the OHCHR, 'Common Approach to Engagement with National Human Rights Institutions' (2017) UN Doc HRI/MC/2017/3, para 33.

[300] *TBB-Turkish Union in Berlin/Brandenburg v Germany*, CERD, Communication No 48/2010 (26 February 2013) UN Doc CERD/C/82/D/48/2010, para 8.1.

[301] M Wąsek-Wiaderek, 'Advisory Opinions of the European Court of Human Rights: Do National Judges Really Need This New Forum of Dialogue?' in PP de Albuquerque and K Wojtyczek (eds), *Judicial Power in a Globalized World* (Springer 2019) 637, 643.

[302] Protocol No 15 amending the Convention on the Protection of Human Rights and Fundamental Freedoms (signed 24 June 2013, entered into force 1 August 2021) CETS No 213.

in 2006,[303] and further discussed during the Izmir and Brighton High-level Conferences on the Future of the Court in 2011[304] and 2012,[305] the advisory procedure was adopted to 'institutionalise the dialogue' between the ECtHR and domestic courts.[306]

The advisory procedure first enables the ECtHR to forge a direct relationship with national courts and convert them into its compliance partners. The ECtHR plays a 'pre-emptive standard-setting'[307] role by providing normative guidance to national courts, which then transpose this guidance into their own national legal systems by applying it in their judgments.[308] Thus, the procedure directly and pre-emptively integrates the national judiciary into the Convention's protection machinery, thereby enabling national judges to enforce the Convention's rights more effectively, in collaboration with the Strasbourg judges.[309] Using this procedure, the ECtHR has provided concrete guidelines for the consideration of national courts, although it avoids imposing a definitive answer on cases pending before them. For example, in the first advisory opinion under Protocol No 16, requested by the French Court of Cassation, and concerning the recognition in domestic law of a legal parent–child relationship between a child born through a gestational surrogacy arrangement abroad and the intended mother in 2016, the ECtHR held that Article 8 requires domestic law to 'provide a possibility of recognition of a legal parent–child relationship with the intended mother'.[310] It elaborated on the necessary factors for such recognition, including prompt and effective implementation, and the assessment of the child's best interests by the courts.[311] However, it refrained from prescribing a specific method of recognition[312] or ruling on whether French adoption laws met these criteria.[313]

The advisory procedure not only positions the national highest courts as the ECtHR's compliance partners. Rule 92(2.1)(e) of the Rules of Court

[303] Report of the Group of Wise Persons to the Committee of Ministers (2006) CM(2006)203, paras 76–86.

[304] High-Level Conference on the Future of the European Court of Human Rights, 'Izmir Declaration' (27 April 2011) Implementation: para 2(b).

[305] Brighton Declaration (n 254) para 12(d).

[306] ECtHR, 'Reflection Paper on the Proposal to Extend the Court's Advisory Jurisdiction' (2009) II-1.

[307] K Dzehtsiarou and N O'Meara, 'Advisory Jurisdiction and the European Court of Human Rights: A Magic Bullet for Dialogue and Docket-Control' (2014) 34 *Legal Studies* 444, 451.

[308] J Gerards, 'Advisory Opinion: European Court of Human Rights (ECtHR)' (last updated December 2018), in Ruiz Fabri (n 159) para 31.

[309] M Entin et al, *Statement on Case-overload at the European Court of Human Rights* (European Law Institute 2012) 35.

[310] *Advisory Opinion Concerning the Recognition in Domestic Law of a Legal Parent-child Relationship between a Child Born through a Gestational Surrogacy Arrangement Abroad and the Intended Mother*, Requested by the French Court of Cassation, ECtHR, Request No P16-2018-001 (10 April 2019) operative para 1.

[311] ibid paras 54–55 and operative para 2.

[312] ibid operative para 2.

[313] ibid para 58.

of the ECtHR provides that the requesting court may provide a statement of the requesting court's own views on the question.[314] This channel addresses a gap in the individual complaint procedure, where national courts cannot introduce new arguments in response to those made by applicants before the ECtHR.[315] It enables national courts to 'influence the case law of the ECtHR more directly'[316] and become 'agents of fundamental rights in Europe' rather than 'mere recipients of the interpretation of fundamental rights provided by the ECtHR'.[317] It also allows national courts 'to voice their disagreement with judgments of the ECtHR adopted in contentious procedures and engage in a direct dialogue over particular interpretations', without the mediation of the executive branch, which represents the respondent state in contentious proceedings.[318] After an advisory opinion is rendered, the requesting national court is invited to inform the ECtHR of any follow-up given to the opinion.[319] This offers another opportunity for national courts to communicate with and influence the ECtHR directly.[320]

In the advisory opinion on the procedural status and rights of a biological parent in proceedings for the adoption of an adult (2023), the requesting court, the Supreme Court of Finland, offered its own analysis of the issues when making a request. This included an analysis of the preparatory materials of the relevant national legislation, national case law and the case law of the ECtHR.[321] The ECtHR relied on the Supreme Court's explanation to find that the rights claimed by the biological mother did not exist in domestic law.[322] Moreover, when interpreting Article 8 ECHR, the ECtHR referred to the Supreme Court's observations and reached an interpretation that 'coincides with the analysis of the Supreme Court' – that the adoption of an adult in this case did not fall under the family life aspect of Article 8.[323]

[314] This rule was inserted on 19 September 2016. For a criticism that this should have been included in the text of Protocol No 16, see Dzehtsiarou and O'Meara (n 307) 464–65.

[315] Wąsek-Wiaderek (n 301) 640.

[316] L Glas and J Krommendijk, 'A Strasbourg Story of Swords and Shields: National Courts' Motives to Request an Advisory Opinion from the ECtHR under Article 16' (2022) 3 *European Convention on Human Rights Law Review* 311, 334.

[317] M Dicosola, C Fasone, and I Spigno, 'The Prospective Role of Constitutional Courts in the Advisory Opinion Mechanism before the European Court of Human Rights: A First Comparative Assessment with the European Union and the Inter-American System' (2015) 16 *German Law Journal* 1387, 1426.

[318] Glas and Krommendijk (n 316) 334.

[319] ECtHR, 'Guidelines on the Implementation of the Advisory-Opinion Procedure Introduced by Protocol No 16 to the Convention' (approved on 18 September 2017, updated on 25 September 2023) para 33.

[320] Wąsek-Wiaderek (n 301) 647–48.

[321] *The Procedural Status and Rights of a Biological Parent in Proceedings for the Adoption of an Adult*, Requested by the Supreme Court of Finland, ECtHR, Request No P-16-2022-001 (13 April 2023) paras 23–26.

[322] ibid para 66.

[323] ibid para 52.

2.4.2.2. National Courts in the Advisory Opinion Procedure of the Inter-American Court of Human Rights

Article 64(1) and (2) ACHR stipulates that 'the member states'/'a member state' of the Organization may file a request for an advisory opinion at the IACtHR. Although some scholars have argued that national courts may use these provisions to request advisory opinions,[324] so far this has not been the case. Moreover, even if it were to be, the IACtHR would be likely to reject it, given its above-cited jurisprudence.[325] Several studies advocate establishing a new advisory procedure similar to that under the ECHR's Protocol No 16 'to facilitate a more fluid interaction between Latin American judges and the [IACtHR]',[326] and 'to improve and to intensify the dialogue and cooperation between the IACtHR and domestic courts',[327] but such a new procedure is yet to be established.

Nevertheless, the IACtHR has recently begun to interact with national courts in a unique manner. Since its advisory opinion OC-28/21 on presidential re-election without term limits in 2021, the IACtHR has directly consulted national courts of states parties on their jurisprudence on the issue concerned based on a memorandum of understanding with the Permanent Secretariat of the Ibero-American Judicial Summit (for this Summit, see Chapter 5, section 5.4.1).[328] For instance, in its advisory opinion OC-29/22 on differentiated approaches with respect to certain groups of persons deprived of liberty, the highest courts from 11 Member States contributed inputs to the IACtHR.[329]

2.5. CONCLUSION

This chapter has explored three interconnected phenomena: first, the demands imposed by treaty organs on individual state organs to enhance the effectiveness of human rights treaty systems (section 2.2); second, the respect treaty organs show for the decision-making competence of individual state organs under their national constitutions (section 2.3); and, third, the recognition by treaty organs of state organs, especially NHRIs, as independent interlocutors (section 2.4). While previous studies have treated these three streams as distinct and isolated

[324] Buergenthal (n 68) 243. However, he stated that national courts should make such requests not directly to the IACtHR, but through their governments (at 244).

[325] *Proposed Amendments to the Naturalization Provisions of the Constitution of Costa Rica* (n 245) para 11.

[326] AE Dulitzky, 'An Inter-American Constitutional Court? The Invention of the Conventionality Control by the Inter-American Court of Human Rights' (2015) 50 *Texas International Law Journal* 45, 87–90.

[327] E Benz, *The Advisory Function of the Inter-American Court of Human Rights* (Nomos 2024) 96.

[328] *Presidential Re-election without Term Limits in the Context of the Inter-American Human Rights System*, IACtHR, Series A No 28, Advisory Opinion OC-28/21 (7 June 2021) para 11.

[329] *Differentiated Approaches with Respect to Certain Groups of Persons Deprived of Liberty*, IACtHR, Series A No 29, Advisory Opinion OC-29/22 (30 May 2022) para 10.

(see particularly Chapter 1, section 1.1.3.1), they should instead be viewed as three facets of a broader phenomenon – the disaggregation of a state. Together, they represent the ongoing blurring of the boundaries between international and national legal orders, and between the spheres in which treaty and state organs respectively operate. On the one hand, the top-down, intrusive approach to the disaggregation, treating state organs as compliance partners, has been a means of increasing the impact of human rights treaties and treaty organs on domestic legal systems. On the other hand, the consequent growing influence of them has also triggered a backlash from national legal orders, often framed as a challenge to democratic legitimacy. This has necessitated a more bottom-up, deferential approach to the disaggregation of the state, where state organs act as primary decision-makers. Finally, the institutionalisation by treaty organs of the roles of state organs as autonomous interlocutors encourages these state organs to act as bridges between human rights treaties and their national legal systems, serving both as compliance partners and primary decision-makers.

Thus, the three forms of disaggregation of a state must be regulated and coordinated in a principled manner, within a comprehensive theoretical framework.

3

Separation of Powers in a Globalised Democratic Society

'Two-Tiered Bounded Deliberative Democracy' as a Guiding Theory

THIS CHAPTER AIMS to establish a normative framework for prescribing the authorities and duties of treaty organs and individual state organs, and regulating their relationship in a principled manner. It first approaches this question from the perspective of legitimacy. International law has long regarded state consent as the primary legitimacy criterion and has remained indifferent to legitimacy standards under national constitutions. Accordingly, international law scholarship has traditionally focused on the division of authority between treaty organs and 'states' as unitary entities, based on the standard of state consent. However, this chapter posits that, given the growing intrusion of human rights treaties and treaty organs into national legal orders, the boundary between international and national sources of legitimacy is increasingly blurred in the human rights law field. We live in 'globalised democratic societies', where democracy is exercised primarily within each national society, but such societies are heavily affected by human rights treaty standards and have become spaces where treaty organs and state organs closely intersect, regardless of their formal origins. Therefore, we must seek a new legitimacy standard for 'globalised democratic societies', one that integrates international and national standards of legitimacy, drawing on the intellectual heritage of national constitutional law scholarship (section 3.1). This chapter thus relies on the framework of the separation of powers, a widely shared fundamental principle in constitutional democracies across the globe, and embodies it within the original theory of 'two-tiered bounded deliberative democracy', leading to what this chapter calls the 'separation of powers in a globalised democratic society' model (section 3.2). This model enables the allocation of respective authorities and duties to both state organs and treaty organs in a concrete manner. Each type of state organ bears a duty to take part in national 'bounded' deliberations in their respective ways. Treaty organs, for their part, must ensure the basis of such deliberations, must respect, regulate and promote them, and must review and contribute to international deliberations on human rights, which will then serve as 'bounds' on national deliberations. The relationships between state and treaty organs should be governed by the 'subsidiarity' and 'principled and continuous dialogue' principles (section 3.3).

This chapter primarily focuses on constructing a normative framework, leaving to Chapter 4 the task of providing a descriptive analysis of the current practices of human rights treaty organs. Nevertheless, when elaborating on elements of the normative framework, this chapter occasionally refers to relevant practices where such reference is not covered by Chapter 4 and is useful in illustrating the concrete design of the normative framework.

3.1. TOWARDS NEW LEGITIMACY STANDARDS FOR A 'GLOBALISED DEMOCRATIC SOCIETY'

3.1.1. The Concept of Legitimacy

Since the seventeenth century, when it became recognised that no one has a natural or divinely ordained authority to rule over human beings, many philosophers have asked why a political entity enjoys the 'right to rule' and why citizens should obey its legal commands.[1] Legitimacy, which underpins the exercise of public authority,[2] provides a framework for debating such questions. Although legitimacy has primarily been studied within national constitutional law frameworks, it has been discussed in the context of international law since around 1990.[3] The question of legitimacy may be even more crucial in international law than in national law, as the former must elicit voluntary compliance from states without the backing of an effective coercive structure, like a national police force.[4]

The concept of legitimacy can be classified into three types:[5] legal (or formal)[6] legitimacy; normative (prescriptive[7] or moral)[8] legitimacy; and social

[1] R Flathman, 'Legitimacy' in R Goodin, P Pettit and T Pogge (eds), *A Companion to Contemporary Political Philosophy*, 2nd edn (Blackwell 2007) 678, 678.

[2] 'Public authority' is generally defined as 'capacity, based on legal acts, to impact other actors in their exercise of freedom, be it legally or simply de facto'. A von Bogdandy and I Venzke, *In Whose Name? A Public Law Theory of International Adjudication* (Oxford University Press 2014) 113.

[3] See generally T Franck, *The Power of Legitimacy Among Nations* (Oxford University Press 1990).

[4] T Franck, 'Legitimacy in the International System' (1988) 82 *AJIL* 705, 707.

[5] CA Thomas, 'The Uses and Abuses of Legitimacy in International Law' (2014) 34 *Oxford Journal of Legal Studies* 729, 733–742; E Gill Pedro, *The International Legal System as a System of Knowledge* (Edward Elgar 2022) 204–05.

[6] J Patrick Kelly, 'Customary International Law in Historical Context: The Exercise of Power without General Acceptance' in BD Lepard (ed), *Reexamining Customary International Law* (Cambridge University Press 2017) 47, 48.

[7] D van Rooyen, 'The Legitimacy of International Law: Re-examining the Theory of State Consent', PhD thesis, Durham University (2019) 54–57.

[8] SC Grover, *The European Court of Human Rights as a Pathway to Impunity for International Crimes* (Springer 2010) 290.

(sociological,[9] descriptive[10] or empirical)[11] legitimacy.[12] This chapter primarily relies on normative legitimacy when discussing the legitimacy of the exercise of authority by human rights treaty organs. As a preliminary observation, it is helpful to briefly examine these three types, as they are often interrelated.

Legal legitimacy equates legitimacy with legal validity and lawfulness. Thus, treaty organs lack legal legitimacy when their actions, including judgments or recommendations, go beyond the competence granted by states parties, constituting an act ultra vires.[13] The fundamental criterion for determining whether an act is ultra vires has been whether it conforms to, and is within the scope of, the consent of the states parties.[14] For example, George Letsas developed a 'commitment-based argument' to defend the legitimacy of the evolutive interpretation of the ECHR by the ECtHR. He argued that such legitimacy is grounded in the principle of *pacta sunt servanda* – the idea that states parties have consented to the ECtHR's legal mandate to provide institutional remedies for human rights violations and have promised to abide by its determinations of whether a violation exists.[15] However, this usage of legitimacy adds little theoretical advantage, as its meaning is exhausted within the existing concepts of legal validity and lawfulness.

The concept of legitimacy gains its theoretical raison d'etre as an autonomous concept when it refers to normative legitimacy. The application of treaty interpretation rules (Articles 31–33 VCLT) rarely leads to a single correct interpretation, leaving considerable discretion to interpreters.[16] Consequently, interpretations made by treaty organs can seldom be deemed invalid, even if they seem inappropriate or suboptimal. Moreover, the acts of treaty organs, including their judgments and Views, enjoy a practically irrebuttable presumption of validity due to their *compétence de la compétence* and the absence of any

[9] A Buchanan and RO Keohane, 'The Legitimacy of Global Governance Institutions' (2006) 20 *Ethics & International Affairs* 405, 405.

[10] A Follesdal, 'The Legitimacy of International Courts' (2020) 28 *Journal of Political Philosophy* 476, 480–81.

[11] A Hurrelmann, S Schneider and J Steffek, 'Introduction: Legitimacy in an Age of Global Politics' in A Hurrelmann, S Schneider and J Steffek (eds), *Legitimacy in an Age of Global Politics* (Palgrave Macmillan 2007) 1, 6–8.

[12] Legal and normative legitimacies are often conflated and grouped together as normative legitimacy *sensu lato*, as they both assess objects against predetermined normative frameworks (Thomas (n 5) 735). Nevertheless, this chapter draws a clear distinction between them and focuses on the normative legitimacy (*sensu stricto*) of the exercise of authority by treaty organs.

[13] R Wolfrum, 'Legitimacy of International Law from a Legal Perspective: Some Introductory Considerations' in R Wolfrum and V Röben (eds), *Legitimacy in International Law* (Springer 2008) 1, 23.

[14] HG Cohen et al, 'Legitimacy and International Courts: A Framework' in N Grossman et al (eds), *Legitimacy and International Courts* (Cambridge University Press 2018) 1, 5.

[15] G Letsas, 'The ECHR as a Living Instrument: Its Meaning and Legitimacy' in A Føllesdal and G Ulfstein (eds), *Constituting Europe: The European Court of Human Rights in a National, European and Global Context* (Cambridge University Press 2013) 106, 136–41.

[16] M Waibel, 'Uniformity versus Specialization (2): A Uniform Regime of Treaty Interpretation?' in CJ Tams, A Tzanakopoulos and A Zimmermann (eds), *Research Handbook on the Law of Treaties* (Edward Elgar 2014) 375, 380–81.

mechanism to invalidate them.[17] Thus, in most cases, the framework of legal validity and lawfulness, based on state consent, cannot effectively control the procedural and substantive quality of treaty organs' judgments and recommendations.[18] Against this backdrop, normative legitimacy offers a framework beyond that of legal validity and lawfulness. It allows for the normative assessment and critique of existing systems and practices, guiding their reform in a principled manner.[19] Based on certain predetermined values, standards and principles, normative legitimacy provides a scale of evaluation rather than the binary distinction between valid/lawful and void/unlawful.[20] Accordingly, this chapter focuses on the normative rather than the legal legitimacy of the exercise of authority by human rights treaty organs.

Acceptance of the concept of normative legitimacy in legal scholarship risks relativising the importance of legal validity and lawfulness.[21] Moreover, numerous criteria for normative legitimacy have been proposed, drawing on political, philosophical and moral theories. Some authors have cautioned that lawyers should adhere to the objective and neutral measure of legal validity and lawfulness, avoiding engagement in philosophical and political debates or imposing subjective preferences disguised as legitimacy.[22] Therefore, when relying on the concept of normative legitimacy for evaluation and reform, it is essential to base the criteria of legitimacy on the fundamental principles and values shared within the relevant society. This is why this chapter begins with the concept of 'democratic society' embedded in human rights treaties[23] and relies on

[17] S Hamamoto, 'Legitimacy of International Adjudication' (last updated 2020) in H Ruiz Fabri (ed), *Max Planck Encyclopedia of International Procedural Law* (Oxford University Press online edition) para 12. An analogy may be drawn with debates concerning the implied power of international organisations and its limit. See generally E Osieke, 'The Legal Validity of Ultra Vires Decisions of International Organization' 77 *AJIL* (1983) 239, 253–55.

[18] H Keller and G Ulfstein, 'Introduction' in H Keller and G Ulfstein (eds), *UN Human Rights Treaty Bodies: Law and Legitimacy* (Cambridge University Press 2012) 1, 7–8. Although some authors discuss treaty organs' broad exercise of authority within the framework of ultra vires, such discussions are not as fruitful as when they are conducted through other standards of normative legitimacy. See, eg, A von Bogdandy and R Urueña, 'International Transformative Constitutionalism in Latin America' (2020) 114 *AJIL* 403, 430–33.

[19] N Grossman, 'The Normative Legitimacy of International Courts' (2013) 86 *Temple Law Review* 61, 64; Hamamoto (n 17) para 42.

[20] A Roberts, 'Legality vs Legitimacy: Can Uses of Force Be Illegal But Justified?' in P Alston and E MacDonald (eds), *Human Rights, Intervention, and the Use of Force* (Oxford University Press 2008) 179, 208–09.

[21] ibid 210.

[22] J Craweford, 'The Problems of Legitimacy Speak' (2004) 98 *ASIL Proceedings* 271, 272–73. See also M Koskenniemi, 'Miserable Comforters: International Relations as New Natural Law' (2009) 15 *European Journal of International Relations* 395.

[23] For previous studies that grounds the need of democratic legitimacy of human rights treaty organs based on the concept of 'democratic society', see S Wheatley, 'On the Legitimate Authority of International Human Rights Bodies' in A Føllesdal, JK Schaffer and G Ulfstein (eds), *The Legitimacy of International Human Rights Regimes: Legal, Political and Philosophical Perspectives* (Cambridge University Press 2013) 84, 103–04; S Greer, 'Constitutionalizing Adjudication under the European Convention on Human Rights' (2003) 23 *Oxford Journal of Legal Studies* 405, 410.

international, transnational and national documents and principles when constructing a framework for legitimacy.

Social legitimacy can play a supplementary role.[24] Unlike legal or normative legitimacy, social legitimacy does not assess legitimacy based on norms, but rather on social facts. It concerns whether members of a community perceive the exercise of public authority as legitimate, which can be empirically measured by observing community members' attitudes, often expressed through interviews, public opinion surveys or actions such as compliance or resistance. For instance, Başak Çalı et al conducted interviews with national politicians, judges and human rights lawyers across different ECHR Member States, finding that the social legitimacy of the ECtHR is grounded in the logic of fair compromise.[25] Social legitimacy should never be equated directly with normative legitimacy, as doing so would subject norms to reality. Nonetheless, community perceptions often reflect the fundamental principles and values shared within society. In this way, social legitimacy can provide a clue to determining the criteria for normative legitimacy.[26]

3.1.2. The Blurred Boundary between International and National Sources of Legitimacy

While national constitutions have based their normative legitimacy (hereinafter simply referred to as 'legitimacy') on constitutional principles and values, most prominently human rights, democracy and the rule of law, in international law, the primary source of legitimacy, both legal and normative, has been state consent.[27] As Nico Krisch observed:

> In the classical picture, national and international law were grounded in distinct forms of legitimacy – domestic law in thick concepts such as liberal democracy, communism, or theocracy; international law in the consent ... of the individual states. The distinction of layers thus allowed for the coordination of very diverse, yet still thick domestic visions of political justice; as long as the two only intersected through consent, wide divergences could be managed.[28]

The separation between international and domestic sources of legitimacy caused no serious issues until recent decades because the limited impact of

[24] See, eg, MK Land, 'Justice as Legitimacy in the European Court of Human Rights' in Grossman et al (n 14) 83, 85.

[25] B Çalı, A Koch and N Bruch, 'The Legitimacy of Human Rights Courts: A Grounded Interpretivist Analysis of the European Court of Human Rights' (2013) 35 *Human Rights Quarterly* 955.

[26] On the relationship between social and normative legitimacies, see JK Schaffer, A Føllesdal and G Ulfstein, 'International Human Rights and the Challenge of Legitimacy' in Føllesdal, Schaffer and Ulfstein (n 23) 1, 12–15.

[27] Wolfrum (n 13) 6; Grossman (n 19) 65–67.

[28] N Krisch, *Beyond Constitutionalism: The Pluralist Structure of Postnational Law* (Oxford University Press 2010) 13.

international law on domestic constitutional orders shielded it from the scrutiny of legitimacy based on national constitutional principles. As Mattias Kumm described, during the Cold War, constitutional democracies viewed international law as ineffective and unreliable, addressing other people or occupying a highly specialised and narrow field.[29] The absence of compulsory dispute resolution mechanisms provided a further guarantee that international law would not ultimately impede constitutional self-government.[30] Shotaro Hamamoto also observed that classical international law scholarship was based on the assumption that 'it is for individual national legal orders to decide whether or not international law norms are directly applicable in their respective national legal orders'.[31] Consequently, the legitimate allocation of authority at the international level and that at the national level were strictly distinguished by the relevant actors and applicable principles, and these realms rarely interacted (see Figure 3.1).

Figure 3.1 Previous theoretical frameworks on allocating authorities

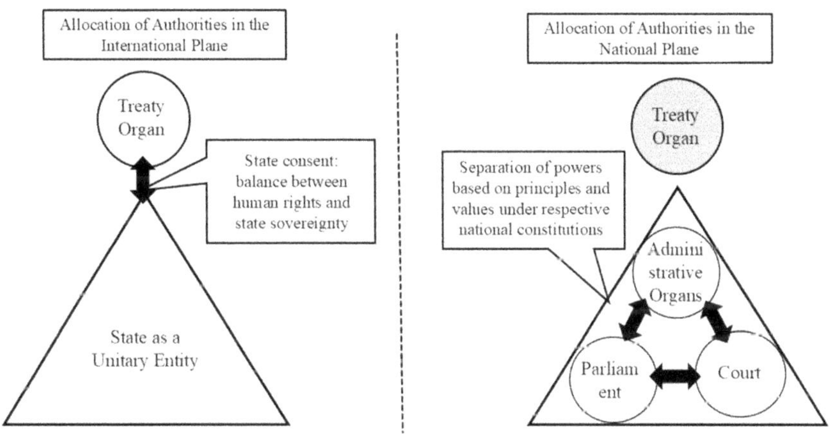

Accordingly, international human rights law scholarship has long adopted the standard of state consent for both normative legitimacy and legal legitimacy.[32] Universal human rights protection, as the object and purpose of the treaty, was placed in a binary and oppositional structure against state sovereignty, with the allocation of authorities between treaty organs and states

[29] M Kumm, 'The Legitimacy of International Law: A Constitutionalist Framework of Analysis' (2004) 15 *EJIL* 907, 911–12.

[30] ibid 912.

[31] S Hamamoto, 'EU-hou to kokusai-hou: Kokusai hougaku no kanten kara [EU Law and International Law: From the Perspective of International Law]' in H Hirano, H Kamemoto and N Kawahama (eds), *Gendaihou no henyou* [*The Transformation of Contemporary Law*] (Yuhikaku 2013) 209, 225.

[32] For this reason, the concept of legitimacy has not played an autonomous role distinct from that of legality and validity when assessing human rights treaty organs.

aiming to achieve equilibrium between the two.[33] This reflects the dominant discursive framework in classical international law scholarship, where the exercise of power by international judiciary was examined in terms of the extent to which state sovereignty could be restricted to enhance the object and purpose of the treaty. On the one hand, some advocated the principle of *in dubio mitius*, which requires interpreters to adopt a meaning that interferes less with state sovereignty when interpreting ambiguous provisions.[34] On the other hand, others were sceptical of this principle and supported the principle of *effet utile*,[35] emphasising the importance of the object and purpose of the treaty agreed upon by the states parties.[36]

In the same vein, the doctrine of the margin of appreciation has long been understood as a tool to properly allocate authority between the ECtHR and states by balancing the universal human rights protection and respect for state sovereignty.[37] For example, Ronald St J McDonald stated in 1993 that:

> The margin of appreciation gives the flexibility needed to avoid damaging confrontations between the Court and Contracting States over their respective spheres of authority and enables the Court to balance the sovereignty of Contracting Parties with their obligations under the Convention.[38]

The same framework also governed the discourse on treaty interpretation, particularly regarding the legitimacy of evolutive interpretation adopted by treaty organs. When the ECtHR held that Article 6 ECHR included a right of access to court in *Golder v UK* (1975), Judge Sir Gerald Fitzmaurice observed that:

> [I]t is for the States upon whose consent the Convention rests, and from which consent alone it derives its obligatory force, to close the gap or put the defect right by an amendment, not for a judicial tribunal to substitute itself for the convention-makers, to do their work for them.[39]

[33] Formally speaking, the scope of a human rights treaty organ's authority must be determined through the interpretation of the relevant provisions of the treaty based on rules of treaty interpretation codified in arts 31–33 VCLT. This chapter instead focuses on the discursive structure and narrative that have substantially controlled the application of such interpretative tools.

[34] See, eg, LFL Oppenheim, *International Law: A Treatise, Vol 1: Peace* (Longmans, Green and Co 1905) 561.

[35] See, eg, Comments by D Guggenheim at the first meeting of the public international law section in 1952's session of l'Institut de Droit International cited in (1952) 44 *Annuaire de l'Institut de Droit International*, at 395.

[36] See, eg, H Lauterpacht, 'Restrictive Interpretation and the Principle of Effectiveness in the Interpretation of Treaties' (1949) 26 *British Year Book of International Law* 48, 60–61.

[37] JG Merrills, *The Development of International Law by the European Court of Human Rights* (Manchester University Press 1988) 157; MR Hutchinson, 'The Margin of Appreciation Doctrine in the European Court of Human Rights' (1999) 48 *ICLQ* 638, 647.

[38] R McDonald, 'The Margin of Appreciation' in R McDonald et al (eds), *The European System for the Protection of Human Rights* (Brill/Nijhoff 1993) 84, 123.

[39] *Golder v UK*, ECtHR, App No 4451/70, Merits and Just Satisfaction (21 February 1975) Separate Opinion of Judge Sir Gerald Fitzmaurice, para 37(c). Similar criticism is often raised, including in different treaty organs and more recent cases. See, eg, *Artavia Murillo et al (In Vitro Fertilization) v Costa Rica*, IACtHR, Series C No 257, Preliminary Objections, Merits, Reparations and Costs (28 November 2012) Dissenting Opinion of Judge Vio Grossi, 'Introduction'.

The practice of treaty organs regarding reparation and remedy has also been assessed within this framework (see Chapter 2, sections 2.2.1 and 2.2.2).

However, this formula – separating international and national sources of legitimacy and focusing on state consent as the sole source of legitimacy in international law – no longer applies to human rights treaty organs today, as they are becoming deeply and 'robustly'[40] embedded in domestic legal orders (see Chapter 2). Moreover, as human rights treaty norms possess an evolutionary character, through the jurisprudence of human rights treaty organs, states often come to bear obligations that they did concretely expect at the time of ratification.[41] This factor further undermines the role of state consent – based on parliamentary approval and other procedures under national constitutions – as a barrier against the unexpected and undesired intrusion of human rights treaties into national legal orders.[42]

Accordingly, the boundary between domestic and international sources of legitimacy has begun to collapse. Not only domestic constitutional lawyers but also international law scholars have started to argue that human rights treaty organs 'should be subject to constitutional standards known from national constitutional law, especially the "[t]rinitarian mantra of the constitutionalist faith": democracy, human rights, and the rule of law'.[43] For this reason, many international lawyers have attempted to extend the debate on the democratic legitimacy of judicial review – accumulated in domestic constitutional law scholarship[44] – to the international plane in order to evaluate and critique human rights treaty organs,[45] a perspective increasingly shared by national politicians, lawyers and the general public (see Chapter 2, section 2.3).

[40] For a concept of 'robust international law', see A Buchanan and R Powell, 'Constitutional Democracy and the Rule of International Law: Are They Compatible?' (2008) 16 *Journal of Political Philosophy* 326.

[41] For some of the prominent examples where treaty organs have imposed new obligations – obligations that did not exist 10–20 years ago – on states parties, see *Christine Goodwin v UK*, ECtHR, App No 28957/95, Merits and Just Satisfaction (11 July 2002); *Roger Judge v Canada*, HRC, Communication No 829/1998 (5 August 2002) UN Doc CCPR/C/78/D/829/1998.

[42] Keller and Ulfstein (n 18) 7–8; A Buchanan, 'The Legitimacy of International Law' in S Besson and J Tasioulas (eds), *The Philosophy of International Law* (Oxford University Press 2010) 79, 91.

[43] G Ulfstein, 'A Transnational Separation of Powers?' in M Saul, A Follesdal and G Ulfstein (eds), *The International Human Rights Judiciary and National Parliaments: Europe and Beyond* (Cambridge University Press 2017) 21, 22.

[44] See, eg, JH Ely, *Democracy and Distrust: A Theory of Judicial Review* (Harvard University Press 1980); L Favoreu, 'La légitimité du juge constitutionnel' (1994) 46 *Revue internationale de droit comparé* 557; M Shigeki, *Shihou shinsa to minshu shugi [Judicial Review and Democracy]* (Yuhikaku 1991).

[45] A Zysset, 'Searching for the Legitimacy of the European Court of Human Rights: The Neglected Role of "Democratic Society"' (2006) 5 *Global Constitutionalism* 16, 21. See, eg, A Føllesdal, 'Why the European Court of Human Rights Might Be Democratically Legitimate: A Modest Defense' (2009) 27 *NJHR* 289, 291; NT Zúñiga, *The Inter American Court of Human Rights: The Legitimacy of International Courts and Tribunals* (Routledge 2022) 20.

3.1.3. The Framework of a 'Globalised Democratic Society'

The blurring of the boundary between international and national sources of legitimacy corresponds to that between international and national societies. Thus, this chapter proposes the framework of a 'globalised democratic society' based on the evolutive interpretation of the term and concept of 'democratic society' embedded in human rights treaties.

Rooted in Article 29(2) of the 1948 UDHR, all three human rights treaties examined in this book, namely the ECHR, the ACHR and the ICCPR, embrace the term 'democratic society' (see Chapter 1, section 1.4.2.2). Although treaty drafters must have had their respective national societies in mind, this chapter posits that today, we live in 'globalised democratic societies'. There is no single global society where human beings constitute a single demos, and democracy is exercised within each national society. International law and national laws do not form a single monist legal order. Nevertheless, respective national democratic societies are greatly affected by human rights treaty standards and have become spaces where treaty organs and state organs closely intersect, regardless of their formal origins. As discussed in Chapter 2, on the one hand, treaty organs substantially participate in the interpretation and application of domestic constitutions and laws by affecting the actions of relevant state organs; on the other hand, state organs claim to and do play roles in the interpretation and application of human rights treaties, as the latter are inextricably integrated into domestic constitutions and laws. Therefore, instead of maintaining distinct sources of legitimacy for human rights law and national laws, it is necessary to develop single and common standards of legitimacy that apply to such globalised democratic societies. The concept of a globalised democratic society serves as a key to integrating the international and national legal orders.

Such legitimacy standards should be based on principles and values widely shared in international and transnational fora as well as national constitutional laws, ensuring that they are acceptable from both the perspectives of human rights treaties and national laws. The acceptability of the frameworks presented in this chapter should be continuously tested within the epistemic community supporting globalised democratic societies, which consist of diverse actors, including treaty organs, states, national courts, parliamentarians, various administrative organs, NHRIs, national and transnational civil society organisations, and academics.[46] As Armin von Bogdandy and René Urueña have argued regarding a similar concept of the 'Latin American human rights community (of practice)', actors in such a community are far from homogeneous and often

[46] The concept of 'epistemic community supporting globalised democratic societies' has been inspired by the concept of transnational communities of practice within the theory of interactional international law advocated by Brunnée and Toope. See generally J Brunnée and SJ Toope, *Legitimacy and Legality in International Law: An Interactional Account* (Cambridge University Press 2010).

produce conflicting views, yet they share a minimum common understanding necessary to build such a community and an identity as its members.[47]

3.2. 'SEPARATION OF POWERS IN A GLOBALISED DEMOCRATIC SOCIETY' MODEL

Having its most prominent origin in Montesquieu's *De l'esprit des lois* in 1748, the separation of powers has become one of the most fundamental and universally accepted principles in the world's constitutional democracies.[48] This chapter uses the framework of the separation of powers to discuss the allocation of authorities and duties among treaty organs and state organs in globalised democratic societies – what it terms the 'separation of powers in a globalised democratic society' model.

This study is not the first to highlight the need for a separation of powers between treaty organs and state organs. Johannes Fahner observed that many states have outsourced part of the constitutional mandate originally allocated to national courts to international human rights courts, and thus the separation of powers requires that human rights courts accord 'constitutional deference' to national decisions.[49] Additionally, relying on the concept of the separation of powers, Christoph Möllers has stated that the ECtHR should act 'with care and political sensitivity' because it restricts 'democratic decision-making from within a democratic vacuum'.[50] Nevertheless, these authors have not elaborated on the specific ways in which their proposals should operate. Although Geir Ulfstein has suggested several broad elements to that effect – such as democracy, human rights, the rule of law, the margin of appreciation, and subsidiarity[51] – further elaboration is necessary. That said, certain authors have examined the transnational separation of powers in global governance within a more general context,[52] which provides useful insights for our case (see section 3.2.1).

3.2.1. Separation of Powers: A Widely Recognised but Incomplete Concept

In classical literature, the concept of the separation of powers was considered equivalent to the strict division of powers in terms of institutions, functions

[47] Von Bogdandy and Urueña (n 18) 416–18.
[48] MJC Vile, *Constitutionalism and the Separation of Powers* (Clarendon Press 1967) 97.
[49] JH Fahner, *Judicial Deference in International Adjudication: A Comparative Analysis* (Hart Publishing 2020) 207–08.
[50] C Möllers, *The Three Branches: A Comparative Model of Separation of Powers* (Oxford University Press 2013) 213.
[51] Ulfstein (n 43) 22–23.
[52] I Venzke and J Mendes, 'The Idea of Relative Authority in European and International Law' (2018) 16 *I-CON* 75, 96; D Haljan, *Separating Powers: International Law before National Courts* (TMC Asser Press 2013) 281–85.

and personnel ('the pure doctrine of the separation of powers'),[53] based on the 'one branch-one function' and 'separation as confinement' views.[54] The primary concern was the effective protection of individuals' liberty by averting the risks of tyranny and the exercise of arbitrary power.[55] However, the pure doctrine has gained little support, as it cannot accommodate the interaction and interdependence between the branches.[56] At present, therefore, the separation of powers is reconstructed to harmonise the division of powers element with the active checks and balances element;[57] it is not only about separation but also about coordination and supervision among powers. Accordingly, another rationale for the separation of powers, in addition to the protection of liberty, is increasingly highlighted: allocating power and assigning tasks to those bodies best suited to execute them in terms of their composition, capacity, decision-making processes, and functions, while coordinating with and supervising one another for the proper fulfilment of their tasks – often referred to as the value of 'efficiency'.[58]

Reconstructed in this way, the separation of powers provides useful guidance for regulating the relationship between treaty organs and state organs in a principled manner.[59] As Ingo Venzke and Joana Mendes argued:

> [The image of the specific tripartite division of powers] does not travel beyond the state. But the core normative program that is vested in separation of powers thinking – above all that authority be divided and connected in specific ways that combines ways of acting with legitimacy assets – is an idea that does travel well and that is insightful for the exercise of authority beyond the state.[60]

Nonetheless, even after these clarifications, the separation of powers remains a 'desiccated concept that waits for the introduction of a stronger normative thesis before it generates a full conception of the doctrine that can provide any institutional considerations'.[61] In fact, the separation of powers as such does

[53] Vile (n 48) 13.

[54] A Kavanagh, 'The Constitutional Separation of Powers' in D Dyzenhaus and M Thorburn (eds), *Philosophical Foundations of Constitutional Law* (Oxford University Press 2016) 221, 225.

[55] See, eg, Supreme Court, *Myers v United States*, 272 US 52, 293 (25 October 1926) (US) (Dissenting Opinion of Judge Brandeis).

[56] E Carolan, *The New Separation of Powers: A Theory for the Modern State* (Oxford University Press 2009) 18–21.

[57] Kavanagh (n 54) 233–34.

[58] See, eg, N Barber, 'Prelude to the Separation of Powers' (2001) 60 *Cambridge Law Journal* 59; K Hesse, *Grundzüge des Verfassungsrechts der Bundesrepublik Deutschland*, 20th edn (CF Müller 1999) 210–11; R Muranishi, 'Kenryokubunritsuron no gendaiteki tenkai: Kinouteki kenryokubunritsuron no kanousei [Recent Developments Concerning the Separation of Powers: Towards Functional Separation of Powers?]' (2005) 90 *Kyudai Law Review* 213.

[59] See Haljan (n 52) 282. Some authors have argued that judicial deference, especially the doctrine of margin of appreciation, is an instrument dealing with the separation of powers beyond the state. See, eg, C Grabenwarter, 'The European Convention on Human Rights: Inherent Constitutional Tendencies and the Role of the European Court of Human Rights' in A von Bogdandy and P Sonnevend (eds), *Constitutional Crisis in the European Constitutional Area: Theory, Law and Politics in Hungary and Romania* (Hart Publishing 2015) 257, 268.

[60] Venzke and Mendes (n 52) 96. See also Barber (n 58) 71.

[61] Barber (n 58) 65–66.

not impose a unified institutional arrangement; rather, it is applied in various ways, reflecting the particularities of the constitutional systems and conceptions of democracy in the state in question.[62] The separation of powers has played determinate roles only with 'hidden normative judgements' based on certain political visions and theories, even though 'in many jurisdictions, these normative assumptions remain untested by political or judicial debate'.[63] Therefore, we need a thicker political theory to be able to derive concrete guidance on the relationship between treaty organs and state organs from the concept of the separation of powers. The original theory of 'two-tiered bounded deliberative democracy', presented in the next subsection, serves this purpose.

3.2.2. 'Two-Tiered Bounded Deliberative Democracy' as a Guiding Theory for a 'Globalised Democratic Society'

Undoubtedly, democracy is one of the fundamental constitutional principles widely shared in constitutional democracies, even though its concrete meaning varies from state to state and is often subject to ongoing debates even within each state. As Samantha Besson observed, although democracy and human rights are mutually dependent and reinforcing sources of legitimacy in the domestic context, they have been decoupled through the internationalisation of these concepts, particularly at the universal level (see also Chapter 1, section 1.4.2.2).[64] Now that we live in 'globalised democratic societies' where the boundary between international and national sources of legitimacy is blurred, democracy and human rights should be recoupled.[65] Thus, this section aims to establish a theory of democracy that should apply to globalised democratic societies.

There is a rich body of previous research on the conception of democracy that should apply to human rights treaties, particularly in the context of the debate regarding the challenge to the democratic legitimacy of human rights treaty organs. Many studies have sought to situate human rights treaty organs within, rather than outside, democracy due to their roles in remedying the failures of domestic democracy,[66] introducing unheard voices into national political processes,[67]

[62] Möllers (n 50) 43.

[63] Carolan (n 56) 33.

[64] S Besson, 'Human Rights and Democracy in a Global Context: Decoupling and Recoupling' (2011) 4 *Ethics & Global Politics* 19, 21.

[65] ibid.

[66] A Føllesdal, 'Much Ado about Nothing? International Judicial Review of Human Rights in Well-Functioning Democracies' in Føllesdal, Schaffer and Ulfstein (n 23) 272, 282; E Benvenisti, 'The Margin of Appreciation, Subsidiarity and Global Challenges to Democracy' (2018) 9 *Journal of International Dispute Settlement* 240, 241.

[67] S Hamamoto, 'An Undemocratic Guardian of Democracy: International Human Rights Complaint Procedures' (2007) 38 *Victoria University of Wellington Law Review* 199, 212.

strengthening participation and consultation,[68] enhancing the quality of democratic deliberations,[69] protecting human rights that are foundational to democracy,[70] and preserving democratic values, such as pluralism and public equality.[71] Some authors have examined international courts in general, arguing that they enhance democratic values like equal participation, accountability and public justification beyond the state.[72] Nevertheless, these accounts remain incomplete, as they generally do not provide a comprehensive definition of 'democracy'. Even when some authors have presented accounts of the conception of democracy, such as Alain Zysset's reliance on Thomas Christiano's 'egalitarian' conception of democracy,[73] and Rory O'Connell's argument that the ECtHR promotes not only representative and liberal models, but also deliberative, participatory and inclusive models of democracy,[74] they have not explored how such conceptions of 'democracy' may extend beyond the state.[75]

A few previous studies have presented original conceptions of democracy that bridge international and national societies.[76] Besson proposed that 'international human rights support domestic democracy by protecting the minimal rights necessary for domestic democracy, and citizens' rights developed within domestic democracy consolidate into international human rights in return'.[77] Steven Wheatley suggested that 'a revised conception' of constitutional courts in deliberative democracy, as proposed by John Rawls, can ground the legitimate role of human rights treaty organs, which is to 'give expression to the overlapping consensus of the subjects of the regime on the issue of human rights'.[78]

[68] R O'Connell, 'Towards a Stronger Conception of Democracy in the Strasbourg Convention' [2006] *European Human Rights Law Review* 281. For the most updated observations of O'Connell, see R O'Connell, *Law, Democracy and the European Court of Human Rights* (Cambridge University Press 2020).

[69] Buchanan and Powell (n 40) 331.

[70] A Mowbray, 'The Role of the European Court of Human Rights in the Promotion of Democracy' [1999] *Public Law* 703. See also A Mowbray, 'Contemporary Aspects of the Promotion of Democracy by the European Court of Human Rights' (2014) 20 *European Public Law* 469.

[71] Zysset (n 45).

[72] JW Kuyper and T Squatrito, 'International Courts and Global Democratic Values: Participation, Accountability, and Justification' (2017) 43 *Review of International Studies* 152.

[73] Zysset (n 45).

[74] O'Connell (n 68).

[75] Exceptionally, Hamamoto (n 67) paid careful attention to the issue of unit of democracy. He argued that while non-binding decisions by UN human rights treaties promote democracy within each national state, the ECHR, with binding judgments of the ECtHR, is recognised as a 'constitutional instrument of European public order' which presupposes 'a Europe-wide democracy'. However, this chapter does not adopt this binary distinction. Armin von Bogdandy proposed the dual-structured and multi-level democratic legitimation of international courts based on the conception of democracy as focusing on civic equality, representation, participation, deliberation and control (A von Bogdandy, 'The Democratic Legitimacy of International Courts: Conceptual Framework' (2013) 14 *Theoretical Inquiries in Law* 361, 364–70). However, as this theory heavily relies on the specific context of the European Union (EU) and is based on the interpretation of the Treaty on European Union, its applicability to human rights treaty organs is limited.

[76] Zúñiga (n 45) 25–33.

[77] Besson (n 64) 33.

[78] Wheatley (n 23) 109.

Discussing the democratic legitimacy of the IACtHR, von Bogdandy and Urueña have proposed the concept of a Latin American community of human rights, comprising various actors such as transnational and grassroots NGOs, IACtHR judges, national courts, other state bodies and scholars, leading to the creation of a 'Latin American public'.[79] Richard Bellamy offered the most comprehensive theory of the 'two-level political constitution', according to which:

> [A] political constitution at the international level renders [human rights courts] subject to the democratic authorization and accountability of the representatives of the contracting democratic states, who are … democratically authorized and accountable to those they represent through a political constitution at the domestic level.[80]

Although these studies represent significant steps towards establishing the theory of democracy beyond the state, they are not without theoretical and practical problems. For instance, Bellamy's conception of the 'two-level political constitution', which excludes undemocratic states from becoming parties to human rights treaties, would not only undermine the value of human rights treaties but would also lead to considerable political challenges in determining which states should qualify as democratic. Moreover, the larger lacuna of prior studies is that they have not fully explored the practical implications of their theories for the authorities and duties of human rights treaty organs and state organs and their interactions.

Against this background, this chapter first demonstrates that consensus on a thicker conception of democracy is emerging in international and transnational fora (section 3.2.2.1). It then presents, drawing lessons from national constitutional scholarship, an original theory of 'two-tiered bounded deliberative democracy' as a guiding theory for globalised democratic societies. This theory harmonises human rights and democracy at the global level by prioritising national deliberations while setting certain frameworks and limits on them based on principles and values that have been firmly established through international deliberations, including human rights treaty standards (section 3.2.2.2).

3.2.2.1. Growing Consensus on a Denser Conception of Democracy: Towards an Evolutive Interpretation of the Concept of 'Democratic Society' in Human Rights Treaties

The ECHR was created to protect Western democracy from the threats of fascism and communism, and the conception of 'democratic society' was inevitably closely linked to the Western understanding of democracy (see Chapter 1, section 1.4.2.2). However, this European conception of 'democracy' was not

[79] Von Bogdandy and Urueña (n 18) 414 and 437.

[80] R Bellamy, 'The Democratic Legitimacy of International Human Rights Conventions: Political Constitutionalism and the European Convention on Human Rights' (2015) 25 *EJIL* 1019, 1033. See also T Christiano, 'Democratic Legitimacy and International Institutions' in Besson and Tasioulas (n 42) 119, 135–36.

universally shared outside the regional framework. As stated in Chapter 1, the term 'democratic society' was understood in a politically neutral manner at the universal level, and no particular political model was a prerequisite for international human rights protection (see Chapter 1, section 1.4.2.2). Such a politically neutral understanding of democracy corresponds to the principles of sovereignty and sovereign equality, under which classical international law has treated all political systems as having equal value (see Chapter 1, section 1.1.1).

However, since the end of the Cold War, a growing consensus on a denser conception of 'democracy' and its relationship with human rights has emerged at the universal level and beyond Europe.[81] One of the primary fora for cultivating this consensus is the Inter-Parliamentary Union (IPU), a global organisation of national parliaments (for detailed information about the IPU, see Chapter 5, section 5.3.1.1). In 1997, the Inter-Parliamentary Council adopted the 'Universal Declaration on Democracy' without a vote.[82] Since then, the IPU Assembly has adopted various resolutions concerning democracy,[83] and in 2017, it unanimously adopted the resolution 'Sharing our Diversity: The 20th Anniversary of the Universal Declaration on Democracy'.[84] Within the framework of the UN, the General Assembly and the Human Rights Council (as well as the former Commission on Human Rights) have advanced debates concerning the conception of 'democracy'.[85] In the Americas, several resolutions and declarations on democracy were adopted in the 1990s within the framework of the OAS,[86] eventually leading to the adoption of the 'Inter-American Democratic Charter' in 2001.[87] While these documents are non-binding and may largely reflect public stances and goals rather than the reality for many countries, the convergence towards a single conception of democracy in the international community greatly facilitates the evolutive interpretation of the concept of 'democratic society' in human rights treaties.

Although this study does not fully elaborate on these documents and related debates, these documents and debates collectively reveal that the essential components of 'democracy' include inclusive representation, participation and deliberation in a climate of respect for diversity and pluralism. For example, the aforementioned IPU Assembly resolution of 2017 recognises that 'building a democratic society requires … respect for diversity and the equitable inclusion

[81] See generally LA Sicilianos, *L'ONU et la démocratisation de l'état: systèmes régionaux et ordre juridique universel* (Pedone 2000). See also articles contained in GH Fox and BR Roth (eds), *Democratic Governance and International Law* (Cambridge University Press 2000).

[82] Inter-Parliamentary Council, 'Universal Declaration on Democracy' (16 September 1997). After the Declaration was adopted, the delegation of China expressed reservations to the text.

[83] For a list of major relevant resolutions, see IPU Assembly, 'Sharing Our Diversity: The 20th Anniversary of the Universal Declaration on Democracy' (18 October 2017) preambular para 6.

[84] ibid.

[85] For a list of major relevant resolutions, see UN Human Rights Council Res 19/36, 'Human Rights, Democracy and the Rule of Law' (23 March 2012) preambular para 1.

[86] See, eg, OAS General Assembly, 'The Declaration of Managua for the Promotion of Democracy and Development' (8 June 1993) AG/DEC. 4 (XXIII-O/93).

[87] OAS General Assembly, 'Inter-American Democratic Charter' (11 September 2001).

of all citizens', and calls on 'parliaments to strengthen citizen engagement and public participation in the democratic process, and … to continue to improve their working methods to facilitate the participation of civil society and ordinary citizens in their deliberations'.[88] A resolution by the UN Human Rights Council in 2012 emphasised the 'crucial role played by the political opposition and civil society in the proper functioning of a democracy'[89] and encouraged 'the use of democratic consultative mechanisms in decision-making processes and disputes as an opportunity for stakeholders to advance their rights and reach well-informed decisions within institutional frameworks'.[90] Moreover, these documents reiterate that 'democracy' and human rights are 'interdependent and mutually reinforcing'.[91] Thus, 'democracy fosters the full realization of all human rights, and vice versa',[92] and the 'full exercise of fundamental freedoms and human rights … can only take place within democratic systems'.[93]

Two conclusions emerge from this brief examination. First, given these international and transnational developments in favour of a richer conception of 'democracy', a politically neutral understanding of the concept of 'democratic society' in human rights treaties is no longer appropriate; therefore, an evolutive interpretation of 'democratic society' is required. Second, the proposition that democracy and human rights are 'interdependent and mutually reinforcing' indicates that the international community does not adopt a simple majoritarian vision of democracy, as such a vision lacks safeguards against the oppression of the minority by the tyranny of the majority and therefore would be in direct conflict with human rights.[94] Thus, an alternative vision of 'democracy' is necessary, one that is not only based on inclusive representation, participation and deliberation, but also facilitates the harmonisation of democracy and human rights at the global level.

3.2.2.2. Harmonisation of Human Rights and Democracy at the Global Level under the Two-Tiered Bounded Deliberative Democracy Theory

As Steven Wheatley observes, deliberative democracy is a strong candidate for a theory that underlies the concept of 'democratic society' in human rights treaties.[95] The theory of democracy experienced a 'deliberative turn' in

[88] IPU Assembly (n 83) paras 2 and 6.
[89] UN Human Rights Council (n 85) para 6.
[90] ibid para 19 (e).
[91] See, eg, UN Commission on Human Rights Res 2003/36, 'Interdependence between Democracy and Human Rights' (23 April 2003) para 2.
[92] UN Commission on Human Rights Res 1999/57, 'Promotion of the Right to Democracy' (27 April 1999) para 1.
[93] UN Commission on Human Rights Res 2002/46, 'Further Measures to Promote and Consolidate Democracy' (23 April 2002) para 2.
[94] S Wheatley, 'Deliberative Democracy and Minorities' (2003) 14 *EJIL* 507, 509–10.
[95] ibid 510; S Wheatley, 'Minorities under the ECHR and the Construction of a "Democratic Society"' [2007] *Public Law* 770, 784–48. See also O'Connell (n 68) 23–26.

around 1990.[96] 'Deliberative democracy' was proposed as an effective alternative to the classical simple majoritarian or 'aggregative' model of democracy.[97] The aggregative model treats the intuitional preferences of individuals as fixed and aims to maximise them.[98] However, the deliberative model suggests that individuals' initial preferences may evolve through open, uncoerced, inclusive and thorough deliberation among equal and reasonable participants. Decisions are not made based on the preferences with the greatest numerical support, but on the proposals supported by the strongest reasoning. In deliberative democracy:

> [F]ree and equal citizens (and their representatives) justify decisions in a process in which they give one another reasons that are mutually acceptable and generally accessible, with the aim of reaching conclusions that are binding in the present on all citizens but open to challenge in the future.[99]

The process of such deliberation itself becomes a source of democratic legitimacy.

Deliberative theory seeks to reconcile democracy with human rights. It not only mandates that all those affected are formally included in the decision-making process, but also requires their substantive participation and representation, ensuring that all voices are carefully heard and thoroughly considered. Jürgen Habermas, a leading deliberative theorist, argues that human rights and democracy are internally connected and 'co-original':[100]

> [Equally enfranchised citizens] can … adequately exercise their public autonomy, guaranteed by rights of communication and participation, only insofar as their private autonomy is guaranteed. A well-secured private autonomy helps 'secure the conditions' of public autonomy just as much as, conversely, the appropriate exercise of public autonomy helps 'secure the conditions' of private autonomy.[101]

In this theory, the specific content of human rights is not derived from a single, objective 'moral truth',[102] but is established through deliberations – the actual exercise of civil autonomy under evolving circumstances.[103]

Although the deliberative model has largely succeeded in assuaging the tension between human rights and democracy, it has not completely eliminated the root cause of the tension. In the 'co-originality' thesis, while equal rights to participate in political deliberation are given intrinsic value as the direct

[96] See generally A Floridia, 'The Origins of the Deliberative Turn' in A Bächtiger et al (eds), *The Oxford Handbook of Deliberative Democracy* (Oxford University Press 2018) 35.

[97] IM Young, *Inclusion and Democracy* (Oxford University Press 2000) 18–26.

[98] ibid 19.

[99] A Gutmann and DF Thompson, *Why Deliberative Democracy?* (Princeton University Press 2004) 7.

[100] J Habermas (translated by W Rehg), *Between Facts and Norms: Contributions to a Discourse Theory of Law and Democracy* (MIT Press 1996) 127.

[101] ibid 408.

[102] *cf* G Letsas, 'The Truth in Autonomous Concepts: How to Interpret the ECHR' (2004) 15 *EJIL* 279.

[103] J Cohen, 'Reflections on Habermas on Democracy' (1999) 12 *Ratio Juris* 385, 393–94.

foundation of democracy, other non-political liberties, which only indirectly contribute to the public autonomy of individuals, are treated as instrumental.[104] This could potentially lead to the problematic conclusion that excessively broad restrictions on non-political liberties might be justified owing to deliberation.

These risks are heightened by the fact that, in practice, ideal deliberation rarely occurs in societies of a certain size and diversity, particularly those with entrenched and permanent divisions between majority and minority groups based on race, religion and other identities. As Wheatley notes, 'individuals cannot easily reject that part of their identity conditioned by membership of a social group. Certain core beliefs are non-negotiable'.[105] Deliberations aim to adopt norms 'to which all possibly affected persons could agree as participants in rational discourses'.[106] However, in most real-world situations, decisions are ultimately made by majority votes following certain deliberations. As a result, the theory of deliberative democracy does not guarantee that its aim of adopting such norms will be realised. To prevent the gradual erosion of human rights for certain individuals by majority votes under the guise of 'deliberation',[107] the pure and unconditional form of deliberative democracy cannot be adopted.

Thus, Sandra Fredman supplemented the theory of deliberative democracy by the concept of 'bounded deliberation'.[108] This approach imposes certain limits ('bounds') on the manner and outcome of deliberation. The reasoning and results of deliberation must align with the principles and values that have been developed over time and are universally accepted within the society in question, including human rights. These 'bounds' are not external to deliberative democracy; they stem from a more careful, long-term and matured deliberation, effectively protecting the integrity of the deliberative process from the irreversible harm that can result from rushed and insufficient decision-making. As Friedrich A Hayek puts it: 'Only a demagogue can represent as "antidemocratic" the limitations which long-term decisions and the general principles held by the people impose upon the power of temporary majorities.'[109]

Building on these previous studies, this chapter constructs the original theory of two-tiered bounded deliberative democracy. It asserts that deliberations should primarily take place within each national society,[110] as only national societies are

[104] R Alexy, 'Basic Rights and Democracy in Jurgen Habermas's Procedural Paradigm of the Law' (1994) 7 *Ratio Juris* 227, 231–32; JK Schaffer, 'The Co-Originality of Human Rights and Democracy in an International Order' (2015) 7 *International Theory* 96, 100.

[105] Wheatley (n 94) 518.

[106] Habermas (n 100) 107.

[107] IY Nugraha, 'Deferring to Consensus and Procedural Rationality: Assessing the European Court of Human Rights' Approach to Majoritarian Will' (2024) 9 *Asian Yearbook of Human Rights and Humanitarian Law* 166, 197.

[108] S Fredman, 'From Dialogue to Deliberation: Human Rights Adjudication and Prisoners' Rights to Vote' in M Hunt, HJ Hooper and P Yowell (eds), *Parliaments and Human Rights: Redressing the Democratic Deficit* (Hart Publishing 2015) 447, 451–54.

[109] FA Hayek, *The Constitution of Liberty* (University of Chicago Press 1960) 181.

[110] This point distinguishes the 'two-tiered bounded deliberative democracy' theory from other major theories on global democracy, such as the 'cosmopolitan democracy' theory advocated by

equipped with dense public spheres, sufficiently shared values and roughly equal stakes necessary for rich and meaningful deliberations.[111] However, deliberations at the national level inevitably face what Eyal Benvenisti calls 'the problem of disregard'.[112] Certain categories of individuals are formally or substantially excluded from deliberations, despite being affected by the state's decisions.[113] These categories typically include asylum seekers and foreigners,[114] but can also encompass nationals who belong to 'discrete and insular minorities'.[115]

To address this issue, the theory of 'two-tiered bounded deliberative democracy' proposes that 'bounds' on national deliberations should be established through long-term and matured deliberations at the international level.[116] Due to the varied population compositions and the diversity of political and social backgrounds across states, deliberations at the international level allow for a broader range of perspectives and interests to be heard and considered, including those overlooked or ignored in national deliberations.[117] In this theory, the two tiers of deliberation – national and international – circulate: the 'bounds' produced through international deliberations set the frameworks and limits for national deliberations, while the outcomes of deliberations within individual national societies contribute to creating new 'bounds' or modifying the existing ones at the international level.

'Bounds' produced through long-term and matured international deliberations are crystallised in the text of human rights treaties. They may also develop after human rights treaties are adopted, in the form of relevant treaties, and resolutions, guidelines and declarations adopted in international organisations and conferences. Setting such 'bounds' for national deliberations based

David Held (D Held, *Democracy and the Global Order: From the Modern State to Cosmopolitan Governance* (Stanford University Press 1995)) and the 'transnational discursive democracy' theory by John Dryzek (J Dryzek, *Deliberative Democracy and Beyond: Liberals, Critics, Contestations* (Oxford University Press 2002) ch 5).

[111] See, eg, W Kymlicka, *Contemporary Political Philosophy: An Introduction*, 2nd edn (Oxford University Press 2001) 314–15.

[112] E Benvenisti, 'Explaining Variations in Standards of Review in International Adjudication' in G Kajtár, B Çali and M Milanovic (eds), *Secondary Rules of Primary Importance in International Law* (Oxford University Press 2022) 21, 23–24. Benvenisti borrowed this concept from RB Stewart, 'Remedying Disregard in Global Regulatory Governance: Accountability, Participation, and Responsiveness' (2014) 108 *AJIL* 211.

[113] S Dothan, *International Judicial Review: When Should International Courts Intervene?* (Cambridge University Press 2020) 29–32.

[114] Benvenisti (n 66) 242–45.

[115] Supreme Court, *United States v Carolene Products Co*, 304 US 144 (25 April 1938) (US), fn 4. See also Ely (n 44) 75–87.

[116] For the discussions on deliberations at the international level, see S Wheatley, 'A Democratic Rule of International Law' (2011) 22 *EJIL* 525, 537–39. Wheatley describes such deliberations as 'deliberative diplomacy'.

[117] Y Shany, 'All Roads Lead to Strasbourg? Application of the Margin of Appreciation Doctrine by the European Court of Human Rights and the UN Human Rights Committee' (2018) 9 *Journal of International Dispute Settlement* 180, 193; B Baade, 'The ECtHR's Role as a Guardian of Discourse: Safeguarding a Decision-Making Process Based on Well-Established Standards, Practical Rationality, and Facts' (2018) 31 *Leiden Journal of International Law* 335, 358.

on subsequent consensus may be perceived as an 'evolutive interpretation' of human rights treaties, making these 'bounds' dynamic rather than static.

There are some caveats to this theory. First, regarding the concept of 'bounds' produced through international deliberations, the quality of such deliberations at the international level does not compare to that within national democracies. As Besson points out:

> [I]nternational human rights have not been deliberated and adopted by highly inclusive international democratic procedures the way constitutional rights have; they are deliberated and adopted by both democratic and non-democratic states, and through procedures that are not necessarily inclusive, egalitarian and transparent.[118]

Although international deliberations are meant to allow for a wider range of positions and interests to be heard and considered, including those overlooked and ignored in national deliberations, they may be deficient in practice, risking the tyranny of the majority at the international level.[119] This concern also applies to the protection of absolute minorities across countries, such as the Roma and persons with disabilities.[120] This concern highlights the importance of treaty organs as fora for international deliberation, involving various participants, including national and transnational civil society organisations (see section 3.3.5.3). It also influences the balance of weight between international and national deliberations (see section 3.3.6.1).

Second, the theory of 'two-tiered bounded deliberative democracy' envisions two tiers of deliberation – national and international – with the latter setting the 'bounds' for the former. However, these tiers could, in fact, be further segmented. Most notably, deliberations at the regional level (such as in Europe or the Americas) can be distinguished from those at the universal level, with the latter setting 'bounds' for the former.[121] In cases where there is regional bias or a delay in regional deliberations, the bounds established through universal deliberations can help to fill these gaps (for analysis of this practice, see Chapter 4, sections 4.1.1.4 and 4.1.2.4). Similarly, deliberations at the national level can be broken down further into those taking place within the national society as a whole and those within local communities. Matthew Saul has underscored the potential contribution of local authorities to the ECHR system for 'their knowledge of the local context and the specific circumstances of individuals; … [their ability] to communicate with those affected by decision making; and

[118] S Besson, 'The Legitimate Authority of International Human Rights: On the Reciprocal Legitimation of Domestic and International Human Rights' in Føllesdal, Schaffer and Ulfstein (n 23) 32, 37.

[119] *cf* Letsas (n 102) 304.

[120] See E Benvenisti, 'Margin of Appreciation, Consensus, and Universal Standards' (1999) 31 *Journal of International Law and Politics* 843, 851.

[121] *cf* C Heyns and M Killander, 'Universality and the Growth of Regional Systems' in D Shelton (ed), *The Oxford Handbook of International Human Rights Law* (Oxford University Press 2013) 670, 673.

their capacity for individualised decision making based upon a proportionality assessment'.[122] Future research should explore the relationships between regional and universal deliberations, as well as between national (central) and local deliberations, in greater depth.

Third, the position of future generations within the framework of two-tiered bounded deliberative democracy requires further discussion. A key case in this context is *Verein KlimaSeniorinnen Schweiz and Others v Switzerland* (2024), in which the ECtHR granted standing to an NGO to claim violations of Article 8 ECHR based on Switzerland's alleged failure to fulfil its positive obligations to mitigate climate change. In doing so, the Court acknowledged that, in the context of climate change:

> [W]here intergenerational burden-sharing assumes particular importance, collective action through associations or other interest groups may be one of the only means through which the voice of those at a distinct representational disadvantage can be heard and through which they can seek to influence the relevant decision-making processes.[123]

The ECtHR's approach can be seen as compensating for the absence of representation for future generations in both national and international deliberations by permitting an NGO to represent their voices and interests before the Court.[124] Future research should examine more closely whether, to what extent and through what legal mechanisms future generations should be represented within the framework of two-tiered bounded deliberative democracy.

3.3. DUTIES OF HUMAN RIGHTS TREATY ORGANS AND EACH TYPE OF STATE ORGAN AND THE ALLOCATION OF AUTHORITY AMONG THEM

As previously discussed, the core philosophy underlying the separation of powers holds that the duties and authorities of organs should be allocated based on their respective legitimacy assets, which derive from their composition, capacity, decision-making process, and function (see section 3.2.1). More specifically, within the framework of the two-tiered bounded deliberative democracy, which serves as a guiding political theory for 'global democratic societies':

> [T]he division of powers and responsibilities among authorities that respectively make, apply, and implement laws follows from the distribution of the possibilities for

[122] M Saul, 'Local Authorities at the European Court of Human Rights' (2024) 28 *IJHR* 1060, 1079.

[123] *Verein KlimaSeniorinnen Schweiz and Others v Switzerland*, ECtHR, App No 53600/20, Merits and Just Satisfaction (9 April 2024) para 489.

[124] This could be explained under the concept of 'proxy representation'. See M Rose, 'All-Affected, Non-identity and the Political Representation of Future Generations: Linking Intergenerational Justice with Democracy' in T Cottier, S Lalani and C Siziba (eds), *Intergenerational Equity: Environmental and Cultural Concerns* (Brill 2019) 32.

access to different sorts of reasons and to the corresponding forms of communication that determine how these reasons are dealt with.[125]

Based on these principles, the separation of powers in a globalised democratic society model posits that treaty organs and state organs should be assigned the following 'duties' (for further discussion on the normative nature and basis of these 'duties', see Chapter 5).[126]

3.3.1. Duties of Parliaments

Parliaments are generally recognised for their representativeness and direct accountability to the public, albeit with a certain deliberative distance from the electorate.[127] Moreover, from the perspective of deliberative democracy, parliaments are the only institutions with unlimited access to normative, pragmatic and empirical reasons.[128] They should therefore be allocated the primary responsibility for deliberating on matters of general public policy involving human rights where there are 'reasonable disagreements'.[129] Such disagreements on human rights often arise concerning the interpretation and application of 'relative' rights[130] – rights that can be balanced against the rights of others and the interests of wider society, as opposed to 'absolute' rights.[131] In making decisions, parliaments must ensure the effective representation and inclusive participation of all sectors of society, including the minorities.[132] This involves not only holding free and genuine elections and protecting the political rights of all individuals,[133] but also conducting thorough, transparent, inclusive and open deliberations. These deliberations should be 'anchored in the informal streams

[125] Habermas (n 100) 192.

[126] On rare occasions, treaty organs have dealt with measures that are directly based on national referenda rather than decided by a specific state organ (see, eg, *Gelman v Uruguay*, IACtHR, Series C No 221, Merits and Reparations (24 February 2011)). Although it is beyond the scope of this book, future research should discuss how direct democracy should be situated within the 'separation of powers in a globalised democratic society'.

[127] D Kyritsis, 'Constitutional Review in Representative Democracy' (2012) 32 *Oxford Journal of Legal Studies* 297, 305.

[128] Habermas (n 100) 192.

[129] J Waldron, 'The Core of the Case against Judicial Review' (2006) 115 *Yale Law Journal* 1346, 1366–69.

[130] PACE, *Handbook for Parliamentarians: National Parliaments as Guarantors of Human Rights in Europe* (Council of Europe 2018) 18.

[131] For absolute and relative rights, see generally M Nowak, 'Absolute and Relative Rights' in C Binder et al (eds), *Elgar Encyclopedia of Human Rights* (Edward Elgar 2022) 8. Notably, absolute rights, such as the right to life, may be subject to a balancing test when positive obligations concerning their protection involve socio-economic aspects. See A Mowbray, 'A Study of the Principle of Fair Balance in the Jurisprudence of the European Court of Human Rights' (2010) 10 *HRLR* 289, 300.

[132] E Brems, 'Key Challenges for the ECHR System: Protecting and Empowering Institutions, Human Rights Defenders and Minorities' (2020) 1 *European Convention on Human Rights Law Review* 7, 9.

[133] Habermas (n 100) 181.

of communication emerging from public spheres that are open to all political parties, associations, and citizens'.[134] To assess whether a national parliament has fulfilled its duty of thorough deliberation, Aruna Sathanapally proposes the following five useful criteria:[135]

(1) The effort and time taken to make the decision: was the decision made after due consideration or hastily?
(2) Reason giving: did deliberation proceed on the basis of public-regarding reasons rather than self-interested motives?
(3) Information: was the relevant information available to decision-makers in their deliberation?
(4) Diversity: was there deliberation that encompassed or invited a diverse range of viewpoints?
(5) Openness to change: were decision-makers open to changing their viewpoints in the course of deliberation – that is, was the deliberation genuine or only symbolic?

Previous studies on the role of parliaments in treaties have tended to focus on enacting and amending legislation at the time of ratifying treaties.[136] However, as human rights treaties often evolve, parliaments must not only conduct deliberations at the time of ratifying human rights treaties, but also continue to review and deliberate on bills, existing legislations, budgets, and government policies and conducts.

Parliamentary deliberations should be 'bounded', meaning they must give due consideration to human rights treaty standards that have been codified and developed through mature international deliberations. According to Alice Donald and Philip Leach, there are broadly three models of parliamentary structures that enable parliamentary deliberations to be 'bounded'.[137] The first is the cross-cutting model, where no committee has a specialised remit for human rights matters, and various committees address these issues as they arise within their respective mandates. The second is the specialised model, where a single standing committee uniformly handles all human rights matters. The third is the hybrid model, where two or more committees specialise in human rights matters. Parliaments are not obligated to adopt a specific model under the separation of powers in a globalised democratic society. Nevertheless, there is a general tendency for the specialised model to enable parliaments to fulfil their

[134] ibid 170–71.

[135] A Sathanapally, 'The Modest Promise of "Procedural Review" in Fundamental Rights Cases' in J Gerards and E Brems (eds), *Procedural Review in European Fundamental Rights Cases* (Cambridge University Press 2017) 40, 59. See also L Lazarus and N Simonsen, 'Judicial Review and Parliamentary Debate: Enriching the Doctrine of Due Deference' in Hunt, Hooper and Yowell (n 108) 385, 403.

[136] See, eg, F Lange, *Treaties in Parliaments and Courts: The Two Other Voices* (Edward Elgar 2024) 93–122.

[137] A Donald and P Leach, *Parliaments and the European Court of Human Rights* (Oxford University Press 2016) 75–84.

duties most effectively and efficiently.[138] Specialised committees, usually referred to as 'parliamentary human rights committees', typically possess the ability to conduct high-quality, focused discussions with sufficient time and expertise in human rights treaties. Additionally, with such committees in place, responsibility becomes clearer, avoiding the problem of 'everyone's responsibility is no one's responsibility'.[139] Establishing such a dedicated committee can also send a symbolic message that human rights are being prioritised in parliamentary activities.

3.3.2. Duties of National Courts

The prominent features of courts include their independence and remoteness from direct democratic control, their triadic structure involving judges and parties to the dispute,[140] and their expertise in law. Consequently, they are best positioned to adjudicate one-off and bilateral disputes between parties – rather than 'polycentric' disputes[141] – in a foreseeable, coherent and fair manner[142] while also serving as guardians against the tyranny of the majority that may arise from the malfunctioning of parliamentary deliberations[143] and filling their 'blind spots' and 'burdens of inertia'.[144] Although the reasons available to courts are limited to those presented by the parties,[145] courts engage in deliberations in their own way. As Habermas stated, '[legal discourse] must remain open to the pragmatic, ethical, and moral reasons brought to bear in the legislative process and bundled together in the legitimacy claim of legal norms'[146] and 'each participant in a trial, whatever her motives, contributes to a discourse that *from the judge's perspective* facilitates the search for an impartial judgment'.[147]

To this end, courts must not only ensure independence and fairness in their composition and procedures, but must also engage in deliberations across all three phases – pre-decisional, decisional and post-decisional, as outlined by

[138] For example, Hunt, Hooper and Yowell empirically showed that the activities of the Joint Committee on Human Rights of the UK Parliament have positively affected the frequency of consideration of human rights in parliamentary discussions. See M Hunt, H Hooper and P Yowell, *Parliaments and Human Rights: Redressing the Democratic Deficit* (Arts and Humanities Research Council 2012) 19–23. Nevertheless, some authors argue that such an increase of consideration of human rights does not necessarily affect the result. See JL Hiebert, 'Governing Like Judges?' in T Campbell, KD Ewing and A Tomkins (eds), *The Legal Protection of Human Rights: Sceptical Essays* (Oxford University Press 2011) 40, 63.

[139] Donald and Leach (n 137) 85.

[140] M Shapiro, *Courts: A Comparative and Political Analysis* (University of Chicago Press 1981) 1.

[141] LL Fuller, 'The Forms and Limits of Adjudication' (1978) 92 *Harvard Law Review* 353, 394–404.

[142] See, Barber (n 58) 74–79.

[143] Ely (n 44) 102–104.

[144] R Dixon, 'Creating Dialogue about Socioeconomic Rights: Strong-Form versus Weak-Form Judicial Review Revisited' (2007) 5 *I-CON* 391, 402–03.

[145] Barber (n 58) 76.

[146] Habermas (n 100) 230.

[147] ibid 231 (emphasis in original).

Conrado Hübner Mendes. In the pre-decisional phase, courts should encourage 'public contestation'. Courts should 'collect, as much as possible, arguments from interlocutors', 'publicly challenge these arguments so that interlocutors have the opportunity to further refine them' and, above all, 'display an institutional openness to the actors that may have something to add to the stock of arguments that bears upon the case'.[148] During the decisional phase, 'collegial engagement' is required. Judges should interact with one another to incorporate their peers' reasoning into their own, whether to concur or dissent, and should examine the widest possible range of reasonable arguments the court was able to collect to pursue consensus (or minimal dissensus).[149] In the post-decisional phase, courts should provide deliberative written decisions showing that courts have made 'an effort to deal with all points of view in a thorough manner'.[150] Furthermore, courts should acknowledge their fallibility and the inevitable continuity of deliberation in the public sphere and potential future cases. Thus, their decisions should convey this understanding through careful and considered rhetoric.[151] Lastly, given the requirement for 'bounded' deliberations, courts' reviews must adhere to human rights treaty-compatible standards, and their decisions should be articulated in accordance with these standards.

3.3.3. Duties of Administrative Organs

The legitimacy of administrative organs stems primarily from their expertise,[152] supported by substantial resources, accumulated experience and continuous, close engagement with issues through the bureaucratic system. Consequently, these organs should be granted special authority to address technical and complex matters in the application and implementation of parliamentary legislation to individual cases. When making such decisions, they must conduct thorough investigations and assessments of the technical aspects involved.

Although administrative organs are not authorised to handle normative reasons in a constructive or reconstructive manner,[153] they can still engage in deliberations by exercising their statutory discretion through dialogue with the affected individuals.[154] According to Geneviève Cartier's theory of 'discretion

[148] CH Mendes, *Constitutional Courts and Deliberative Democracy* (Oxford University Press 2013) 108.

[149] ibid 108–09.

[150] ibid 110.

[151] ibid.

[152] On detailed accounts of how administrative expertise concretely operates, see M Teo, 'Administrative Expertise and *Wednesbury* Unreasonableness' [2025] *Public Law* (forthcoming, available at SSRN at: https://papers.ssrn.com/sol3/papers.cfm?abstract_id=4915508).

[153] Habermas (n 100) 192 and 231.

[154] G Cartier, 'Deliberative Ideals and Constitutionalism in the Administrative State' in R Levy et al (eds), *The Cambridge Handbook of Deliberative Constitutionalism* (Cambridge University Press 2018) 57, 60–64.

as dialogue', individuals should first present the specifics of their case to inform the administrative organ's decision-making process about the context in which the decision will be made.[155] Second, administrative organs and citizens interact in various spaces, allowing informal opinion and will formation to influence formal decision-making.[156] Third, administrative organs must exercise their discretion in accordance with the norms and values that emerge from this dialogue.[157] Thus, administrative organs are required to follow a decision-making process that is transparent and open to the public, consulting those affected, considering a wide range of factors and interests involved, as well as the specific circumstances of the individuals affected, and providing reasons that demonstrate how these factors and circumstances were considered and weighted.[158]

3.3.4. Duties of National Human Rights Institutions

It has been generally observed that NHRIs 'do not sit well within the tripartite model of separation of powers (the *trias politica*) … among the executive, legislative and judicial organs of the state'.[159] Previous studies have pointed out the *sui generis* functions performed by NHRIs within the separation of powers, such as their participation in national litigation.[160] However, these *sui generis* functions have not yet been systematically theorised. This chapter argues that NHRIs have significant potential to enhance the two-tiered bounded deliberative democracy, due to their independent and pluralistic structure, their expertise in human rights and their unique status as 'acteurs de troisième type'[161] – positioned between the state and civil society, despite formally being a state organ.

As Habermas posited, deliberative democracy can function properly and serve as a source of political legitimacy only through the continuous interaction of two deliberative processes (the 'two-track model'): non-institutionalised

[155] ibid 63.
[156] ibid.
[157] ibid 64.
[158] JL Mashaw, *Reasoned Administration and Democratic Legitimacy: How Administrative Law Supports Democratic Government* (Cambridge University Press 2018) 168.
[159] RE Kapindu, 'Separation of Powers and the Accountability Role of NHRIs: The Malawi Human Rights Commission through the Courts' in D Bilchitz and D Landau (eds), *The Evolution of the Separation of Powers* (Edward Elgar 2018) 206, 233.
[160] ibid.
[161] G Fellous, *Les institutions nationales des droits de l'homme: Acteurs de trsoisème type* (La documentation française 2006) 11. See also K Roberts, 'The Role and Functioning of the International Coordinating Committee of National Human Rights Institutions in International Human Rights Bodies' in K Meuwissen and J Wouters (eds), *National Human Rights Institutions, in Europe: Comparative, European and International Perspectives* (Intersentia 2013) 223, 227; A Smith, 'The Unique Position of National Human Rights Institutions: A Mixed Blessing?' (2006) 28 *Human Rights Quarterly* 904, 908.

deliberations in the informal public sphere, where civil society is at the core,[162] and institutionalised deliberations in the formal public sphere within political systems such as parliaments and courts.[163] The former provides a space for open-ended debates on all sorts of issues, both political and otherwise,[164] and acts as a 'context of discovery',[165] sensitively identifying emerging problems[166] as 'a sounding board'.[167] The latter serves as the 'context of justification',[168] where deliberations are conducted under the pressure of reaching decisions within limited forms, procedures, timeframes and reasons, culminating in binding decisions.[169] The quality of deliberations in the formal public sphere largely depends on the supply of public opinions generated in the informal public sphere.[170] However, the active interplay between these deliberative processes is often hindered by the fact that 'the signals [movements and initiatives within civil society] send out and the impulses they give are generally too weak' to reach the formal public sphere in the short term.[171]

In this context, NHRIs, particularly those with A-status, can serve as a unique bridge between these two deliberative processes. The Paris Principles and the General Observations of the Sub-Committee on Accreditation (SCA) (for a detailed explanation of these documents, see Chapter 5, section 5.2.2) require NHRIs to work closely with civil society in both their composition and activities. This enables them to reach 'sections of the populations who are geographically, politically or socially remote' and to engage with vulnerable groups.[172] At the same time, NHRIs are mandated to advise the national parliament, government and courts actively and regularly.[173] Given their broad human rights mandate and resulting 'home-made' human rights expertise,[174] NHRIs ensure that national deliberations are properly 'bounded' – conducted within the framework of human rights treaty standards – while also considering local values and realities.[175] In this way, NHRIs are positioned at the heart of bounded national deliberations.

[162] Habermas (n 100) 307–08 and 367.
[163] ibid 307–08 and 371.
[164] J Flynn, 'Communicative Power' in A Allen and E Mendieta (eds), *The Cambridge Habermas Lexicon* (Cambridge University Press 2019) 53, 53.
[165] Habermas (n 100) 307.
[166] ibid 308.
[167] ibid 359.
[168] ibid 307.
[169] Flynn (n 164) 53.
[170] Habermas (n 100) 308.
[171] ibid 373.
[172] GANHRI, 'General Observations of the Sub-Committee on Accreditation' (2018) s 1.5.
[173] Paris Principles, s A-3 (a); see also GANHRI (n 172) ss 1.6 and 1.11.
[174] MM Qafisheh, 'The International Status of National Human Rights Institutions: A Comparison with NGOs' (2013) 31 *NJHR* 55, 73.
[175] M Lafourcade, 'Le réseau des institutions nationales des droits de l'homme à l'épreuve de la politization' (2019) 20 *Annuaire français de relations internationales* 917, 920. See also E Gonzalez-Ocantos and W Sandholtz, 'The Sources of Resilience of International Human Rights Courts: The Case of the Inter-American System' (2022) 47 *Law & Social Inquiry* 95, 110.

Accordingly, first, NHRIs bear a duty to enrich national deliberations and ensure they are 'bounded' by bringing inclusive perspectives, including those of minorities and marginalised groups, and information on relevant international human rights law into national deliberations in parliaments, courts and other governmental bodies. Second, NHRIs bear a duty to actively provide inputs regarding the broader background and national contexts of the issues at hand to treaty organs, enabling them to supplement national deliberations when necessary. To fulfil these duties effectively, NHRIs must have a composition and procedures that are independent of the government while ensuring pluralism and openness to civil society.[176]

In relation to the second duty – providing inputs to treaty organs – it is helpful to distinguish the role of NHRIs from that of NGOs, as previous studies have often treated their participation in treaty organs' activities and proceedings as parallel. Some studies have suggested that the participatory roles of NHRIs 'largely concur'[177] with those of NGOs, or that NHRIs 'supplement' the functions of NGOs.[178] There has been some scepticism about the added value of NHRIs' provision of inputs to treaty organs.[179] However, this chapter posits that the duty of NHRIs – to provide inputs to treaty organs to help supplement national deliberations – is unique to NHRIs and does not apply to NGOs in the same way. International NGOs, being outsiders and distanced from national societies, generally have little involvement in national deliberations.[180] Local NGOs, as part of the national civil society, can engage in national deliberations by lobbying political systems; their voices should primarily be considered and addressed within the national political framework rather than bypassing national deliberative processes by appealing directly to treaty organs.[181] Thus, while NHRIs can present the state of national deliberations and the interaction between informal and formal public spheres to treaty organs from an impartial perspective, NGOs cannot perform this role in the same way.

[176] Nicole Bürli argues the criteria of independence and pluralism give NHRIs the authority to represent interests of the whole population in a given country. See N Bürli, *Third-Party Interventions before the European Court of Human Rights Amicus Curiae, Member-State and Third-Party Interventions* (Intersentia 2017) 64.

[177] K Meuwissen, 'NHRI Participation to United Nations Human Rights Procedures: International Promotion versus Institutional Consolidation?' in Meuwissen and Wouters (n 161) 263, 274. See also R Murray, *The Role of National Human Rights Institutions at the International and Regional Levels: The Experience of Africa* (Hart Publishing 2007) 65.

[178] S Egan, 'Strengthening the United Nations Human Rights Treaty Body System' (2013) 13 *HRLR* 209, 227. See also D Langtry and K Roberts Lyer, *National Human Rights Institutions: Rules, Requirements, and Practice* (Oxford University Press 2021) 25.

[179] G de Beco, 'National Human Rights Institutions in Europe' (2007) 7 *HRLR* 331, 354–55. See also F McGaughey, 'From Gatekeepers to GONGOs: A Taxonomy of Non-governmental Organisations Engaging with United Nations Human Rights Mechanisms' (2018) 36 *Netherlands Quarterly of Human Rights* 111, 131.

[180] See K Anderson, 'The Ottawa Convention Banning Landmines, the Role of International Non-governmental Organizations and the Idea of International Civil Society' (2000) 11 *EJIL* 91, 117–18.

[181] See Benvenisti (n 112) 28.

Nevertheless, it should be noted that local NGOs can trigger treaty organs' intervention when national deliberations are dysfunctional. They may provide treaty organs with views, positions and perspectives that have not been adequately addressed by the national political system, allowing treaty organs to offer guidance for more effective bounded national deliberations.[182] For example, in *Jovsset Ante Sara v Norway* in 2024, concerning the compatibility of a culling order by Norway's Reindeer Husbandry Board with Article 27 ICCPR, the HRC permitted the Sami Parliament of Norway, joined by the Sami Reindeer Herders' Association of Norway, to intervene as a third party.[183] It heavily relied on their submissions and held that 'the State party has not demonstrated that the methods chosen to implement said reindeer reduction policy in the present case, [which are inconsistent] with the position of the Sami Parliament and the Sami Reindeer Herders' Association, was based on reasonable and objective justifications'.[184]

3.3.5. Duties of Human Rights Treaty Organs

As judicial/quasi-judicial organs, human rights treaty organs share structural and functional similarities with national courts. Nevertheless, treaty organs have higher expertise in international human rights law, are far more remote from national influence and control, and enjoy a higher degree of diversity in their composition in terms of national, cultural and legal backgrounds.[185] Therefore, treaty organs should bear the following three duties.

3.3.5.1. Protecting the Foundations of Deliberative Democracy

The first duty of human rights treaty organs is to protect the basic preconditions for the appropriate functioning of deliberation by adopting protective standards for those rights that directly relate to deliberations. To introduce treaty organs' practice that is representative of this, the ECtHR[186] has declared that 'freedom of political debate is at the very core of the concept of a democratic society which prevails throughout the Convention'[187] and that '[t]he essence of democracy is its capacity to resolve problems through open debate'.[188] Thus, the

[182] Bürli (n 176) 32. See also L Hodson, 'Women's Rights and the Periphery: CEDAW's Optional Protocol' (2014) 25 *EJIL* 561, 575.

[183] *Jovsset Ante Sara v Norway*, HRC, Communication No 3588/2019 (19 July 2024) UN Doc CCPR/C/141/D/3588/2019, para 1.2.

[184] ibid para 10.10.

[185] See, eg, art 31(2) ICCPR.

[186] For a comprehensive examination of the ECtHR's jurisprudence on the protection of the foundations of a democratic society, see M Levinet, 'La Convention européenne des droits de l'homme socle de la protrection des droits de l'homme dans le droit constitutionnel européen' (2011) 86 *Revue française de droit constitutionnel* 227, 237–62; Zysset (n 45).

[187] *Lingens v Austria*, ECtHR, App No 9815/82, Merits and Just Satisfaction (8 July 1986) para 42.

[188] *Stankov and the United Macedonian Organisation Ilinden v Bulgaria*, ECtHR, App Nos 29221/95 and 29225/95, Merits and Just Satisfaction (2 October 2001) para 97.

ECtHR has ruled that restrictions on the rights of the press, civil society organisations and political parties call for 'the most careful scrutiny'[189] or 'a limited margin of appreciation'.[190] Even among cases concerning the same provision of the freedom of expression, the ECtHR has applied a stricter standard of review for the restriction of journalism compared to artistic expressions.[191] Similarly, the HRC emphasised 'the paramount importance, in a democratic society, of the right to freedom of expression and of a free and uncensored press or other media'.[192] It clarified that the right is 'not to be assessed by reference to a "margin of appreciation"'.[193] The IACtHR also held that '[t]he just demands of democracy must ... guide the interpretation of the Convention' and 'free debate and the possibility that dissenting voices be fully heard' are essential conditions for democracy.[194] Thus, it ruled that different protection standards should be applied to expressions that concern public interests and those that do not.[195]

3.3.5.2. Supplementing National Deliberations: Subsidiary Position of Human Rights Treaty Organs

Given that national deliberations have primary roles in the two-tiered bounded deliberative democracy, the second duty of human rights treaty organs is to respect the outcome of the national deliberation as far as the deliberative process properly works. However, if a national deliberative process has deficiencies, human rights treaty organs must fill the gaps by conducting intrusive examinations on the substance of the decision. Although previous studies have criticised the intrusive review by human rights treaty organs as undermining national democracies (see Chapter 2, section 2.3), their interventions in national decisions that were not the outcomes of adequate deliberations should not be considered undemocratic, as these national decisions do not enjoy democratic legitimacy from the outset under the two-tiered bounded deliberative democracy. Rather, their intervention enhances the two-tiered bounded deliberative democracy because the disadvantageous effects that accompany the insufficiency of

[189] *Bladet Tromsø and Stensaas v Norway*, ECtHR, App No 21980/93, Merits and Just Satisfaction (20 May 1999) para 64; *Társaság a Szabadságjogokért v Hungary*, App No 37374/05, Merits and Just Satisfaction (14 April 2009) para 27.

[190] *United Communist Party of Turkey and Others v Turkey*, ECtHR, App No 133/1996/752/951, Merits and Just Satisfaction (30 January 1998) para 46.

[191] P Mahoney, 'Universality versus Subsidiarity in the Strasbourg Case Law on Free Speech: Explaining Some Recent Judgments' [1997] *European Human Rights Law Review* 364, 371–72.

[192] *Rafael Marques de Morais v Angola*, HRC, Communication No 1128/2002 (29 March 2005) UN Doc CCPR/C/83/D/1128/2002, para 6.8.

[193] HRC, 'General Comment No. 34: Article 19: Freedoms of Opinion and Expression' (2011) UN Doc CCPR/C/GC/34, para 36.

[194] *Compulsory Membership in an Association Prescribed by Law for the Practice of Journalism (Arts. 13 and 29 American Convention on Human Rights)*, IACtHR, Series A No 5, Advisory Opinion OC-5/85 (13 November 1985) paras 44 and 69.

[195] *Herrera-Ulloa v Costa Rica*, IACtHR, Series C No 107, Preliminary Objections, Merits, Reparations and Costs (2 July 2004) para 129.

national deliberations can incentivise domestic authorities to engage in proper deliberations.[196] In fulfilling this duty, human rights treaty organs must first examine the quality of the national deliberative process that has led to the contested decision. In other words, treaty organs should review whether the particular state organ that has substantially adopted the decision concerned fulfilled its duty prescribed above (see sections 3.3.1–3.3.3). They should then defer to the national decision that has emerged from the adequate deliberative process – that is, the decision adopted by the state organ fulfilling its duty – while conducting an intrusive review on the substance in other cases.

In this approach, treaty organs are not required to examine the democratic qualities of 'states' as such. Previous studies have argued that since the democratic legitimacy of national decisions is an important basis of deference, treaty organs should differentiate states according to their democratic qualities and apply greater deference to democratic states while tightening the standard of review for non-democratic states, which do not deserve deference deriving from democratic legitimacy.[197] However, such arguments are not feasible given that categorising democratic and non-democratic states is difficult both politically and legally. By focusing on the quality of the deliberative process leading to each decision instead of a 'state' in general, this approach overcomes such political and legal challenges, and provides a more tailored regulation for each case.[198] Even in a state that normally functions consistently with the two-tiered bounded deliberative democracy theory, there may be particular cases of dysfunction, which should lead to no or less deference. In contrast, even in states that are generally inconsistent with the theory, a particular state organ may acquire deference by fulfilling its duties under the separation of powers in a globalised democratic society model.

Some previous studies are sceptical of whether treaty organs are well placed to review the quality of national decision-making processes, especially those of national parliaments, as 'the grammar of politics is different from the grammar of law'.[199] They argue that 'political debate is partial, personal, sometimes principled, sometimes symbolic, and, crucially, underpinned by radically different conceptions of the common good and demands of rights'.[200] However, the requirement that parliamentary deliberations should be 'bounded' – paying due consideration to human rights treaty standards – mitigates such concerns.

[196] Sathanapally (n 135) 56.

[197] See, eg, Y Shany, 'Toward a General Margin of Appreciation Doctrine in International Law?' (2005) 16 *EJIL* 907, 921; K Hessler, 'Resolving Interpretive Conflicts in International Human Rights Law' (2005) 13 *Journal of Political Philosophy* 29, 47–48.

[198] A Føllesdal, 'Subsidiarity and International Human-Rights Courts: Respecting Self-Governance and Protecting Human Rights – or Neither?' (2016) 79 *Law and Contemporary Problems* 147, 160; N Tsereteli, 'Emerging Doctrine of Deference of the Inter-American Court of Human Rights?' (2016) 20 *IJHR* 1097, 1106.

[199] M Jackson, 'Judicial Avoidance at the European Court of Human Rights: Institutional Authority, the Procedural Turn, and Docket Control' (2022) 20 *I-CON* 112, 123.

[200] ibid 123–24.

From a procedural perspective, the inclusion of the relevant state organs in the proceedings of treaty organs (for example, through amicus curiae or third-party intervention procedures) could address such concerns. Such procedures give the relevant state organs an opportunity to directly elaborate on the quality of their deliberative process for the decision concerned.

When national deliberations suffer deficiencies, human rights treaty organs must serve as an alternative forum for deliberation by conducting intrusive examinations on the substance of the decision. They must consider various relevant perspectives and factors that should have been considered in a properly functioning national deliberative process, and, in doing so, they should satisfy the same procedural requirements as those imposed on national courts elaborated above (section 3.3.2). The ECtHR and the IACtHR seem to fulfil these requirements largely. First, they hold and webcast public oral hearings in legally and politically important cases.[201] Oral hearings are essential for effective deliberations, as they enable treaty organs to clarify points of divergence accurately, and directly compare which party has adduced reasons with more persuasive force. Second, the ECtHR and the IACtHR widely accept third-party and amicus curiae submissions, respectively, including those from NHRIs and NGOs. As human rights treaty organs have insufficient expertise and knowledge of national situations, such submissions play an indispensable role in making treaty organs aware of comprehensive factors and perspectives. Third, cases before the IACtHR have been examined by the IACmHR (Article 61 ACHR), and judgments of the Chamber of the ECHR may be referred to the Grand Chamber under certain conditions (Article 43 ECHR). Thereby, parties to the dispute and other interested actors can fully employ opportunities to express their views after an IACmHR report and an ECHR Chamber judgment are issued, and the IACtHR and the ECtHR's Grand Chamber may consider them. In fact, in some cases, such as *Lautsi v Italy* and *Al-Khawaja and Tahery v UK*, the Chamber judgments of the ECtHR[202] induced various observations not only from the respondent governments but also from national courts,[203] other states parties and civil society organisations, which had not been expressed previously. Thus, the Grand Chamber was able to consider these new observations to hold richer deliberations, which led to different conclusions from the Chamber.[204] Fourth, the judgments of both courts are based on detailed reasons, and judges

[201] K Reid, *A Practitioner's Guide to the European Convention on Human Rights*, 6th edn (Sweet & Maxwell 2015) 11–12; JM Pasqualucci, *The Practice and Procedure of the Inter-American Court of Human Rights*, 2nd edn (Cambridge University Press 2012) 159–61.

[202] *Lautsi v Italy*, ECtHR [Second Section], App No 30814/06, Merits and Just Satisfaction (3 November 2009); *Al-Khawaja and Tahery v UK*, ECtHR [Fourth Section], App Nos 26766/05 and 22228/06 (20 January 2009).

[203] Supreme Court, *R v Horncastle and Others* [2009] UKSC 14 (9 December 2009) (UK).

[204] *Lautsi v Italy*, ECtHR [GC], App No 30814/06, Merits and Just Satisfaction (18 March 2011); *Al-Khawaja and Tahery v UK*, ECtHR [GC], App Nos 26766/05 and 22228/06, Merits and Just Satisfaction (5 December 2011).

are allowed to write concurring and dissenting opinions, which ensure that their judgments are the outcome of a comprehensive examination of relevant factors and possible legal constructions. The combination of these factors provides a guarantee that relevant perspectives are fully presented and comprehensively considered.

Due to the significant time[205] and resource constraints,[206] the HRC have limited capabilities to conduct thorough deliberations.[207] Nevertheless, in recent years, they have advanced important reforms in their procedures towards fully ensuring that all relevant perspectives and factors are presented and considered in their review. First, whereas the HRC had examined individual communications only based on written submissions, in 2016, the HRC decided that it may invite parties to offer oral comments on other parties' submissions in important and complex cases.[208] The 'Guidelines on Making Oral Comments concerning Communications', adopted in 2017, set out the procedures for the initial statements, follow-up questions, requests for clarification and closing statements.[209] In the same year, the Committee held the first oral hearings through video conference in *Miller & Carroll v New Zealand*.[210] Second, previously, the HRC had no procedure to accept third-party/amicus curiae submissions and had admitted submissions from non-parties such as NGOs only through the authors as 'legal opinions'.[211] The HRC amended its Rules of Procedure in 2018 to insert a provision on third-party submissions,[212] which was not previously admitted formally. In 2019, the Committee adopted the 'Guidelines on Third-Party Submissions', which provide that 'the third-party submissions and observations and comments of the parties to the communication concerned may be used in the Committee's deliberations and reflected in the Committee's Views or decision on the communication'.[213] In practice, the possibility of third-party interventions is limited,[214] as the HRC only publishes the table of pending cases with very

[205] The HRC is not a permanent body and holds three regular sessions a year; each session lasts for three to four weeks.

[206] HRC Report on its Work on its 138th–140th Sessions (2024) UN Doc A/79/40, paras 19, 37 and 42.

[207] For a criticism that the HRC's individual communications procedure offers limited opportunities for the parties to express their views, see, eg, High Court, *Roach v Electoral Commissioner*, 233 CLR 162 (26 September 2007) (Australia) 224–25 (Dissenting Opinion of Judge Heydon).

[208] HRC Report on its Work on Its 117th–119th Sessions (2017) UN Doc A/72/40, para 36.

[209] HRC, 'Guidelines on Making Oral Comments concerning Communications' (2017) UN Doc CCPR/C/159, paras 3 (g)-(i).

[210] HRC Report on its Work on its 120th–122nd Sessions (2018) UN Doc A/73/40, para 53.

[211] *Irina Fedotova v Russia*, HRC, Communication No 1932/2010 (31 October 2012) UN Doc CCPR/C/106/D/1932/2010, para 5.8; *Nell Toussaint v Canada*, HRC, Communication No 2348/2014 (24 July 2018) UN Doc CCPR/C/123/D/2348/2014, para 7.4.

[212] Rules of Procedure of the HRC, UN Doc CCPR/C/3/Rev.11 (2019), Rule 96.

[213] HRC, 'Guidelines on Information and Documentation Submitted by Third Parties' (2019) UN Doc CCPR/C/160, para 4.

[214] International Service for Human Rights, *Guide for Third Party Interventions before UN Human Rights Treaty Bodies* (2022), https://ishr.ch/defenders-toolbox/resources/guide-for-tpis-before-untbs, 34.

brief descriptions, which only include the name of the state party concerned, the articles involved and the subject matter in one phrase.[215] Nevertheless, this procedure has been occasionally applied. In *Daniel Billy and Others v Australia* in 2022, concerning damages suffered by Torres Strait Islanders due to adverse climate change impacts, several experts, including the former and the current UN Special Rapporteurs on human rights and the environment, presented third-party submissions (see also *Jovsset Ante Sara v Norway* (2024), which was introduced in section 3.3.4).[216] These recent reforms indeed show the HRC's intention to improve its procedures as a deliberative forum.

3.3.5.3. Setting 'Bounds' to National Deliberations

The third duty of human rights treaty organs under the separation of powers in a globalised democratic society model is to set 'bounds' on national deliberations through the outcomes of long-term and matured deliberations at the international level. Human rights treaty organs are especially well placed to perform such duties, due to their expertise in international human rights law, remoteness from national influence and control, and higher degree of diversity in their composition.[217] 'Bounds' may be identified based on the texts of human rights treaties, and consensus among the treaty Member States that have emerged after the adoption of the treaties. When the national deliberation leading to a contested measure is not conducted within the 'bounds', treaty organs must not defer to the outcome of the national deliberation. This duty plays a key role in preventing the 'tyranny of the majority' in a national society under the disguise of deliberation.

In theory, placing such 'bounds' on national deliberations is consistent with the value of 'democracy' within the two-tiered bounded deliberative democracy, as doing so addresses national deliberation gaps, and 'bounds' themselves are outcomes of international deliberations. In practice, however, identification of 'bounds' by treaty organs inevitably accompanies a very wide discretion due to the highly discursive and underdeveloped nature of international deliberations and the absence of a centralised political organ that can legislate on newly emerged consensus in a unified manner and monitor whether human rights treaty organs have identified 'bounds' properly. As will be analysed in Chapter 4, treaty organs' identification of bounds requires improvement in terms of consistency and transparency. Otherwise, the delicate balance between national and international deliberations may be at risk.

[215] The HRC's table of pending cases is available on the 'Individual Communications' page on its website: www.ohchr.org/en/treaty-bodies/ccpr/individual-communications.

[216] *Daniel Billy and Others v Australia*, HRC, Communication No 3624/2019 (21 July 2022) UN Doc CCPR/C/135/D/3624/2019, para 1.2.

[217] Dothan demonstrated, based on Condorcet's Jury Theorem, that human rights treaty organs have unique institutional advantages in collecting the wisdom of national decisions: Dothan (n 113) ch 3. See also Donald and Leach (n 137) 131.

To minimise such problems, diverse actors, including state parties (composed of multiple actors, such as national courts, governments, parliaments and NHRIs), civil society organisations,[218] and other organs of regional organisations and the UN (eg, the Council of Europe's CoM and PACE, and the General Assemblies of the OAS and the UN), must actively and continuously participate in the deliberations on 'bounds' in treaty organs. Such participation can occur before human rights treaty organs render their decisions (for the participation of NHRIs as amicus curiae, see Chapter 2, section 2.4.1 and Chapter 4, section 4.3) or between the Chamber and the Grand Chamber judgments in the ECtHR (see section 3.3.5.2 above). In the case of the HRC, the drafting process of General Comments, which serve as important guidance of 'bounds', is a valuable opportunity for such participation (see Chapter 4, section 4.1.3.4). Moreover, as will be discussed in more detail later (see section 3.3.6.2), the deliberation on 'bounds' should continue even after treaty organs render their decisions.

3.3.6. Principles Regulating the Relationship between Human Rights Treaty Organs and State Organs

As noted above (see section 3.1.2), previously, when discussing the allocation of authorities between international and national levels, international human rights law scholarship relied on the binary and oppositional structure of state sovereignty versus the universality of human rights. However, as Kumm observes:

> The idea of sovereignty does not … in and of itself provide any indication whatsoever of how large that domain [over which a national community may govern itself without regard to the international community] should be or even how to meaningfully structure debates about the boundaries of sovereignty.[219]

Thus, such a binary and oppositional structure has not been effective in normatively regulating the allocation of authorities in concrete cases. In contrast, this chapter proposes two principles – subsidiarity (section 3.3.6.1) and principled and continuous dialogue (section 3.3.6.2) – which provide concrete guidelines for regulating specific cases. These principles place relevant actors – treaty organs and state organs – into a cooperative structure where each contributes to the common goal of the flourishing of individuals under the two-tiered bounded deliberative democracy in their own ways and asserts authority or defer to

[218] See generally L van den Eynde, 'The Consensus Argument in NGOs' Amicus Curiae Briefs: Defending Minorities through a Creatively Used Majoritarian Argument' in P Kapotas and VP Tzevelekos (eds), *Building Consensus on European Consensus: Judicial Interpretation of Human Rights in Europe and Beyond* (Cambridge University Press 2019) 96.

[219] M Kumm, 'The Cosmopolitan Turn in Constitutionalism: On the Relationship between Constitutionalism in and beyond the State' in JL Dunoff and JP Trachtman (eds), *Ruling the World? Constitutionalism, International Law, and Global Governance* (Cambridge University Press 2009) 258, 292.

another actor depending on which actor is most suitable for achieving the goal in a given situation.

3.3.6.1. Subsidiarity

Many constitutional legal systems, especially those of the EU[220] and federal states[221] recognise, whether expressly or implicitly, subsidiarity as a principle to allocate authorities among different levels of societies and organs. As Paolo Carozza argued, this principle stands on the conviction that:

> [E]ach human individual is endowed with an inherent and inalienable worth, or dignity … Because of this value, all other forms of society, from the family to the state and the international order, ought ultimately to be at the service of the human person. Their end must be the flourishing of the individual.[222]

Precisely because the principle of subsidiarity treats societies and organs as instruments to achieve the ultimate goal of the flourishing of individuals, no societies and organs, including 'states', are sovereign in the world of subsidiarity.[223] The concept of subsidiarity thus reforms the classical paradigm of state sovereignty, where states, not individuals, have inalienable worth and thus are treated as the absolute and irreversible source of authority (see Chapter 1, section 1.1.1). In this sense, it concurs with previous studies that aim at restructuring the concept of sovereignty. Through historical studies on the concept of state sovereignty, Shigejiro Tabata showed that the argument of Emmerich de Vattel, who first introduced the concept of state sovereignty as a general foundation for international relations, was based on the premise that 'a state is created for the well-being of its citizens and its freedom and independence are necessary precisely to achieve such goals'.[224] Christian Tomuschat argued that:

> Today, these functional aspects [that States have a special public interest task to ensure law and order within its territory] have by far outpaced the notion of sovereignty as a natural gift enjoyed by every State just by virtue of its existence. The international

[220] See, eg, K Granat, *The Principle of Subsidiarity and its Enforcement in the EU Legal Order: The Role of National Parliaments in the Early Warning System* (Hart Publishing 2020).

[221] See, eg, A Ladner, 'Switzerland: Subsidiarity, Power-Sharing, and Direct Democracy' in F Hendriks et al (eds), *The Oxford Handbook of Local and Regional Democracy in Europe* (Oxford University Press 2011) 196; SG Calabresi and LD Bickford, 'Federalism and Subsidiarity: Perspectives from US Constitutional Law' (2014) 55 *Nomos* 123; J Bröhmer, 'Subsidiarity and the German Constitution' in M Evans and A Zimmermann (eds), *Global Perspectives on Subsidiarity* (Springer 2014) 129; H Kong, 'Subsidiarity, Republicanism, and the Division of Powers in Canada' (2015) 45 *Revue de droit de l'Université de Sherbrooke* 13.

[222] PG Carozza, 'Subsidiarity as a Structural Principle of International Human Rights Law' (2003) 97 *AJIL* 38, 42.

[223] K Endo, 'Subsidiarity and its Enemies: To What Extent is Sovereignty Contested in the Mixed Commonwealth of Europe?' (2001) *EUI Working Papers* No RSC 2001/24 1, 34.

[224] S Tabata, *Kokkashuken to Kokusaihou* [*State Sovereignty and International Law*] (Nihonhyouronsha 1950) 30–31.

community, as already described, views the State as a unit at the service of the human beings for whom it is responsible.[225]

The theories of 'popular sovereignty' by W Michael Reisman,[226] 'sovereignty as responsibility' by Francis M Deng et al,[227] and 'responsible sovereignty' by Richard Falk[228] are also on the same track.

Subsidiarity possesses duality, which is often described as a 'paradox'.[229] While it prioritises the smaller/lower unit that is closer to the affected individuals in fulfilling certain aims ('negative subsidiarity'), this priority should be reversed in favour of the intervention by the larger/higher unit when the smaller/lower unit cannot properly fulfil the aim, or when the larger/higher one can do so better ('positive subsidiarity').[230] It opens up a way to harmoniously understand the universal impetus of human rights and their plurality not as a clash between human rights protection and state sovereignty, but rather as finding an appropriate balance between universalism and pluralism under the ultimate purpose of the flourishing of individuals.[231]

The principle of subsidiarity and the theory of two-tiered bounded deliberative democracy are in a mutually reinforcing relationship. By prioritising the decision-making in the smaller/lower unit, where those who are affected by the decision are more closely represented in the decision-making process, subsidiarity generally promotes the proper functioning of deliberative democracy.[232] This applies even more so between international and national societies, where deliberations at the international level remain discursive and underdeveloped due to the absence of centralised international political organs, and each national society has unique historical, cultural, religious and social backgrounds. The duality of subsidiarity enables the appropriate regulation of the relationship between the two tiers of deliberations: although national deliberations should be given priority as far as they are assumed to be properly functioning (negative subsidiarity), such priority is reversed in favour of international intervention when the national deliberative process fails to properly represent the rights and

[225] C Tomuschat, 'International Law: Ensuring the Survival of Mankind on the Eve of a New Century' (1999) 281 *Recueil des cours de l'Académie de La Haye* 9, 95.

[226] WM Reisman, 'Sovereignty and Human Rights in Contemporary International Law' (1990) 84 *AJIL* 876, 872.

[227] FM Deng et al, *Sovereignty as Responsibility: Conflict Management in Africa* (Brookings Institution Press 1996).

[228] R Falk, 'Sovereignty and Human Dignity: The Search for Reconciliation' in FM Deng and T Lyons (eds), *African Reckoning: A Quest for Good Governance* (Brookings Institution Press 1998) 12, 14.

[229] C Delsol, *L'État Subsidiaire: Ingérence et non-ingérence de l'Etat: Le principe de subsidiarité aux fondements de l'histoire européenne* (Presses universitaires de France 1992) 8.

[230] For the negative and positive aspects of subsidiarity, see Carozza (n 222) 44.

[231] ibid 67–68.

[232] D Shelton, 'Subsidiarity and Human Rights Law' (2006) 27 *HRLJ* 4, 6–7. See also A Follesdal, 'Subsidiarity, Democracy, and Human Rights in the Constitutional Treaty of Europe' (2006) 37 *Journal of Social Philosophy* 61, 69.

interests of those affected – most likely, non-nationals and discrete and insular minorities – or deviates from 'bounds' (positive subsidiarity).

In the same vein, this duality is a key to harmonising the effectiveness and democratic legitimacy of human rights treaties, which were considered to be in a potential tension (see Chapter 1, section 1.2). On the one hand, treaty organs' intrusive approach towards malfunctioning national decision-making processes, where the state organs fail to fulfil the above-stated duties concerning bounded deliberation, contributes to the effectiveness. On the other hand, their deferential approach towards well-functioning national decision-making processes, where state organs properly fulfil their duties of bounded deliberation, promotes democratic legitimacy within the meaning of the two-tiered bounded deliberative democracy. These two approaches of the treaty organs can be harmoniously understood as two sides of the same coin, namely positive subsidiarity and negative subsidiarity, respectively.

One may argue that self-restraint by treaty organs under 'negative subsidiarity', such as employing a deferential standard of review or refraining from ordering specific remedies, may compromise their effectiveness.[233] This chapter does not embark on empirical studies on the short-term and long-term impact of treaty organs' self-restraint on human rights protection in Member States. Nevertheless, the 'effectiveness' of human rights treaty systems could be understood not just from a sociological perspective but also from a more normative perspective, especially based on Yuval Shany's 'goal-based approach'.[234] Under this approach, the effectiveness of a treaty organ is measured based on the extent to which it has achieved the goals set for it by its relevant constituencies.[235] In the separation of powers in a globalised democratic society model, the goal of treaty organs is to contribute to the flourishing of individuals within the two-tiered bounded deliberative democracy by fulfilling the above-stated duties (see section 3.3.5). Thus, according to the 'goal-based approach', treaty organs' self-restraint to respect and promote the exercise of authority by well-functioning state organs reinforces rather than undermines their effectiveness.

3.3.6.2. *Principled and Continuous Dialogue*

The concept of 'dialogue' has played an important role in national constitutional law contexts, especially in Canada[236] and other Commonwealth countries,[237] to

[233] For example, the margin of appreciation doctrine of the ECtHR has been criticised as detrimental to effective protection of human rights. See Y Arai-Takahashi, *The Margin of Appreciation Doctrine and the Principle of Proportionality in the Jurisprudence of the ECHR* (Intersentia 2002) 233–34.

[234] Y Shany, *Assessing the Effectiveness of International Courts* (Oxford University Press 2014) 4–8.

[235] ibid 6.

[236] PW Hogg and AA Bushell, 'The Charter Dialogue between Courts and Legislatures (or Perhaps the Charter of Rights isn't Such a Bad Thing after All)' (1997) 35 *Osgoode Hall Law Journal* 75.

[237] See, eg, Dixon (n 144); S Jackson, 'Designing Human Rights Legislation: "Dialogue", the Commonwealth Model and the Roles of Parliaments and Courts' (2007) 13 *Auckland University*

facilitate checks and balances[238] and to guide the separation of powers.[239] They posited that the interpretation of constitutional rights should be produced through a shared elaboration between the judiciary and other constitutional organs.[240] These lessons from constitutional studies are transposable to our context,[241] though with two refinements in accordance with the requirements of the two-tiered bounded deliberative democracy, to avoid the 'misleading' and 'distorting' effects caused by the oversimplified metaphor of 'dialogue'.[242] First, the dialogue between treaty and state organs must be based on the values and principles widely shared in the epistemic community supporting globalised democratic societies, which consists of various actors, including the treaty organs, states, national courts, parliaments, administrative organs, NHRIs, national and transnational civil society organisations and academics. This requirement is endorsed by the concept of a 'culture of justification', where every exercise of power should be justified by reference to reasons that are publicly available and compatible with society's fundamental commitments.[243] Second, the dialogue must be continuous. Habermas describes the decisions of competent organs as 'the rationally motivated yet fallible result of a process of argumentation that has been interrupted in view of institutional pressures to decide, but is in principle resumable'.[244] Even when a treaty organ decides that a measure is compatible (or incompatible) with a treaty, this should not be taken as final and conclusive. State organs can and must continue to engage in dialogue, considering the evolving situations.[245] Treaty organs, on their part, should be open to changing their previous positions when state organs provide persuasive reasons for having to do so, although they must also duly consider the principle of legal security.

Democratic critics of treaty organs have insisted that domestic decision-makers, not international courts, should have the 'final say' in human rights issues.[246] However, the two-tiered bounded deliberative democracy conceives that no single actor should have the exclusive authority to make final decisions.

Law Review 89; S Stephenson, 'Constitutional Reengineering: Dialogue's Migration from Canada to Australia' (2013) 11 *I-CON* 870.

[238] AL Young, *Democratic Dialogue and the Constitution* (Oxford University Press 2017) 156–58.

[239] CH Mendes, 'Neither Dialogue nor Last Word: Deliberative Separation of Powers III' (2011) 5 *Legisprudence* 1.

[240] C Bateup, 'The Dialogic Promise: Assessing the Normative Potential of Theories of Constitutional Dialogue' (2006) 71 *Brooklyn Law Review* 1109, 1109.

[241] See M Gillis, 'Can We Talk? The Application of the Public Law Democratic Dialogue Model to the Interactions between Domestic Legislatures and the European Courts' (2022) 23 *German Law Journal* 56.

[242] A Kavanagh, 'The Lure and the Limits of Dialogue' (2016) 66 *University of Toronto Law Journal* 83.

[243] M Hunt, 'Introduction' in Hunt, Hooper and Yowell (n 108) 1, 15–16.

[244] Habermas (n 100) 179.

[245] *cf* A Føllesdal, 'Law Making by Law Breaking? A Theory of Parliamentary Civil Disobedience against International Human Rights Courts' in Saul et al (n 43) 329, 344–48.

[246] Bellamy (n 80) 1030.

Every relevant actor should engage in the ongoing process of deliberation with an openness towards changing their previous positions when faced with better reasons. The resumability of deliberations is even more essential in our context, given the discursive and underdeveloped nature of international deliberations. Therefore, when a human rights treaty organ establishes a 'bound' in one case, it should not be final and definitive. Rather, a judgment or View of treaty organs should be conceived as a 'catalyst'[247] for further deliberations, which may lead to the change of the 'bound' or establishment of a new 'bound' in the future. Thus, in practice, a more important question than that of the 'final say' could be which body gets the 'first say' – an opportunity to first frame the question and present its own interpretation.[248]

In the case of UN human rights treaty bodies, the non-binding but 'authoritative'[249] character of their Views, in that states parties should furnish cogent reasons if they do not follow the Views, provides a solid foundation for such ongoing deliberations. While governments can express their opinions in the follow-up procedure, other actors, such as national parliaments and NHRIs, should also be provided with opportunities to participate in the procedure. Domestic courts could express their views via their judgments, thus engaging in a 'judicial dialogue'.[250] Moreover, the UN General Assembly can also be a forum of deliberation on the content of 'bounds' by examining annual reports submitted by UN human rights treaty bodies.[251]

Non-binding advisory opinions rendered by regional human rights courts similarly provide a basis for continued deliberations.[252] In contrast, in contentious cases, regional human rights courts render judgments that are final and binding under international law, which seemingly suggests that they are not open to further deliberations. However, the very fact that coercive enforcement mechanisms do not accompany their judgments, where states therefore

[247] Mendes (n 239) 39.

[248] *cf* N Lupo, 'The Advantage of Having the "First Word" in the Composite European Constitution' (2018) 2 *Italian Journal of Public Law* 186.

[249] HRC, 'General Comment No. 33: The Obligations of States Parties under the Optional Protocol to the International Covenant on Civil and Political Rights' (2008) UN Doc CCPR/C/GC/33, para 13. See also *Affaire Ahmadou Sadio Diallo (République de Guinée c République démocratique du Congo) (fond)* [2010] CIJ Recueil 639, para 66.

[250] See generally A Müller (ed), *Judicial Dialogue and Human Rights* (Cambridge University Press 2017).

[251] H Keller and L Grover, 'General Comments of the Human Rights Committee and Their Legitimacy' in Keller and Ulfstein (n 18) 116, 180–81.

[252] C Giannopoulos, 'Considerations on Protocol N°16: Can the New Advisory Competence of the European Court of Human Rights Breathe New Life into the European Convention on Human Rights?' (2015) 16 *German Law Journal* 337, 342; M Wąsek-Wiaderek, 'Advisory Opinions of the European Court of Human Rights: Do National Judges Really Need This New Forum of Dialogue?' in PP de Albuquerque and K Wojtyczek (eds), *Judicial Power in a Globalized World* (Springer 2019) 637, 645–46. However, for a critical opinion that the advisory procedure is detrimental to fruitful dialogue, see G Lübbe-Wolff, 'How Can the European Court of Human Rights Reinforce the Role of National Courts in the Convention System?' (2012) 32 *HRLJ* 11, 13.

retain the ultimate de facto power not to comply,[253] opens up, albeit cautiously, opportunities for further deliberations. When states and relevant state organs do not agree with the identification of 'bounds' by regional human rights courts, they may choose to protest at their own risk and expense. As Andreas Føllesdal argues, building upon Rawls' theory of civil disobedience, when states and relevant state organs resort to this exceptional option, they must strictly abide by certain requirements, including the following: the incorrect nature of the judgment must be clear; other means must be exhausted; the international legal order must not be destabilised; and injury to the innocent must be avoided.[254] Most importantly, such protests must not be based on self-interested reasons, such as sovereignty or historical and cultural reasons, but based on objective reasons conforming with widely accepted values in the epistemic community supporting globalised democratic societies.[255] They will then be met by support or denouncement by other actors, further enhancing deliberations, and may eventually lead to the consolidation or change of a 'bound'.

3.4. CONCLUSION

This chapter first argued that we must search for a new legitimacy standard for 'globalised democratic societies' to integrate international and national standards of legitimacy, drawing lessons from the intellectual heritage of national constitutional law scholarship (section 3.1). To provide such new standards, it constructed the original normative framework of 'separation of powers in a globalised democratic society' as embodied by the theory of 'two-tiered bounded deliberative democracy' (section 3.2). It then proposed, by way of deduction from the normative framework, the authorities and duties of treaty organs and individual state organs, as well as the principles to regulate their relationship (section 3.3). Chapter 4 will use this framework to examine the actual practice of human rights treaty organs and propose reforms where necessary.

As opposed to the traditional segregation between the allocation of authorities in the international plane and that in the national plane in terms of relevant actors and applicable principles (see Figure 3.1 above), this chapter has integrated them under the 'separation of powers in a globalised democratic society' model (see Figure 3.2). In this model, treaty organs and each type of state organ directly interact as actors of a globalised democratic society. Authorities and duties are allocated to treaty organs and each type of state organ in accordance

[253] Bellamy observes that regional human rights courts apply 'a "soft" version of strong review' because they cannot disapply national laws, which remain in force until the relevant domestic legislature changes them, and can only offer a remedy in international not domestic law. See Bellamy (n 80) 1037.

[254] Føllesdal (n 245) 344–48.

[255] *cf* B Çalı, 'The Legitimacy of International Interpretive Authorities for Human Rights Treaties: An Indirect-Instrumentalist Defence' in Føllesdal et al (n 23) 141, 157.

with their particular legitimacy assets by virtue of their composition, capacity, decision-making process and function, considering the requirements of the two-tiered bounded deliberative democracy. Their relationship is regulated based on the principles of subsidiarity and principled and continuous dialogue.

Figure 3.2 Allocation of authorities according to the 'separation of powers in a globalised democratic society' model

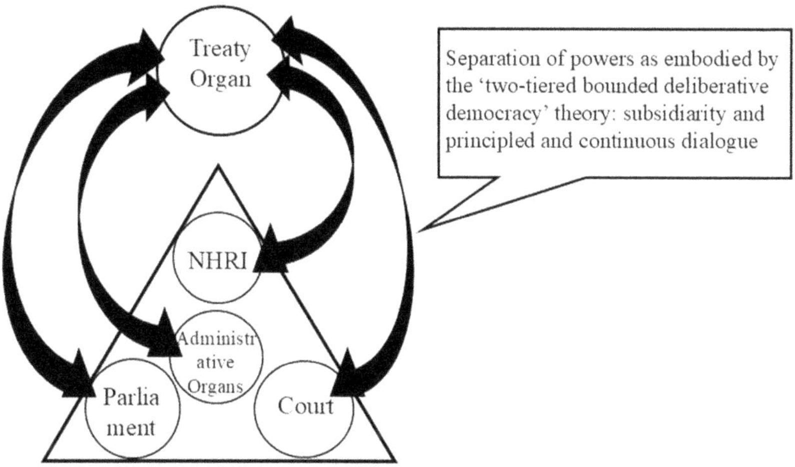

In this model, although international and national laws do not form a single monist order, fulfilment of their own duties by human rights treaty organs and state organs can be a driving force for their integration. This way, this model provides a new perspective on the issue of the relationship between international and national laws – it sheds light on the duties of and relationship between relevant *actors* instead of that between *legal orders* as such. Furthermore, to strengthen this perspective, Chapter 5 will discuss the emergence of 'inter-state organ norms' as a normative device to incentivise state organs to fulfil their duties.

4

Assessing Human Rights Treaty Organs' Practices under the Separation of Powers in a Globalised Democratic Society Model

This chapter examines the actual practices of treaty organs in allocating authority to state organs and analyses such practices through a comparative approach. It not only describes treaty organs' relevant practices from a neutral perspective but also critically evaluates the compatibility of such practices with the 'separation of powers in a globalised democratic society' model, with reforms proposed where necessary.

To this end, this chapter first examines treaty organs' practices of allocating authority to state organs and analyses how treaty organs treat each type of state organ differently, and when and under what conditions they take intrusive and top-down approaches or deferential and bottom-up approaches. Specifically, it covers the following two areas where the decision-making authority is fiercely contested between treaty and state organs: the treaty organs' approach to reviewing the necessity and proportionality of the measure in question (section 4.1) and their practice in ordering/recommending remedial measures after finding a violation of the treaty (section 4.2). The allocation of authority between treaty and state organs may be contested in other areas, including the review of exhaustion of local remedies,[1] fact-finding,[2] and where treaty organs review the composition and procedures of state organs themselves through the right to a fair trial or judicial remedy,[3] and the right to free elections and parliamentarians' freedom of expression.[4] Integrating these aspects into descriptive studies is left

[1] See, eg, A Zysset and B Çalı, 'Exhausting Domestic Remedies or Exhausting the Rule of Law? Revisiting the Normative Basis of Procedural Subsidiarity in the European Human Rights System' (2023) 14 *Transnational Legal Theory* 157.

[2] See, eg, T Stirner, *The Procedural Law Governing Facts and Evidence in International Human Rights Proceedings* (Brill 2021) ch 4.

[3] See, eg, D Kosař and L Lixinski, 'Domestic Judicial Design by International Human Rights Courts' (2015) 109 *AJIL* 713.

[4] See, eg, M Saul, 'How Does, Could and Should the International Human Rights Judiciary Interact with National Parliaments?' in M Saul, A Follesdal and G Ulfstein (eds), *The International Human Rights Judiciary and National Parliaments: Europe and Beyond* (Cambridge University Press 2017) 135, 153–56.

for future research. Second, it examines how treaty organs treat the information and views submitted by NHRIs and how these submissions helped treaty organs to assess, supplement and promote national bounded deliberations in accordance with the separation of powers in a globalised democratic society model (section 4.3). Third, it analyses how treaty organs address 'triangular relationships' among a treaty organ and two state organs within one state that take different positions regarding the interpretation and application of the treaty. As such triangular relationships were invisible under the classical paradigm that treats 'states' as unitary entities, the ability to regulate these relationships is a unique advantage of the separation of powers in a globalised democratic society model (section 4.4). Finally, this chapter conducts a comparative analysis of the three treaty organs in terms of the modes of their practices of interacting with state organs. It finds that although treaty organs tend to adopt the separation of powers in a globalised democratic society model, they differ substantially in terms of the extent and mode of adopting it (section 4.5).

4.1. HUMAN RIGHTS TREATY ORGANS' PRACTICES IN REVIEWING THE NECESSITY AND PROPORTIONALITY OF A MEASURE

4.1.1. The European Court of Human Rights

The ECtHR has recently shown an increasing tendency to act consistently with the separation of powers in a globalised democratic society model. Previously, in reviewing the necessity and proportionality of the measure, and in deciding whether and to what extent to defer to a national decision on the matter, the ECtHR dealt with a 'state' as a totality and paid little attention to the state's internal factors, such as which specific state organ adopted a decision and how that particular organ arrived at the decision.[5] When applying the margin of appreciation doctrine, the ECtHR has consistently invoked the nature of the purpose of the restriction, the existence and extent of consensus among the state parties, and the nature of the rights/activities involved[6] – all of which are factors external to the state.

However, from the 2000s to the 2010s, the ECtHR began to adopt a new approach, often called a 'procedural' approach,[7] focusing on the quality of the decision-making process of a particular state organ that has substantially adopted the decision concerned. It has become the ECtHR's consolidated jurisprudence to require national courts, parliaments and administrative organs to fulfil certain procedural criteria in their decision-making processes.

[5] B Çalı, 'Coping with Crisis: Whither the Variable Geometry in the Jurisprudence of the European Court of Human Rights' (2017) 35 *Wisconsin International Law Journal* 237, 255.

[6] See, eg, *S. and Marper v UK*, ECtHR, App Nos 30562/04 and 30566/04, Merits and Just Satisfaction (4 December 2008) para 102.

[7] See generally J Gerards and E Brems (eds), *Procedural Review in European Fundamental Rights Cases* (Cambridge University Press 2017).

These procedural criteria, which differ according to the type of state organ, largely correspond to those proposed in Chapter 3. Compliance by the state organ concerned with those criteria is treated as a weighty, and sometimes decisive, 'second-order reason'[8] by the ECtHR when it decides whether and to what extent to impose its own first-order assessment of necessity and proportionality or refrain from doing so.[9] In other words, the ECtHR defers to state organs that fulfil those criteria, endorsing 'negative subsidiarity', and conducts an intrusive review when they fail to do so, endorsing 'positive subsidiarity'.

The ECtHR has also promoted national deliberations by not immediately finding a violation in the case at hand, but instead by giving a prior warning for a future violation, thereby endorsing 'principled and continuous dialogue' with state organs. Moreover, the ECtHR's 'European consensus' approach largely corresponds to its duty under the separation of powers in a globalised democratic society model to set a bound on national deliberations based on the product of long-term and mature international deliberations.

4.1.1.1. *Review of National Courts*

Since around 2010, the ECtHR has gradually begun to pay attention to how domestic courts have functioned.[10] For example, in *MGN Limited v UK* (2011), concerning the restriction of the freedom of expression of a newspaper company, the ECtHR closely examined the decision-making process in the national courts when determining whether the interference was 'necessary in a democratic society'. It found that:

> The High Court examined this issue over 5 days and, in a detailed and lengthy judgment, found the publication of the additional material unjustified. The Court of Appeal, following a hearing of 2 days and by another detailed judgment, allowed the applicant's appeal finding the publication of the additional material to be justified. Having heard the appeal over 2 days and, each of the five members giving detailed judgments, the House of Lords found by a majority (3 to 2) that the publication of the additional material exceeded the latitude accorded to editorial assessment and was not justified.[11]

Therefore, the ECtHR gave large deference to the decision by the domestic courts, stating that '[a]gainst this background … the Court would require

[8] J Raz, *Practical Reason and Norms* (Oxford University Press 1999) 36–40. For an application of Raz's theory to the context of treaty organs' deference and margin of appreciation, see A Legg, *The Margin of Appreciation in International Human Rights Law: Deference and Proportionality* (Oxford University Press 2012) 18–23.

[9] According to Patricia Popelier, the use of a procedural approach can be categorised as: (i) a substitute for substantive review; (ii) an escape route; and (iii) a tool to strengthen the proportionality analysis. See P Popelier, 'Procedural Rationality Review after Animal Defenders International: A Constructively Critical Approach' (2019) 15 *European Constitutional Law Review* 272, 279.

[10] For a comprehensive review of such cases, see ECtHR, 'Background Document: Judicial Seminar 2024: Revisiting Subsidiarity in the Age of Shared Responsibility' (2024) 12–14.

[11] *MGN Limited v UK*, ECtHR, App No 39401/04, Merits (18 January 2011) para 149.

strong reasons to substitute its view for that of the final decision of the House of Lords'.[12]

In *Von Hannover v Germany (No 2)* in 2012, the ECtHR established, as a general jurisprudence, that special attention should be paid to the decision-making processes of national courts. Both *Von Hannover v Germany (No 1)* in 2004 and *Von Hannover v Germany (No 2)* concern domestic courts' refusal to issue an injunction against the further publication of photographs of Princess Caroline von Hannover. While the ECtHR conducted a rigorous review in *(No 1)* to find a violation of Article 8 (right to respect for private and family life),[13] in *(No 2)*, it adopted the following approach: 'where the balancing exercise has been undertaken by the national authorities in conformity with the criteria laid down in the Court's case-law, the Court would require strong reasons to substitute its view for that of the domestic courts'.[14] Başak Çalı called this approach the 'responsible domestic courts doctrine',[15] while Oddný Mjöll Arnardóttir referred to it as the 'rebuttable presumption of Convention compliance for diligent national courts'.[16] In *Von Hannover v Germany (No 2)*, the ECtHR confirmed that the German domestic courts carefully balanced the rights at stake, and 'explicitly took account of' and 'undert[ook] a detailed analysis of' the ECtHR's relevant case law, including the ECtHR judgment on *Von Hannover v Germany (No 1)*.[17] Accordingly, the ECtHR granted large deference to the national court's decision and found no violation.[18]

This approach led the ECtHR to defer to national courts and find no violation, despite the existence of a seemingly opposing precedent. In *Humpert and Others v Germany* (2023), concerning a general prohibition of strikes for civil servants, the ECtHR rejected the application of the less restrictive measures test or the requirement that the aim was not achievable without the measure; instead, it admitted a large margin of appreciation to national courts. This was precisely because the measure 'reflects a long-standing democratic consensus in Germany as well as the outcome of the weighing-up and balancing of different, potentially competing, interests' by the German Federal Constitutional Court.[19] The applicant relied heavily on the ECtHR's judgment in *Enerji Yapi-Yol Sen v Turkey* (2009),[20] which

[12] ibid para 150.

[13] *Von Hannover v Germany*, ECtHR, App No 59320/00, Merits (24 June 2004) paras 61–75.

[14] *Von Hannover v Germany (No 2)*, ECtHR, App Nos 40660/08 and 60641/08, Merits and Just Satisfaction (7 February 2012) para 107.

[15] B Çalı, 'From Flexible to Variable Standards of Judicial Review' in OM Arnardóttir and A Buyse (eds), *Shifting Centres of Gravity in Human Rights Protection* (Routledge 2016) 144, 155.

[16] OM Arnardóttir, 'Res Interpretata, Erga Omnes Effect and the Role of the Margin of Appreciation in Giving Domestic Effect to the Judgments of the European Court of Human Rights' (2017) 28 *EJIL* 819, 832.

[17] *Von Hannover v Germany (No 2)* (n 14) para 125.

[18] ibid paras 124–26.

[19] *Humpert and Others v Germany*, ECtHR, App Nos 59433/18, 59477/18, 59481/18 and 59494/18, Merits and Just Satisfaction (14 December 2023) para 142.

[20] *Enerji Yapi-Yol Sen v Turkey*, ECtHR, App No 68959/01, Merits and Just Satisfaction (21 April 2009).

had found that Article 11 (freedom of peaceful assembly) was violated when a circular deprived all public servants of the right to strike.[21] However, the ECtHR carefully distinguished the case from this precedent in that the circular in question was issued in *Enerji Yapi-Yol Sen* 'without any balance having been struck', while the measure in this case 'reflect[s] the balancing and weighing-up of different, potentially competing, constitutional interests'.[22] Authors have observed that the diligent efforts by the German Federal Constitutional Court in engaging with the Strasbourg jurisprudence 'have been rewarded'.[23]

The same approach led to a narrowing of deference where the decision-making process of the national court failed to satisfy the required quality. In *Matúz v Hungary* (2014), concerning the dismissal of a journalist for publishing a book criticising his employer in breach of a confidentiality clause, the ECtHR explicitly recognised that:

> [T]he fairness of proceedings and the procedural guarantees afforded … are factors to be taken into account when assessing the proportionality of an interference … If the reasoning of the national court demonstrates a lack of sufficient engagement with the general principles of the Court under Article 10 of the Convention, the degree of margin of appreciation afforded to the authorities will necessarily be narrower.[24]

Following this approach, the ECtHR afforded only a limited margin of appreciation to domestic courts because they had confined their analysis to contractual obligations and failed to examine the applicant's freedom of expression in accordance with the ECHR standards.[25]

Nevertheless, inconsistency and uncertainty remain in the Court's approach, especially in determining whether the domestic court applied standards consistent with the ECHR. For example, in *Bărbulescu v Romania*, the applicant was dismissed for using the company's internet network during working hours for private purposes in breach of internal regulations. In its judgment in 2016, the Chamber positively evaluated the decision-making process of the domestic courts because 'the applicant was able to raise his arguments related to the alleged breach of his private life and correspondence by his employer before the domestic courts … [and] they duly examined his arguments'.[26] Accordingly, the Chamber deferred to domestic courts' findings[27] and found no violation. Remarkably, the Grand Chamber's judgment in 2017 reached a directly opposite evaluation. The Grand Chamber set out factors that the domestic courts should

[21] *Humpert and Others v Germany* (n 19) para 124.

[22] ibid para 145.

[23] J Batura, 'A European Dialogue on Strike Action: The Strike Ban for German Civil Servants between Karlsruhe and Strasbourg' *Verfassungsblog* (20 December 2023), https://verfassungsblog.de/a-european-dialogue-on-strike-action.

[24] *Matúz v Hungary*, ECtHR, App No 73571/10, Merits and Just Satisfaction (21 October 2014) para 35.

[25] ibid para 49.

[26] *Bărbulescu v Romania*, ECtHR [Fourth Section], App No 61496/08 (12 January 2016) para 56.

[27] ibid para 57.

have considered more elaborately than the Chamber: the scope of the monitoring and degree of interference by the employer, reasons to justify monitoring the applicant's communications, the existence of less intrusive means and the seriousness of consequences.[28] The Grand Chamber found that the domestic courts failed to consider these factors and therefore 'the Court of Appeal's conclusion that a fair balance was struck between the interests at stake ... is questionable'.[29]

4.1.1.2. Review of National Parliaments

The ECtHR consolidated its jurisprudence on the quality of the parliamentary decision-making process from the 2000s to the 2010s.[30] In *Maurice v France* (2005), concerning the compatibility of the restriction of the scope of compensation for errors in pre-natal diagnosis with Article 8 (right to respect for private and family life), the ECtHR placed decisive weight on the decision-making process of the French Parliament in examining fair balance. It stated:

> [T]he French parliament, after consulting the various persons and interest groups concerned, decided to intervene to establish a new system of compensation ... These rules were the result of comprehensive debate in Parliament, in the course of which account was taken of legal, ethical and social considerations, and concerns relating to the proper organisation of the health service and the need for fair treatment for all disabled persons.[31]

Given this, the ECtHR, without examining the law's substantive content, found that the law in question was within the wide margin of appreciation.[32] In this case, the ECtHR indicated that such an approach has a theoretical basis in 'the fundamentally subsidiary role of the Convention' and the 'direct democratic legitimation' of domestic policy-makers.[33]

By contrast, the lack of adequate parliamentary deliberation has resulted in the deprivation or narrowing of the margin of appreciation. In *Hirst v UK (No 2)*, concerning a blanket ban on convicted prisoners voting in elections, the Chamber (2004) first pointed to the lack of clear consensus among Member States on the issue, which should normally lead to a wider margin of appreciation.[34] However, the Chamber emphatically stated that 'a Contracting State may [not] rely on the margin of appreciation to justify restrictions on the right to vote

[28] *Bărbulescu v Romania*, ECtHR [GC], App No 61496/08, Merits and Just Satisfaction (5 September 2017) paras 134–37.

[29] ibid para 139.

[30] See generally M Saul, 'The European Court of Human Rights' Margin of Appreciation and the Processes of National Parliaments' (2015) 15 *HRLR* 745. See also ECtHR (n 10) 14–16.

[31] *Maurice v France*, ECtHR, App No 11810/03, Merits and Just Satisfaction (6 October 2005) para 121.

[32] ibid para 124.

[33] ibid para 117.

[34] *Hirst v UK (No 2)*, ECtHR [Fourth Section], App No 74025/01, Merits and Just Satisfaction (30 March 2004) para 40.

which have not been the subject of considered debate in the legislature'.[35] It denied a margin of appreciation to the Parliament because 'there is no evidence that the legislature … has ever sought to weigh the competing interests or to assess the proportionality of the ban'.[36] The Grand Chamber upheld this evaluation and added that the legislature failed to provide 'continued justification in light of modern-day penal policy and of current human rights standards'.[37]

The quality of the parliamentary decision-making process may play a decisive role in the ECtHR's evaluation of necessity and proportionality. In *Sukhovetskyy*, concerning an allegedly excessively high electoral deposit, the ECtHR allowed a wide margin of appreciation to the Parliament and carefully distinguished this case from *Hirst (No 2)* by stating that: 'Unlike in the aforementioned cases [including *Hirst (No 2)*], the impugned measure has been the subject of considerable parliamentary scrutiny.'[38]

The same approach was adopted even in politically sensitive and controversial cases[39] such as *A, B and C v Ireland* (2010), concerning the prohibition of abortion for reasons of health and well-being. In this case, the Oireachtas (parliamentary) Committee on the Constitution conducted serious deliberations on the conditions of legal abortion, ensuring the inclusive representation and consideration of various positions and interests, including those of the minority. The Committee received over 100,000 submissions from individuals and organisations, and heard the views and opinions of experts in the fields of obstetrics, gynaecology and psychiatry through public hearings.[40] After positively evaluating the seriousness and comprehensiveness of these processes, the ECtHR decided to defer to the choice that has emerged 'from the lengthy, complex and sensitive debate in Ireland … as regards the content of its abortion laws'.[41]

The parliamentary decision-making process contributed to the substantial reversal of the precedent in *Animal Defenders International v UK* (2013),[42] where the ECtHR found that the general prohibition of political advertising was compatible with Article 10 (freedom of expression) ECHR, even though it had previously found that an 'essentially identical'[43] measure violated Article 10 in *VgT Verein gegen Tierfabriken v Switzerland* (2001).[44]

[35] ibid para 41.

[36] ibid para 51.

[37] *Hirst v UK (No 2)*, ECtHR [GC], App No 74025/01, Merits and Just Satisfaction (6 October 2005) para 79.

[38] *Sukhovetskyy v Ukraine*, ECtHR, App No 13716/02, Merits (28 March 2006) para 65.

[39] For other such cases, see ECtHR (n 10) 16.

[40] *A, B and C v Ireland*, ECtHR, App No 25579/05, Merits and Just Satisfaction (16 December 2010) paras 70–76.

[41] ibid para 239.

[42] *Animal Defenders International v UK*, ECtHR, App No 48876/08, Merits and Just Satisfaction (22 April 2013).

[43] ibid Joint Dissenting Opinion of Judge Ziemele et al, para 1.

[44] *VgT Verein gegen Tierfabriken v Switzerland*, ECtHR, App No 24699/94, Merits and Just Satisfaction (28 June 2001).

In *Animal Defenders International*, the ECtHR established the following criterion:

> [I]n order to determine the proportionality of a general measure, the Court must primarily assess the legislative choices underlying it .... The quality of the parliamentary and judicial review of the necessity of the measure is of particular importance ... to the operation of the relevant margin of appreciation.[45]

Thus, it gave great weight to the following facts: the draft bill considered the diversity of views and positions through wide consultation; the parliamentary bodies, including the Joint Committee on Human Rights, thoroughly deliberated on the implications of the *VgT* judgment, including an analysis of comparative law and consideration of possible alternative measures; hence, the prohibition was enacted with cross-party support and with no dissenting vote. In short: 'The prohibition was ... the culmination of an exceptional examination by parliamentary bodies of the cultural, political and legal aspects of the prohibition.'[46]

Further advancing its jurisprudence,[47] in *LB v Hungary* (2023), concerning the publication of taxpayers' identifying data for failing to fulfil their tax obligations, the ECtHR treated the quality of parliamentary review as an independent and decisive criterion of proportionality by inserting a section titled 'General measures and the quality of parliamentary review'.[48] It considered that even though 'the choice of such a general scheme is not in itself problematic',[49] the failure of the legislature to make efforts to strike a fair balance between the relevant competing individual and public interests was decisive in finding a violation of Article 8.[50]

However, because this approach is relatively new, the ECtHR has not yet established a consolidated framework to assess whether the parliament of a respondent state has fulfilled its duty. In *Belcacemi and Oussar v Belgium* (2017), concerning the ban on full-face veils in public by the 2011 Law, the ECtHR positively valued the decision-making process of the Belgian Parliament, stating that 'the decision-making process leading to the ban in question lasted several years and was marked by an extensive debate in the House of Representatives',[51] and thus granted a wide margin of appreciation. Yet, Eva Brems, a world-renowned international human rights law scholar and then member of the Chamber of Representatives, criticised this evaluation by the ECtHR:

> [T]he reason why the process lasted several years was not because the discussion took a lot of time, but rather because the process had to be re-started after early elections.

[45] *Animal Defenders International v UK* (n 42) para 108.

[46] ibid para 114.

[47] H Ní Chinnéide, 'Balancing Privacy and the Public Interest: The Application of the "General Measures" Doctrine in *L.B. v Hungary* in the Absence of Any Substantive Proportionality Assessment' (2024) 20 *European Constitutional Law Review* 146, 156–57.

[48] *LB v Hungary*, ECtHR, App No 36345/16, Merits and Just Satisfaction (9 March 2023) paras 124–26.

[49] ibid para 130.

[50] ibid para 138.

[51] *Belcacemi and Oussar v Belgium*, ECtHR, App No 37798/13 (11 July 2017) para 54.

> What is more, the 'extensive debate' in the Chamber was characterized by the absence of human rights considerations, and all measures that could have been employed to provide more thorough discussion (expert hearings, advice of the Council of State, re-examination by the Senate) were rejected in this case.[52]

As suggested in Chapter 3, section 3.3.5.2, the direct participation of the parliament concerned in the ECtHR proceeding – including the opportunities for the parliament to submit its own views on the deliberative process leading to the contested measure, and to respond to the applicant's submissions and possible questions by the Court – would be useful for the Court to properly evaluate the quality of parliamentary deliberations. The third-party intervention procedure could be used for this purpose. Parliaments can be represented by parliamentary human rights committees (see Chapter 5, section 5.3 for the recent development concerning parliamentary human rights committees).

Another strand of practice consistent with the separation of powers in a globalised democratic society model is the ECtHR's occasional instruction for the national parliament to conduct continuous deliberations while not finding a violation in the case at hand.[53] In *SH and Others v Austria* (2011), concerning the prohibition of the use of donor gametes for *in vitro* fertilisation, the ECtHR did not find a violation of Article 8 because of the lack of an established consensus. However, it critically noted that:

> [T]he Austrian Parliament has not, until now, undertaken a thorough assessment of the rules governing artificial procreation, taking into account the dynamic developments in science and society ... [T]his area, in which the law appears to be continuously evolving and which is subject to a particularly dynamic development in science and law, needs to be kept under review by the Contracting States.[54]

Similarly, in *Zdanoka v Latvia* (2006), while finding no violation in the case, the ECtHR indicated that 'the Latvian parliament must keep the statutory restriction under constant review' and 'the failure by the Latvian legislature ... may result in a different finding by the Court'.[55]

4.1.1.3. *Review of National Administrative Organs*

The ECtHR has developed criteria for the administrative decision-making process that differ from those imposed on national courts and parliaments. In *Chapman v UK* (2001), concerning the refusal to give planning permission to gypsies to station residential caravans, the ECtHR highlighted the expertise of

[52] E Brems, 'Positive Subsidiarity and its Implications for the Margin of Appreciation Doctrine' (2019) 37 *Netherlands Quarterly of Human Rights* 210, 222–23.

[53] See also A Müller, 'Domestic Authorities' Obligations to Co-develop the Rights of the European Convention on Human Rights' (2016) 20 *IJHR* 1058, 1061.

[54] *SH and Others v Austria*, ECtHR [GC], App No 57813/00, Merits and Just Satisfaction (3 November 2011) paras 117–18.

[55] *Zdanoka v Latvia*, ECtHR [GC], App No 58278/00, Merits and Just Satisfaction (16 March 2006) para 135.

the administrative organs, stating that '[b]ecause planning inspectors visit the site, hear the arguments on all sides and allow the examination of witnesses, they are better placed than the Court to weigh the arguments'.[56] Thus, the ECtHR examined 'whether the decision-making process ... was fair and such as to afford due respect to the interests safeguarded to the individual by Article 8'.[57] Eventually, the ECtHR deferred to the planning inspectors' decision and found no violation of Article 8 because the inspector's reports showed 'that there were strong, environmental reasons for the refusal of planning permission and that the applicant's personal circumstances had been taken into account in the decision-making process'.[58] By contrast, in *Connors v UK* (2004), concerning the eviction of a gypsy family from a caravan site, the ECtHR did not defer to the local administrative organ because 'the eviction ... was not attended by the requisite procedural safeguards, namely the requirement to establish proper justification'.[59]

Starting from *Hatton and Others v UK* (2003), concerning sleep disturbance caused by aircraft noise, the ECtHR has divided its enquiry regarding compliance with Article 8 into two aspects in cases involving administrative measures on environmental issues: substantive and procedural.[60] It directly scrutinises the administrative decision-making processes, leaving the substantive weighing of rights and interests to properly functioning processes. In examining the substantive merits – whether a fair balance was struck between competing rights and interests – the ECtHR allowed a wide margin of appreciation.[61] In return, the ECtHR rigorously scrutinised the procedural aspect, 'including the type of policy or decision involved, the extent to which the views of individuals (including the applicants) were taken into account throughout the decision-making procedure, and the procedural safeguards available'.[62] In *Hatton*, the ECtHR emphasised the following facts: first, the scheme of night-flying restrictions in question was 'preceded by a series of investigations and studies carried out over a long period of time';[63] second, the measures 'were announced to the public by way of a Consultation Paper', and this paper was 'sent to bodies representing the aviation industry and people living near airports';[64] and, third, 'it would have been open to [the applicants] to make any representations they felt appropriate' and 'they could have challenged subsequent decisions, or the

[56] *Chapman v UK*, ECtHR, App No 27238/95, Merits (18 January 2001) para 92.

[57] ibid.

[58] ibid para 110.

[59] *Connors v UK*, ECtHR, App No 66746/01, Merits and Just Satisfaction (27 May 2004) para 95.

[60] *Hatton and Others v UK*, ECtHR [GC], App No 36022/97, Merits and Just Satisfaction (8 July 2003) para 99. See also OM Arnardóttir, 'The "Procedural Turn" under the European Convention on Human Rights and Presumptions of Convention Compliance' (2017) 15 *I-CON* 9, 14.

[61] ibid para 100.

[62] ibid para 104.

[63] ibid para 128.

[64] ibid.

scheme itself, in the courts'.[65] Based on these elements, the ECtHR found no violation of Article 8.

In *Taşkın and Others v Turkey* (2004), the ECtHR elaborated on additional criteria that administrative organs must follow in determining complex and technical environmental matters:

> [T]he decision-making process must firstly involve appropriate investigations and studies in order to allow them to predict and evaluate in advance the effects of those activities ... and to enable them to strike a fair balance between the various conflicting interests at stake ... The importance of public access to the conclusions of such studies and to information ... is beyond question ... Lastly, the individuals concerned must also be able to appeal to the courts against any decision, act or omission.[66]

The development of procedural standards for administrative organs focusing on participation in decision-making, especially in environmental matters, has been facilitated by international initiatives such as the adoption of the 1998 Convention on Access to Information, Public Participation in Decision-Making and Access to Justice in Environmental Matters (Aarhus Convention).[67]

4.1.1.4. Setting Bounds on National Deliberations

The ECtHR has developed a unique approach called the 'European consensus'[68] to mediate between evolutive interpretation and the margin of appreciation.[69] While a wide consensus (the ECtHR uses various terms including 'common European standards', 'common ground' and 'general trend')[70] serves as a basis for the ECtHR to develop an evolutive interpretation and tighten the margin of appreciation accorded to states, little consensus is a determinative factor that inhibits evolutive interpretation and widens the margin of appreciation. While previous studies have struggled to ground the democratic legitimacy of the European consensus approach,[71] these functions of European consensus largely correspond to those of the 'bounds' within the meaning of the two-tiered bounded deliberative democracy theory. For instance, in *Konstantin Markin v Russia* (2012), concerning the difference in treatment between male and female military personnel regarding rights to parental leave, the Russian Constitutional

[65] ibid.

[66] *Taşkın and Others v Turkey*, ECtHR, App No 46117/99, Merits and Just Satisfaction (10 November 2004) para 119.

[67] Convention on Access to Information, Public Participation in Decision-Making and Access to Justice in Environmental Matters (adopted 25 June 1998, entered into force 30 October 2001) 2161 UNTS 447. See *Tătar v Romania*, ECtHR, App No 67021/01, Merits and Just Satisfaction (27 January 2009) para 118.

[68] See generally K Dzehtsiarou, *European Consensus and the Legitimacy of the European Court of Human Rights* (Cambridge University Press 2015).

[69] ibid 23.

[70] ibid 11.

[71] See, eg, P Łącki, 'Consensus as a Basis for Dynamic Interpretation of the ECHR: A Critical Assessment' (2021) 21 *HRLR* 186, 198–99.

Court and the legislature deliberated on the measure and justified it based on 'the limited participation of women in military service' and 'the special social role of women associated with motherhood'.[72] However, the ECtHR placed a 'bound' on such national deliberations based on the solid European consensus that rejects the traditional distribution of gender roles in society as a justification for treating mothers and fathers differently. It stated that:

> [T]he advancement of gender equality is today a major goal in the member States of the Council of Europe and very weighty reasons would have to be put forward before such a difference of treatment could be regarded as compatible with the Convention ... [R]eferences to traditions, general assumptions or prevailing social attitudes in a particular country are insufficient justification for a difference in treatment on grounds of sex.[73]

When examining European consensus, the ECtHR dedicates a distinct section for 'relevant international and European material' (or similar title) and relies on: (i) comparative law materials such as national legislation and jurisprudence; (ii) treaties (including those not yet in force) and other non-binding instruments such as resolutions and declarations; and (iii) judgments and recommendations of other international judicial organs and expert bodies.[74] The ECtHR usually invokes all or some of these materials. For example, to interpret the applicability of Article 11 to civil servants in *Demir and Baykara v Turkey* (2008), the ECtHR referred to the practice of all ECHR Member States, in addition to the EU's Charter of Fundamental Rights, the European Social Charter, the ICESCR, the ICCPR, a relevant International Labour Organization (ILO) Convention, the views of the ILO Committee of Experts on the Application of Conventions and Recommendations and of the ILO Committee on Freedom of Association, and a recommendation by the CoM of the Council of Europe.[75] When listing these documents, the ECtHR did not distinguish between legally binding treaties and other non-binding instruments. Moreover, the ECtHR explicitly stated that it would consider international instruments, including those that are not ratified by the respondent state, as long as they 'denote a continuous evolution' and show that 'there is common ground in modern societies'.[76]

From the perspective of the two-tiered bounded deliberative democracy theory, which underlies the separation of powers in a globalised democratic society model, relying on item (ii) above is the most consistent with the concept of 'bounds', as these documents have been subject to deliberations at the

[72] *Konstantin Markin v Russia*, ECtHR [GC], App No 30078/06, Merits and Just Satisfaction (22 March 2012) para 34.

[73] ibid para 127.

[74] For a comprehensive examination, see J Ferrero, *L'interprétation évolutive des conventions internationales des droits de l'homme* (Pedone 2019) 88–116.

[75] *Demir and Baykara v Turkey*, ECtHR [GC], App No 34503/97, Merits and Just Satisfaction (12 November 2008) paras 85 and 98–106.

[76] ibid para 86.

international level. The ECtHR's reliance on documents of the PACE,[77] made up of 306 parliamentarians from the Council of Europe Member States, is particularly welcome, as its diverse members can represent and bring into the debate a wider range of positions and perspectives than diplomatic conferences. Item (iii) could also constitute a 'bound' as long as the judicial organs and expert bodies have carefully deliberated on the matter by considering diverse perspectives across different countries and inputs from the transnational civil society. However, the ECtHR should not establish a bound based on item (i) by merely counting the number of states that have adopted a particular position, as that would amount to the simple majoritarian or 'aggregative' theory of democracy,[78] which directly clashes with human rights protection of the minorities[79] and thus is something that the theory of deliberative democracy strives to overcome.[80] Nevertheless, the fact that the ECtHR usually supplements comparative law materials with items (ii) and (iii) and inputs from other states parties, transnational civil society organisations and NHRIs greatly mitigates such problems.

Another inevitable problem associated with the ECtHR's process of identifying consensus is inconsistency and non-transparency.[81] For instance, in *Leyla Şahin v Turkey* (2005), the ECtHR noted 'the diversity of the approaches taken by national authorities' in 'regulating the wearing of religious symbols in educational institutions'.[82] Thus, without placing a tight 'bound' on national deliberations, the ECtHR granted a wide margin of appreciation to the national deliberation outcome. However, many criticised this approach,[83] arguing that the Court should have limited its comparative law survey on university education, 'which is intended for young adults, who are less amenable to pressure',[84] and that such survey would have led the Court to a different conclusion.

As mentioned in Chapter 3, section 3.2.2.2, in some cases, the ECtHR supplemented the lack of 'bounds' at the European level with 'bounds' at the universal

[77] See, eg, *Vallianatos and Others v Greece*, ECtHR, App Nos 29381/09 and 32684/09, Merits and Just Satisfaction (7 November 2013) para 91.

[78] Some authors call this a 'pan-European majoritarian approach'. See IY Nugraha, 'Deferring to Consensus and Procedural Rationality: Assessing the European Court of Human Rights' Approach to Majoritarian Will' (2024) 9 *Asian Yearbook of Human Rights and Humanitarian Law* 166.

[79] See, eg, G Letsas, 'Strasbourg's Interpretive Ethic: Lessons for the International Lawyer' (2010) 21 *EJIL* 509, 531; Łącki (n 71) 199.

[80] A Yoshida, 'Jinken jouyaku kaishaku ni okeru jouyaku jisshi kikan to touji-koku no "tairitsu" to "taiwa" [Confrontation and Dialogue between Treaty Monitoring Bodies and States Parties in the Interpretation of Human Rights Treaties]' PhD thesis, Waseda University (2023) 170.

[81] See, eg, LR Helfer, 'Consensus, Coherence and the European Convention on Human Rights' (1993) 26 *Cornell International Law Journal* 133.

[82] *Leyla Şahin v Turkey*, ECtHR, App No 44774/98, Merits and Just Satisfaction (10 November 2005) para 109.

[83] See, eg, D Regan, 'European Consensus: A Worthy Endeavour for the European Court of Human Rights' (2011) 14 *Trinity College Law Review* 51, 61.

[84] *Leyla Şahin v Turkey* (n 82) Dissenting Opinion of Judge Tulkens, para 3.

level. In *Christine Goodwin v UK* (2002), concerning the legal recognition of the new sexual identity of post-operative transsexuals, the ECtHR held that:

> The Court accordingly attaches less importance to the lack of evidence of a common European approach ..., than to the clear and uncontested evidence of a continuing international trend in favour ... of legal recognition of the new sexual identity of post-operative transsexuals.[85]

4.1.2. The Inter-American Court of Human Rights

Unlike the ECtHR, which has developed a deferential approach under the doctrine of margin of appreciation, the IACtHR has rejected this approach and instead consolidated an interventionist approach[86] to prioritise the *pro homine/pro persona* principle – the maximisation of human rights protection.[87] Presumably, two factors led to this contrast (see Chapter 1, section 1.4.2.1).[88] First, unlike the ECHR, whose main respondents were mature democracies (especially before the 1990s), when the IACtHR initiated its activities in the late 1980s, most ACHR Member States were in the midst of a transition to democracy and peace; thus, the IACtHR had insufficient trust in national systems. Second, unlike the ECtHR, whose main cases concerned good-faith restrictions of rights for public purposes (especially before the 1990s), most cases before the IACtHR concerned gross and systematic violations of human rights, which did not reasonably tolerate divergent understandings and applications by state organs.

Nevertheless, the practice of the IACtHR is not inconsistent with the separation of powers in a globalised democratic society model, although the IACtHR's application of the model differs from that of the ECtHR. The IACtHR has highlighted the duties of national courts among other state organs and emphasised the positive aspect of subsidiarity while applying negative subsidiarity in rare cases where national courts fulfilled their duties properly.

[85] *Christine Goodwin v UK*, ECtHR, App No 28957/95, Merits and Just Satisfaction (11 July 2002) para 85. See also *DH and Others v Czech Republic*, ECtHR, App No 57325/00, Merits and Just Satisfaction (13 November 2007) paras 181–82. For a detailed analysis of how the consensus approach was used in *DH and Others*, see D Kagiaros, 'When to Use European Consensus: Assessing the Differential Treatment of Minority Groups by the European Court of Human Rights' in P Kapotas and VP Tzevelekos (eds), *Building Consensus on European Consensus: Judicial Interpretation of Human Rights in Europe and Beyond* (Cambridge University Press 2019) 283, 292–97.

[86] See generally G Candia Falcón, 'Standard of Review: Inter-American Court of Human Rights (IACtHR)' (last updated 2022) in H Ruiz Fabri (ed), *Max Planck Encyclopedia of International Procedural Law* (Oxford University Press online edition).

[87] L Burgorgue-Larsen, 'Les methods d'interprétation de la Cour interaméricaine des droits de l'homme: Justice in Context' (2014) 97 *Revue trimestrielle des droits de l'homme* 31, 33 and 35.

[88] PG Carozza, 'The Anglo-Latin Divide and the Future of the InterAmerican System of Human Rights' (2015) 5 *Notre Dame Journal of International & Comparative Law* 153, 168.

4.1.2.1. Review of National Courts

As introduced in Chapter 2, section 2.2.2, the IACtHR established the doctrine of 'conventionality control' to directly address national courts. Previous studies have characterised this doctrine as 'vertical',[89] 'an extraordinary and unprecedented degree of intrusion into domestic legal systems'[90] and 'the direct opposite of the "margin of appreciation"'.[91] Based on this understanding, the doctrine has often been criticised as institutionalising judicial 'monologue' instead of judicial dialogue and being detrimental to democracy.[92] The IACtHR mostly used the doctrine to effectively export its jurisprudence to domestic legal orders, treating national courts as obedient messengers who mechanically implement the IACtHR's jurisprudence in their domestic legal orders.[93] In *Almonacid-Arellano et al v Chile* (2006), where the IACtHR first applied the doctrine, the IACtHR went so far as to state that the amnesty law in question 'does not have any legal effect'.[94]

However, in recent years, thanks to successful democratisation in ACHR Member States, the independence and quality of the decision-making process of national courts have greatly improved. There are more 'less "obvious"' cases,[95] deriving from the good faith restriction of rights for the general welfare and freedom of others. Thus, the aforementioned situations that have necessitated the IACtHR to adopt an interventionist approach have greatly changed. Governments, politicians (see Chapter 2, section 2.3.2), and scholars[96] have called on the IACtHR to modify its interventionist approach.

Although the IACtHR is generally reluctant to abandon its interventionist approach, it has shown signs of deference in a few cases, albeit sporadically and in an ad hoc manner. This tendency first emerged in the practices of the

[89] H Nogueira Alcalá, 'El control de convencionalidad y el diálogo interjurisdiccional entre tribunales nacionales y Corte Iberoamericana de Derechos Humanos' (2013) 19 *Revista de derecho constitucional europeo* 221, 246–47.

[90] PG Carozza, 'The Problematic Applicability of Subsidiarity to International Law and Institutions' (2016) 61 *American Journal of Jurisprudence* 51, 65.

[91] LE Barreiros, 'Emerging Voices: Freedom or Restraint? On the Comparison between the European and Inter-American Human Rights Courts' *Opinio Juris* (11 August 2014), http://opiniojuris.org/2014/08/11/emerging-voices-freedom-restraint-comparison-european-inter-american-human-rights-courts.

[92] For a summary of such views, see L Burgorgue-Larsen, 'Chronique d'une théorie en vogue en Amérique latine Décryptage du discours doctrinal sur le contrôle de conventionalité' (2014) 100 *Revue française de droit constitutionnel* 831, 859–60.

[93] AE Dulitzky, 'An Inter-American Constitutional Court? The Invention of the Conventionality Control by the Inter-American Court of Human Rights' (2015) 50 *Texas International Law Journal* 45, 83.

[94] *Almonacid-Arellano et al v Chile*, IACtHR, Series C No 154, Preliminary Objections, Merits, Reparations and Costs (26 September 2006) para 119.

[95] J Contesse, 'Inter-American Constitutionalism: The Interaction between Human Rights and Progressive Constitutional Law in Latin America' in CA Rodríguez Garavito (ed), *Law and Society in Latin America: A New Map* (Routledge 2015) 220, 227.

[96] See, eg, J Contesse, 'Contestation and Deference in the Inter-American Human Rights System' (2016) 79 *Law and Contemporary Problems* 123, 145.

IACmHR.[97]In *Dudley Stokes v Jamaica* (2008), concerning freedom of expression (Article 13 ACHR) and the imposition of a high amount of civil damage for libel, the IACmHR emphasised that 'domestic courts are generally best situated to assess the numerous factors required' for the evaluation of the appropriate amount of damages.[98] The IACmHR then confirmed that domestic courts applied the standards of reasonableness and proportionality and considered diverse relevant factors.[99] Accordingly, it adopted a deferential standard of '[a]bsent clear errors or due process violations' and respected the decision of the national court.[100]

The IACtHR followed such an approach in *Mémoli v Argentina* (2013), concerning criminal sanctions for the applicants' statements in newspaper articles and radio broadcasts. It stated that:

> [I]n strict observance of its subsidiary competence, the Court ... must verify whether the State authorities made a reasonable and sufficient weighing up between the two rights in conflict, without necessarily making an autonomous and independent weighing, unless the specific circumstances of the case require this.[101]

In this case, the IACtHR positively valued the fact that the domestic courts 'examined thoroughly the characteristics of the statements [in question]'[102] based on the standards that are compatible with the IACtHR's jurisprudence.[103] Thus, the IACtHR deferred to the domestic courts, holding that 'domestic judicial authorities were in a better position to assess which right suffered most harm',[104] and found no violation of Article 13.

In addition, even in cases where the IACtHR eventually refused to give deference to the national court, it attributed this refusal to the national court's failure to exercise adequate conventionality control based on ACHR standards, including the IACtHR's jurisprudence.[105] This implies that the IACtHR may have deferred to the national court if the latter had carefully done so.

Considering these new practices, the doctrine of conventionality control must be reconstructed.[106] Rather than blindly implementing the

[97] For the development of the 'fourth instance formula' by the IACmHR, see B Duhaime, 'Subsidiarity in the Americas: What Room is There for Deference in the Inter-American System?' in L Gruszczynski and W Werner (eds), *Deference in International Courts and Tribunals: Standard of Review and Margin of Appreciation* (Oxford University Press 2014) 289, 291–96.

[98] *Dudley Stokes v Jamaica*, IACmHR, Report no 23/08, Petition 12.468, Merits (14 March 2008) para 85.

[99] ibid paras 83 and 88.

[100] ibid para 93.

[101] *Mémoli v Argentina*, IACtHR, Series C No 265, Preliminary Objections, Merits, Reparations and Costs (22 August 2013) para 140.

[102] ibid para 141.

[103] ibid para 142.

[104] ibid para 143.

[105] *Gomes Lund et al v Brazil*, IACtHR, Series C No 219, Preliminary Objections, Merits, Reparations, and Costs (24 November 2010) para 177.

[106] *cf* P Gonzalez-Dominguez, *The Doctrine of Conventionality Control: Between Uniformity and Legal Pluralism in the Inter-American Human Rights System* (Intersentia 2018) ch 4.

jurisprudence of the IACtHR, domestic courts are required to conduct a comprehensive and thorough review of all relevant factors based on standards that are consistent with the ACHR, with the guarantee of procedural fairness. The IACtHR should then be ready to listen to the views of national courts that have properly exercised conventionality control. When redefined in this way, the doctrine of conventionality control promotes the principle of principled and continuous dialogue advocated by the separation of powers in a globalised democratic society model.[107] Judge Ferrer Mac-Gregor Poisot, in his concurring opinion in *Cabrera García and Montiel Flores v Mexico* (2010), stated that:

> The doctrine does not seek to establish which body has the final word, but to encourage creative, responsible jurisprudential dialogue .... Domestic judges now become the first Inter-American judges. It is they who bear the greatest responsibility in harmonizing national legislation within the Inter-American parameters. The Inter-American Court must monitor this process ... considering also the 'national margin of discretion'.[108]

The doctrine of conventionality control thus understood endorses the duality of subsidiarity. The interventionist and top-down nature of the doctrine of conventionality control, which has drawn attention and criticism from previous studies,[109] is only one side of the coin (positive subsidiarity), in which the IACtHR takes an interventionist approach when the domestic court in question does not fulfil its duty. Antônio Augusto Cançado Trindade, the former President of the IACtHR, advocated for the interventionist and top-down approach, stating:

> How could we apply [the margin of appreciation doctrine] in the context of a regional human rights system where many countries' judges are subject to intimidation and pressure? How could we apply it in a region where the judicial function does not distinguish between military jurisdiction and ordinary jurisdiction?[110]

This logic precisely reflects positive subsidiarity.[111] The other side of the same coin (negative subsidiarity) will necessarily be that if the domestic court fulfils its duty, the IACtHR shall defer to its decision. In fact, in the order concerning compliance with the judgment in *Gelman v Uruguay* (2013), the IACtHR expressly asserted that the concept of conventionality control has a

[107] See PG Carozza and P González, 'The Final Word? Constitutional Dialogue and the Inter-American Court of Human Rights: A Reply to Jorge Contesse' (2017) 15 *I-CON* 436, 440–41; C Orunesu, 'Control de convencionalidad y supremacía de los tribunales internacionales' (2022) 46 *Revues*, para 45.

[108] *Cabrera García and Montiel Flores v Mexico*, IACtHR, Series C No 220, Preliminary Objection, Merits, Reparations, and Costs (26 November 2010) Concurring Opinion of Judge Ferrer Mac-Gregor Poisot, para 87.

[109] See previous studies cited in nn 89–93.

[110] AA Cançado Trindade, *El derecho internacional de los derechos humanos en el siglo XXI*, 2nd edn (Editorial Jurídica de Chile 2006) 389–90.

[111] Carozza (n 90) 65.

close connection with the principle of subsidiarity, which underlies the ACHR system.[112] Relatedly, Judge Mac-Gregor Poisot posited that while domestic organs cannot adopt an interpretation different from that of the IACtHR on a particular case to which the state was a party by virtue of the principle of *res judicata*, in other situations, they enjoy 'margen interpretativo nacional' (national interpretive margin) to pursue their own interpretations by building upon the jurisprudence of the IACtHR.[113] Oswaldo Ruiz-Chiriboga observed that the less firmly consolidated the IACtHR's jurisprudence is on the matter, the broader the national courts' discretion would be in exercising conventionality control.[114]

4.1.2.2. Review of National Parliaments

As the IACtHR has mostly dealt with the conduct of the military and police and laws adopted under undemocratic regimes, it has had few opportunities to develop the procedural approach on national parliaments. The most relevant yet highly controversial case was *Gelman v Uruguay* (2011). In this case, the amnesty law in question was passed by the democratic Parliament in 1986 and was subsequently reaffirmed twice in the national referenda, in 1989 and 2009. However, the IACtHR asserted that:

> The fact that the Expiry Law of the State has been approved in a democratic regime and yet ratified or supported by the public, on two occasions, namely, through the exercise of direct democracy, does not automatically or by itself grant legitimacy under International Law ... The democratic legitimacy of specific facts in a society is limited by the norms of protection of human rights recognized in international treaties, such as the American Convention.[115]

Thus, despite Leiv Marsteintredet's observation that '[i]f there ever was one case in which the margin of appreciation would be granted to a member state on the basis of high-quality parliamentary and democratic procedures, *Gelman* v. *Uruguay* should be it',[116] the IACtHR did not grant deference to the national deliberation. It held that the failure to investigate, prosecute and punish the crimes in question constituted a violation of the right to a fair trial and judicial protection enshrined in Articles 8 and 25 ACHR. The *Gelman* judgment has often been criticised from a democratic perspective because the IACtHR

[112] *Gelman v Uruguay*, IACtHR, Order on Monitoring Compliance with Judgment (20 March 2013) para 70.

[113] ibid Separate Opinion of Judge Mac-Gregor Poisot, paras 67–72.

[114] O Ruiz-Chiriboga, 'The Conventionality Control: Examples of (Un)Successful Experiences in Latin-America' (2010) 3 *Inter-American and European Human Rights Journal* 200, 215.

[115] *Gelman v Uruguay*, IACtHR, Series C No 221, Merits and Reparations (24 February 2011) 238–39.

[116] L Marsteintredet, 'The Inter-American Court of Human Rights and the Mobilisation of Parliaments' in Saul, Follesdal and Ulfstein (n 4) 248, 257.

allegedly replaced the outcome of national democratic deliberation with its own value judgement.[117]

However, through the lens of the separation of powers in a globalised democratic society, the IACtHR's approach is justified as it precisely set 'bounds' to national deliberations per the outcome of international deliberations.[118] Given that amnesty laws had been consistently declared unlawful by the IACtHR and such judgments had been generally accepted by domestic courts of Member States citing one another,[119] the mere existence of a national deliberation on the matter was insufficient for the IACtHR to accord deference unless the national deliberation was persuasively shown to be 'bounded' – based on and within the standards embodied in ACHR texts and the consensus among Member States.[120] As Rene Urueña noted, previous studies' criticism on the anti-democratic nature of the *Gelman* judgment 'is too reductive' as it focuses 'solely on national electoral democracy'.[121] He posits that the *Gelman* judgment instead highlights the IACtHR's 'pivotal role as key promoter of a *regional* democracy, that complements and reinforces national democracies'.[122] This book's theory of two-tiered bounded deliberative democracy precisely incarnates what he conceived as regional democracy.

4.1.2.3. *Review of National Administrative Organs*

The IACtHR also reviews the quality of administrative decision-making processes. In *Granier v Venezuela* (2015), concerning telecommunication authorities' refusal to renew broadcasting licences, after highlighting the need for a clear and precise procedure and objective criteria,[123] the IACtHR determined that the administrative authorities' failure to follow such procedures demonstrated that their refusal was based on illegitimate rather than technical grounds.[124]

In the context of the protection of indigenous people's right to communal property under Article 21 ACHR, the IACtHR has consistently required administrative authorities to fulfil procedural standards, including the effective

[117] R Gargarella, 'Democracy and Rights in *Gelman v. Uruguay*' (2015) 109 *AJIL Unbound* 115, 119; LF Mex Ávila, 'Caso "Gelman vs Uruguay": Una Revisión bajo la Idea de Razón Pública de John Rawls' (2020) 42 *Andamios* 167.

[118] See L Lixinski, 'The Inter-American Court of Human Rights' Tentative Search for Latin American Consensus' in Kapotas and Tzevelekos (n 85) 337, 354.

[119] *Gelman v Uruguay* (n 115) paras 215–29.

[120] *cf* N Tsereteli, 'Emerging Doctrine of Deference of the Inter-American Court of Human Rights?' (2016) 20 *IJHR* 1097, 1106.

[121] R Urueña, 'The Democracy We Want: Standards of Review and Democratic Embeddedness at the Inter-American Court of Human Rights' in H Ruiz Fabri et al (eds), *International Judicial Legitimacy: New Voices and Approaches* (Nomos 2020) 227, 246.

[122] ibid 247.

[123] *Granier et al (Radio Caracas Television) v Venezuela*, IACtHR, Series C No 293, Preliminary Objections, Merits, Reparations and Costs (22 June 2015) para 171.

[124] ibid para 252.

participation of and informed consultation with the community concerned in conformity with their customs and traditions, and the prior environmental and social impact assessment.[125] The IACtHR has also referred to Article 23(1) ACHR (right to take part in the conduct of public affairs) as one of the bases of the obligation to ensure the participation of indigenous people in decision-making affecting them.[126] The IACtHR later extended these procedural standards beyond the rights of indigenous people.[127] In Advisory Opinion OC-23/17, concerning the environment and human rights in 2017, the IACtHR developed the concept of 'procedural obligations', including the 'obligation to ensure the participation of persons subject to their jurisdiction in decision-making and policies that could affect the environment, without discrimination and in a fair, significant and transparent manner' and the obligation to ensure access to necessary information in advance.[128] Moreover, the IACtHR stated, albeit in a recommendatory tone, that as part of the obligation of prevention, an environmental impact assessment should be conducted with the participation of interested parties.[129] Nevertheless, unlike the ECtHR (see section 4.1.1.3), the IACtHR currently treats these procedural criteria simply as additional to, and not as a factor tightening or loosening, the substantive criteria. From the perspective of the separation of powers in a globalised democratic society model, the IACtHR should consider applying different levels of deference depending on compliance with procedural criteria by the administrative organs concerned or loosening its review on the substantive merits of the case in return for a vigorous procedural review.

4.1.2.4. Setting Bounds on National Deliberations

The IACtHR also relies on consensus in its interpretation, although less consistently than the ECtHR does.[130] Compared with the ECtHR, the IACtHR's approach to consensus has two distinct features. First, the IACtHR tends to rely more frequently on documents and materials at the universal level than those at the regional level,[131] thereby supplementing the lack of 'bounds' at the

[125] *Saramaka People v Suriname*, IACtHR, Series C No 172, Preliminary Objections, Merits, Reparations and Costs (28 November 2007) paras 129 and 133.

[126] *Kaliña and Lokono Peoples v Suriname*, IACtHR, Series C No 309, Merits, Reparations and Costs (25 November 2015) para 196.

[127] *La Oroya Population v Peru*, IACtHR, Series C No 511, Preliminary Objections, Merits, Reparations and Costs (27 November 2023) paras 256–61.

[128] *The Environment and Human Rights*, IACtHR, Series A No 23, Advisory Opinion OC-23/17 (15 November 2017) para 231.

[129] ibid paras 166–68.

[130] See generally Lixinski (n 118).

[131] GL Neuman, 'Import, Export, and Regional Consent in the Inter-American Court of Human Rights' (2008) 19 *European Journal of International Law* 101, 107; M de Pauw, 'The Inter-American Court of Human Rights and the Interpretive Method of External Referencing: Regional Consensus v. Universality' in Y Haeck, O Ruiz-Chiriboga and C Burbano Herrera, *The Inter-American Court of Human Rights: Theory and Practice, Present and Future* (Intersentia 2015) 3.

inter-American level with 'bounds' at the universal level. In *Atala Riffo and Daughters v Chile* (2012), concerning the denial of the right of custody based on sexual orientation, Chile argued that sexual orientation is not a suspect category, as little consensus on the matter exists at the inter-American level.[132] However, the IACtHR held that:

> [T]he alleged lack of consensus in some countries regarding full respect for the rights of sexual minorities cannot be considered a valid argument to deny or restrict their human rights … The fact that … it is not necessarily a matter of consensus, cannot lead this Court to abstain from issuing a decision.[133]

Instead of relying on 'regional' consensus, the IACtHR carefully examined the consensus at the universal level, including the UN General Assembly Resolution titled 'Declaration on Human Rights, Sexual Orientation, and Gender Identity' in 2008, to develop an evolutive interpretation and hold that sexual orientation is included in the suspect categories of discrimination under Article 1(1) ACHR.[134] Tainá Garcia Maia called this approach 'internationalized consensus', as opposed to regional consensus.[135] According to Gerald Neuman, the IACtHR relies more heavily on consensus at the universal level than at the regional level because the comparative prevalence of systematic and serious human rights abuses in Latin American countries meant that reliance on their national practices would risk the adoption of very low targets.[136] In addition, unlike the Council of Europe and the EU, the OAS has not been active in elaborating human rights standards.[137]

Second, compared with the ECtHR, which has placed a relatively high weight on the level of conversion among legislation and jurisprudence of Member States when ascertaining European consensus, the IACtHR tends to accord a greater weight on soft law documents adopted at the universal and regional levels and the jurisprudence of other human rights expert bodies and courts[138] under the concept of 'corpus juris'.[139] For example, in *Claude-Reyes et al v Chile* (2006),

[132] *Atala Riffo and Daughters v Chile*, Series C No 239, IACtHR, Merits, Reparations and Costs (24 February 2012) para 75.

[133] ibid para 92.

[134] *Atala Riffo and Daughters v Chile* (n 132) paras 87–90.

[135] T Garcia Maia, 'Challenging the Use of External Sources by the Inter-American Court of Human Rights' (2023) 72 *ICLQ* 977, 999. See also Y Negishi, *Conventionality Control of Domestic Law: Constitutionalised International Adjudication and Internationalised Constitutional Adjudication* (Nomos 2022) 56.

[136] Neuman (n 131) 107.

[137] ibid.

[138] A Yoshida, 'Jinken jouyaku no hatten-teki kaishaku ni okeru konsensasu no yakuwari (2) [The Role of Consensus in the Evolutive Interpretation of Human Rights Treaties (2)]' (2021) 72 *Waseda Law Journal* 89, 91–92. The IACtHR does cite national practices and jurisprudences, but in a selective rather than comprehensive manner. See Tsereteli (n 120) 1101.

[139] P Contreras, 'Notas sobre el corpus juris interamericano' in H Nogueira and G Aguilar (eds), *Control de Convencionalidad, Corpus Iuris y Ius Commune Interamericano* (Editorial Triángulo 2017) 145.

where the IACtHR examined whether Article 13 included the right to access state-held information, the IACtHR relied on the 'regional consensus' reflected in OAS General Assembly Resolutions, along with the UDHR and ICCPR, other treaties, and declarations and recommendations at the universal and European levels, to answer in the positive.[140] This approach to consensus by the IACtHR, as with that of the HRC (see section 4.1.3.4), appears more consistent with the two-tiered bounded deliberative democracy theory than the ECtHR's and may therefore offer a useful lesson for the ECtHR. This is because treaties, resolutions and declarations tend to reflect the outcome of international deliberations whereas the simple counting of Member States' practices would risk upholding the aggregative democracy as opposed to deliberative democracy.[141]

4.1.3. The UN Human Rights Committee

The HRC has also shown a tendency consistent with the separation of powers in a globalised democratic society model, especially regarding national courts and administrative organs. However, it is generally reluctant to review the decision-making processes of national parliaments. In setting bounds on national deliberations, the production of General Comments offers the HRC unique opportunities to provide a forum for inclusive and participatory international deliberations.

4.1.3.1. Review of National Courts

Since the 2000s, the HRC has ascribed a special role to national courts. It has consistently asserted that 'it is generally for the courts of the States parties to the Covenant to evaluate facts and evidence of a particular case, unless it is found that the evaluation was clearly arbitrary or amounted to a denial of justice'.[142] This formulation was first introduced in the context of fact-finding and the interpretation and application of domestic law, especially in the context of Article 14 ICCPR (right to a fair trial).[143] However, the scope of this formulation quickly expanded to include the interpretation and application of the ICCPR in general. For example, in *Rupert Althammer et al v Austria* (2003), concerning the allegedly discriminatory effect of the abolition of household entitlements on retired persons, the national court conducted a comprehensive and thorough

[140] *Claude-Reyes et al v Chile*, IACtHR, Series C No 151, Merits, Reparations and Costs, Judgment (19 September 2006) paras 76–82. See also *The Pacheco Tineo Family v Bolivia*, IACtHR, Series C No 272, Preliminary Objections, Merits, Reparations and Costs (25 November 2013) paras 156–58.

[141] Yoshida (n 80) 170.

[142] See, eg, *Mehrez Ben Abde Hamida v Canada*, HRC, Communication No 1544/2007 (18 March 2010) UN Doc CCPR/C/98/D/1544/2007, para 8.4.

[143] See, eg, *Sergei Anatolievich Cheban et al v Russia*, HRC, Communication No 790/1997 (24 July 2001) UN Doc CCPR/C/72/D/790/1997, para 6.5.

review of the measure in question under the standards of objectiveness and proportionality.[144] Thus, the Committee found without substantive review that 'the measure, as was stressed by the Austrian courts ... was based on objective and reasonable grounds'.[145]

The same approach led the HRC to apply a rigorous review when the domestic court failed to satisfy the required standards. In *Evelio Ramón Giménez v Paraguay* (2018), concerning the prohibition of the author's participation in assemblies for two years, the Committee critically observed that 'neither the appellate court nor the Supreme Court ... expressed any view on the restriction of the author's right of peaceful assembly or on the grounds for its imposition'.[146] Therefore, the Committee held that 'the domestic authorities failed to demonstrate' the necessity and proportionality of the measure.[147]

4.1.3.2. Review of National Parliaments

In *Oulajin and Kaiss v The Netherlands* (1992), concerning the alleged discrimination between foster children and own children in family allowances, the HRC took a deferential approach and found that the distinctions were compatible with Article 26 (prohibition of discrimination).[148] Although the Committee did not provide reasons for the deferential approach, the individual opinions of the four members were telling:

> It is for the legislature of each country, which best knows the socio-economic needs of the society concerned, to try to achieve social justice in the concrete context. Unless the distinctions made are manifestly discriminatory or arbitrary, it is not for the Committee to reevaluate the complex socio-economic data and substitute its judgment for that of the legislatures of States parties.[149]

In *Haraldsson v Iceland* (2007), concerning the differential treatment between the group of fishers under fisheries management legislation, Iceland emphasised the high quality of parliamentary deliberation on the matter.[150] Nevertheless, the HRC conducted a rigorous review on its own and concluded that the distinction between fishers was not based on reasonable grounds.[151] Mr Iwasawa, in his dissenting opinion, observed that '[t]he Committee should be mindful of the limits of its own expertise in reviewing economic policies

[144] *Rupert Althammer et al v Austria*, HRC, Communication No 998/2001 (8 August 2003) UN Doc CCPR/C/78/D/998/2001, para 2.3.

[145] ibid para 10.2.

[146] *Evelio Ramón Giménez v Paraguay*, HRC, Communication No 2372/2014 (25 July 2018) UN Doc CCPR/C/123/D/2372/2014, para 8.4.

[147] ibid para 8.5.

[148] *Oulajin and Kaiss v The Netherlands*, HRC, Communication Nos 406/1990 and 426/1990 (23 October 1992) UN Doc CCPR/C/46/D/406/1990 and 426/1990, para 7.4.

[149] ibid Individual Opinion of Mr Herndl et al, para 3.

[150] *Erlingur Sveinn Haraldsson and Örn Snævar Sveinsson v Iceland*, HRC, Communication No 1306/2004 (24 October 2007) UN Doc CCPR/C/91/D/1306/2004, para 8.7.

[151] ibid paras 10.2–10.4.

which have been formed carefully through democratic processes'.[152] Three other HRC members also pointed out that 'the State party has carried out a careful balance, through its legislative and judicial processes, between the general interest and the interest of the individual fishers', thus criticising the non-deferential approach of the Committee.[153]

However, despite such calls from individual HRC members and increasing reliance by the concerned parties themselves on the quality of parliamentary deliberations,[154] the HRC has been generally reluctant to focus on the quality of parliamentary deliberations. In *Siobhán Whelan v Ireland* (2017), concerning abortion law, the HRC refused to uphold Ireland's argument on the democratic and inclusive decision-making process,[155] stating that 'the legality of a particular conduct or action under domestic law does not mean that it cannot infringe article 7 of the Covenant'.[156] Similarly, in *Sonia Yaker v France* (2018), where Act No 2010-1192 prohibiting the wearing of garments in public places to conceal the face was at issue, France emphasised the following:

> Act No. 2010-1192 was adopted by the National Assembly and the Senate with only one vote against, after a broad democratic debate … [A] parliamentary commission was set up, bringing together elected representatives from across the political spectrum, and proceeded to hear the different views of many persons within civil society, including Muslims and non-Muslims.[157]

Moreover, even the author of the communication discussed the quality of the parliamentary debate.[158] Nevertheless, the HRC failed to assess the decision-making process in the Parliament and conducted an interventionist review.[159] Mr José Manuel Santos Pais critically highlighted this oversight in his dissenting opinion.[160] The HRC's general reluctance to consider the quality of parliamentary debates in these two cases clearly contrasts with the ECtHR's judgments on similar issues in *A, B and C v Ireland*[161] and *SAS v France*.[162] In these cases, the ECtHR found no violation of the relevant rights, given the large margin of appreciation derived from the high quality of parliamentary deliberations.

[152] ibid Dissenting Opinion of Mr Iwasawa, para 3.
[153] ibid Dissenting Opinion of Ms Palm, Mr Shearer and Ms Motoc, para 4.
[154] In addition to the cases cited below, see, eg, *Bikramjit Singh v France*, HRC, Communication No 1852/2008 (1 November 2012) UN Doc CCPR/C/106/D/1852/2008, para 5.2; *Luiz Inácio Lula da Silva v Brazil*, HRC, Communication No 2841/2016, Initial Proceedings (17 March 2022) UN Doc CCPR/C/134/D/2841/2016, para 4.28.
[155] *Siobhán Whelan v Ireland*, HRC, Communication No 2425/2014 (17 March 2017) UN Doc CCPR/C/119/D/2425/2014, para 4.4.
[156] ibid para 7.4.
[157] *Sonia Yaker v France*, HRC, Communication No 2747/2016 (17 July 2018) UN Doc CCPR/C/123/D/2747/2016, para 7.1.
[158] ibid para 3.5.
[159] ibid paras 8.5–8.12.
[160] ibid Dissenting Opinion of Mr. José Manuel Santos Pais, para 8.
[161] *A, B and C v Ireland* (n 40) para 239. Note that while the *Siobhán Whelan* case concerned abortion in cases of non-viable pregnancy, the *A, B and C* case concerned abortion for health and well-being reasons (A and B).
[162] *SAS v France*, ECtHR, App No 43835/11, Merits and Just Satisfaction (1 July 2014) paras 153–55.

Nevertheless, in its concluding observations, the HRC has increasingly recognised the importance of the roles of parliaments in conducting bounded deliberations, and this approach could well be extended to the individual communications procedure. For example, in its concluding observations to Hungary in 2018, the HRC recommended that the state party:

> [S]trengthen its legislative process, especially in relation to laws affecting the enjoyment of human rights, by ensuring that mechanisms are in place to guarantee a transparent, inclusive and participatory process that involves opposition politicians, civil society, other relevant stakeholders and the general public, and provides adequate opportunity and time for the meaningful review and proper debate of legislative proposals and amendments.[163]

Moreover, in the context of Article 27 ICCPR (rights of persons belonging to minorities), the HRC tends to place considerable weight on the parliamentary decision-making process, particularly regarding the representation and participation of minorities.[164] In *Apirana Mahuika et al v New Zealand* (2000), the alleged victims, belonging to the Maori people, claimed a violation of Article 27 by virtue of the Treaty of Waitangi (Fisheries Claims) Settlement Act of 1992. In this case, the HRC commended the decision-making process in the Parliament and confirmed the following:

> [T]he State party undertook a complicated process of consultation in order to secure broad Maori support to a nation-wide settlement and regulation of fishing activities. Maori communities and national Maori organizations were consulted and their proposals did affect the design of the arrangement … In the consultation process, special attention was paid to the cultural and religious significance of fishing for the Maori.[165]

The HRC found no violation of Article 27 without strictly reviewing the substantive aspect of the Act in question. The HRC's heavy focus on participation and consultation, which is unique to Article 27 cases, may have been influenced by the international trends on minority protection[166] reflected in the UN General Assembly Resolution 'Declaration on the Rights of Persons Belonging to National or Ethnic, Religious and Linguistic Minorities' (1992)[167] and the Framework Convention for the Protection of National Minorities (1994).[168] It is yet to be seen whether this approach remains relevant solely to Article 27 or has a wider scope.

[163] HRC, 'Concluding Observations on the Sixth Periodic Report of Hungary' (2018) UN Doc CCPR/C/HUN/CO/6, para 8.

[164] S Wheatley, 'Deliberative Democracy and Minorities' (2003) 14 *EJIL* 507, 523–24.

[165] *Apirana Mahuika et al v New Zealand*, HRC, Communication No 547/1993 (27 October 2000) UN Doc CCPR/C/70/D/547/1993, paras 9.6 and 9.8.

[166] Wheatley (n 164) 523.

[167] UNGA Res 47/135, 'Declaration on the Rights of Persons Belonging to National or Ethnic, Religious and Linguistic Minorities' (18 December 1992) art 2(3).

[168] Framework Convention for the Protection of National Minorities (adopted 1 February 1995, entered into force 1 February 1998) CETS No 157, art 15. See also 'Towards Effective Participation of Minorities', Expert Seminar organised by the European Centre for Minority Issues, Flensburg, Germany, UN Doc E/CN.4/Sub.2/AC.5/1999/WP.4 (1999).

4.1.3.3. Review of National Administrative Organs

The HRC also scrutinises the administrative decision-making processes.[169] In *Mansour Leghaei and Others v Australia* (2015), concerning the Minister of Immigration's refusal to grant the author a permanent visa despite his long-settled family life in Australia, the HRC made the criticism that '[t]he author was never formally provided with the reasons for the refusal'.[170] Thus, without closely examining the substantive aspect of the measure, the HRC held that the measure was arbitrary within the meaning of Article 17 ICCPR (right to privacy, family, and home). Similarly, in *Q v Denmark* (2015), where the Ministry of Refugee, Immigration and Integration Affairs rejected the author's application for Danish naturalisation due to a lack of language proficiency, not allowing an exemption based on his mental and learning disabilities, the HRC observed that '[t]he Ministry was unable to give details about the reasons for the Naturalization Committee's decision' and also criticised the lack of transparency in the procedure.[171] Thus, without examining the substantive merits of the case, the HRC held that the measure in question was not based on reasonable and objective grounds under Article 26.

By contrast, when administrative organs thoroughly examined the relevant factors through transparent procedures, the HRC defers to their decisions. In *MGC v Australia* (2015), concerning the cancellation of author's visa despite the existence of his son born in Australia, given that the Minister for Immigration and the courts carefully considered relevant elements, including the best interests of the child, the HRC observed that 'the author's personal family situation has been thoroughly assessed by the competent authorities'. Thus, without assessing the substantive merits, it held that the measure was not arbitrary under Articles 17 and 23(1) (protection of a family) ICCPR.[172]

4.1.3.4. Setting Bounds on National Deliberations

The HRC has also used a consensus approach, especially to support an evolutive interpretation, thereby setting 'bounds' on national deliberations. In *Judge v Canada* (2003), concerning the extradition by an abolitionist state of a person to a state in which he or she would be executed, the HRC changed its jurisprudence in *Kindler v Canada* (1993), stating that:

> [T]he abovementioned jurisprudence was established some 10 years ago, and … since that time there has been a broadening international consensus in favour of abolition

[169] V Engström, 'Deference and the Human Rights Committee' (2016) 34 *NJHR* 73, 79.

[170] *Mansour Leghaei and Others v Australia*, HRC, Communication No 1937/2010 (26 March 2015) UN Doc CCPR/C/113/D/1937/2010, para 10.4.

[171] *Q v Denmark*, HRC, Communication No 2001/2010 (19 May 2015) UN Doc CCPR/C/113/D/2001/2010, para 7.5.

[172] *MGC v Australia*, HRC, Communication No 1875/2009 (26 March 2015) UN Doc CCPR/C/113/D/1875/2009, para 11.9.

> of the death penalty, and in states which have retained the death penalty, a broadening consensus not to carry it out.[173]

Although the HRC did not elaborate on what materials were used as the basis for ascertaining a 'broadening international consensus', it seems to have considered the adoption of the Second Optional Protocol to the ICCPR, aiming at the abolition of the death penalty in 1998, along with a judgment by the Supreme Court of Canada and state practices cited therein.[174] As Akinaga Yoshida has shown,[175] the HRC has cited various international documents, including other treaties,[176] UN General Assembly Resolutions,[177] and recommendations and guidelines adopted by other human rights treaty organs[178] and expert bodies.[179]

By contrast, the HRC has generally been reluctant to rely on individual states' legislation and jurisprudence. Even when it does, such as in *Jong-Cheol v Republic of Korea* (2005), where the HRC stated 'similar restrictions can be found in many jurisdictions',[180] the HRC does not cite specific legislations. The HRC's prioritisation of international documents, which had been subject to international deliberations, over the convergence of national practices, which may reflect the aggregative form of democracy, is welcoming from the perspective of two-tiered bounded deliberative democracy. Nevertheless, such an approach presumably derives more from practical reasons than from normative reasons, given the special difficulties encountered by the HRC in conducting a comprehensive comparative analysis owing to the lack of resources and broad diversity in the Member States.

As mentioned in Chapter 3, section 3.3.5.3, the production of General Comments offers the HRC unique opportunities to provide a forum for international deliberations. General Comments, which have a legal basis in Article 40(4) ICCPR, are non-binding guidance on specific treaty provisions and/or the relationship between treaty provisions and specific themes.[181] Because of their

[173] *Roger Judge v Canada*, Communication No 829/1998 (5 August 2002) UN Doc CCPR/C/78/D/829/1998, para 10.3.

[174] ibid.

[175] Yoshida (n 138) 98–100.

[176] See, eg, *Mourad Kimouche et al v Algeria*, Communication No 1328/2004 (10 July 2007) UN Doc CCPR/C/90/D/1328/2004, para 7.8.

[177] See, eg, *Tiina Sanila-Aikio v Finland*, HRC, Communication No 2668/2015 (1 November 2018) UN Doc CCPR/C/119/D/2668/2015, paras 6.6, 6.8 and 6.9; *Suleimenov v Kazakhstan*, HRC, Communication No 2146/2012 (21 March 2017) UN Doc CCPR/C/119/D/2146/2012, para 8.7.

[178] See, eg, *NK v The Netherlands*, HRC, Communication No 2326/2013 (18 July 2017) UN Doc CCPR/C/120/D/2326/2013/Rev.1, para 9.10; *Francisco Juan Larrañaga v The Philippines*, HRC, Communication No 1421/2005 (24 July 2006) UN Doc CCPR/C/87/D/1421/2005, para 7.11.

[179] See, eg, *MM v Denmark*, HRC, Communication No 2345/2014 (14 April 2019) UN Doc CCPR/C/125/D/2345/2014, para 8.7.

[180] *Jong-Cheol v Republic of Korea*, HRC, Communication No 968/2001 (27 July 2005) UN Doc CCPR/C/84/D/968/2001, para 8.3. See also *Juliet Joslin et al v New Zealand*, HRC, Communication No 902/1999 (17 July 2002) UN Doc CCPR/C/75/D/902/1999, para 8.2.

[181] Twenty-Seventh Meeting of Chairpersons of the Human Rights Treaty Bodies, 'Consultation Process for the Elaboration of Treaty Body General Comments' (2015) UN Doc HRI/MC/2015/4, para 2.

'general' character – that is, they do not address specific cases or specific states – General Comments possess 'quasi-legislative'[182] and 'law-making'[183] functions, and represent 'a new species of soft law',[184] and thus effectively act as 'bounds' on national deliberations. For example, in *Siobhán Whelan v Ireland* (2017), cited above, the HRC used General Comments Nos 16, 18, 20, and 28 to limit national deliberations on abortion.[185]

In recent years, the HRC has broadly invited submissions from states parties and other actors at various stages of the drafting process of General Comments and ensured the transparency of such participation by publicising stakeholder submissions and records of the HRC's deliberations.[186] For example, in drafting the HRC's General Comment No 37 on Article 21 (right of peaceful assembly), given the advance posting of the draft general comment on the HRC's website, 55 NGOs, 25 states parties, 13 academic institutions/individual experts, 12 NHRIs, nine bodies and experts associated with the UN, and three actors associated with regional organisations and/or courts submitted written comments before the second reading.[187] A comprehensive examination of the summary records of the second reading[188] shows that HRC members made 400 direct references to stakeholder submissions. Of these, 176 came from NGOs, 89 from states parties, 45 from academic institutions or individual experts, 41 from actors associated with the UN and other UN treaty bodies, 39 from actors associated with regional organisations and/or courts, and six from NHRIs. While the traditional rules of treaty interpretation consider states as authentic interpreters,[189] the rapporteur and other members of the HRC did not privilege the views of state parties over those of NGOs and other stakeholders, but treated them as equally contributing to deliberations. For example, in drafting paragraph 48 of General Comment No 37, which concerns the degree to which restrictions on the right of peaceful assembly were justified in the interests of national security, the rapporteur,

[182] T Opsahl, 'The Human Rights Committee' in P Alston (ed), *The United Nations and Human Rights: A Critical Appraisal* (Clarendon Press 1992) 369, 415.

[183] E Klein and D Kretzmer, 'The UN Human Rights Committee: The General Comments: The Evolution of an Autonomous Monitoring Instrument' (2015) 58 *German Yearbook of International Law* 189, 203.

[184] Y Tyagi, *The UN Human Rights Committee: Practice and Procedure* (Cambridge University Press 2011) 301.

[185] *Siobhán Whelan v Ireland* (n 155) paras 7.7 and 7.12 and fns 18 and 19.

[186] Increased participation and transparency in the elaboration process of General Comments are partly the product of reforms led within the framework of the meetings of chairpersons of UN human rights treaty bodies. See Twenty-Seventh Meeting of Chairpersons of the Human Rights Treaty Bodies (n 181) 'E. Elements for Endorsement by the Treaty Body Chairpersons'.

[187] 'Call for Comment: No. 37 on Article 21 of the International Covenant on Civil and Political Rights: Right of Peaceful Assembly' *HRC* (17 September 2020), www.ohchr.org/en/calls-for-input/call-comment-no-37-article-21-international-covenant-civil-and-political-rights.

[188] The 3,707th, 3,710th, 3,711th, 3,712th, 3,713th, 3,714th, 3,715th, 3,716th, 3,717th, 3,718th, 3,719th, 3,720th, 3,721st, 3,722nd, 3,724th, 3,725th, 3,726th, 3,727th, 3,728th, 3,730th, 3,731st and 3733rd meetings were covered.

[189] See art 31(3)(a) and (b) and (4) VCLT.

Mr Heyns, introduced the contradicting views of Russia and the Consortium of Latin American NGOs, and proposed the wording that 'represented [a] middle ground between those two approaches'.[190] Moreover, Article 40(5) ICCPR provides that states parties may submit their observations on General Comments after they are adopted. Famously, the US, the UK and France have made detailed critical observations on General Comment No 24 on reservations.[191] The inclusive participation and thorough deliberations in the elaboration process of General Comments, as well as the formal opportunity for states parties to submit observations after their adoption, have contributed to the higher legitimacy of the General Comments as 'bounds' limiting national deliberations, within the meaning of the two-tiered bounded deliberative democracy.

4.2. HUMAN RIGHTS TREATY ORGANS' PRACTICES IN ORDERING/ RECOMMENDING REMEDIES AND REPARATIONS

After finding a violation of one or more rights enshrined in the respective treaties, regional human rights courts issue orders, and the HRC issues recommendations, concerning remedies and reparations. As shown in Chapter 2, section 2.2, in recent years, individual state organs have become substantial targets for remedial orders. This section shows that such practices tend to conform to the requirements of the separation of powers in a globalised democratic society model. On the one hand, such orders indicate a top-down relationship between treaty organs and state organs, where the former directly impose their demands on specific state organs. On the other hand, treaty organs have increasingly recognised the bottom-up aspect of the relationship by deferring to trustworthy state organs as the primary decision-making forum, thereby endorsing the negative subsidiarity. Treaty organs have also encouraged the adoption of concrete measures through national bounded deliberations, providing elements of 'bounds' as guidance without prescribing specific measures.

4.2.1. The European Court of Human Rights

The ECtHR has issued remedial orders that were substantially addressed to parliaments in the context of the pilot judgment procedure (Chapter 2,

[190] HRC, 129th Session, 3718th mtg (9 July 2020) UN Doc CCPR/C/SR.3718, para 33.

[191] 'Observations of States Parties under Article 40, paragraph 5, of the Covenant: United States of America' and 'Observations of States Parties under Article 40, paragraph 5, of the Covenant: Kingdom of Great Britain and Northern Ireland' in HRC Report (1995) UN Doc A/50/40, 126–134; 'Observations of States Parties under Article 40, Paragraph 5, of the Covenant: France' in HRC Report (1996) UN Doc A/51/40, 104–06.

section 2.2.1). Although the ECtHR's application of the procedure has often been criticised for being an 'ad hoc rather than well-crafted jurisprudential approach',[192] a general tendency can be discerned in its approach in determining whether to apply the pilot judgment procedure. It has considered, in addition to the formal requirement of 'the existence of a structural or systemic problem or other similar dysfunction which has given rise or may give rise to similar applications',[193] whether the parliament can reasonably be expected to act promptly and in good faith. When the ECtHR finds the parliament to be trustworthy, it refrains from applying the pilot judgment procedure, even when the aforementioned criteria are formally met. If it finds otherwise, it applies the procedure and indicates the timing and content of the legislative amendment to the national parliament.[194]

In *Sürmeli v Germany* (2006), the formal criteria for applying the pilot judgment procedure seemed to have been fulfilled, as the violation occurred from a systemic failure in the German legal system to provide adequate redress for the excessive length of civil proceedings. Nevertheless, the ECtHR refrained from applying this procedure because it positively valued the fact that a bill to remedy the violation had been introduced to the Parliament.[195] However, thereafter, the enactment process in the German Parliament made little progress. Thus, the ECtHR initiated the pilot judgment procedure in *Rumpf v Germany* (2010) concerning similar sets of facts to indicate specific measures, criticising the Parliament's 'complete reluctance to resolve the problems at hand in a timely fashion'.[196] In other cases, the ECtHR has also been reluctant to apply the pilot judgment procedure immediately, even when the formal requirements for its application have been met. It applies this procedure only after confirming that the national parliament concerned is unwilling or unable to implement effective measures.[197] For example, in *Greens and MT v UK* (2010), the ECtHR applied the pilot judgment procedure and ordered the amendment of the legislation concerned only after confirming that the UK Parliament had been unwilling to comply with the *Hirst (No 2)* (2005) judgment and 'the lengthy delay' has occurred in the legislative process.[198]

[192] D Kurban, 'Forsaking Individual Justice: The Implications of the European Court of Human Rights' Pilot Judgment Procedure for Victims of Gross and Systematic Violations' (2016) 16 *HRLR* 731, 739.

[193] Rule 61 (1) of the Rules of Court of the ECtHR.

[194] *cf* N Tsereteli, 'The Role of the European Court of Human Rights in Facilitating Legislative Change in Cases of Long-Term Delays in Implementation' in Saul, Follesdal and Ulfstein (n 4) 223, 239.

[195] *Sürmeli v Germany*, ECtHR, App No 75529/01, Merits and Just Satisfaction (8 June 2006) paras 138–39.

[196] *Rumpf v Germany*, ECtHR, App No 46344/06, Merits and Just Satisfaction (2 September 2010) para 72.

[197] L Cornejo Chavez, 'New Remedial Responses in the Practice of Regional Human Rights Courts: Purposes beyond Compensation' (2017) 15 *I-CON* 372, 384.

[198] *Greens and MT v UK*, ECtHR, App Nos 60041/08 and 60054/08, Merits and Just Satisfaction (23 November 2010) paras 112 and 115.

By contrast, when the parliament concerned clearly cannot be expected to act effectively, the ECtHR may issue pilot judgments immediately. In *Broniowski v Poland* (2004), the contested acts and omissions of the national Parliament were taken against the judgment of the Polish Constitutional Court, indicating that the Parliament could not reasonably be expected to adopt remedial measures on its own initiative. Therefore, the ECtHR initiated the pilot judgment procedure from first sight by relying largely on the judgment of the Constitutional Court. 'Endorsing [the Polish courts'] assessment', the ECtHR found a systemic nature of the problem.[199]

When indicating specific measures in pilot judgments, the ECtHR has been keen to promote parliamentary deliberation.[200] In *Manushaqe Puto and Others v Albania* (2012), it indicated that the 'decision-making process for the type of compensation to be awarded requires the utmost transparency and efficiency'[201] and that 'wide public discussions' on the matter are necessary.[202]

As for the ECtHR's relationship with national courts, its jurisprudence concerning ordering the re-opening of national proceedings has not yet been fully consolidated.[203] Nevertheless, signs that the ECtHR is willing to defer to a trustworthy national court regarding its need for re-opening the proceedings are emerging. In *Moreira Ferreira v Portugal* (2011), after finding a violation of Article 6(1) ECHR (right to a fair trial), the ECtHR indicated that a retrial would constitute an appropriate remedy in principle.[204] However, when the applicant later relied on this ECtHR judgment to request a retrial, the Supreme Court dismissed the request, and the applicant lodged a new complaint with the ECtHR, claiming that the dismissal violated Article 6(1). Given that the Supreme Court analysed the content of the 2011 ECtHR judgment in good faith, the ECtHR relied on the principle of subsidiarity and held that the Supreme Court's refusal was not arbitrary.[205] These interactions between the ECtHR and Portugal's national courts have been positively valued as 'open[ing] up an entirely new path of a *sensu stricto* judicial dialogue'.[206]

[199] *Broniowski v Poland*, ECtHR, App No 31443/96, Merits (22 June 2004) para 189.

[200] *cf* M Fyrnys, 'Expanding Competences by Judicial Lawmaking: The Pilot Judgment Procedure of the European Court of Human Rights' in A von Bogdandy and I Venzke (eds), *International Judicial Lawmaking: On Public Authority and Democratic Legitimation in Global Governance* (Springer 2011) 329, 357–58.

[201] *Manushaqe Puto v Albania*, ECtHR, App Nos 604/07, 43628/07, 46684/07 and 34770/09, Merits and Just Satisfaction (31 July 2012) para 114.

[202] ibid para 118.

[203] A Donald and AK Speck, 'The European Court of Human Rights' Remedial Practice and its Impact on the Execution of Judgments' (2019) 19 *HRLR* 83, 114–15.

[204] *Moreira Ferreira v Portugal*, ECtHR, App No 19808/08, Merits and Just Satisfaction (5 July 2011) para 41.

[205] *Moreira Ferreira v Portugal (No 2)*, ECtHR, App No 19867/12, Merits and Just Satisfaction (11 July 2017) para 98.

[206] M Wąsek-Wiaderek, 'Advisory Opinions of the European Court of Human Rights: Do National Judges Really Need This New Forum of Dialogue?' in PP de Albuquerque and K Wojtyczek (eds), *Judicial Power in a Globalized World* (Springer 2019) 637, 642.

4.2.2. The Inter-American Court of Human Rights

Contrary to the ECHR's practice, since around 2000, the IACtHR has ordered concrete measures addressing specific organs in a categorical manner without examining whether a particular state organ is expected to act responsibly in the individual cases at hand. In addition, the IACtHR's orders often included more than what was strictly necessary for restitution.[207] Undoubtedly, a principal factor that enabled the IACtHR's interventionist approach is the wording of Article 63(1) ACHR, which authorises it to take wider measures along with financial compensation (see Chapter 2, section 2.2.2).[208] At the same time, an equally important factor is that state organs in many ACHR Member States lack the willingness and ability to take reparation measures on their own.[209]

However, given the progress of democratisation in Member States, the IACtHR has recently refined its approach to reparation by recognising the roles of national courts and parliaments as the primary decision-makers, to the extent that some authors consider that the traditionally different approaches of the ECtHR and the IACtHR to reparations are now converging.[210] In *Manuel Cepeda Vargas v Colombia* (2011), the IACtHR held, based on its 'subsidiary and complementary competence', that the domestic court has awarded compensation to the victims through processes that meet the 'criteria of objectivity, reasonableness and effectiveness'.[211] Thus, it refrained from ordering additional reparations even though the concrete criteria applied by the domestic court for calculation differed from the IACtHR's precedent.[212]

In 2018, the IACtHR examined whether the presidential pardon on humanitarian grounds of former Peruvian President Alberto Fujimori, who had been convicted and imprisoned for his role in crimes against humanity, was compatible with the obligation to investigate, prosecute and punish, as established in the *Barrios Altos* and *La Cantuta* judgments. Despite the submissions of petitioners and the IACmHR calling for the IACtHR to revoke the pardon, the IACtHR referred to the doctrine of conventionality control and decided that it was the Peruvian courts that should address the matter, considering the ACHR and

[207] Cornejo Chavez (n 197) 389.

[208] *Baena-Ricardo et al v Panama*, IACtHR, Series C No 104, Competence (28 November 2003) para 64.

[209] Cornejo Chavez (n 197) 390–91.

[210] C Binder, 'Die Zukunft des regionalen Menschenrechtsschutzes: Europa und Amerika – oder: Subsidiarität revisited' (2022) 77 *Zeitschrift fur Offentliches Recht* 5, 22.

[211] *Manuel Cepeda Vargas v Colombia*, IACtHR, Series C No 213, Preliminary Objections, Merits, Reparations and Costs (26 May 2010) para 246. For discussions on this formula, see C Sandoval, 'Two Steps Forward, One Step Back: Reflections on the Jurisprudential Turn of the Inter-American Court of Human Rights on Domestic Reparation Programmes' (2018) 22 *IJHR* 1192, 1201–02.

[212] *Manuel Cepeda Vargas v Colombia* (n 211) Partially Dissenting Opinion of Judge Pérez Pérez, para 8.

IACtHR's order.[213] The IACtHR then clarified the multiple factors that national courts should consider, including the person's health condition, compensation paid to the victims, the person's recognition of the seriousness of the crimes, his rehabilitation and the impact that his release could have on society and the victims.[214] As Jorge Contesse describes, this order shows 'a novel form of engagement' of the IACtHR with national courts by giving them 'constrained deference' under the principle of subsidiarity.[215] Unfortunately, the IACtHR's invitation for principled dialogue was not well received by the Peruvian Constitutional Court, which, in March 2022, reinstated the pardon and ordered the release of Fujimori while failing to examine many of the factors indicated by the IACtHR.[216] Thus, criticising the Constitutional Court's failure to engage in conventionality control for disregarding those factors,[217] in April 2022 the IACtHR ordered the state not to execute the Constitutional Court's judgment.

In *Fontevecchia and D'Amico v Argentina* (2011), the IACtHR found that orders by the Supreme Court of Argentina of monetary compensation for publishing articles and photographs on a public official and his family violated Article 13 ACHR. The IACtHR then ordered the state to 'set aside [*dejar sin efecto*] the civil sentence … as well as all of its consequences'.[218] In 2017, the Supreme Court refused to execute this reparation order after closely examining the order in light of the ACHR, general international law and the Constitution, and criticising the IACtHR for disregarding the principles of the fourth instance and subsidiarity.[219] Given this reasoned and principled disagreement expressed by the Supreme Court, the IACtHR took a deferential approach in its order on monitoring compliance.[220] It clarified that the term 'dejar sin efecto' does not necessarily mean nullifying the civil sentence and that national courts have various means to implement the order, such as removing the case from the Supreme Court's website or inserting some type of annotation indicating

[213] *Barrios Altos and La Cantuta v Peru*, IACtHR, Resolution on Monitoring Compliance with Judgment (30 May 2018) paras 64–66.

[214] ibid para 57.

[215] J Contesse, 'International Decisions: Case of *Barrios Altos and La Cantuta v. Peru*' (2019) 113 *AJIL* 568, 573–74.

[216] Constitutional Court, *Alberto Fujimori*, No 02010-2020-PHC/TC (17 March 2022) (Peru).

[217] *Barrios Altos and La Cantuta v Peru*, IACtHR, Resolution on Provisional Measures and Monitoring Compliance with Judgment (7 April 2022) para 40.

[218] *Fontevecchia and D'Amico v Argentina*, IACtHR, Series C No 238, Merits, Reparations, and Costs (29 November 2011) operative para 2 (reparation).

[219] Supreme Court, *Ministerio de Relaciones Exteriores y Culto s/ informe sentencia dictada en el caso 'Fontevecchia y D'Amico vs. Argentina' por la Corte Interamericana de Derechos Humanos*, CSJ 368/1998 (34-M)/CS1 (14 February 2017) (Argentina).

[220] Marisa Iglesias Vila argues that the Supreme Court of Argentina should have engaged in a more serious examination such as considering alternative remedies. She thus characterises this series of interaction as 'successful statist resistance' instead of 'an effective institutional dialogue'. See M Iglesias Vila, 'The Conventionality Control and the Fontevecchia Case: Is the Margin of Appreciation the Panacea?' (2022) 46 *Revus*, paras 31–35.

that the sentence was declared in violation of the ACHR.[221] The Supreme Court reacted immediately by issuing a resolution stating that the judgment should be recorded with a caption stating that it was declared incompatible with the ACHR by the IACtHR.[222] Thus, in 2020, the IACtHR held that Argentina has complied with the obligation to 'set aside [*dejar sin efecto*] the civil sentence … as well as all of its consequences'.[223] This series of exchanges 'illustrates how an initial act of noncompliance may be only the starting point of a wider process' of principled interactions between the IACtHR and national courts.[224]

Signs of a new approach to national parliaments are also emerging. In 2019, the IACtHR received a request for provisional measures to suspend the Legislative Assembly of El Salvador's processing of the bill on the National Reconciliation Law, which would allegedly negatively affect the execution of the reparation order in 2012's *Massacres of El Mozote and Nearby Places* judgment. However, the IACtHR refrained from ordering a provisional measure, ascribing great weight to the fact that the Legislative Assembly intended to ensure the participation of different social sectors in the deliberations and seek a wide consensus among them.[225] This demonstrates the IACtHR's willingness to respect and promote the deliberations of the national parliament.

4.2.3. The UN Human Rights Committee

The HRC has also shown signs of respecting the primary decision-making competence of national courts on remedial measures, on the condition that the latter conduct a comprehensive and thorough review under ICCPR-compatible standards and with the guarantee of procedural fairness. In *Mehrez Ben Abde Hamida v Canada* (2010), the Immigration and Refugee Board rejected the author's asylum application mainly because the protection under the Refugee Convention did not apply to him by virtue of his complicity in crimes against humanity. The Federal Court upheld this decision. When examining whether his expulsion to Tunisia would violate his rights under the ICCPR, the Committee first endorsed the principle that 'it is generally for the courts of the States parties to the Covenant to evaluate facts and evidence of a particular case'.[226] However,

[221] *Fontevecchia and D'Amico v Argentina*, IACtHR, Order on Monitoring Compliance with Judgment (18 October 2017) paras 20–21.

[222] Supreme Court, Resolution 4015/17 (5 December 2017) (Argentina), cited in *Fontevecchia and D'Amico v Argentina*, IACtHR, Order on Monitoring Compliance with Judgment (11 March 2020) para 7.

[223] *Fontevecchia and D'Amico v Argentina* (2020) (n 222) operative para 1.

[224] A von Bogdandy and R Urueña, 'International Transformative Constitutionalism in Latin America' (2020) 114 *AJIL* 403, 427–28.

[225] *Massacres of El Mozote and Surrounding Areas v El Salvador*, IACtHR, Resolution on Provisional Measures and Monitoring Compliance with Judgment (3 September 2019) paras 23 and 41.

[226] *Mehrez Ben Abde Hamida v Canada* (n 142) para 8.4.

the Committee pointed out that the administrative bodies and domestic courts solely focused on the applicability of the Refugee Convention and gave 'inadequate consideration' to his rights under the ICCPR.[227] Therefore, the HRC conducted its own assessment of the evidence and concluded that if enforced, the expulsion of the author would violate Article 7 (prohibition of torture and other treatments or punishments).[228] Nonetheless, the Committee did not recommend the expulsion order to be revoked and, instead, deferred the decision to the domestic courts with a recommendation for 'a full reconsideration of his expulsion order, taking into account the State party's obligations under the Covenant'.[229] After this View was issued, the administrative bodies and domestic courts conducted a review and fully considered relevant factors such as the author's marriage to a Canadian citizen and the human rights situation in Tunisia, considering ICCPR standards.[230] Although they eventually upheld the expulsion order, in the follow-up procedure, the HRC valued this measure positively with an A rank.[231]

4.3. HUMAN RIGHTS TREATY ORGANS' PRACTICES IN RELYING ON NATIONAL HUMAN RIGHTS INSTITUTIONS' SUBMISSIONS TO ASSESS, SUPPLEMENT AND PROMOTE NATIONAL DELIBERATIONS

As discussed in Chapter 3, section 3.3.4, under the separation of powers in a globalised democratic society model, NHRIs have a duty to become a bridge between national formal and informal public spheres and make such deliberations 'bounded'. They must also provide inputs regarding the broader background and national contexts of the issues at hand to treaty organs, enabling them to assess national deliberations and to supplement those deliberations when necessary. This section probes the extent to which treaty organs respect and promote such duties.

4.3.1. The European Court of Human Rights

The ECtHR has widely admitted third-party submissions from NHRIs and has not hesitated to cite them. For instance, in *Khan v France* (2019), concerning the living conditions of unaccompanied foreign minors, France's Commission nationale consultative des droits de l'homme (CNCDH) made detailed

[227] ibid para 8.5.
[228] ibid para 8.7.
[229] ibid para 10.
[230] HRC, 'Follow-up Progress Report on Individual Communications Adopted by the Committee at its 116th Session' (2016) UN Doc CCPR/C/116/3, 7–8.
[231] ibid 8.

submissions based on its previous opinions and statements on the issue.[232] The ECtHR repeatedly cited these opinions and statements when determining the general situation concerning care for unaccompanied foreign minors and the effectiveness of the government's measures.[233] Even in cases where the ECtHR does not expressly cite NHRIs' submissions, they have assisted the ECtHR in assessing national deliberations and conducting deliberations on its own by raising issues and perspectives 'not addressed by either party',[234] including wider social background and structural problems surrounding the case.[235] Antoine Buyse calls this role 'factual contextualisation'.[236] For example, in *O'Keeffe v Ireland* (2014), the Irish Human Rights Commission provided a detailed explanation of Ireland's educational system and its operations, the proper understanding of which was crucial for assessing the extent of the state's positive obligation. It persuasively pointed out the fact, which neither party referred to, that the Act in question rendered parents subject to criminal proceedings and other sanctions if they failed to ensure that their children attended school.[237] Such information has presumably assisted the ECtHR to conclude that 'the applicant had no "realistic and acceptable alternative" other than attendance'.[238]

The NHRIs' submissions have contributed to thorough deliberations in the ECtHR by inducing parties to rebut and elaborate further. For example, in *Donohoe v Ireland* (2013), concerning the fairness of the applicant's trial and conviction before the Special Criminal Court that are partly based on confidential information, the Irish Human Rights Commission made a third-party submission. It explained the background, legal basis and features of the Special Criminal Court system, and domestic jurisprudence and practice regarding convictions based on belief evidence.[239] The respondent government 'responded

[232] *Khan v France*, ECtHR, App No 12267/16, Merits and Just Satisfaction (28 February 2019) paras 60–62.

[233] ibid paras 79, 82, 83, and 86. See also *Hakobyan and Others v Armenia*, ECtHR, App No 34320/04, Merits and Just Satisfaction (10 April 2012) paras 90 and 103.

[234] *McCaughey and Others v UK*, ECtHR, App No 43098/09, Merits and Just Satisfaction (16 July 2013) para 119.

[235] B Dickson, 'The Contribution of Human Rights Commissions to the Protection of Human Rights' [2003] *Public Law* 272, 282; LA Sicilianos, 'La tierce intervention devant la Cour européenne des droits de l'homme' in H Ruiz-Fabri and JM Sorel (eds), *Le tiers à l'instance devant les juridictions internationales* (Pedone 2005) 123, 137. De Beco suggests that given their advantage in grasping the overall picture of national structural problems, NHRIs should play greater roles in pilot judgments. See G de Beco, 'La contribution des institutions nationales des droits de l'homme au renforcement de l'efficacité de la Court européenne des droits de l'homme' (2009) 77 *Revue Trimestrielle des Droits de l'Homme* 165, 178.

[236] A Buyse, 'The Court's Ears and Arms: National Human Rights Institutions and the European Court of Human Rights' in J Wouters and K Meuwissen (eds), *National Human Rights Institutions in Europe: Comparative, European and International Perspectives* (Intersentia 2013) 173, 179.

[237] Irish Human Rights Commission, 'Amicus Brief in the European Court of Human Rights: Application No. 35810/09' (30 September 2011) paras 26–27.

[238] *O'Keeffe v Ireland*, ECtHR, App No 35810/09, Merits and Just Satisfaction (28 January 2014) para 151.

[239] *Donohoe v Ireland*, ECtHR, App No 19165/08, Merits and Just Satisfaction (12 December 2013) paras 70–72.

in detail to the [Irish Human Rights Commission's] submissions'.[240] It discussed whether the non-jury character of the Special Criminal Court was pertinent to the protection of the applicant's defence rights in this case and stressed the self-imposed restraint exercised by the Special Criminal Court.[241]

The ECtHR has used NHRIs' submissions to give states the opportunity and basis for continued national bounded deliberation after judgment. In *Brannigan and McBride v UK* (1993), while holding that the derogation was valid, as was also held by the submission of the Northern Ireland Standing Advisory Commission on Human Rights,[242] the ECtHR encouraged the UK to take 'a process of continued reflection' and 'permanent review' of the need for emergency measures.[243] Judge Martens, in his concurring opinion, recommended that during the process of continued reflection, the UK should 'consider the advice submitted by [UK's] own Standing Advisory Commission on Human Rights stressing the possibility of introducing some form of judicial review of extended detention'.[244] In *Kelly and Others v UK* (2001), the Northern Ireland Human Rights Commission intervened and 'urged the Court to take the opportunity to give precise guidance as to the form which investigations into the use of lethal force by State agents should take'.[245] Although the ECtHR did not expressly cite this request, it gave detailed guidance on this point in the 'General Principles' section,[246] thereby assisting national authorities to conduct 'bounded' deliberations on the matter after the judgment.

In recent years, European NHRIs have begun to collectively interact with the ECtHR through the European Network of National Human Rights Institutions (ENNHRI, formerly the European Group of NHRIs – see Chapter 2, section 2.4.1.1). In 2008, the legal working group of the European Group of NHRIs began to monitor pending cases before the ECtHR, aiming to make third-party interventions in the Court in appropriate cases. Since its first submission to the ECtHR in *DD v Lithuania*,[247] the European Group (later the ENNHRI) has intervened in numerous cases. The most unique element of these submissions is that they provide extensive materials on comparative law concerning social and normative changes in European societies. For example, in *Strøbye and Rosenlind v Denmark*, concerning the restriction of the right to vote for people under guardianship, the ENNHRI submitted a 12-page report to the ECtHR in 2019, gathering information from 17 member NHRIs concerning

[240] ibid para 64.
[241] ibid.
[242] *Brannigan and McBride v UK*, ECtHR, App Nos 14553/89; 14554/89, Merits and Just Satisfaction (25 May 1993) para 45.
[243] ibid para 54.
[244] ibid Concurring Opinion of Judge Martens, para 1.
[245] *Kelly and Others v UK*, ECtHR, App No 30054/96, Merits and Just Satisfaction (4 May 2001) para 90.
[246] ibid paras 95–98.
[247] *DD v Lithuania*, ECtHR, App No 13469/06, Merits and Just Satisfaction (14 February 2012) para 113.

their domestic legislation and relevant practices and analysing them.[248] This role to provide comparative law data, which Buyse calls 'legal contextualisation',[249] is best undertaken by a group of NHRIs rather than a single NHRI. As ENNHRI's submissions reflect the outcome of a thorough consultation process among its member NHRIs,[250] they help fill the gap in the ECtHR's European consensus approach – namely, its heavy reliance on the simple counting of states (see section 4.1.1.4) – and contribute to international deliberations at the ECtHR.

Nevertheless, whether and to what extent the ECtHR recognises the unique roles of NHRIs, especially those accredited with A-status, as distinct from those of NGOs (see Chapter 3, section 3.3.4) are undetermined. The ECtHR sometimes conflates NHRIs with NGOs,[251] and often cites NHRIs together with NGOs and other sources.[252] Moreover, when admitting NHRIs' submissions, the ECtHR is indifferent as to whether the NHRI has been accredited by the GANHRI with an A-status. The ECtHR should consider reforming its procedure and practice to further recognise and promote the unique role of A-status NHRIs and ENNHRI, for example, by providing a distinct procedure for their participation.

4.3.2. The Inter-American Court of Human Rights

As introduced in Chapter 2, section 2.4.1.2, the IACtHR has also welcomed NHRIs' submissions as amicus curiae, considering them 'useful',[253] and has often invited NHRIs as expert witnesses. It occasionally cites NHRIs' submissions. For example, in *Four Ngöbe Indigenous Communities and Their Members v Panama*, when examining the IACmHR's request for provisional measures, the IACtHR requested that Panama's Defensoría del Pueblo submit a report on the potential impact of the construction of the Chan-75 hydroelectric project on the rights of the Ngöbe indigenous communities and on the consultation processes that have been carried out.[254] The IACtHR referred to the Defensoría del Pueblo's report at length,

[248] ENNHRI, 'Written Observations in Applications Nos. 25802/18 and 27338/18 Strøbye v. Denmark and Rosenlind v. Denmark' (12 August 2019) 6–10.

[249] Buyse (n 236) 179.

[250] ENNHRI, *Procedure for Third Party Interventions before the European Court of Human Rights* (2020) 4–5. For the function of the ENNHRI as a forum of European-level deliberations, see K Meuwissen, 'European National Human Rights Institutions as Multi-layered Actors Characteristics, Challenges and Opportunities' in S Lopez Escarcena et al (eds), *National Human Rights Institutions in Europe and Latin America: International and Comparative Perspectives* (Intersentia 2024) 29, 37.

[251] *Strøbye and Rosenlind v Denmark*, ECtHR, App Nos 25802/18 and 27338/18, Merits and Just Satisfaction (2 February 2021) para 90.

[252] See, eg, *MSS v Belgium and Greece*, ECtHR, App No 30696/09, Merits and Just Satisfaction (21 January 2011) para 348; *CN v UK*, ECtHR, App No 4239/08, Merits and Just Satisfaction (13 November 2012) para 80.

[253] See, eg, *Acevedo-Jaramillo et al v Peru*, IACtHR, Series C No 144, Preliminary Objections, Merits, Reparations and Costs (7 February 2006) para 197.

[254] *Four Ngöbe Indigenous Communities and Their Members*, IACtHR, Order on Request for Provisional Measures (28 May 2010) para 6.

particularly regarding the satisfactory nature of the national consultation process on the issue.[255] It concluded that the IACmHR 'fail[ed] to demonstrate prima facie the situation of extreme gravity and urgency of preventing irreparable damage',[256] partly because '[t]he Commission did not develop specific arguments on the report by [the Defensoría del Pueblo]'.[257] This case demonstrates how NHRIs' participation may place the burden of justification on relevant interlocutors, thereby enhancing the quality of deliberations at the IACtHR.

4.3.3. The UN Human Rights Committee

As introduced in Chapter 2, section 2.4.1.3, UN human rights treaty bodies, including the HRC, have increasingly permitted and encouraged NHRIs to participate in their activities, especially in state reporting procedures. HRC members have frequently relied on NHRIs' submissions when considering state reports. For example, in examining the fifth periodic report of Georgia in 2022, an HRC member pointed out that '[a]lthough the Office of the Public Defender had called for a reform of the selection process for judges in May 2021, the authority to select them still remained with influential judges'.[258] She then asked the delegation 'what action would be taken to prevent the misuse of such authority'.[259] As some other treaty bodies, such as the CEDAW and the CERD, permit A-status NHRIs to make speeches in the examination of state reports, in addition to the submission of written reports, such opportunities have further promoted treaty body members to pay attention to NHRIs' information and views. For example, in the CEDAW's consideration of Gambia's report in its 83rd Session, a CEDAW member expressly cited the speech of Gambia's NHRI representative[260] in her question.[261]

The HRC has also incorporated NHRIs' submissions into its recommendations.[262] For example, in its concluding observations on the fifth periodic report of the Philippines, the HRC recommended that the state party '[s]trengthen the legal framework on climate change, including by implementing the recommendations of the Commission on Human Rights contained in the report of the National Inquiry on Climate Change'.[263] An empirical study

[255] ibid 'Considering' para 7.
[256] ibid 'Considering' para 12.
[257] ibid 'Considering' para 11(g).
[258] HRC, 135th Session, 3,889th mtg (6 July 2022) UN Doc CCPR/C/SR.3889, para 14.
[259] ibid.
[260] CEDAW, 83rd Session, 1,925th mtg (20 October 2022) UN Doc CEDAW/C/SR.1925, paras 14–18 (especially para 18).
[261] CEDAW, 83rd Session, 1,926th mtg (20 October 2022) UN Doc CEDAW/C/SR.1926, para 24.
[262] As early as 2003, Brice Dickson, then chief commissioner of the Northern Ireland Commission, stated that 'in each case we feel that [Concluding Observations were] influenced by the points we made'. Dickson (n 235) 277.
[263] HRC, 'Concluding Observations on the Fifth Periodic Report of the Philippines' (2022) UN Doc CCPR/C/PHL/CO/5, para 24 (a).

recently conducted by Domenico Zipoli indicated that treaty bodies are influenced by NHRIs' submissions in numerous cases, although those treaty bodies do not explicitly refer to such submissions.[264]

Moreover, the HRC has recommended that states parties conduct participatory consultations with NHRIs when reviewing and amending legislation. For example, in the aforementioned concluding observations on the Philippines, the HRC recommended that the state party review and amend the Anti-Terrorism Act, 'ensur[ing] a participatory consultations process with relevant stakeholders, including the Commission on Human Rights and civil society organizations'.[265]

As mentioned in Chapter 3, section 3.3.5.2, the HRC, in its individual communication procedure, has established a procedure for third-party/amicus curiae submissions, which is open to NHRIs. Although this procedure has rarely been used in practice (for analysis of this problem, see Chapter 3, section 3.3.5.2), the CERD's case of *TBB-Turkish Union in Berlin/Brandenburg v Germany* (2013) shows that deliberations at the HRC have the potential to benefit greatly from NHRI participation through this procedure. In this case, the CERD admitted an amicus curiae brief by the German Institute for Human Rights (GIHR), the A-status NHRI of Germany, submitted through the petitioner.[266] The GIHR provided the Committee with information that neither the petitioner nor the state party had brought up, such as the reaction to the statement in question in German society, and presented its observations that the statements constituted racist ideas prohibited under the Convention.[267] This observation induced a detailed rebuttal by the state party, which even stated that 'it rejects [GIHR's] opinions … The GIHR's brief conveys a fundamental misconception of the relationship between freedom of expression and the Convention',[268] eventually helping to enrich the deliberation and improve the quality of the CERD's review.

4.4. WHEN MORE THAN TWO STATE ORGANS TAKE DIFFERENT POSITIONS: REGULATING THE TRIANGULAR RELATIONSHIP

It is not rare for more than two state organs within one state to take different positions in the interpretation and application of human rights treaties (see Chapter 1, section 1.1.1). Unlike the classical framework, which considers states as unitary and monolithic entities, the framework of the separation of powers

[264] D Zipoli, 'NHRI Engagement with UN Human Rights Treaty Bodies: A Goal-Based Approach' (2019) 37 *NJHR* 259, 275–77.

[265] HRC's Concluding Observations on the Philippines (n 263) para 14(a).

[266] *TBB-Turkish Union in Berlin/Brandenburg v Germany*, CERD, Communication No 48/2010 (26 February 2013) UN Doc CERD/C/82/D/48/2010, para 8.1.

[267] ibid paras 8.1–8.4.

[268] ibid para 10.1.

in a globalised democratic society makes such situations visible and regulates them by establishing the relationship between treaty organs and respective state organs. Treaty organs examine not only what the 'state' – as represented by the executive branch – argues before them, but also the decision-making processes of the relevant state organs separately, and defer to the one that has properly fulfilled its duty (negative subsidiarity) while adopting an intrusive review vis-a-vis the one that has not (positive subsidiarity).

From a procedural perspective, these practices clearly highlight the limit of the current treaty organs' procedure. While the 'state' is represented by the executive branch, most often by the ministry of foreign affairs, in making pleadings before treaty organs, the executive branch is not well placed to represent the positions and views of other state organs. Thus, treaty organs should consider improving their procedure for the participation of state organs other than the executive. They should consider providing opportunities for the relevant state organs to elaborate on their decision-making process in the case concerned, to respond to submissions of the applicants, governments and other state organs and to address the questions of treaty organs when necessary.

4.4.1. The Relationship Among the Human Rights Treaty Organ, the National Courts and the National Human Rights Institution

In *TV and AG v Uzbekistan* (2016), a case before the HRC, the authors alleged that their forced placement in a psychiatric hospital violated Article 9 ICCPR (right to liberty and security). In this case, the Ombudsman, the NHRI of Uzbekistan, conducted an investigation and qualified the actions of officials as an abuse of authority and a violation of domestic law.[269] Although the Ombudsman forwarded the authors' complaints to the domestic courts, referring to the outcome of the investigation, and requested that the Supreme Court take measures to protect the authors' rights, all those claims were dismissed without substantive examination of the facts and authors' rights.[270] Accordingly, the HRC refused to defer to the domestic courts because they had 'not responded to the findings of the Ombudsman's office, which confirmed the abuse of authority and violation of the procedure prescribed by the national legislation'.[271]

This case may be analysed according to the separation of powers in a globalised democratic society model. On the one hand, the HRC gave great weight to the NHRI's view as the latter had satisfactorily fulfilled its duty by providing information to the national courts and urging them to conduct

[269] *TV and AG v Uzbekistan*, HRC, Communication No 2044/2011 (11 March 2016) UN Doc CCPR/C/116/D/2044/2011, para 2.6.
[270] ibid paras 2.6–2.9.
[271] ibid para 7.7.

bounded deliberations (negative subsidiarity). On the other hand, the national courts could not enjoy deference because they did not thoroughly examine the relevant facts and authors' rights, and ignored the information provided by the NHRI (positive subsidiarity).

4.4.2. The Relationship Among the Human Rights Treaty Organ, the Parliament and the National Human Rights Institution

In *Vallianatos and Others v Greece* (2013), the ECtHR dealt with the allegation that Greece violated Article 14 (prohibition of discrimination) taken in conjunction with Article 8 ECHR because the new legislation introducing the system of 'civil union' excluded same-sex couples. Prior to the enactment of the law in question, the National Human Rights Commission of Greece had unanimously adopted a report criticising the Parliament for having proceeded 'in a fragmentary, hasty and inadequately reasoned manner, without prior public consultation of the social, academic and professional stakeholders'.[272] The Commission further observed, relying on the ECtHR's relevant jurisprudence, that despite the tendency in other European countries to introduce civil unions for same-sex couples, the explanatory report on the bill offered no justification for excluding same-sex couples.[273] In other words, the Greek NHRI properly fulfilled its duty by making the Parliament fully aware of the relevant ECHR standards and their implications for the bill. Thus, the ECtHR has repeatedly cited and assigned considerable weight to the opinions of the Greek National Human Rights Commission (negative subsidiarity).[274] Conversely, it gave no deference to the Parliament, which did not properly conduct bounded deliberations, and held that it has 'not offered convincing and weighty reasons capable of justifying the exclusion of same-sex couples from the scope of Law no 3719/2008' (positive subsidiarity).[275]

In *G v Australia* (2017) before the HRC, the compatibility of the Births, Deaths and Marriages Registration Act 1995, which provides that a person must be unmarried to register a change of sex, with Articles 17 and 26 ICCPR was disputed. Relatedly, the Australian Human Rights Commission had published a report of more than 50 pages in 2009 on the issue.[276] After carefully considering international human rights law standards, the Commission recommended a legislative change and that 'marital status should not be a relevant consideration

[272] *Vallianatos and Others v Greece* (n 77) para 22.
[273] ibid paras 23–24.
[274] ibid para 89.
[275] ibid para 92.
[276] Australian Human Rights Commission, 'Sex Files: The Legal Recognition of Sex in Documents and Government Records' (2009).

as to whether or not a person can request a change in legal sex'.[277] Considering this recommendation by the Commission (negative subsidiarity),[278] the HRC refrained from deferring to the decision of the Parliament (positive subsidiarity) because of a lack of 'convincing explanations' concerning the differential treatment between married and unmarried persons who have undergone a sex affirmation procedure.[279]

4.4.3. The Relationship Among the Human Rights Treaty Organ, the Parliament and the National Courts

In *A and Others v UK* (2009), the ECtHR examined the compatibility of the detention of terrorist suspects under the Anti-Terrorism, Crime and Security Act 2001 (hereinafter the '2001 Act') with Articles 5 (right to liberty and security) and 15 (derogation) ECHR. When the House of Lords, acting as the highest court of appeal, examined the legality of the measures, it considered comprehensive elements in light of the ECHR standards, such as the facts that the detention scheme applied only to non-nationals, that suspected terrorists could leave the UK and continue their threatening activities abroad, and that the legislation was drafted too broadly.[280] The majority held that the detention scheme under the 2001 Act was disproportionate and thus granted a quashing order with respect to the derogation order, and a declaration of incompatibility regarding the 2001 Act. However, the government failed to take appropriate measures, including the release of detained terrorist suspects. When the applicants lodged a complaint with the ECtHR, the government argued that 'the House of Lords had erred' in the interpretation and application of the ECHR and emphasised that the 2001 Act was the outcome of the parliamentary debate.[281] In this case, while the House of Lords successfully implemented its duties by thoroughly reviewing the relevant facts in light of the ECHR standards, the Parliament failed to do so by not properly taking into account the ECHR standards and instead hastily passed the bill.[282] Therefore, while noting the abnormal character of the present case as 'Governments do not normally resort to challenging … decisions of their own highest courts before [the ECtHR]',[283] the ECtHR expressly relied on its subsidiarity role and granted a wide margin of appreciation

[277] *G v Australia*, HRC, Communication No 2172/2012 (17 March 2017) UN Doc CCPR/C/119/D/2172/2012, para 2.13.
[278] ibid para 7.13.
[279] ibid para 7.15.
[280] *A and Others v UK*, ECtHR, App No 3455/05, Merits and Just Satisfaction (19 February 2009) para 20.
[281] ibid para 150.
[282] ibid para 12.
[283] ibid para 157.

specifically to the domestic court.[284] It stated that 'it would be justified in reaching a contrary conclusion only if satisfied that the national court had misinterpreted or misapplied Article 15 or the Court's jurisprudence under that Article or reached a conclusion which was manifestly unreasonable'.[285]

Similarly, in *Oliari and Others v Italy* (2015) before the ECtHR, concerning the lack of legal recognition of same-sex partnerships, the Constitutional Court and the Court of Cassation had repeatedly called on the Parliament to enact a law for such recognition.[286] However, the Italian legislature was unable to enact such a law and could not show that substantive deliberation on the issue had taken place.[287] '[I]n the light of domestic courts' conclusions on the matter which remained unheeded',[288] the ECtHR determined that the Italian Parliament had overstepped its margin of appreciation.

While the cases mentioned above concerned the phase of reviewing the necessity and proportionality of the measures, the same regulation applies to the phase of ordering reparation/remedial measures. In *Hutten-Czapska v Poland* (2006) before the ECtHR, concerning the compatibility of the legislation governing housing matters and relations between landlords and tenants with Article 1 of Protocol No 1 (protection of property), the Polish Constitutional Court declared the relevant legislation unconstitutional in 2005 and issued a set of recommendations directed at the parliament. The Constitutional Court's judgment was based on inclusive participation of relevant stakeholders,[289] contained 'extensive reasoning and a thorough assessment of the various social, political and economic circumstances',[290] and 'paid particular attention' to the 2005 Chamber judgment of the ECtHR.[291] Because the Parliament failed to implement this judgment of the Constitutional Court and structural violations continued, the ECtHR applied the pilot judgment procedure. In ordering legislative measures, the ECtHR encouraged the Parliament to consider recommendations by the Constitutional Court.[292] Thus, the ECtHR applied negative subsidiarity with regard to the Constitutional Court, and positive subsidiarity with the Parliament.[293]

[284] ibid para 174.

[285] ibid.

[286] *Oliari and Others v Italy*, ECtHR, App Nos 18766/11 and 36030/11, Merits and Just Satisfaction (21 July 2015) para 180.

[287] ibid para 183.

[288] ibid para 185.

[289] *Hutten-Czapska v Poland*, ECtHR [GC], App No 35014/97, Merits and Just Satisfaction (19 June 2006) para 135.

[290] ibid para 136.

[291] ibid para 139.

[292] ibid para 239.

[293] *cf* W Sadurski, 'Partnering with Strasbourg: Constitutionalisation of the European Court of Human Rights, the Accession of Central and East European States to the Council of Europe, and the Idea of Pilot Judgments' (2009) 9 *HRLR* 397, 421.

4.4.4. When Both State Organs Fulfil their Duties, but Reach Opposing Conclusions

When both state organs fulfil their duties and still come to differing views concerning the interpretation and application of human rights treaties, it is not the task of the treaty organ to choose which one prevails. The treaty organ shall give priority to the state organ that has the authority over the matter in the domestic legal order of the state concerned. For example, in *Marie-Louise Jungelin v Sweden* (2014), before the Committee on the Rights of Persons with Disabilities (CRPD), the case concerned the Social Insurance Agency's failure to consider the author for the vacant post on the grounds that taking adaptation measures to accommodate her sight impairment would be difficult. This was examined under Articles 5 (equality and non-discrimination) and 27 (work and employment) of the Convention on the Rights of Persons with Disabilities. The Swedish Disability Ombudsman (now the Equality Ombudsman) filed an application with the Labour Court on behalf of the author and provided detailed proposals for adaptation measures that the agency could reasonably have taken, thereby fulfilling its duty in the separation of powers in a globalised democratic society model. The Labour Court thoroughly assessed all the relevant elements and fully considered the Ombudsman's proposals,[294] thus also fulfilling its duty. Although the Labour Court eventually dismissed the Ombudsman's application, the CRPD emphasised that 'State parties enjoy a certain margin of appreciation' in assessing the reasonableness and proportionality of the measures,[295] and supported the decision of the Labour Court, which has the authority over the matter in the Swedish legal order,[296] as being 'based on objective and reasonable considerations'.[297]

4.5. ANALYSING THE FINDINGS

4.5.1. Emerging General Patterns

The analyses in the previous sections are far from comprehensive, and practices remain inconsistent. Nevertheless, they reveal the following emerging patterns across different treaty organs and state organs, which largely endorse the separation of powers in a globalised democratic society model.

First, in both reviewing the necessity and proportionality of the measure and ordering remedial or reparation measures, treaty organs have increasingly

[294] *Marie-Louise Jungelin v Sweden*, CRPD, Communication No 5/2011 (2 October 2014) UN Doc CRPD/C/12/D/5/2011, para 10.6.
[295] ibid para 10.5.
[296] ibid.
[297] ibid para 10.6.

recognised the primary roles of various state organs, which differ depending on their respective composition, competence, decision-making process and functions, and have placed themselves in a subsidiary position. In principle, it is for the national courts to hear the arguments of relevant authorities and individuals, evaluate the relevant facts and determine whether the measure is compatible with treaty standards; it is for national parliaments to balance between different values and interests when deciding matters of general policy; and it is for the administrative organs with expertise to deal with the technically complex evaluations in individual cases.

Second, treaty organs require national courts, parliaments and administrative organs to adhere to different procedural standards: National courts must conduct comprehensive and thorough reviews under human rights treaty-compatible standards, with the guarantee of procedural fairness. Parliaments must hold rich deliberations that ensure the inclusive representation, participation and consideration of various positions and interests, including the human rights of those affected. Administrative organs must conduct sufficient investigations, follow a decision-making process that is transparent and open to the public, including those affected, and provide reasons for their decisions.

Third, treaty organs increasingly endorse the duality of subsidiarity in their relationships with state organs. They take a deferential and bottom-up approach to state organs when the latter fulfil or are reasonably expected to fulfil the aforementioned procedural requirements, by deferring to the decisions of those state organs and refraining from ordering/recommending specific measures to them (negative subsidiarity). By contrast, treaty organs take an intrusive and top-down approach when a state organ has not fulfilled or cannot be expected to fulfil them, by replacing state organ decisions and evaluations with their own and ordering/recommending detailed measures for specific state organs (positive subsidiarity). This practice indicates that a new conception of deference is emerging.[298] While the classical conception has been concerned with the allocation of authority between treaty organs and states solely in the international plane, where deference is given unconditionally and equally to all states because treaty organs must respect the sovereignty inherent in any state,[299] the new conception concerns the separation of powers in a globalised democratic society, where deference is given to each state organ under the condition that it fulfils certain standards. Although the first conception of deference was dominant in the twentieth century,[300] reflecting the clear boundary between international and domestic laws and actors, in recent years, the second version has gradually prevailed, corresponding to the blurring of the boundary.

[298] *cf* M Iglesias Vila, 'Subsidiarity, Margin of Appreciation and International Adjudication within a Cooperative Conception of Human Rights' (2017) 15 *I-CON* 393, 407.

[299] Vila calls this type of deference a 'voluntarist version' of the margin of appreciation, which reflects a statist view of the principle of subsidiarity. See ibid.

[300] See, eg, R McDonald, 'The Margin of Appreciation' in R McDonald et al (eds), *The European System for the Protection of Human Rights* (Brill/Nijhoff 1993) 84, 123.

Fourth, regarding NHRIs, treaty organs have endorsed the authority of NHRIs in enriching national deliberations and making them 'bounded', by expressly relying on and endorsing their information and views, especially those concerning the wider background and context of the issue. Treaty organs have refrained from deferring to other decision-making state organs when these organs failed to properly consider NHRIs' views, and have recommended that states consider NHRIs' views in taking measures.

Fifth, treaty organs have played a significant role in identifying 'bounds' to be placed on national deliberations based on international and comparative law materials, and submissions from transnational civil society organisations and other stakeholders. The fact that the examined treaty organs do not make qualitative distinctions between binding and non-binding instruments[301] and between documents to which all Member States (especially including the respondent state) are party and those to which they are not, clearly indicates their departure from the state consent-based approach to treaty interpretation.[302] Their approach of identifying 'bounds' cannot be fully justified based on Article 31(3)(b) – a subsequent practice which establishes the agreement of *all*[303] states parties – or on Article 31(3)(c) – relevant *binding*[304] rules of international law *applicable between the states parties* – of the VCLT.[305] Rather, it seems to be a pursuit of 'ordinary meaning to be given to the terms' under Article 31(1) – with 'ordinary meaning' understood not within the inter-state community, but within the epistemic community supporting globalised democratic societies, which consists of various actors, including treaty organs, national courts, parliaments, administrative organs, NHRIs, civil society organisations and academics.

Last, treaty organs have shown a certain willingness, though not always, to accept the 'principled and continuous dialogue', by refraining from making a determinate decision on the matter and entrusting the deliberations to national parliaments and courts (see *SH and Others v Austria*; *Zdanoka v Latvia; Manushaqe Puto and Others v Albania; Barrios Altos and La Cantuta [Monitoring Compliance]* (2018); *Massacres of El Mozote and Surrounding Areas v*

[301] Nevertheless, Angelika Nußberger argued that hard law is given a relatively heavier weight than soft law in the ECtHR. See A Nußberger, 'Hard Law or Soft Law – Does it Matter? Distinction between Different Sources of International Law in the Jurisprudence of the ECtHR' in A van Aaken and I Motoc (eds), *The European Convention on Human Rights and General International Law* (Oxford University Press 2018) 41.

[302] See, eg, Letsas (n 79).

[303] Although the text of the VCLT is unclear on this point, see *Whaling in the Antarctic (Australia v Japan: New Zealand intervening) (Merits)* [2014] ICJ Rep 226, para 83. See also ILC, 'Draft Conclusions on Subsequent Agreements and Subsequent Practice in Relation to the Interpretation of Treaties, with Commentaries' (2018) UN Doc A/73/10, 16, Commentary to Conclusion 3, para 12.

[304] Although the text of the VCLT is not explicit on this point, see ME Villiger, *Commentary on the 1969 Vienna Convention on the Law of Treaties* (Nijhoff 2009) 433.

[305] G Ulfstein, 'Evolutive Interpretation in the Light of Other International Instruments: Law and Legitimacy' in A van Aaken, and I Motoc (eds), *The European Convention on Human Rights and General International Law* (Oxford University Press 2018) 83. However, some authors consider that the treaty organs' consensus approach enlarges the criteria of art 31(3)(b) and (c) VCLT instead of deviating from them. See, eg, Ferrero (n 74) 156 and 166.

El Salvador [Provisional Measures and Monitoring Compliance]), and by relaxing the substantive standards established in previous cases when faced with the state organs' arguments based on bounded national deliberations (see *Animal Defenders International v UK*, *Humpert and Others v Germany* and *Manuel Cepeda Vargas v Colombia*).

4.5.2. Differences Among the Three Human Rights Treaty Organs

Despite the common elements described above, the extent to and manner in which the treaty organs have endorsed the separation of powers in a globalised democratic society model vary. In addition to the differences noted earlier (in particular, those concerning the identification of 'bounds'; see section 4.1.2.4), two fundamental differences merit closer analysis. First, on the one hand, the ECtHR has elaborated on the roles of respective state organs in detail and established general formulas. On the other hand, the IACtHR and the HRC have acknowledged the roles of state organs only in an ad hoc and restrained manner. This difference presumably derives from the fact that the relativisation of the boundary between international and domestic legal orders, which constitutes the rationale for developing the separation of powers between treaty organs and state organs (see Chapter 2), is much more advanced in the ECHR framework; it is clearly the least advanced in UN human rights treaties owing to the lack of binding powers in treaty bodies' decisions. Nonetheless, the ECtHR's reaction to the integration between international and domestic legal orders and actors can provide useful lessons for other treaty organs, not only where such integration advances under those treaty regimes in the future, but also where the treaty organs wish to promote such integration.

Second, although the ECtHR has acknowledged the roles of the respective state organs in an equal manner, allocating different functions to each, the IACtHR and the HRC place greater weight on the roles of national courts than on those of others. In fact, the IACtHR invented the doctrine of conventionality control primarily to address national courts. The HRC established the formula that 'it is generally for the courts … to evaluate facts and evidence in a particular case', but has been reluctant to show a deferential attitude to parliaments. This difference may be attributed to the fact that while the ECHR largely consists of well-functioning representative democracies whose minimum democratic qualities are guaranteed by membership criteria in the Council of Europe,[306] the ACHR and the ICCPR contain a wider variety of states parties, including those without consolidated representative democracy. Thus, the IACtHR and the HRC have placed greater trust and expectations on national courts, which, owing to their independent nature

[306] See Statute of the Council of Europe (signed 5 May 1949, entered into force 3 August 1949) 87 UNTS 103, arts 3 and 4.

from the majority's will and their professional knowledge of law and human rights, appear to become partners of these treaty organs more easily than other state organs.[307] Moreover, the separation of powers in a globalised democratic society model does not require treaty organs to review the democratic qualities of 'states' or that of parliaments in general and only requires reviewing the deliberative process of the particular decision concerned. Nevertheless, conducting such a review, especially over the parliamentary decision-making process, may indirectly lead to a 'double standard'[308] between states that have mature representative democracy and states that do not,[309] thereby deviating from the traditional premise of 'equality between political regimes' based on the principles of state sovereignty and non-intervention in the internal affairs of states (see Chapter 1, section 1.1.1).[310] The relative reluctance of the IACtHR and the HRC to scrutinise the decision-making process of parliaments may reflect their oscillation between acceptance of a particular political theory of two-tiered bounded deliberative democracy and respecting the traditional premise of 'equality between political regimes'. Again, the ECtHR's approach in relation to parliaments can provide valuable lessons for other treaty organs when the parliaments in their Member States generally begin to function responsibly.[311] At the same time, the careful approach of the IACtHR and the HRC in relation to parliaments may be instructive to the ECtHR if the recent global rise of populism, including in several European countries,[312] results in a general decline in the quality of parliamentary decision-making processes.

4.6. CONCLUSION

This chapter has examined treaty organs' practices of interacting with state organs in three areas: reviewing the necessity and proportionality of the

[307] As such, previous studies on the IACtHR and the HRC have largely focused on deference to national courts. See, eg, S Bertelsen, 'A Margin for the Margin of Appreciation: Deference in the Inter-American Court of Human Rights' (2021) 19 *I-CON* 887, 897–900. The importance of national courts in the ACHR system has also been explained from the perspective of Ius Constitutionale Commune in América Latina. See A von Bogdandy et al, 'Ius Constitutionale Commune in América Latina: A Regional Approach to Transformative Constitutionalism' in A von Bogdandy et al (eds), *Transformative Constitutionalism in Latin America: The Emergence of a New Ius Commune* (Oxford University Press 2017) 1, 10.

[308] R Spano, 'The Future of the European Court of Human Rights: Subsidiarity, Process-Based Review and the Rule of Law' (2018) 18 *HRLR* 473, 493.

[309] Çalı (n 5) 274.

[310] For similar discussions in international investment arbitration, see A Roberts, 'The Next Battleground: Standards of Review in Investment Treaty Arbitration' (2011) 16 *International Council for Commercial Arbitration Congress Series* 170, 178; C Henckels, *Proportionality and Deference in Investor-State Arbitration* (Cambridge University Press 2015) 41–42.

[311] *cf* D McGoldrick, 'A Defence of the Margin of Appreciation and an Argument for its Application by the Human Rights Committee' (2016) 65 *ICLQ* 21, 43.

[312] See generally J Vidmar (ed), *European Populism and Human Rights* (Brill/Nijhoff 2020).

measure (section 4.1), ordering/recommending remedial and reparation measures (section 4.2), and relying on NHRIs' information and views (section 4.3). It also analysed how treaty organs have treated cases in which two organs within a single state disagree in the interpretation and application of human rights treaties – cases that could not be properly described and regulated under the classical paradigm of a unitary and monolithic state (section 4.4). The key finding is that treaty organs have increasingly endorsed, although with inconsistencies and varying degrees among treaty organs owing to their unique backgrounds, the separation of powers in a globalised democratic society model as embodied by the two-tiered bounded deliberative democracy theory (section 4.5).

As stated in Chapter 1, section 1.1.3.1, abundant literature on one or some aspects of these practices exists, and one of this book's ambitions lies in its proposal to grasp and regulate these practices as an integral whole under the separation of powers in a globalised democratic society model. Through an in-depth descriptive analysis of the practices of the ECtHR, the IACtHR and the HRC, this chapter has demonstrated that such ambition is grounded not only in theory but also in practice, at least to a certain extent. Thus, recent developments regarding individual state organs are not sporadic, haphazard or opportunistic, but rather, systemic and consistent. They do bear significance that may shake the foundational assumptions of traditional international law where 'states' have been the necessary unit of regulation.

5

The Emergence of 'Inter-State Organ Norms'

Their Cooperative Interactions with Human Rights Treaties under Global Legal Pluralism

In the 'separation of powers in a globalised democratic society' model, in addition to treaty obligations owed by 'states' as unitary and monolithic entities, individual state organs themselves bear their own 'duties', and human rights treaty organs directly interact with them. What is the normative nature of these duties? Are they equivalent to international law obligations owed by states? If so, does that mean that state organs are new subjects of international law? If not, what is the status of state organs in human rights treaties?

This chapter posits that the duties of individual state organs under the separation of powers in a globalised democratic society model have a unique normative nature that is distinct from states' international law obligations. On the one hand, such duties could be considered a part of the existing international law rules concerning the doctrine of deference, as treaty organs apply different levels of deference to national decisions depending on the level of state organs' compliance with their duties. From this perspective, the 'duties' of state organs may be paraphrased as conditions for the operation of deference. On the other hand, and of greater importance, state organs' duties stand on an additional normative basis, that is, on the cooperative interactions between 'inter-state organ norms' and human rights treaties. These interactions enable state organs to become autonomous actors in human rights treaties that are distinct from their states, and a bridge between human rights treaties and their respective national legal systems.

This chapter elaborates on the latter normative basis, namely, the cooperative interactions between 'inter-state organ norms' and human rights treaties in the following order. First, it introduces the original concept of 'inter-state organ norms' as an autonomous normative order of, by and for individual state organs and not states (section 5.1). Second, it examines inter-state organ norms on human rights for each type of state organs, namely, NHRIs (section 5.2), parliaments (section 5.3) and courts (section 5.4), which endorse these state organs' duties under the separation of powers in a globalised democratic society model. The chapter then argues, through the lens of global legal pluralism, that inter-state organ norms on human rights and human rights treaties should, and already do to some extent, interact with each other in a cooperative manner under the shared values in globalised democratic societies. Such cooperative interactions are key to transforming state organs into organs with triple identities and duties – not only those under national constitutions, but also those within transnational communities of state organs and those under human rights treaties. Efforts by state organs to simultaneously fulfil their triple duties will contribute to the gradual permeation of the separation of powers in a globalised democratic society model into national legal systems and practices, and thus to harmonisation between human rights treaties and national laws (section 5.5).

Regarding the scope of this chapter, first, although inter-state organ norms on human rights for administrative organs are both conceivable and desirable, they remain underdeveloped, presumably because the types and mandates of administrative organs are highly segmented and do not necessarily match among different states. Therefore, they are outside the scope of this chapter and are best left for future studies. Second, governmental structures known as 'national mechanisms for implementation, reporting and follow-up (NMIRFs)' have recently been developed under the initiative of the UN.[1] Although inter-NMIRF norms seem to be in the process of emerging,[2] this chapter does not deal with NMIRFs, as their functions are, in principle, confined to contributing to reporting procedures.[3] Nevertheless, as their functions are broadening[4] and partially overlapping with those of NHRIs,[5] it is a task for future studies to locate such mechanisms within the separation of powers in a globalised democratic society model, clarifying their relationship with NHRIs.

[1] UN Human Rights Council Res 42/30, 'Promoting International Cooperation to Support National Mechanisms for Implementation, Reporting and Follow-up' (27 September 2019).

[2] See, eg, Danish Institute for Human Rights, 'Report on the International Seminar on National Mechanisms for Implementation, Reporting and Follow-up in the Field of Human Rights (Marrakech, 7–8 December 2022)', www.humanrights.dk/publications/report-international-seminar-national-mechanisms-implementation-reporting-follow-field.

[3] See generally OHCHR, *National Mechanisms for Reporting and Follow-up: A Practical Guide to Effective State Engagement with International Human Rights Mechanisms* (2016), www.ohchr.org/sites/default/files/Documents/Publications/HR_PUB_16_1_NMRF_PracticalGuide.pdf.

[4] OHCHR, 'Regional Consultations on Experiences and Good Practices Relating to the Establishment and Development of National Mechanisms for Implementation, Reporting and Follow-up' (2022) UN Doc A/HRC/50/64, para 53.

[5] See generally *Danish Institute for Human Rights, Interactions between NHRIs and NMIRFs: Research and Recommendations* (2023), www.humanrights.dk/publications/interactions-between-nhris-nmirfs-research-recommendations.

5.1. THE ORIGINAL CONCEPT OF 'INTER-STATE ORGAN NORMS'

International law, as traditionally understood, is a legal system of, by and for states. First, international law is created, interpreted and developed by states. Treaties are concluded by states, typically represented by the heads of state, heads of government and ministers for foreign affairs,[6] and are interpreted and sometimes developed in light of the subsequent practices and agreements of states.[7] Customary international law is generated, ascertained and developed based on the general practices and *opinio juris* of states.[8] Second, international law governs the relationship between states[9] and thus addresses states. Third, states are held accountable by other states to secure compliance with international law. Under the law of state responsibility, an injured state (or any other state in the case of a breach of obligations *erga omnes*) may invoke the responsibility of another state that has breached an international obligation.[10] Although the development of international law has created notable exceptions to the above premises, such as international organisations[11] and individuals[12] that partially assume these prerogatives of states, the conception of a unitary and monolithic state remains unchanged. Therefore, when two or more state organs within a state adopt different practices in the context of formation or identification of customary international law, such practices are still assessed as 'a whole' as a practice of a unitary state, resulting in a reduced weight of that state's contribution to the general practice.[13] Similarly, even when an international law rule regulates the conduct of a particular state organ, such as a rule of jurisdictional immunity requiring a national judiciary's conduct, the rule is considered as addressing a state, and its violation incurs the responsibility of the state as a whole.

In contrast, the 'inter-state organ norms' that this chapter proposes are an autonomous normative system of, by and for respective types of state organs – parliaments, courts, NHRIs or administrative organs. The most well-established and mature inter-state organ norms on human rights are the Paris Principles on NHRIs (see section 5.2); however, equivalent norms regarding other types of state organs are emerging (see sections 5.3–5.4). Inter-state organ norms are created, interpreted and developed by state organs rather than by states.

[6] Articles 6 and 7 VCLT.

[7] ibid art 31(3)(a) and (b).

[8] ILC, 'Draft Conclusions on Identification of Customary International Law, with Commentaries' (2018) UN Doc A/73/10, 119, Conclusion 4(1).

[9] *Affaire du 'Lotus' (France c Turquie)* [1927] CPJI série A No 10, 18.

[10] ILC, 'Draft Articles on Responsibility of States for Internationally Wrongful Acts, with Commentaries' (2001) UN Doc A/56/10, 26, arts 42 and 48.

[11] See, eg, J Klabbers, *An Introduction to International Organizations Law*, 4th edn (Cambridge University Press 2022) 41–70.

[12] See, eg, A Peters, *Beyond Human Rights: The Legal Status of the Individual in International Law* (Cambridge University Press 2016).

[13] ILC (n 8) Conclusion 7 and its commentary, paras 3–4.

Inter-state organ norms are addressed to state organs rather than to states. To ensure compliance with such norms, state organs are held accountable by their foreign counterparts, ie, the same type of state organs in other states. Just as 'states' are subjects of international law, individual state organs are subjects of inter-state organ norms.

Figure 5.1 Unique features of inter-state organ norms

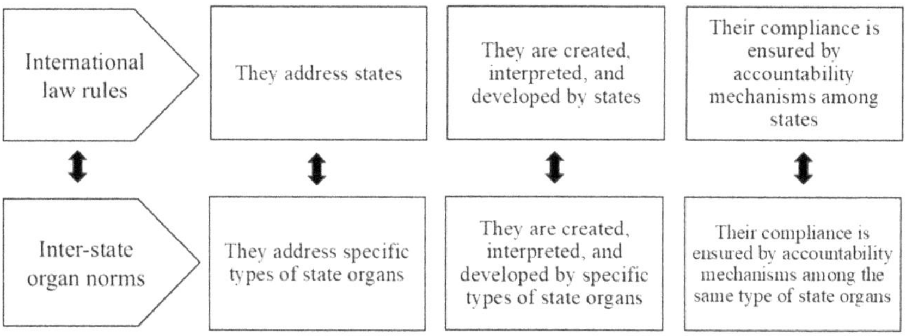

The introduction of the concept of inter-state organ norms builds on previous studies that have discussed the nature of such norms, especially those regarding the Paris Principles on NHRIs. Most of these studies have focused solely on their non-binding nature. Anna-Elina Pohjolainen wrote that 'the Paris Principles do not possess the quality of legally binding international rules. … Nonetheless … the Principles have gained considerable political and moral weight'.[14] Similarly, Sanzhuan Guo characterised them as 'soft law' because they are not treaties, customary international law or general principles of law.[15] Katerina Linos and Tom Pegram described the Paris Principles as acquiring 'the gravitas' but not 'the status' of an international treaty.[16] Several other authors have noted the unique nature of the Paris Principles, which distinguishes them from typical international soft law such as UN General Assembly resolutions and outcome documents of international conferences. According to Domenico Zipoli: 'The Paris Principles represent a unique example of partly bypassing State preferences, in that [they] were the result of deliberations by NHRIs themselves as opposed to UN Member States.'[17] Gauthier de Beco and Rachel Murray pointed out that the Paris Principles directly regulate NHRIs, as opposed to unitary

[14] AE Pohjolainen, *The Evolution of National Human Rights Institutions: The Role of the United Nations* (Danish Institute for Human Rights 2006) 9.

[15] S Guo, 'Independence of National Human Rights Institutions and Linkage between International Law and Domestic Law: A Case Study of the National Human Rights Commission of Korea' (2017) 1 *Asian Yearbook of Human Rights and Humanitarian Law* 264, 279.

[16] K Linos and T Pegram, 'Architects of Their Own Making: National Human Rights Institutions and the United Nations' (2016) 38 *Human Rights Quarterly* 1109, 1126.

[17] D Zipoli, 'NHRI Engagement with UN Human Rights Treaty Bodies: A Goal-Based Approach' (2019) 37 *NJHR* 259, 267.

states, and observed that 'this does not fit easily within the international human rights framework – which addresses itself to States, not non-State actors'.[18] Nevertheless, none of these studies have offered a comprehensive and systematic explanation of the nature of the Paris Principles and equivalent norms concerning other state organs.

Inter-state organ norms could be categorised as a branch of the concept of 'informal international lawmaking' advocated by Joost Pauwelyn, Ramses A Wessel and Jan Wouters. They argued that informal international law-making, which has not been a subject of international legal studies previously, produces significant normative effects in actual global governance practices. 'Informal' here means, first, that such laws do not fall under the definition of a treaty or any other formal sources of international law within the meaning of Article 38(1) of the Statute of the ICJ;[19] rather, they take the form of guidelines, standards, declarations and informal policy coordination and exchanges (output informality).[20] Second, informal international lawmaking 'occurs in a loosely organized network or forum rather than a traditional international organization' (process informality).[21] Third, informal international lawmaking 'does not engage traditional diplomatic actors (such as heads of State, foreign ministers, or embassies) but rather other ministries, domestic regulators, independent or semi-independent agencies … sub-federal entities … or the legislative or judicial branch' (actor informality).[22]

However, as the project of informal international lawmaking primarily focuses on securing its accountability and legitimacy, important theoretical questions remain. In discussing whether informal international laws are part of international law, Pauwelyn, Wessel and Wouters set out two options: first, 'international law can adapt and incorporate … [such a new type of lawmaking], thereby increasing its societal relevance'.[23] This option 'would require a radical transformation of international law, both procedurally and substantively'.[24] Second, 'international law can entrench itself and stick to its traditional typologies',[25] and in this case, 'the core question would then be how traditional international law interacts with [such informal forms of lawmaking]'.[26]

[18] G de Beco and R Murray, *A Commentary on the Paris Principles on National Human Rights Institutions* (Cambridge University Press 2015) 137.

[19] Statute of the International Court of Justice (signed 26 June 1945, entered into force 24 October 1945) XV UNCIO 355.

[20] J Pauwelyn, 'Informal International Lawmaking: Framing the Concept and Research Questions' in J Pauwelyn, R Wessel and J Wouters (eds), *Informal International Lawmaking* (Oxford University Press 2012) 13, 15–16.

[21] ibid 17.

[22] ibid 19.

[23] J Pauwelyn, R Wessel and J Wouters, 'Informal International Lawmaking: An Assessment and Template to Keep It Both Effective and Accountable' in Pauwelyn, Wessel and Wouters (n 20) 500, 506.

[24] ibid 507.

[25] ibid 506.

[26] ibid 507.

However, they have left choice between these two options open. Furthermore, although Pauwelyn briefly touched upon the question of whether state organs other than those authorised to represent the state could produce international law norms that bind themselves as subjects under international law, he gave no clear answer.[27]

In contrast, the concept of inter-state organ norms takes a clear position regarding these theoretical questions. Inter-state organ norms are autonomous normative orders that are distinct from and outside international law. As this chapter will show in the following sections, inter-state organ norms possess their own set of secondary-rules – meta-rules 'that define the normative context within which primary norms function and that thereby affect the operation of such primary norms'[28] – such as rules concerning the creation, development and interpretation of norms, and rules concerning accountability that are distinct from those of international law. Pretending that inter-state organ norms are part of international law would excessively dilute and distort the normative integrity of international law. It would also deprive inter-state organ norms of their unique advantages – namely, the ability to circumvent the government to directly address individual state organs and give them a transnational identity. For example, the fact that the Paris Principles are an autonomous normative order of, by and for NHRIs has shielded NHRIs from state politics,[29] thus strengthening their independence from the government – one of the most essential requirements for NHRIs to be able to play their duties in the separation of powers in a globalised democratic society (see section 5.2.2.1). Thus, although individual state organs are subjects of inter-state organ norms, they cannot be regarded as subjects of international law, at least not in the same way as states, since inter-state organ norms are not part of international law.

Nevertheless, international law scholarship should not place inter-state organ norms outside its scope. As will be observed in section 5.5, inter-state organ norms should, and already do to some extent, closely interact with human rights treaties in a cooperative manner under the shared values in globalised democratic societies, thereby serving as a normative basis for state organs' duties. If international law studies close their eyes to norms other than those traditionally called international law, such studies may fail to properly understand the reality surrounding such norms that have traditionally been called international law, nor can it achieve the values that such norms aim to realise.

[27] J Pauwelyn, 'Is it International Law or Not, and Does it Even Matter?' in Pauwelyn, Wessel, and Wouters (n 20) 125, 142–43.

[28] A Nollkaemper, 'The Power of Secondary Rules to Connect the International and National Legal Orders' in T Broude and Y Shany (eds), *Multi-sourced Equivalent Norms in International Law* (Hart Publishing 2011) 45, 47.

[29] C Sidoti, 'National Human Rights Institutions and the International Human Rights System' in R Goodman and T Pegram (eds), *Human Rights, State Compliance, and Social Change Assessing National Human Rights Institutions* (Cambridge University Press 2011) 93, 98.

5.2. THE PARIS PRINCIPLES AS INTER-NHRI NORMS ON HUMAN RIGHTS

The Paris Principles on NHRIs are the typical and most well-developed inter-state organ norms in the field of human rights. The Paris Principles were created by NHRIs rather than by states (section 5.2.1) and are interpreted and applied by NHRIs themselves in accordance with unique interpretative principles that are different from rules of treaty interpretation (section 5.2.2). To ensure an NHRI's compliance with the Paris Principles, other NHRIs hold it accountable (section 5.2.3). The Paris Principles primarily address NHRIs (section 5.2.4).

5.2.1. Creation of the Paris Principles by National Human Rights Institutions

The debate surrounding NHRIs first developed within the inter-state framework of the UN. Having their origins in the resolution of the UN Economic and Social Council in 1946[30] and then in the drafting process of the ICCPR,[31] the inter-state initiatives to establish certain criteria for NHRIs were advanced through a series of resolutions adopted by the UN Commission on Human Rights.[32]

However, it was not states but NHRIs themselves that codified such criteria for NHRIs. In 1991, the UN Centre for Human Rights organised the first International Workshop on National Institutions for the Promotion and Protection of Human Rights in Paris. Representatives of the then-existing NHRIs across all regions (24 national institutions and 15 ombudsman and similar institutions) participated in this workshop, along with representatives of the regional human rights courts, UN specialised agencies, NGOs and governments.[33] Discussions during the workshop were marked by the constructive participation of the NHRIs themselves, which spoke in their own right and not as state representatives, about their own experiences and challenges.[34] The rich and intensive debates that emerged during the three-day workshop[35] resulted in the adoption of a set of principles concerning the basic competence, responsibilities, composition and methods of operation of the NHRIs – the

[30] UN Economic and Social Council Res 9 (II) (21 June 1946) para 5.

[31] UNGA, Plenary Meeting, GAOR 21st Session 1496th plenary mtg (16 December 1966) 1, paras 6–7.

[32] See, eg, UN Commission on Human Rights Res 24 (XXXV), 'National Institutions for the Promotion and Protection of Human Rights' (14 March 1979).

[33] For the list of participants, see the note by the Secretariat attached to the Report of the 1991 International Workshop on NHRIs (n 35) UN Doc E/CN.4/1992/43/Add.1 (1992).

[34] E Decaux, 'Le dixième anniversaire des principes directeurs des institutions nationales des droits de l'homme dits "principes de Paris"' (2003) 3 *Droits fondamentaux* 11, 19–20.

[35] For the summary record of the workshop, see UN Commission on Human Rights, 'Further Promotion and Encouragement of Human Rights and Fundamental Freedoms, Including the Question of the Programme and Methods of Work of the Commission: Report of the International Workshop on National Institutions for the Promotion and Protection of Human Rights' (1991) UN Doc E/CN.4/1992/43 (hereinafter 'Report of the 1991 International Workshop on NHRIs').

principles later called the 'Principles Relating to the Status of National Human Rights Institutions' or 'Paris Principles'.[36]

After effective lobbying by NHRI members, the principles were endorsed in the Vienna Declaration and Programme of Action in 1993[37] and adopted as an annex to a UN Commission on Human Rights resolution[38] and a UN General Assembly resolution[39] in 1992 and 1993, respectively.[40] The fact that the Commission on Human Rights and General Assembly did not adopt the Paris Principles as their own, but annexed them to resolutions illustrates that the Paris Principles were initiatives of NHRIs themselves rather than those of 'states'.[41]

Independence, pluralism and effectiveness are the pillars of the Paris Principles. These factors directly connect to NHRIs' duties in the separation of powers in a globalised democratic society model, namely, enriching national deliberations and making them 'bounded' by bringing inclusive perspectives, and assisting treaty organs to properly assess and supplement national deliberations (see Chapter 3, section 3.3.4). First, the principle of independence requires NHRIs to function autonomously and without interference from external entities, particularly national governments. The Paris Principles provide various means for securing independence – legal and operational autonomy (sections A-2[42] and B-2 of the Paris Principles), financial autonomy (section B-2), autonomy in appointment and dismissal procedures (sections B-2 and B-3), and political neutrality and expertise in the composition of members and pluralism (section B-1).[43] Independence is a prerequisite for NHRIs to act as a bridge between formal and informal public spheres, by not being part of either the political system or civil society.

Second, pluralism, which is closely related to independence, requires the representation and participation of a wide range of sectors in the society in the composition and activities of NHRIs, and prevents the monopoly of NHRIs by certain powerful sectors.[44] Section B-1 of the Paris Principles requires 'the pluralist representation of the social forces (of civilian society)' in the

[36] ibid 45–49.

[37] UN World Conference on Human Rights, 'Vienna Declaration and Programme of Action' (25 June 1993) UN Doc A/CONF.157/23, para 36.

[38] UN Commission on Human Rights Res 1992/54, 'National Institutions for the Promotion and Protection of Human Rights' (3 March 1992).

[39] UNGA Res 48/134, 'National Institutions for the Promotion and Protection of Human Rights' (20 December 1993).

[40] For a historical analysis of the Paris Principles from their drafting to their inclusion in the Vienna Declaration and the UN General Assembly resolution, see T Pegram, 'The Untold Story of the Paris Principles' (18 June 2019), http://tompegram.com/2019/06/untold-story-paris-principles.

[41] G de Beco, 'National Human Rights Institutions in Europe' (2007) 7 *HRLR* 331, 334.

[42] Although the original Paris Principles text does not use the A, B, C and D numbering, the GANHRI's Sub-Committee on Accreditation labels the four sections A–D. This chapter follows this numbering.

[43] A Smith, 'The Unique Position of National Human Rights Institutions: A Mixed Blessing?' (2006) 28 *Human Rights Quarterly* 904.

[44] *cf* ibid 928.

composition of NHRIs, and section C requires NHRIs to develop relationships with NGOs. Pluralism enables NHRIs to facilitate inclusive deliberations.

Third, the principle of effectiveness requires that NHRIs engage in activities to protect and promote human rights at both the national and international levels. Thus, the Paris Principles set out various competences and responsibilities for NHRIs, including: advising the government and parliament (section A-3-(a)), which contributes to the NHRIs' function as a bridge between formal and informal public spheres by informing the political systems of the signals and impulses arising in the civil society; promoting compliance with human rights treaties (section A-3-(b)), which enables NHRIs to place 'bounds' on national deliberations; and contributing to the international state reporting procedure (section A-3-(d)) and cooperating with the UN and regional human rights systems (section A-3-(e)), which allow NHRIs to provide the treaty organs with input concerning the wider background and national contexts of the issue concerned, thereby assisting them in properly assessing and supplementing national deliberations.

5.2.2. Interpretation of the Paris Principles by the Global Alliance of National Human Rights Institutions

5.2.2.1. The Global Alliance of National Human Rights Institutions as the Authoritative Interpreter of the Paris Principles

The Paris Principles do not provide for rules of interpretation or designate a specific body that interprets and applies them authoritatively. However, in practice, the Global Alliance of National Human Rights Institutions (GANHRI) enjoys de facto authority over their interpretation and application, as the GANHRI's accreditation of NHRIs in accordance with the Paris Principles is accepted by NHRIs and other relevant actors as authoritative.

Established in 1993, the GANHRI (formerly the International Coordinating Committee of National Institutions for the Promotion and Protection of Human Rights (ICC)) is an organisation comprising NHRIs worldwide. Although its structure is similar to that of an international organisation, with internal organs such as a general assembly, bureau, chairperson, secretariat and head office, the GANHRI should be distinguished from international organisations in that its members are NHRIs and not states. It can be considered an 'inter-NHRI organisation' or 'inter-state organ organisation' in more general terms. According to the Statute of the GANHRI, its objective is to promote and strengthen NHRIs to operate in line with the Paris Principles and to provide leadership in the promotion and protection of human rights.[45]

[45] Article 5 of the GANHRI Statute (version adopted in 2023). Documents from the GANHRI cited below are all available on the GANHRI website at: https://ganhri.org.

Two factors justify the central role of the GANHRI in interpreting the Paris Principle. First, as a global organisation comprised of NHRIs, the GANHRI is best positioned to conduct a comprehensive survey of NHRIs and to understand the practical needs and challenges faced by NHRIs.[46] Second, given the essential importance of the independence of NHRIs in the Paris Principles, the central role of the GANHRI, instead of other bodies comprising states, is justified on the grounds of shielding their interpretation and application from the influence of governments. Transgovernmental networking theory (see section 5.5.4) also provides support for the view that the GANHRI can be an effective safeguard to protect member NHRIs' independence[47] by assisting in the forming of coalitions of NHRIs against pressure and intervention by their governments.[48]

The Sub-Committee on Accreditation (SCA), comprising one A-status NHRI from each of the four regional groups (Africa, the Americas, Asia and the Pacific, and Europe),[49] is entrusted with reviewing and accrediting NHRIs in accordance with the Paris Principles,[50] through a procedure sometimes described as 'quasi-judicial'.[51] The SCA prepares a report recommending the granting of A-status to NHRIs that comply with the Paris Principles, and B-status to those that partially comply (it used to give C-status to NHRIs that failed to comply with the Paris Principles, but C-status was abolished in 2011).[52] In addition to the reasons for the accreditation, these reports contain recommendations for improving NHRI's compliance with the Paris Principles. As of November 2024, 91 NHRIs had been accredited with A-status and 27 with B-status.[53] Only those with A-status can become voting members of the GANHRI and its regional groups and may be elected to sit in the Bureau and other committees.[54]

After considering NHRIs' initial applications, the SCA reviews them every five years[55] and may conduct a 'Special Review' if an NHRI's compliance with the Paris Principles is in question because of a change in circumstances.[56] The SCA assesses accreditation applications based on a 'Statement of Compliance

[46] GANHRI, 'General Observations of Sub-Committee on Accreditation' (2018) (hereinafter 'SCA's General Observations') 'Introduction', para 5.

[47] For an empirical study on the positive impact of the GANHRI on the durability of NHRIs, see C Lacatus, 'Explaining Institutional Strength: The Case of National Human Rights Institutions in Europe and its Neighbourhood' (2019) 26 *Journal of European Public Policy* 1657.

[48] For application of transgovernmental networking theory to NHRIs, see A Wolman, 'Sub-national Human Rights Institutions and Transgovernmental Networks' (2015) 33 *NJHR* 110. However, for an argument that the current GANHRI system is not sufficiently resilient against governmental actions to weaken NHRIs, see M Lafourcade, 'Le réseau des institutions nationales des droits de l'homme à l'épreuve de la politization' (2019) 20 *Annuaire français de relations internationals* 917, 926–27.

[49] Rule 3.1 of the Rules of Procedure for the GANHRI SCA (amended version adopted in 2024).

[50] For the SCA's accreditation procedure, see D Langtry and K Roberts Lyer, *National Human Rights Institutions: Rules, Requirements, and Practice* (Oxford University Press 2021) ch 2.

[51] See Lafourcade (n 48) 929.

[52] Langtry and Roberts Lyer (n 50) 44.

[53] GANHRI, 'Chart of the Status of National Institutions' (2024) 1.

[54] Articles 24.1 and 31.4 of the GANHRI Statute.

[55] ibid art 15.

[56] ibid arts 16.1 and 16.2.

with the Paris Principles' and related documents submitted by the NHRI, recommendations and observations of international human rights mechanisms, teleconference interviews,[57] and submissions from third parties such as civil society organisations and individuals.[58] An applicant NHRI may file a challenge against the accreditation recommendation by the SCA. If there is no challenge or the challenge is rejected by the Bureau, the recommendation becomes final.[59]

As the Paris Principles were not originally intended to serve as criteria for evaluating NHRIs, they do not set forth elaborate standards.[60] To fill the gap, since 2006, the SCA has developed 'General Observations' concerning the interpretation and application of the Paris Principles to be used in accreditation, and has periodically renewed and enriched them. For example, when the 'human rights mandate' section was first inserted in the General Observations in the March 2007 Session, it simply provided that '[a]ll NHRIs should be mandated with specific functions to both *protect* and *promote* human rights, such as those listed in the Paris Principles'.[61] In contrast, in the current version of the General Observations, the same section, 'human rights mandate', has a detailed interpretative guideline, closely defining the concepts of 'protection' and 'promotion', providing that the NHRIs' mandate should be interpreted in a broad, liberal and purposive manner, and listing the specific mandates to be given to and exercised by NHRIs.[62] It also explains, under a separate 'justification' heading, that sections A-1 and A-2 of the Paris Principles are the basis of such observations.[63] In 2011, the SCA also adopted a formalised multi-stage process for renewing the General Observations.[64]

What, then, are the principles governing the interpretation[65] of the Paris Principles within the accreditation system? Although previous research addressing the content of the Paris Principles is relatively rich,[66] such research

[57] Rules 6.1 and 8.2 of the Rules of Procedure for the GANHRI SCA.

[58] The procedure for third-party submissions was initiated in 2008. See ICC, 'Report and Recommendations of the Session of the Sub-Committee on Accreditation' (3–6 November 2008) para 2.4 (the Reports and Recommendations of the SCA are hereinafter cited as 'SCA Report (Month Year)').

[59] Article 12.1 of the GANHRI Statute.

[60] J Mertus, 'Evaluating NHRIs: Considering Structure, Mandate, and Impact' in Goodman and Pegram (n 29) 74, 79.

[61] SCA Report (March 2007) 11 (emphasis in original).

[62] SCA's General Observations (n 46) s 1.2.

[63] ibid.

[64] ibid 'Introduction', paras 10–11.

[65] In general, 'interpretation' is defined as the process of 'determining the meaning of a rule' and may be distinguished from 'application' as the process of 'determining the consequences which the rule attaches to the occurrence of a given fact' (*Affaire relative à usine de Chorzów (Allemagne c Pologne (compétence)* [1927] CPJI série A No 9, 35, 39 (Opinion dissidente de M Ehrlich)). Although this chapter primarily deals with the former, in light of the essential 'inseparable link' between the two concepts (F Berman, 'International Treaties and British Statutes' (2005) 26 *Statute Law Review* 1, 10), the examination in this chapter broadly covers the sequence of processes starting from the text of the Paris Principles to reach specific recommendations.

[66] For the most comprehensive studies, see de Beco and Murray (n 18); Langtry and Roberts Lyer (n 50).

has not fully explored the principles governing their interpretation and has been confined to general descriptions of the accreditation procedure.[67] This gap may derive from the relative indifference of international law scholarship towards norms that do not form part of the traditional sources of international law.[68] However, this study finds that at least three interpretative principles appear in the practice of the GANHRI that are unique and different from those concerning interpretation of treaties: first, the dynamic interpretation principle, which consists of evolutive interpretation and de facto amendment; second, the normative gradation principle; and, third, the overall evaluation principle.[69]

5.2.2.2. *The Dynamic Interpretation Principle*

5.2.2.2.1. Evolutive Interpretation of the Paris Principles

The SCA's evolutive interpretation of the Paris Principles, especially through the constant renewal of General Observations, makes them a 'living instrument'[70] adapting to changes in the environment to provide appropriate solutions to current problems faced by NHRIs.[71] When the Paris Principles were drafted in 1991, comparatively few countries had NHRIs. Thus, the Paris Principles focused primarily on supporting the establishment of NHRIs by regulating their basis of establishment and design[72] in terms of law on paper, not in practice.[73] However, 'the environment in which [NHRIs] function has evolved since the

[67] See, eg, R Murray, *The Role of National Human Rights Institutions at the International and Regional Levels: The Experience of Africa* (Hart Publishing 2007) 78–82; G de Beco, 'Compliance with the Paris Principles and the ICC Sub-Committee on Accreditation' in K Meuwissen and J Wouters (eds), *National Human Rights Institutions in Europe: Comparative, European and International Perspectives* (Intersentia 2013) 247, 255–60; K Linos and T Pegram, 'What Works in Human Rights Institutions?' (2017) 111 *AJIL* 628, 641–43.

[68] Nevertheless, certain studies from politics and international relations approaches exist. Linos and Pegram argued that the Paris Principles contain both strong recommendations that use firm language and weak recommendations that use flexible language. Linos and Pegram then empirically demonstrated that strong and weak recommendations produce different effects on state behaviour, especially in the case of authoritarian regimes. See K Linos and T Pegram, 'The Language of Compromise in International Agreements' (2016) 70 *International Organization* 587. Although my current study confines its scope to the interpretation of the Paris Principles by the GANHRI, which is the authoritative interpreter, it is a task for future research to incorporate into my analysis the interpretative methods used by states.

[69] This chapter confines itself to descriptively analysing these principles. For my previously published article, which makes normative proposals to improve the application of these principles, see H Takata, 'How are the Paris Principles on NHRIs Interpreted? Towards a Clear, Transparent, and Consistent Interpretative Framework' (2022) 40 *NJHR* 285.

[70] De Beco and Murray (n 18) 23–24.

[71] Ad hoc SCA Working Group on the Proposed Review of General Observations, 'Discussion Paper on the Proposed Review of the General Observations Developed by the ICC Sub-Committee on Accreditation' (2010) reproduced in Annex IV of the SCA Report (March 2010) 42, 56.

[72] De Beco (n 67) 261.

[73] R Murray, 'National Human Rights Institutions: Criteria and Factors for Assessing Their Effectiveness' (2007) 25 *Netherlands Quarterly of Human Rights* 189, 190.

adoption of the Paris Principles in 1991 and the creation of the ICC'.[74] Now that NHRIs have been established in many countries, it is also necessary to regulate the substance of their activities more rigorously. Therefore, through the revision of the General Observations and their application, the SCA has evolutively interpreted the requirements that originally concerned the scope of NHRIs' mandate to require NHRIs' actual exercise of that mandate effectively. For instance, in its review of the Danish Institute for Human Rights (DIHR) in the October 2018 Session, the SCA interpreted sections A-1, A-2 and A-3 of the Paris Principles to encourage 'the DIHR to continue to interpret its protection mandate in a broad manner and to conduct a range of protection actions, including monitoring, enquiring, investigating, and reporting'.[75]

Such an evolutive approach has sometimes resulted in tightening the criteria for accreditation.[76] For instance, the SCA accredited the National Human Rights Commission of Malaysia (SUHAKAM) with A-status in 2002,[77] but intended to downgrade it to B-status in the re-accreditation procedure in 2008, relying on four of its General Observations,[78] even though there had been no substantial change in the SUHAKAM's structure, procedure or activities.[79]

5.2.2.2.2. De Facto Amendment of the Paris Principles

Although such evolutive interpretation has commonality with treaty interpretation,[80] the SCA has often gone further by substantially amending the Paris Principles through its General Observations, which is hardly conceivable in treaty interpretation.

The SCA's General Observations are divided into two categories: section 1, entitled 'Essential Requirements of the Paris Principles'; and section 2, entitled 'Practices That Directly Promote Paris Principles Compliance'. On the one hand, section 1 contains a direct interpretation of the Paris Principles, clarifying and elaborating existing terms and phrases.[81] For example, section A-3-(d) of the Paris Principles provides that NHRIs shall have the responsibility to contribute to state reports submitted to international human rights bodies 'with due respect for their independence'. In section 1.4 of the General Observations, the

[74] ICC Working Group on Accreditation, 'Decision Paper on the Review of ICC Accreditation Procedures for National Human Rights Institutions (NHRI)' (2008) reproduced in Annex 5 of SCA Report (April 2008) 18, at p 5.

[75] SCA Report (October 2018) 8.

[76] *cf* ICC Working Group on Accreditation (n 74) 12. See also Langtry and Roberts Lyer (n 50) 76.

[77] SCA Report (April 2002) 2.

[78] SCA Report (April 2008) 5.

[79] See C Renshaw, A Byrnes and A Durbach, 'Testing the Mettle of National Human Rights Institutions: A Case Study of the Human Rights Commission of Malaysia' (2011) 1 *Asian Journal of International Law* 165, 194.

[80] For the evolutive interpretation of treaties, see generally E Bjorge, *The Evolutionary Interpretation of Treaties* (Oxford University Press 2014).

[81] SCA Report (May 2013) Annex III, para 9.

phrase 'with due respect for their independence' is interpreted as requiring that 'NHRIs should not participate as part of a government delegation', and even where such independent participation right does not exist, 'the manner of their participation must clearly distinguish them as an independent NHRI'.[82]

On the other hand, the General Observations in section 2 are not based on specific texts, but are drawn from the SCA's extensive experience in identifying proven practices to ensure the independence and effectiveness of NHRIs in line with the Paris Principles.[83] For instance, the Paris Principles are silent on the issue of functional immunity, but section 2.3 of the General Observations provides that 'members and staffs of an NHRI should be protected from both criminal and civil liability for acts undertaken in good faith in their official capacity'.[84] As this example shows, General Observations in section 2 often amount to de facto amendment of the Paris Principles, going beyond the original text and lacking a textual basis.[85] The SCA does not hesitate to rely on them in its accreditation review.[86] De facto amendment of the Paris Principles by the SCA, instead of formal amendment, is preferred from a practical point of view, as there is a risk that 'by revising the Paris Principles, we will not necessarily end up with a better product',[87] especially if states are involved in the process.[88] It is a 'Pandora's box'.[89]

5.2.2.3. *The Normative Gradation Principle*

Another feature in the SCA's interpretative approach is normative gradation. Instead of taking the binary approach of examining whether a specific principle is complied with or not, the SCA gives recommendations to all NHRIs,

[82] SCA's General Observations (n 46) s 1.4.

[83] SCA Report (May 2013) Annex III, para 9.

[84] SCA's General Observations (n 46) s 2.3.

[85] Drawing lessons from the law of treaties, the dividing line between interpretation and amendment is often blurred, as both can narrow or expand the scope of rights and obligations that would have existed under the natural and ordinary meaning of the terms (see Special Rapporteur Sir Humphrey Waldock, 'Third Report on the Law of Treaties' (1964) UN Doc A/CN.4/167 and Add. 1-3, 60, para 25). Nonetheless, whereas the identification of one of the possible meanings of a norm, which remains within the frame (ie, the parameters of the original treaty's provisions) is characterised as an interpretation, any application extending beyond such a frame amounts to an amendment (G Hafner, 'Subsequent Agreements and Practice: Between Interpretation, Informal Modification, and Formal Amendment' in G Nolte (ed), *Treaties and Subsequent Practice* (Oxford University Press 2013) 105, 114). From this perspective, the SCA's approach in terms of producing the General Observations not based on specific provisions of the Paris Principles, but rather on its own experiences, has an effect that is equivalent to an amendment.

[86] Nevertheless, in practice, the SCA tends to rely on General Observations in section 1 more frequently than those in section 2. For example, in the October 2024 Session, the SCA referred 85 times to General Observations in section 1 and 24 times to those in section 2.

[87] De Beco and Murray (n 18) 146.

[88] Mertus (n 60) 89.

[89] E Decaux, 'Evolution and Perspectives for National Institutions for the Promotion and Protection of Human Rights: Their Contribution to the Prevention of Human Rights Violations' in LA Sicilianos and C Bourloyannis Vrailas (eds), *The Prevention of Human Rights Violations* (Kluwer Law International 2001) 233, 236.

regardless of whether they are eventually accredited with A-status, to further improve their levels of compliance with the Paris Principles. The SCA considers that compliance with the Paris Principles is a question of degree.

This normative gradation principle derives from one of the primary functions of the Paris Principles – to promote the establishment and proper functioning of independent and effective NHRIs. From this perspective, unlike the interpretation and application of treaties by judicial organs, the SCA's interpretation and application of the Paris Principles aim not to determine the legality of a certain measure in a black-or-white manner, but to hold a constructive dialogue with the NHRI concerned to identity problems and discuss solutions for improvements.

However, the Paris Principles have also played another function as the standard of accreditation.[90] The outcomes of the accreditation have increasingly played a decisive role as the 'filter' for participatory opportunities[91] in various international human rights law fora[92] and in the GANHRI itself,[93] and as the source of NHRI's legitimacy and credibility at both the national and international levels.[94] From this viewpoint, the SCA's approach of normative gradation raises an issue in terms of the need for clear, transparent, foreseeable and consistent accreditation. This was especially so until 2017, where the SCA pointed out deficiencies and gave recommendations to all NHRIs in an equal manner, while not explaining the relationship between such recommendations and accreditation outcomes.

Therefore, since the May 2018 Session, the SCA has adopted a new practice to harmonise these two functions of the Paris Principles: it categorises its recommendations as either those that 'the SCA notes' or those that 'the SCA notes with concern'. If an NHRI receives negative evaluations and recommendations under 'the SCA notes' section, this does not affect its fulfilment of a satisfactory level of compliance with the Paris Principles; the NHRI can still be (re-)accredited with A-status. However, when an NHRI receives any recommendation under 'the SCA notes with concern' heading, this means that the problem(s) is/are sufficiently severe to impact the NHRI's ability to

[90] De Beco and Murray (n 18) 30.

[91] G Fellous, *Les institutions nationales des droits de l'homme: Acteurs de troisième type* (La Documentation Française 2006) 75.

[92] For example, the UN Human Rights Council grants A-status NHRIs special participatory opportunities (UN Human Rights Council Res 16/21, 'Review of the Work and Functioning of the Human Rights Council' (25 March 2011) Annex, paras 13, 22 (a), and 28). For practices in other fora, see UN Human Rights Council, 'Activities of the Global Alliance of National Human Rights Institutions in Accrediting National Institutions in Compliance with the Principles Relating to the Status of National Institutions for the Promotion and Protection of Human Rights (the Paris Principles): Report of the Secretary-General' (2020) UN Doc A/HRC/45/43, para 36.

[93] Only A-status NHRIs can become voting members of the GANHRI and its regional groups and may be elected to sit in the Bureau and other committees. See nn 49 and 54 above.

[94] ENNHRI and Commission nationale consultative des droits de l'homme, *The Accreditation of National Human Rights Institutions: Practical Guide* (2018), https://ennhri.org/wp-content/uploads/2019/09/ENNHRI-CNCDH-Practical-Guide-on-the-Accreditation-of-NHRIs.pdf, 12–13.

satisfy the necessary level of compliance.[95] It is accordingly accredited with or downgraded to B-status.[96] While maintaining that compliance with the Paris Principles is a question of degree, this new practice of the SCA enables NHRIs to know the exact causes for receiving B-status instead of A-status, thereby introducing a certain level of clarity and foreseeability to the SCA's interpretation of the Paris Principles.

5.2.2.4. *The Overall Evaluation Principle*

Finally, the SCA follows the principle of overall evaluation, where it does not assess the requirement on its own, but considers the compliance situations of other requirements and their combined effect on the level of compliance with the Paris Principles as a whole.[97] In other words, whether an issue is categorised under the 'SCA notes' section or the 'SCA notes with concern' section depends not only on the seriousness of the issue in question but also on the compliance situations concerning other requirements. For example, in section 2.3 of its General Observations, the SCA states that when the NHRI cannot comply with the specific requirements of functional immunity:

> [T]he NHRI under review should provide sufficient information to explain why this is the case given its particular national context. This information will be reviewed in line with other guarantees provided at the national level to ensure independence, security of tenure, and the ability to engage in critical analysis on human rights issues.[98]

This principle of overall evaluation presumably derives from the need to flexibly consider and respect the wide diversity of NHRIs, both in their institutional structures and in the legal and social situations surrounding them.

5.2.3. The Global Alliance of National Human Rights Institutions as the Accountability Mechanism for National Human Rights Institutions' Compliance with the Paris Principles

In the GANHRI's accreditation procedure, NHRIs, rather than states, are the subjects of accreditation, and the performance of the NHRI, and not that of the state, is reviewed.[99] Consequently, as Meg Brodie pointed out, the accreditation

[95] Canadian Human Rights Commission (on behalf of GANHRI), *A Practical Guide to the Work of the Sub-Committee on Accreditation (SCA)* (2018), https://ganhri.org/wp-content/uploads/2019/11/GANHRI-Manual_online1.pdf, 36.

[96] SCA Report (May 2018) 5–6. Sometimes, the accreditation of the NHRI that receives recommendations under 'the SCA notes with concern' section is deferred for several sessions so that the NHRI may take necessary measures to ameliorate the issue.

[97] Canadian Human Rights Commission (n 95) 16.

[98] SCA's General Observations (n 46) s 2.3.

[99] Langtry and Roberts Lyer (n 50) 342–43.

outcome may sometimes be 'counter-intuitive', in that the NHRI of a state with a poor human rights record may be accredited A-status or vice versa.[100]

Thus, the GANHRI's accreditation procedure functions as an accountability mechanism that directly addresses NHRIs to ensure their compliance with the Paris Principles. In most cases, unlike parliaments, courts or the executive branch, NHRIs do not have domestic origins; they are products of international and transnational initiatives, for which the adoption of the Paris Principles is symbolic.[101] Accordingly, an NHRI's identity is substantially linked to its compliance with the Paris Principles.[102] If an NHRI fails to be accredited with A-status, its credibility is seriously impaired in both the domestic and international arenas, and its legitimacy and raison d'etre are undermined (see section 5.2.2.3). It is beyond the scope of this chapter to conduct empirical research on the effect of the GANHRI's accreditation procedure on NHRIs' compliance with the Paris Principles. Nevertheless, it is noteworthy that the comprehensive research on NHRIs' submissions to the SCA from 1999 to 2011 by Sulini Sarugaser-Hug revealed at least 15 cases in which the SCA's recommendations prompted NHRIs' actions towards their implementation.[103]

5.2.4. National Human Rights Institutions as Addressees of the Paris Principles

As the Paris Principles are framed in terms of the phrase '[a] national institution shall', it is not clear whom they address. On the one hand, such provisions may be interpreted as addressing states, as certain requirements, such as the establishment of NHRIs based on the constitution or law (section A-2 of the Paris Principles), can only be realised by states. On the other hand, other parts of the principles may be understood as addressing NHRIs, regulating the ways in which they themselves interpret and exercise their mandates under domestic laws.[104] For example, as mentioned earlier, in the October 2018 Session, the SCA

[100] M Brodie, 'Progressing Norm Socialisation: Why Membership Matters. The Impact of the Accreditation Process of the International Coordinating Committee of National Institutions for the Promotion and Protection of Human Rights' (2011) 80 *Nordic Journal of International Law* 143, 144–45.

[101] In 1991, only around 30 NHRIs existed. See Report of the 1991 International Workshop on NHRIs (n 35) para 28. Today, approximately 120 exist. Linos and Pegram have empirically shown that the Paris Principles are likely to have contributed to the rapid spread of NHRIs globally. See Linos and Pegram (n 16) 1114–15.

[102] Brodie (n 100) 152–53. Many NHRIs emphasise their compliance with the Paris Principles and accreditation with A-status on their websites and leaflets.

[103] S Sarugaser-Hug, 'How a Peer-Review Mechanism Can Influence the Implementation of International Human Rights Standards: Why the Work of the Sub-Committee on Accreditation of the International Coordinating Committee of National Institutions for the Promotion and Protection of Human Rights Matters' (2012) 18 *Australian Journal of Human Rights* 45.

[104] De Beco and Murray (n 18) 136–38.

relied on sections A-1, A-2 and A-3 of the Paris Principles to encourage 'the DIHR to continue to interpret its protection mandate in a broad manner and to conduct a range of protection actions'.[105]

Importantly, even in cases where legislative amendments are necessary for compliance, the SCA focuses on the efforts of the NHRI itself by reviewing whether the NHRI has actively advocated for such legislative amendments.[106] In its review of the Institution of Human Rights Ombudsmen of Bosnia and Herzegovina (IHROBH) in 2009, the SCA expressed its concerns regarding several problems, including the lack of pluralism in the appointment process. The SCA then indicated its intention to downgrade the IHROBH to B-status and gave it a one-year moratorium to rectify the problems.[107] In response to the recommendation, the IHROBH worked hard to convince the Parliament to change the laws concerning its structure. Therefore, in 2010, the SCA 'commend[ed] the efforts undertaken by the IHROBH' and recommended that the IHROBH be re-accredited with A-status, even though the laws in question had not yet been amended.[108] While advancing such practices in recent years, the SCA has begun to recommend that NHRIs 'advocate for amendments to its enabling law' so that they can fully comply with the Paris Principles.[109] Accordingly, the practice of the SCA has transformed the Paris Principles into norms that directly address NHRIs.

5.3. EMERGING INTER-PARLIAMENTARY NORMS ON HUMAN RIGHTS

Although not as consolidated as the Paris Principles on NHRIs, 'inter-parliamentary norms' – an autonomous normative order of, by and for national parliaments – are emerging in the field of human rights law. 'Inter-parliamentary organisations/bodies' – transnational organisations/bodies composed of national parliaments and parliamentarians, especially the Inter-Parliamentary Union (IPU) and the Parliamentary Assembly of the Council of Europe (PACE) – have contributed to the creation of such norms, some of which are codified in documents such as the 'Draft Principles on Parliaments and Human Rights' (section 5.3.1). Although the procedure for the interpretation and application of such norms, as well as the methods of their interpretation, have not been developed, inter-parliamentary organisations/bodies have become fora for ensuring the accountability of parliaments for their compliance with inter-parliamentary norms (section 5.3.2). Most inter-parliamentary norms address parliaments rather than states (section 5.3.3).

[105] SCA Report (October 2018) 8.
[106] K Roberts Lyer, 'The Role and Functioning of the International Coordinating Committee of National Human Rights Institutions in International Human Rights Bodies' in Meuwissen and Wouters (n 67) 223, 235.
[107] SCA Report (November 2009) 6–7.
[108] SCA Report (October 2010) 5.
[109] See, eg, SCA Report (October 2019) 8.

5.3.1. Creation of Inter-parliamentary Norms on Human Rights in Inter-parliamentary Organisations and Bodies

5.3.1.1. The Inter-Parliamentary Union

The IPU is an inter-parliamentary organisation composed of parliaments across the globe, with 182 member parliaments and 15 associate members. Article 1(2) of the Statute of the IPU stipulates that the IPU shall function '[a]s the focal point for worldwide parliamentary dialogue'. It also provides that the IPU shall 'contribute to the defence and promotion of human rights'. The Assembly (formerly known as the Inter-Parliamentary Conference) is the main political body composed of all member parliaments, and its sessions are held twice a year to adopt resolutions. Draft resolutions are prepared by standing committees.

Under the initiative of the Standing Committee on Democracy and Human Rights, the IPU has highlighted the importance of parliamentary roles in human rights protection. The turning point was the IPU's hosting of an inter-parliamentary symposium 'Parliament: Guardian of Human Rights' in 1993, in which the participants affirmed that 'parliamentary activity … could and should be oriented more deliberately towards consideration of human rights'.[110] To trace the major developments since then, in the Inter-Parliamentary Conference, the resolutions entitled 'Strengthening National Structures, Institutions and Organizations of Society Which Play a Role in Promoting and Safeguarding Human Rights' (1994)[111] and 'Strong Action by National Parliaments in the Year of the 50th Anniversary of the Universal Declaration of Human Rights to Ensure the Promotion and Protection of All Human Rights in the 21st Century' (1998)[112] were adopted. In 2004, the seminar 'Strengthening Parliament as a Guardian of Human Rights' was held and attended by parliamentarians from more than 50 states.[113] In 2016, the IPU Assembly adopted an outcome document of the General Debate 'Human Rights Abuses as Precursors of Conflict: Parliaments as Early Responders'.[114]

These developments address a wide range of aspects concerning parliamentary composition, working methods and activities. First, they emphasise the importance of the inclusive representation of all sectors of society in

[110] 'Summing-up of the Deliberations by the President of the Symposium', *Inter-Parliamentary Symposium: Parliament: Guardian of Human Rights* (Budapest, 19–22 May 1993) para 38.

[111] Inter-Parliamentary Conference Res, 'Strengthening National Structures, Institutions and Organizations of Society Which Play a Role in Promoting and Safeguarding Human Rights' (17 September 1994).

[112] Inter-Parliamentary Conference Res, 'Strong Action by National Parliaments in the Year of the 50th Anniversary of the Universal Declaration of Human Rights to Ensure the Promotion and Protection of All Human Rights in the 21st Century' (11 September 1998).

[113] *Seminar: Strengthening Parliament as a Guardian of Human Rights* (organised by the IPU and the UNDP with the support of the OHCHR) (Geneva, 15–17 March 2004).

[114] IPU Assembly, 'Outcome Document of the General Debate: Human Rights Abuses as Precursors of Conflict' (27 October 2016).

parliaments, including minorities and vulnerable groups, in both the composition and decision-making process of parliaments.[115] For this purpose, parliamentarians should be chosen through free and fair elections by universal and equal suffrage,[116] and the opposition must be given opportunities to freely perform its role in the parliament.[117] Moreover, parliaments are required to foster a partnership with civil society and NGOs.[118] Second, parliaments should scrutinise legislation in light of international human rights standards[119] and supervise the government's compliance with such standards.[120] Third, parliaments should interact with and contribute to the activities of international human rights monitoring bodies.[121] Finally, parliaments are encouraged to create parliamentary human rights committees to exercise their responsibilities effectively in relation to these requirements.[122] All these elements directly contribute to the parliaments' duties in the separation of powers in a globalised democratic society model, namely, to conduct thorough, transparent and open 'bounded' deliberations while ensuring the representation and participation of all sectors of society.

In addition, since the 2000s, the IPU has held numerous national and regional-level seminars for parliamentarians aimed at improving the role of parliaments in the implementation of human rights treaties.[123] For example, in the seminar held in Mauritania in 2008, the participants discussed general strategies such as producing annual reports on parliamentary actions related to human rights, as well as solutions for concrete human rights issues.[124]

Inspired by the IPU's initiatives, the UN has taken various actions to enhance parliamentary roles in human rights treaties.[125] In 2010, the General Assembly adopted Resolution 65/123 entitled 'Cooperation between the United Nations, National Parliaments and the Inter-Parliamentary Union'. The General Assembly acknowledged 'the role and responsibility of national parliaments in regard to national plans and strategies, as well as in ensuring greater transparency and

[115] ibid 'Recommendations', para 3.

[116] 'Summing-up of the Deliberations by the President of the Symposium' (n 110) para 10.

[117] ibid para 21.

[118] ibid para 37; Inter-Parliamentary Conference (n 111) para 19.

[119] Inter-Parliamentary Conference (n 112) para 1(iii); IPU Assembly (n 114) 'Recommendations', para 1.

[120] 'Summing-up of the Deliberations by the President of the Symposium' (n 110) para 24.

[121] Loretta Ann P Rosales (Chairperson), 'Concluding Observations' *Seminar: Strengthening Parliament as a Guardian of Human Rights* (organised by the IPU and the UNDP with the support of the OHCHR) (Geneva, 15–17 March 2004). Note that this was not what the participants agreed on, but rather what the chairperson of the seminar introduced as a favourable practice.

[122] IPU Assembly (note 114) 'Recommendations', para 1.

[123] For summaries of the proceedings of the seminars, see the IPU's website on 'Parliamentary Work on Human Rights' at: http://archive.ipu.org/hr-e/parliaments.htm.

[124] 'Résumé et conclusions' *Séminaire: Le rôle du parlement mauritanien dans les travaux des organes de traités relatifs aux droits de l'homme* (organised by the IPU and the OHCHR in collaboration with the National Assembly of Mauritania) (Nouakchott, 12–14 May 2008).

[125] See generally K Roberts Lyer, 'Parliaments as Human Rights Actors: The Potential for International Principles on Parliamentary Human Rights Committees' (2019) 37 *NJHR* 195.

accountability'[126] and encouraged the IPU 'to strengthen its contribution to the United Nations human rights treaty body system'.[127]

Most importantly, since 2017, the UN Human Rights Council has taken initiatives in drafting the 'Principles on Parliaments and Human Rights' through considering the Paris Principles on NHRIs as a model.[128] To offer a guide, the OHCHR carried out a survey of parliamentary practices worldwide in cooperation with the IPU and published a report in 2018. The 'Draft Principles on Parliaments and Human Rights' is annexed to this report and primarily focuses on 'the setting up of parliamentary human rights committees' and 'ensuring their effective functioning'.[129] The Draft Principles provide the mandates, responsibilities, functions, composition and working methods of parliamentary human rights committees. Parliamentary human rights committees shall introduce and review bills, existing legislation and draft national budgets to ensure compatibility with international human rights obligations; lead parliamentary oversight of the government's compliance with human rights obligations; provide human rights-related information and training to parliamentarians; lead parliamentary actions such as legislative initiatives, parliamentary enquiries, public hearings, public debates, requesting information and documentation, summoning and hearing witnesses; and issue reports on national human rights issues and developments. Moreover, parliamentary human rights committees shall participate in the national mechanism for reporting and follow-up on international and regional human rights mechanisms and interact with human rights treaty organs. In fulfilling these responsibilities and functions, they shall possess human rights expertise, respect the principles of pluralism and non-partisanship, and consult with NHRIs, civil society and relevant experts. Parliamentary human rights committees fulfilling these requirements will surely enable a parliament to effectively fulfil its duties in separation of powers in a globalised democratic society.

Although the Draft Principles on Parliaments and Human Rights were not formerly written by parliaments themselves, they are still considered as a product of 'a parliamentarian-driven exercise' as they 'were based on a study of best practices in parliaments' widely collected through the IPU.[130] Thus, parliaments have emphasised that '[p]arliamentarians should own the next steps of the process, including the adoption of such draft principles'.[131] One such step

[126] UNGA Res 65/123, 'Cooperation between the United Nations, National Parliaments and the Inter-Parliamentary Union' (13 December 2010) preambular para 13.

[127] ibid para 7.

[128] UN Human Rights Council Res 35/29, 'Contribution of Parliaments to the Work of the Human Rights Council and its Universal Periodic Review' (23 June 2017) para 5.

[129] Report of the OHCHR, 'Contribution of Parliaments to the Work of the Human Rights Council and its Universal Periodic Review' (2018) UN Doc A/HRC/38/25, Annex I: Draft Principles on Parliaments and Human Rights (hereinafter 'Draft Principles on Parliaments and Human Rights') preambular para 10.

[130] UN Human Rights Council, 'Report of the Chair: Second Session of the Forum on Human Rights, Democracy and the Rule of Law', UN Doc A/HRC/40/65 (2019) para 65.

[131] ibid.

would be to discuss the Draft Principles widely and adopt them with necessary amendments within the IPU.

The Draft Principles have enjoyed authority among parliaments despite being only a 'draft'. For example, when the Scottish Parliament's Equalities and Human Rights Committee conducted a study of its own and Scotland's practices related to human rights, involving wide consultations with stakeholders in 2018,[132] it relied on the Draft Principles when publishing an outcome report and recommendations.[133] Additionally, inspired by the Draft Principles, the Uzbek Parliament created a parliamentary commission on international human rights in 2020.[134] The chairperson of the parliamentary commission reportedly committed to 'strengthen[ing] interaction and consultation with the parliamentary ombudsman, NHRIs and representatives of civil society on human rights issues' and to intensifying participation in the work of the UN human rights treaty bodies.[135]

In 2023, after receiving direct inputs from a cross-regional panel of parliamentarians, the IPU and the OHCHR jointly launched a 'self-assessment toolkit' for parliaments and human rights. The toolkit contains a series of checklists for parliaments to self-assess the level of implementation of their human rights roles, such as: 'Does the [parliamentary human rights] committee comprise parliamentarians with human rights expertise?'[136] and 'Have public events on human rights been organized in parliament or by parliament [in the past 12 months]?'[137] These self-assessment checklists largely build on the Draft Principles on Parliaments and Human Rights and other principles reiterated in the above-summarised IPU documents, thereby practically assisting parliaments' implementation of these inter-parliamentary norms on human rights.

5.3.1.2. The Parliamentary Assembly of the Council of Europe

As the deliberative organ of the Council of Europe, the PACE[138] is an inter-parliamentary body[139] made up of 306 parliamentarians from the national

[132] B Chang and M Hunt, 'The Role of Parliaments in Implementing Decisions and Recommendations from Supranational Human Rights Bodies' in R Murray and D Long (eds), *Research Handbook on Implementation of Human Rights in Practice* (Edward Elgar 2022) 140, 159 60.

[133] Equalities and Human Rights Committee, Scotland's Parliament, 'Getting Rights Right: Human Rights and the Scottish Parliament' (26 November 2018), https://digitalpublications.parliament.scot/Committees/Report/EHRiC/2018/11/26/Getting-Rights-Right--Human-Rights-and-the-Scottish-Parliament-3.

[134] Chang and Hunt (n 132) 157–58.

[135] Cited in ibid 158.

[136] IPU and OHCHR, *Parliaments and Human Rights: A Self-Assessment Toolkit* (2023), www.ipu.org/resources/publications/toolkits/2023-10/parliaments-and-human-rights-self-assessment-toolkit, 44.

[137] ibid 53.

[138] See generally P Leach, 'The Parliamentary Assembly of the Council of Europe' in S Schmahl and M Breuer (eds), *The Council of Europe: Its Law and Policies* (Oxford University Press 2017) 166.

[139] The PACE is an organ of the Council of Europe and is different from other independent inter-parliamentary organisations, such as the IPU, which possess their own organs. Thus, this chapter refers to the PACE as an inter-parliamentary 'body'.

parliaments of the Council of Europe's 46 Member States. It generally meets four times a year for a week-long plenary session in Strasbourg. The PACE has highlighted the unique duties of national parliaments in human rights protection. In 2011, in Resolution 1787 concerning the implementation of ECtHR's judgments, the PACE stressed that national parliaments must play 'a much more proactive role' in the execution of ECtHR judgments, warning that otherwise, the whole ECHR system 'is likely to be put in jeopardy'.[140] Following this, in the same year, it adopted Resolution 1823 entitled 'National Parliaments: Guarantors of Human Rights in Europe',[141] where a large part of inter-parliamentary norms on human rights in Europe is codified. In this resolution, which plays a leading role and is regularly cited in subsequent resolutions,[142] the PACE regrets that while obligations under the ECHR concern all state organs, '[n]ational parliaments are often overlooked in this context'.[143] It then calls on national parliaments/parliamentarians to fulfil various duties concerning the implementation of international human rights obligations, especially the ECHR and the ECtHR's judgments, and monitoring their implementation by other state organs.[144] This resolution refers to the Paris Principles and emphasises that 'similar benchmarks should be drawn up for parliamentary bodies',[145] thereby presenting 'Basic Principles for Parliamentary Supervision of International Human Rights Standards' in its appendix. These Principles provide that

> National parliaments shall establish appropriate parliamentary structures to ensure rigorous and regular monitoring of compliance with and supervision of international human rights obligations, such as dedicated human rights committees or appropriate analogous structures.[146]

Such structures shall be given remits that are clearly defined and enshrined in law, assisted by experts and specialised secretariats, and cooperate with relevant national and international bodies and civil society.[147] They shall have the following competences: systematically verifying the compatibility of draft legislation with international human rights obligations; requiring governments to regularly submit reports on relevant ECtHR judgments and their implementation; initiating legislative proposals and amendments to laws; and subpoena powers over witnesses and documents.[148] These principles share large parts of their contents with the above-mentioned Draft Principles on Parliaments and Human Rights.

[140] PACE Res 1787, 'Implementation of judgments of the European Court of Human Rights' (26 January 2011) para 2.

[141] PACE Res 1823, 'National Parliaments: Guarantors of Human Rights in Europe' (23 June 2011).

[142] See, eg, PACE Res 2055, 'The Effectiveness of the European Convention on Human Rights: The Brighton Declaration and Beyond' (24 April 2015) para 6; PACE Res 2178, 'Implementation of Judgments of the European Court of Human Rights' (29 June 2017) para 10.

[143] ibid paras 1–2.

[144] ibid para 6.

[145] PACE Res 1823 (n 141) para 4.

[146] ibid Appendix, para 1.

[147] ibid paras 1–3.

[148] ibid paras 1.

In 2018, the PACE published a 100-page handbook for parliamentarians entitled 'National Parliaments as Guarantors of Human Rights in Europe', elaborating on each of the above-mentioned elements with guiding practices.[149] The handbook stressed that where a parliament had conducted 'reasoned participatory deliberations' and done its best 'to review and ensure the compatibility of the proposed measure with Convention', that parliament can 'earn' deference from the ECtHR.[150]

5.3.1.3. Other Regional Inter-parliamentary Organisations

The Commonwealth Parliamentary Association, which comprises over 180 parliaments from the 53 member countries of the Commonwealth, has also made significant contributions to the mainstreaming of human rights in parliament by holding joint workshops with the IPU and adopting its own declarations on the topic.[151] In 2014, the Mahé Declaration was adopted as an outcome of the 'Africa Regional Seminar for Members of Parliament on the Role of Parliamentarians in the Promotion and Protection of Human Rights'. In 2015 and 2016, the Pipitea Declaration and Kotte Declaration were adopted after similar regional seminars in the Pacific and Asia, respectively.[152] They all recognise that parliaments are 'a key institution' that protects and promotes human rights. The participants in these declarations were committed to ensuring that human rights norms and principles are reflected in legislation, increasing engagement with international and human rights mechanisms, and establishing parliamentary human rights committees.

The Parliamentary Assembly of the Mediterranean (PAM) is a relatively new inter-parliamentary organisation established in 2005; it is composed of 34 parliaments in the Euro-Mediterranean and Gulf regions. In 2019, the PAM adopted a resolution 'PAM MPs for Human Rights',[153] calling on its member parliaments to play their legislative, oversight and other functions to implement international human rights obligations and recommendations, and to engage with international human rights mechanisms. Notably, the resolution repeatedly relied on the Draft Principles on Parliaments and Human Rights and invited the member parliaments to set up parliamentary human rights committees in conformity with the Draft Principles.[154]

[149] PACE, *Handbook for Parliamentarians: National Parliaments as Guarantors of Human Rights in Europe* (Council of Europe 2018).

[150] ibid 83–84.

[151] See generally Commonwealth Secretariat and Universal Rights Group, *The Global Human Rights Implementation Agenda: The Role of National Parliaments* (2018), www.universal-rights.org/urg-policy-reports/the-global-human-rights-implementation-agenda-the-role-of-national-parliaments-2/, 10–11.

[152] These declarations are available at the Commonwealth Parliamentary Association's website on 'The CPA and Human Rights' at: www.cpahq.org/about-us/our-principles/the-cpa-and-human-rights.

[153] Parliamentary Assembly of the Mediterranean Res, 'PAM MPs for Human Rights' (22 February 2019).

[154] ibid para VII.

5.3.2. Inter-parliamentary Organisations and Bodies as the Accountability Mechanism for Parliaments' Compliance with Inter-parliamentary Norms

The appointment and dismissal of NHRI members and their activities are (supposed to be) independent of government interference and the majority's will. In contrast, parliaments are closely related to governments, most prominently in states adopting a parliamentary system in which the party (or parties) with the greatest representation in parliament forms the government. Sometimes, a parliament is degraded to being a mere 'rubber stamp' that uncritically passes the bills submitted by the government and fails to effectively exercise its oversight functions. Moreover, the position of parliamentarians is insecure and depends directly on elections – majority voting. Thus, compared with NHRIs, parliaments are much less independent of the government and other external factors, especially the majority's will. Improving the independence of parliaments is essential for them to fulfil their duties as human rights actors in their own right;[155] therefore, creating an accountability mechanism for parliaments at the transnational level is an effective strategy to this effect (see the discussion on transgovernmental networking theory in section 5.5.4).

Unlike the Paris Principles, which are interpreted by the GANHRI's SCA in a centralised and authoritative manner based on its 'jurisprudence',[156] interpretation of inter-parliamentary norms on human rights is still largely left to individual parliaments and the interpretative method is underdeveloped. The lack of a clear, consistent and transparent interpretative framework and an authoritative mechanism to determine compliance is detrimental to ensuring an effective and legitimate accountability mechanism. Nevertheless, there are signs that accountability mechanisms for parliaments are emerging within the frameworks of inter-parliamentary organisations/bodies, though in an underdeveloped and modest manner.

The PACE has developed several procedures to hold parliament(arian)s accountable for the fulfilment of their duties under the inter-parliamentary norms on human rights. First, in its Resolution 1516 entitled 'Implementation of Judgments of the European Court of Human Rights' in 2006, the PACE highlighted that it:

> [R]eserves the right to take appropriate action, notably by making use of Rule 8 of its Rules of Procedure (namely, challenging the credentials of a national delegation), … should the national parliament fail to exert the necessary pressure on the government to implement judgments of the Court.[157]

Although there has been no case of suspension of credentials solely for that specific reason, when the PACE adopted a resolution not to ratify the credentials

[155] M Krennerich, *Human Rights Politics: An Introduction* (Springer 2024) 59–60.
[156] Canadian Human Rights Commission (n 95) 11.
[157] PACE Res 1516, 'Implementation of Judgments of the European Court of Human Rights' (2 October 2006) para 22.7.

of the delegation of Azerbaijan in 2024, it stated that Azerbaijan's failure to respect human rights, as illustrated by the ECtHR judgments, was one of the reasons for the suspension.[158] Although the criticism in this resolution was largely directed towards the state as a whole, it also criticised the 'Azerbaijani [parliamentary] delegation's lack of co-operation with the Rapporteur for the Committee on Legal Affairs and Human Rights' on human rights issues.[159] Moreover, in this resolution, the PACE referred to its Resolution 2494 (2023),[160] which called on member parliaments to implement the Basic Principles for Parliamentary Supervision of International Human Rights Standards and to engage in monitoring the implementation of ECtHR judgments.[161] The possibility of suspension of credentials itself can provide PACE members with strong incentives to advocate that their respective national parliaments fulfil their duties under the inter-parliamentary norms on human rights.

Second, since 2012, the PACE's Committee on Legal Affairs and Human Rights has held a series of hearings with the heads of parliamentary delegations from the states that have had serious problems in the implementation of ECtHR judgments.[162] In these hearings, detailed information notes on the unimplemented judgments by the state under hearing are circulated in advance,[163] and the heads of parliamentary delegations are requested by other PACE members to account for the concrete parliamentary actions and plans towards implementation. The fact that these hearings are open to the public and that NGOs can attend them strengthens their function as accountability mechanisms directed at the parliament(arian)s.

Third, the PACE has criticised the failure to implement ECtHR judgments within the context of its monitoring activities, led by the Committee on the Honouring of Obligations and Commitments by Member States of the Council of Europe (hereinafter 'Monitoring Committee'). For example, in PACE Resolution 2459 (2022) entitled 'The Honouring of Obligations and Commitments by Türkiye', adopted based on the reports of the Monitoring Committee, the PACE repeatedly called for the implementation of major ECtHR judgments against Turkey.[164] Although the monitoring procedure targets Member States instead of

[158] PACE Res 2527, 'Challenge, on Substantive Grounds, of the Still Unratified Credentials of the Parliamentary Delegation of Azerbaijan' (24 January 2024) para 2.

[159] ibid para 6.

[160] ibid para 3.

[161] PACE Res 2494, 'Implementation of Judgments of the European Court of Human Rights' (26 April 2023) para 8.

[162] PACE's Committee on Legal Affairs and Human Rights, 'Implementation of Judgments of the European Court of Human Rights: Extracts from the Minutes of Hearings, Organised by the Committee, Held in Strasbourg in April 2012, in June 2012, in October 2012 and in January 2013' (2013) AS/Jur(2013)13.

[163] See, eg, PACE's Committee on Legal Affairs and Human Rights, Mr Constantinos Efstathiou (Rapporteur), 'The Implementation of Judgments of the European Court of Human Rights: 11th Report Information Note in Preparation of a Hearing in Relation to Türkiye' (2023) AS/Jur (2023) 06.

[164] PACE Res 2459, 'The Honouring of Obligations and Commitments by Türkiye' (12 October 2022) para 8.

parliaments/parliamentarians, it may contribute to raising awareness among PACE members of the state subject to monitoring. The PACE could consider expressly referring to the duties of parliaments in this procedure.

Additionally, as a softer accountability mechanism, in its Resolution 2494 (2023), the PACE reiterated its willingness to hold targeted events at the parliamentary level, such as conferences and seminars, in countries where parliamentary involvement would be effective in the implementation of ECtHR judgments.[165]

Unlike the PACE, which has an institutional tie with the ECHR system as part of the Council of Europe system, the IPU has no such ties with the UN or other regional human rights treaty systems. For the reason, the IPU is not equipped with accountability mechanisms comparable to those within the PACE. Nevertheless, the various initiatives of the IPU on human rights, including those referred to in the previous subsection, not only facilitate the creation of inter-parliamentary norms on human rights but also incentivise parliaments/parliamentarians to comply with these norms through peer pressure. For example, given her experience in the IPU, a Japanese MP, Ms Yoko Kamikawa, made the following statement in the National Diet of Japan:

> [W]e discussed the issues of the worst forms of child labour, human trafficking and child sexual exploitation [at the IPU's Coordinating Committee of Women Parliamentarians] ... As Japan is widely known as one of the major destination countries for human trafficking, I felt deeply ashamed ... In light of this, I would like to request that the speaker from the Ministry of Foreign Affairs elaborate on the current initiatives taken by the government and the future strategies in this regard.[166]

The IPU could provide a more powerful and effective accountability mechanism by institutionalising sanctions, such as the suspension of membership or reduction of voting rights against parliaments that continuously fail to fulfil their human rights duties. For example, for enhancing gender equality, the Statutes of the IPU provides that '[a]ny delegation that for two consecutive sessions of the Assembly is composed exclusively of parliamentarians of the same sex shall automatically be reduced by one person'.[167] A similar sanction could be introduced regarding the fulfilment of duties under inter-parliamentary norms on human rights.

5.3.3. Parliaments as Addressees of Inter-parliamentary Norms

Unlike the Paris Principles on NHRIs, which are codified into a single document, inter-parliamentary norms on human rights exist in more scattered forms. Nevertheless, PACE Resolution 1823 and the appended Basic Principles for

[165] PACE Res 2494, 'Implementation of Judgments of the European Court of Human Rights' (26 April 2023) para 10.

[166] Yoko Kamikawa, Special Committee on Youth Affairs of the House of Representatives, 159th Session of the National Diet, No 6 (3 June 2004) 2 (Japan).

[167] Article 10(4) of the Statutes of the IPU (last amended in 2024).

Parliamentary Supervision of International Human Rights Standards, as well as the Draft Principles on Parliaments and Human Rights prepared by the OHCHR in cooperation with the IPU, are representative of inter-parliamentary norms on human rights. They directly address parliaments. PACE Resolution 1823 repeatedly uses terms such as 'the Assembly urges parliamentarians to …' and 'the Assembly calls on parliaments to …'.[168] The first principle of the PACE's Basic Principles for Parliamentary Supervision of International Human Rights Standards begins with '[n]ational parliaments shall establish appropriate parliamentary structures …'.[169] Similarly, the preamble of the Draft Principles on Parliaments and Human Rights states that '[t]he following Principles should guide parliaments in the setting up of parliamentary human rights committees, as well as in ensuring their effective functioning'.[170] Other relevant documents also largely address national parliaments and parliamentarians,[171] although they sometimes contain recommendations directed at government and states.[172]

5.4. IMMATURE BUT SLOWLY DEVELOPING INTER-NATIONAL COURT NORMS ON HUMAN RIGHTS

It has been widely shared that national courts are important players for the effective implementation of international (human rights) law.[173] Therefore, many previous studies exist on the application of human rights treaties by national courts and the judicial dialogue/dialogue between judges (see Chapter 1, section 1.1.3.1). Nonetheless, 'inter-national court norms' – an autonomous normative order of, by and for national courts – have not yet been consolidated in the field of human rights, as debates on the role of national courts in human rights treaties within 'inter-national court organisations/networks' – transnational organisations/networks composed of national courts – are only at an early and undeveloped stage (section 5.4.1). A 'global community of courts' created through horizontal judicial dialogue among national courts on human rights treaties may function as a unique accountability mechanism for national courts (section 5.4.2).

5.4.1. Discussion on National Courts' Duties in Inter-National Court Organisations and Networks

Carsten Smith, then the Chief Justice of the Norwegian Supreme Court, stated in 1998 that: 'The Supreme Court has to an increasing degree taken part in

[168] PACE Res 1823 (n 141) para 6.
[169] ibid Appendix, para 1.
[170] Draft Principles on Parliaments and Human Rights (n 129) preambular para 10.
[171] See, eg, Inter-Parliamentary Conference (n 112) paras 1, 2, 4 and 5.
[172] See, eg, PACE Res 1823 (n 141) paras 6.3 and 6.4.
[173] See, eg, RA Falk, *The Role of Domestic Courts in the International Legal Order* (Syracuse University Press 1964) 65.

international collaboration among the highest courts. It is a natural obligation that ... we should take part in European and international debate and mutual interaction.'[174] Recently, such a view has become more widely shared as opportunities to debate the roles of national courts in human rights treaties have increased within inter-national court organisations/networks.

The World Conference on Constitutional Justice (WCCJ) is a universal inter-national court organisation with the General Assembly, Bureau and the Secretariat; it is composed of 120 constitutional courts/councils and supreme courts. According to Article 1 of the WCCJ Statute, the objective of the WCCJ is to 'promote[] constitutional justice – understood as constitutional review, including human rights case-law – as a key element for democracy, the protection of human rights and the rule of law'.[175] A 'flagrant violation' by a member court of such principles serves as the basis for suspension of its membership.[176] Since its first conference in 2009, the WCCJ has held five conferences, and the role of national courts in human rights protection has been one of the most important topics. Albeit only occasionally, the participants exchange information and views regarding their experiences with the application of and reference to human rights treaty standards.[177] At the universal level, the International Association of Judges, established in 1953 and comprising 93 national associations of judges, could also potentially serve as a forum for discussing the roles of national courts in human rights treaties.

At the regional level, since 2005, the ECtHR has annually hosted the seminar 'Dialogue between Judges', in which judges of the ECtHR and national courts of Member States make speeches and conduct discussions on common topics.[178] The common topics often concern the duties of domestic courts in the ECHR, such as 'How Can We Ensure Greater Involvement of National Courts in the Convention System?' in 2012 and 'Implementation of the Judgments of the European Court of Human Rights: A Shared Judicial Responsibility?' in 2014. In these seminars, while mindful of the constitutional limits on the application of and reference to the ECHR and the ECtHR jurisprudence by national courts,[179] the participants have emphasised that national courts should act as if 'they are delegated with the task of reviewing the conventionality of national decisions, with the Strasbourg Court entitled to act as a

[174] Statement of Carsten Smith quoted in AM Slaughter, 'A Global Community of Courts' (2003) 44 *Harvard International Law Journal* 191, 194–95.

[175] Article 1 of the Statute of the World Conference on Constitutional Justice (amended in 2017).

[176] ibid art 9.

[177] See, eg, Han-Chul Park (President of the Constitutional Court of the Republic of Korea), 'Session II Keynote Speech: International Standards for Social Integration' *3rd Congress of the WCCJ* (Seoul, 29 September 2014).

[178] A list of these seminars and their proceedings are available on the ECtHR's website at 'Opening of the Judicial Year' at: www.echr.coe.int/opening-of-the-judicial-year.

[179] See, eg, Andreas Voßkuhle (President of Bundesverfassungsgericht, Germany), 'Pyramid or Mobile? Human Rights Protection by the European Constitutional Courts' in ECtHR, *Proceedings of the Seminar: Dialogue between Judges: Implementation of the Judgments of the European Court of Human Rights* (31 January 2014) 36, 37.

guiding body',[180] and that 'national courts should be incentivised not only to adopt the language, but also to think and reason in terms of the protection of European rights'.[181]

The ECtHR established the Superior Courts Network in 2015, comprising 111 courts from 46 Council of Europe Member States.[182] The Preamble to the Cooperation Charter of the Superior Courts Network states that the ECtHR and national courts have a 'shared responsibility' for the implementation of the ECHR. The Network aims at creating 'a Community of European human rights judges, who, each and every one of them, act as "Strasbourg" judges at the domestic level'.[183] It has held meetings known as 'SCN Focal Points Forums' with workshops annually,[184] on specific topics such as 'National Courts and the Challenge of Climate Change Litigation'.[185] National judges have observed that the Network has helped institutionalise the perception of engagement with the 'same mission, similar language, and shared concerns' among European courts.[186]

For the Americas, la Cumbre Judicial Iberoamericana (the Ibero-American Judicial Summit) has been the most active regional inter-national court organisation. Composed of the supreme courts of 23 countries from the Ibero-American region, the Summit has adopted various important inter-national court norms. For example, it adopted the 'Ibero-American Code of Judicial Ethics' in 2006 and the 'Ibero-American Charter of Victims' Rights' in 2012,[187] providing the duties of member courts in terms of their composition, procedure and working methods. However, these documents do not expressly deal with the courts' roles over interpretation and application of human rights treaties.

The Conferencia Iberoamericana de Justicia Constitucional (CIJC), composed of constitutional courts in the Ibero-American region, is another regional inter-national court organisation. Its objectives include the promotion and defence of human rights.[188] It regularly holds conferences and seminars, many of which touch upon human rights issues. Owing to the only partial overlap of membership between the ACHR and the CIJC, the roles of national courts in the ACHR are not directly discussed there. Nevertheless, member

[180] Sabino Cassese (Judge Emeritus of the Constitutional Court of Justice, Italy), 'Ruling Indirectly: Judicial Subsidiarity in the ECtHR' in ECtHR, *Proceedings of the Seminar: Dialogue between Judges 2015: Subsidiarity: A Two-Sided Coin?* (31 January 2015) 11, 17.

[181] Michal Bobek (Judge, Supreme Administrative Court of the Czech Republic), 'Subsidiarity: A View from a National Judiciary', in ECtHR, *Proceedings of the Seminar: Dialogue between Judges 2024: Revisiting Subsidiarity in the Age of Shared Responsibility* (24 January 2024) 27, 30.

[182] See generally O Andreotti, 'The Superior Courts Network of the European Court of Human Rights: An Innovative Working Tool Allowing a Structured Dialogue with National Courts' (2021) 41 *HRLJ* 329.

[183] R Spano, 'International and Supranational Catalogues of Human Rights in Theory and in Practice' (2021) 41 *HRLJ* 1, 3.

[184] A list of these events and related documents are available on the ECtHR's website at 'Superior Courts Network' at: https://prd-echr.coe.int/web/echr/superior-courts-network.

[185] See Superior Courts Network, 'Superior Courts Network Forum 6–7 June 2024: Agenda' (2024).

[186] Bobek (n 181) 30.

[187] These documents are available at 'Productos Axiológicos' on the Ibero-American Judicial Summit's website: www.cumbrejudicial.org/productos-axiologicos.

[188] Article 2(1) of the Statute of the CIJC.

courts often refer to the IACtHR's jurisprudence in the CIJC's conferences and seminars,[189] thereby raising awareness of the ACHR among peer courts.

In addition, the European Commission for Democracy through Law of the Council of Europe, known as the 'Venice Commission', has set up the Sub-Commission for Latin America, which regularly holds meetings for the presidents and judges of the Latin-American constitutional/supreme courts and the IACtHR. For example, in 2013, it held the International Congress on the Implementation of International Human Rights Treaties in National Legislation in Mexico.[190]

5.4.2. Potential Emergence of a Global Community of Courts Through Horizontal Judicial Dialogue on Human Rights Treaties

The previous subsection has shown that the roles of national courts in human rights treaties have been addressed only sporadically within inter-national court organisations/networks, and that such discussions have not yet led to the development of effective inter-national court norms on human rights. This may be because the mandates of national courts are strictly defined under their respective constitutions, laws and jurisprudence; national courts possess less flexibility and discretion compared to parliaments and NHRIs. Nevertheless, as judges across the world share the legal mindset and reasoning unique to lawyers, dialogue between national judges (horizontal judicial dialogue) through reference to one another's jurisprudence on human rights treaties could create a non-institutionalised but effective 'global community of courts'. This may potentially serve as a unique accountability mechanism, though much softer and voluntary compared to that provided by the GANHRI or the PACE, for ensuring compliance by national judges with their duties.

In a 2003 article, Anne-Marie Slaughter argued that a 'global community of courts' is emerging through judges reading and citing each other's opinions.[191] Such a community may be 'as close as it is possible to come to a formal global legal system' when sufficiently developed,[192] where judges 'see each other not only as servants and representatives of a particular polity, but also as fellow professionals in an endeavor that transcends national borders'.[193] Slaughter argues that in order to become a genuine community, judges 'must share the common values and principles that constitute the normative understandings of a community'.[194] Nevertheless, she did not clarify the specific

[189] See, eg, Argentina's Questionnaire Responses in the CIJC's Seminar on Access to Constitutional Justice for Indigenous People (17–20 October 2023), www.cijc.org/es/seminarios/2023-Cartagena-Indias/Paginas/documentos-trabajo.aspx.

[190] Venice Commission, 'Annual Report of Activities 2013' (2014), www.venice.coe.int/webforms/documents/?pdf=CDL-RA(2013)001-e, 69.

[191] Slaughter (n 174).

[192] ibid 218.

[193] ibid 193.

[194] ibid 215.

content of these common values and principles or how they are to be identified. Udi Sommer and Olga Frishman further advanced this vision, arguing that references by national courts to international law are a necessary condition for the creation of an 'epistemic community' of judges.[195] Once judges belong to such a community, judges would rely on international law 'by the power of being members of an international epistemic community', 'notwithstanding whether they are required to do so by constitutional mandate or due to legal reasons'.[196] Eyal Benvenisti and George W Downs argued, with some examples of national courts extensively relying on international law and citing each other in its interpretation, that:

> Co-operative courts will be cited with approval and approbation by their counterparts, whereas courts which step out of line by either refusing to give force to a new standard or setting a different standard will be criticized, sometimes quite severely, in judgments.[197]

5.5. COOPERATIVE INTERACTIONS BETWEEN INTER-STATE ORGAN NORMS ON HUMAN RIGHTS AND HUMAN RIGHTS TREATIES BASED ON SHARED VALUES

The previous sections have shown that inter-state organ norms on human rights are emerging for NHRIs, parliaments and courts, albeit to varying degrees and in varying modes. This section examines the relationship between these inter-state organ norms and human rights treaties.

To approach this question, this chapter adopts the theoretical lens of 'global legal pluralism'. This lens enables observation of what was previously unobservable under the classical approach – that is, cooperative interactions between inter-state organ norms on human rights and human rights treaties on an equal footing (section 5.5.1). This chapter adopts 'constitutional legal pluralism' over 'radical pluralism', to argue that inter-state organ norms and human rights treaties should interact closely and cooperatively under shared values in 'globalised democratic societies' (section 5.5.2). It then examines the signs of cooperative interactions between inter-state organ norms and human rights treaties, and proposes ways to further facilitate such interactions (section 5.5.3). This examination focuses on the Paris Principles and inter-parliamentary norms on human rights, excluding inter-national court norms, which are much less developed.

Thus, the normative basis of the 'duties' of individual state organs in the separation of powers in a globalised democratic society model is the cooperative interactions between inter-state organ norms and human rights treaties. Such

[195] U Sommer and O Frishman, 'Translating Justice: The International Organization of Constitutional Courts' (2016) 38 *Law & Policy* 124, 129–30.

[196] ibid 131.

[197] E Benvenisti and GW Downs, 'National Courts, Domestic Democracy, and the Evolution of International Law' (2009) 20 *EJIL* 59, 65–68.

cooperative interactions are a key to transforming state organs into organs with triple identities and duties – not only those under national constitutions, but also those within the transnational communities of state organs and those under human rights treaties. Efforts by state organs to simultaneously fulfil their triple duties will contribute to the gradual permeation of the separation of powers in a globalised democratic society model into national legal systems and practices, and thus to harmonisation between human rights treaties and national laws (section 5.5.4).

5.5.1. Inter-State Organ Norms as Part of the Global Legal Universe under the Theory of Global Legal Pluralism

The theory of 'global legal pluralism' posits that:

> Formal international law is [only] a part of the interplay of normative orders, domestic and international, formal and informal, public and private. … Pluralists do not necessarily see international law as entirely deformalized – they can accept that international law emerges from a distinct social practice, characterized by convergence on common principles of law ascertainment and centred on a particular idea of the relevant actors, sources and processes. But from a pluralist perspective, this particular practice is not the only one in town – it exists alongside other practices that may be seen to equally constitute (legal) normativities, with different participants, different addressees or different forms and degrees of bindingness. Retaining formal international law as the sole focus of attention would mean losing sight of its place in the broader complex of post-national, or global law, in which different social practices may generate competing rules of recognition, or parallel (and often interlinked) sets of rules.[198]

Thus, global legal pluralism relativises the place of the state and state sovereignty in the concept of law and legal practice in the global sphere.

Certain legal pluralists have strived to re-define 'law' by focusing on sociological facts,[199] thus broadly including in the concept of 'law' normative orders that are institutionalised and perceived as authoritative in the society concerned.[200] If this approach was adopted, inter-state organ norms on human rights, most undoubtedly the Paris Principles, would be considered as law because they possess institutionalised mechanisms for interpretation, application and ensuring accountability, and are perceived as authoritative in the transnational community of the type of state organs.[201] However, this broad definition of law is not without problems. As Martti Koskenniemi critically observes, '[t]he wider

[198] N Krisch, 'Pluralism' in J d'Aspremont and S Singh (eds), *Concepts for International Law: Contributions to Disciplinary Thought* (Edward Elgar 2019) 691, 700–01.

[199] PS Berman, 'Can Global Legal Pluralism Be Both "Global" and "Pluralist"?' (2019) 29 *Duke Journal of Comparative & International Law* 381, 393.

[200] See, eg, BZ Tamanaha, *A General Jurisprudence of Law and Society* (Oxford University Press 2001) 166; H Lindahl, *Authority and the Globalisation of Inclusion and Exclusion* (Cambridge University Press 2018) 1.

[201] For this reason, the Paris Principles and treaties have often been treated in parallel, as have the SCA and treaty bodies. See Linos and Pegram (n 16) 1126.

the laws grasp, the weaker its normative force'.[202] The appropriate concept of 'law' depends on the specific purpose that one intends to achieve by defining this concept. While it may make no sense to characterise certain norms as law for the sake of applying them before an international court to examine states' rights and obligations, the same could be valid for other purposes. As Nico Krisch observes, 'what matters in practice is not the abstract qualification of a norm as "law", but its qualification as part of the "relevant" law or normative order – its "relative legality"'.[203] Thus, this book does not rely on global legal pluralism to abstractly label inter-state organ norms as 'law', and is satisfied with calling them 'norms'. It relies on global legal pluralism to grasp the complex reality of human rights legal practice in the global sphere in a more accurate manner and explore how – with what procedural and institutional means and by what principles – interactions between inter-state organ norms on human rights and human rights treaties are and should be governed.[204]

Under the classical approach, which tightly confines the concept of law to formal and public norms and privileges law thus defined over non-legal norms, scholars of international law have located human rights treaties at the centre of their research and marginalised the normative importance of other norms, including inter-state organ norms. However, in reality, inter-state organ norms on human rights and human rights treaties have established a cooperative relationship on an equal footing, and this relationship should be further strengthened to facilitate the permeation of the separation of powers in a globalised democratic society model at the domestic level and to promote the harmonisation between international and national laws on human rights, as will be shown below (see sections 5.5.3–5.5.4). The theoretical lens of global legal pluralism effectively enables international law scholars to examine and regulate the relationship from a legal perspective, and properly understand the normative basis of state organs' duties in a separation of powers in a globalised democratic society.

5.5.2. Shared Values in a 'Globalised Democratic Society' as the Basis of the Cooperative Relationship between Inter-State Organ Norms and Human Rights Treaties

Broadly categorised, there are two strands of global legal pluralism. One is the so-called 'constitutional legal pluralism', which assumes the existence of overarching values and principles that bring order among the norms.[205] The other

[202] See, eg, M Koskenniemi, 'The Fate of Public International Law: Between Technique and Politics' (2007) 70 *Modern Law Review* 1, 23.

[203] Krisch (n 198) 700.

[204] ibid 700–01.

[205] See, eg, M Kumm, 'The Cosmopolitan Turn in Constitutionalism: On the Relationship between Constitutionalism in and beyond the State' in JL Dunoff and JP Trachtman (eds), *Ruling the World: Constitutionalism, International Law, and Global Governance* (Cambridge University Press 2009) 258.

can be labelled 'radical pluralism', which denies the existence of overarching values and principles, and, instead, contends that the relationship between norms is ultimately determined by politics.[206] This chapter considers that the relationship between inter-state organ norms on human rights and human rights treaties is better understood, and should be further promoted, within the framework of constitutional legal pluralism, in that the two operate in harmony based on the shared values in globalised democratic societies. Such values include, in particular, human rights protection, democracy – participation, inclusion and deliberation – and subsidiarity.

These values, which are incorporated into human rights treaties in an interrelated manner under the theory of two-tiered bounded deliberative democracy (see Chapter 3, section 3.2.2), are also embedded in the inter-state organ norms on human rights. First, it is obvious that both the Paris Principles and inter-parliamentary norms on human rights are committed to protecting human rights.

Second, regarding the value of democracy, especially participation, inclusion and deliberation, the Preamble to the Paris Principles[207] expressly refers to 'the fundamental importance of the role of the national institutions in … promoting democracy [and] strengthening dialogue between the Government and civilian society'.[208] By requiring NHRIs to ensure pluralistic composition and openness to civil society,[209] thus reaching 'sections of the populations who are geographically, politically or socially remote' and 'engag[ing] with vulnerable groups',[210] and to advise parliament and other decision-making bodies on human rights issues,[211] the Paris Principles are committed to the realisation of better-informed and inclusive deliberation. Regarding inter-parliamentary norms on human rights, the importance of pluralism and wide consultation and close interaction with civil society and stakeholders is reiterated in the multiple documents already mentioned.[212]

Finally, the principle of subsidiarity is inherent in both the Paris Principles and inter-parliamentary norms on human rights, in that they are founded on the idea that human rights protection must be primarily achieved at the national level, considering the specific context and particularities of the society in question, before intervention from the international level. The GANHRI's SCA has emphasised the importance of reflecting the national concerns and human rights priorities of each country in the activities of NHRIs.[213] Similarly, the

[206] See, eg, N Krisch, *Beyond Constitutionalism: The Pluralist Structure of Postnational Law* (Oxford University Press 2010).

[207] Originally, the Paris Principles adopted in the 1991 Workshop were accompanied by a preamble containing 10 paragraphs. However, the preamble was not included in the subsequent resolutions of the UN Commission on Human Rights (Resolution 1992/54) and UN General Assembly (Resolution 48/134). For that reason, the preamble of the Paris Principles is not well known.

[208] Report of the 1991 International Workshop on NHRIs (n 35) 45.

[209] Paris Principles, ss B-1 and C (g).

[210] SCA's General Observations (n 46) s 1.5.

[211] Paris Principles, s A-3-(a).

[212] See, eg, Draft Principles on Parliaments and Human Rights (n 129) paras 4 and 9; IPU Assembly (n 114) para 3.

[213] SCA's General Observations (n 46) ss 1.4, 1.5, and 1.9.

above-mentioned resolution by the Inter-Parliamentary Conference in 1998 emphasised that 'international action in the field of human rights must be based on awareness of the political, economic and social realities of each society'.[214] The background report prepared for PACE Resolution 1823 expressly connects the principle of subsidiarity to the roles of national parliaments in protecting human rights at the national level.[215]

5.5.3. The Cooperative Relationship between Inter-State Organ Norms on Human Rights and Human Rights Treaties

Norms do not interact on their own; they interact via vectors. Thus, the cooperative relationship between inter-state organ norms on human rights and human rights treaties is realised through the interactions between inter-state organ organisations/bodies/networks, such as the GANHRI, the IPU and the PACE, and human rights treaty organs. Inter-state organ organisations/bodies/networks respect and promote human rights treaties when they interpret and apply inter-state organ norms on human rights, and treaty organs recognise the authority of and facilitate compliance with inter-state organ norms on human rights when interpreting and applying human rights treaties.

Currently, these cooperative interactions are not truly mutual and rather unbalanced. On the one hand, as has been examined in previous sections, inter-state organ norms on human rights frequently cite human rights treaties expressly, and inter-state organ organisations/bodies/networks rely on and endorse the recommendations and jurisprudence of human rights treaty organs. Reference in PACE Resolution 1823 to the ECHR and the ECtHR (see section 5.3.1.2) is an example. Also, the GANHRI's SCA has often recommended NHRIs to take measures to facilitate compliance with judgments of regional human rights courts.[216] On the other hand, human rights treaty organs do not frequently refer to inter-state organ norms on human rights. Nevertheless, in recent years, such mutual interactions have gradually developed between the Paris Principles and UN human rights treaties (section 5.5.3.1), and inter-parliamentary norms on human rights and UN human rights treaties, especially the Convention on the Elimination of All Forms of Discrimination against Women[217] (section 5.5.3.2). Human rights treaty organs should further facilitate cooperative relationships between inter-state organ norms on human rights and human rights treaties (section 5.5.3.3).

[214] Inter-Parliamentary Conference (n 112) preambular para 6.

[215] PACE's Committee on Legal Affairs and Human Rights, Mr. Christos Pourgourides (Rapporteur), 'National Parliaments: Guarantors of Human Rights in Europe' (2011) PACE Doc 12636, para 58.

[216] See, eg, SCA Report (May 2018) 29–30.

[217] Convention on the Elimination of All Forms of Discrimination against Women (adopted 18 December 1979, entered into force 3 September 1981) 1249 UNTS 13.

5.5.3.1. *The Cooperative Relationship between the Paris Principles and UN Human Rights Treaties*

The GANHRI's SCA often relies on UN human rights treaties and treaty bodies' recommendations when interpreting and applying the Paris Principles. For example, in the March 2015 Session, in the review of the National Commission on Human Rights and Freedoms of Cameroon (NCHRF), the SCA encouraged the NCHRF to consider the recommendations by the CEDAW and the CERD to expand its mandate as part of its duty under section A-2 of the Paris Principles.[218] This practice is facilitated by the procedural design of the accreditation system that requires the SCA to consider relevant treaty bodies' recommendations.[219]

The UN human rights treaty bodies also respect and promote the Paris Principles. First, UN human rights treaty bodies have constantly encouraged Member States to establish NHRIs or strengthen existing NHRIs in accordance with the Paris Principles.[220] Some have done so through their General Comments. The most prominent example is General Comment No 2 of the Committee on the Rights of the Child (CRC) in 2002, which stated that establishing Paris Principles-compliant NHRIs is part of the states parties' obligations to undertake all measures for the implementation of the Convention.[221] The HRC regularly spares a separate section for 'national human rights institutions' in its concluding observations and recommends that the state party establish NHRIs or improve existing ones in accordance with the Paris Principles and acquire accreditation by the GANHRI.[222] In some cases, the HRC has given more specific recommendations, such as on the budget of NHRIs,[223] the procedure for selection, appointment and removal from the office of members of NHRIs,[224] and the geographical coverage of the operations of NHRIs.[225] In making such recommendations, the Committee refers to relevant recommendations made by the GANHRI's SCA.[226]

Second, in recognising the autonomous status of NHRIs in UN human rights treaties, treaty bodies have highlighted the importance of compliance by NHRIs

[218] SCA Report (March 2015) 34.

[219] Rule 8.1 of the Rules of Procedure for the GANHRI SCA.

[220] See generally LC Reif, *Ombuds Institutions, Good Governance and the International Human Rights System*, 2nd edn (Brill 2020) 198–203.

[221] CRC, 'General Comment No 2: The Role of Independent National Human Rights Institutions in the Promotion and Protection of the Rights of the Child' (2002) UN Doc CRC/GC/2002/2 (2002) paras 1 and 4.

[222] See, eg, HRC, 'Concluding Observations on the Fourth Periodic Report of Czechia' (2019) UN Doc CCPR/C/CZE/CO/4, para 8.

[223] HRC, 'Concluding Observations on the Second Periodic Report of the Niger' (2019) UN Doc CCPR/C/NER/CO/2, para 8.

[224] HRC, 'Concluding Observations on the Fourth Periodic Report of Paraguay' (2019) UN Doc CCPR/C/PRY/CO/4, paras 10–11.

[225] HRC, 'Concluding Observations on the Second Periodic Report of Angola' (2019) UN Doc CCPR/C/AGO/CO/2, paras 9–10.

[226] See, eg, HRC, 'Concluding Observations on Nigeria in the Absence of its Second Periodic Report' (2019) UN Doc CCPR/C/NGA/CO/2, para 11.

with the Paris Principles and their accreditation by the GANHRI. The HRC adopted the 'Paper on the Relationship of the Human Rights Committee with National Human Rights Institutions' in 2012 in close consultation with NHRIs. This paper provides that 'by virtue of their mandates under the Paris Principles, national human rights institutions have an independent and distinct relationship with the Committee'.[227] It also states that 'the Committee provides ICC [today's GANHRI]-accredited national human rights institutions with opportunities to engage with it that are distinct from those of other actors' and that 'Paris Principles-compliant national human rights institutions can contribute to all stages of the reporting process under the Covenant'.[228] Some treaty bodies, such as the CEDAW and the CERD, offer only NHRIs accredited with A-status by the GANHRI an opportunity to present an opening statement during the examination of state reports.[229]

5.5.3.2. *The Cooperative Relationship between Inter-parliamentary Norms and UN Human Rights Treaties*

The most successful form of cooperation between inter-parliamentary norms on human rights and human rights treaties has been achieved through interactions between the IPU and the CEDAW.[230] In 1998, the Inter-Parliamentary Council adopted a decision to urge parliamentarians to ensure that their states submit reports to the CEDAW and that the reports are detailed, complete and comply with the standards laid down by the CEDAW.[231] Since then, the IPU has promoted parliamentary engagement in CEDAW activities. It regularly holds seminars to support parliamentarians and parliamentary staffs whose states are scheduled for review by the CEDAW in the coming year to better understand the obligations under the Convention on the Elimination of All Forms of Discrimination Against Women and the CEDAW's activities, as well as the parliaments' roles in implementing the Convention and cooperating with the CEDAW.[232] These seminars are also attended by CEDAW members and other stakeholders.[233] After the

[227] HRC, 'Paper on the Relationship of the Human Rights Committee with National Human Rights Institutions' (2012) UN Doc CCPR/C/106/3, para 7.

[228] ibid paras 7–8.

[229] CEDAW, 'Paper on the Cooperation between the Committee on the Elimination of Discrimination against Women and National Human Rights Institutions' (2019) para 26; CERD, 'Guidelines on the Cooperation of the Committee with National Human Rights Institutions' (2012) UN Doc CERD/C/505, paras 7 and 17.

[230] Report of the UN Secretary-General, 'Interaction between the United Nations, National Parliaments and the Inter-Parliamentary Union' (2012) UN Doc A/66/770, paras 23–24.

[231] Inter-Parliamentary Council, 'Co-operation with the United Nations System: Parliamentary Action for National Follow-up to International Agreements and Treaties Regarding Women' (11 April 1998) Decision No 1, para 1.

[232] See, eg, IPU, 'Concept Note and Provisional Programme for the December 2023 Webinar on Parliamentary Engagement on CEDAW' (14 December 2023).

[233] IPU and UN, *The Convention on the Elimination of All Forms of Discrimination against Women and its Optional Protocol: Handbook for Parliamentarians*, 2nd edn (2023) 164.

CEDAW's review of state reports, the IPU sends follow-up letters to the parliaments to encourage parliamentary debate on the concluding observations.[234]

For its part, the CEDAW has appointed a focal point for the IPU among its members and has closely liaised with it.[235] In 2008, the CEDAW began to include a paragraph on the role of parliament in most concluding observations, which generally reads as follows:

> [T]he Committee ... invites the State party to encourage its national parliament ... to take the necessary steps with regard to the implementation of these concluding observations and the Government's next reporting process under the Convention.[236]

The CEDAW established a working group on the role of parliaments in 2009[237] and adopted the 'Statement on the Relationship of the Committee on the Elimination of Discrimination against Women with Parliamentarians' in 2010.[238] The Statement recognises the important roles of the IPU in promoting the implementation of the Convention among parliamentarians and in providing country-specific information and data on parliaments regarding the states whose reports are under consideration, and cites the practical guide published by the IPU.[239] The Statement recommends that national parliaments be informed of the Committee's work, their members be included in the delegation for the examination of state reports, and parliaments exercise their various functions to implement the Convention.[240] Motivated by these CEDAW initiatives, many national parliaments have become involved in the CEDAW's reporting procedure. For example, Japanese MP Ms Nono served as the head of the delegation in the consideration of Japan's report and made statements concerning her experiences of working for women's rights in the parliament.[241] In the resulting concluding observation, the CEDAW 'commend[ed]' Japan that its delegation was headed by a parliamentarian.[242]

Although in a much less institutionalised and ad hoc form, the IPU and the HRC also interact in a cooperative manner. For instance, in 2010, the IPU held a parliamentary seminar on the implementation of the ICCPR and the ICESCR,

[234] ibid.

[235] IPU and UN, *The Convention on the Elimination of All Forms of Discrimination against Women and its Optional Protocol Handbook for Parliamentarians*, 1st edn (2003) 26.

[236] See, eg, CEDAW, 'Concluding Observations on the Sixth Periodic Report of Japan' (2009) UN Doc CEDAW/C/JPN/CO/6, para 14.

[237] CEDAW Report on its 42nd and 43rd Sessions (2009) UN Doc A/64/38, 10.

[238] CEDAW, 'Statement on the Relationship of the Committee on the Elimination of Discrimination against Women with Parliamentarians' (2010) reproduced in CEDAW Report on its 45th Session (2010) UN Doc A/65/38(SUPP) Annex VI.

[239] ibid para 9.

[240] ibid paras 4–6, 11 and 18.

[241] Statement by Chieko Nohno (Member, House of Councillors) on the Occasion of the Consideration of Japan's sixth Periodic Report (23 July 2009), www.gender.go.jp/international/int_kaigi/int_teppai/pdf/statement_e.pdf.

[242] CEDAW (n 236) para 3.

and cooperation with the HRC and the Committee on Economic, Social and Cultural Rights, with members of these treaty bodies.[243]

5.5.3.3. *Proposals for Further Facilitation of Cooperation*

Cooperation between inter-state organ norms on human rights and human rights treaties should be further facilitated, as this would help promote the permeation of the separation of powers in a globalised democratic society model at the domestic level and foster greater harmonisation between international and national laws on human rights, as shown below (see section 5.5.4). In addition, human rights treaty organs increasingly set out duties for each type of state organs, alongside the relativisation of the boundary between international and national laws (see Chapters 2 and 4). Nevertheless, they do not have the expertise to elaborate on the concrete duties for each type of state organ, given the diversity and complexities of state organ structures and of the distinctive realities they face worldwide. Nor do they possess accountability mechanisms of their own to hold individual state organs accountable for fulfilling their duties. Inter-state organ organisations/bodies/networks are better placed to perform these tasks. Thus, human rights treaty organs should outsource these tasks to such organisations/bodies/networks and endorse their authority in creating, interpreting, applying and developing inter-state organ norms on human rights, and in ensuring accountability.

The most effective way to commit treaty organs to such cooperation would be to insert express reference to the Paris Principles and inter-parliamentary norms on human rights into newly adopted human rights treaties or amendments to existing human rights treaties. The 2002 Optional Protocol to the Convention against Torture and Other Cruel, Inhuman or Degrading Treatment or Punishment (Article 18(4))[244] and the 2006 Convention on the Rights of Persons with Disabilities (Article 33(2)) oblige states parties to 'give due consideration to' and 'take into account' the Paris Principles when designating or establishing 'national preventive mechanisms' and 'a framework, including … independent mechanisms, to promote, protect and monitor implementation of [the Convention]' (national monitoring mechanisms), respectively.[245]

However, even in the absence of such express references, human rights treaty organs should rely on the Paris Principles and inter-parliamentary norms on

[243] *Seminar on Implementing the International Covenant on Civil and Political Rights and the International Covenant on Economic, Social and Cultural Rights: What Part for Parliaments?* (organised by the IPU and the OHCHR) (Geneva, 7 October 2010), http://archive.ipu.org/splz-e/hr10.htm.

[244] Optional Protocol to the Convention against Torture and Other Cruel, Inhuman or Degrading Treatment or Punishment (adopted 18 December 2002, entered into force 22 June 2006) 2375 UNTS 237.

[245] The concepts of 'national preventive mechanisms' and 'national monitoring mechanisms' are distinct from NHRIs; however, in practice, many NHRIs also serve as such mechanisms.

human rights when reviewing and interacting with NHRIs and national parliaments, respectively. For example, when receiving amicus curiae/third-party submissions from NHRIs, treaty organs should distinguish between NHRIs that fully comply with the Paris Principles (ie, A-status NHRIs) and those that do not. Treaty organs should consider giving the former privileges both procedurally and substantially by, for instance, increasing the word limit of their submissions, giving them the right to oral intervention and giving greater weight to their information and views. Regarding inter-parliamentary norms, as the ECtHR has established the quality of parliamentary deliberation as an important factor for deference (see Chapter 4, section.4.1.1.2), it should consider relying on PACE Resolution 1823 with its Basic Principles for Parliamentary Supervision of International Human Rights Standards when examining this factor. Similarly, when the HRC makes recommendations regarding the quality of parliamentary scrutiny in its concluding observations, or reviews the quality of parliamentary deliberations in its individual communication procedure albeit in limited circumstances (see Chapter 4, section 4.1.3.2), it should consider relying on inter-parliamentary norms on human rights, especially the Draft Principles on Parliaments and Human Rights.

5.5.4. Towards the 'Triple Identity' of State Organs

Lastly, this chapter proposes the original 'triple identity' theory. This theory builds on transgovernmental networking theory, which was developed mainly by international relations scholars. As early as 1974, Robert O Keohane and Joseph S Nye argued that sub-units of different governments build 'transgovernmental coalitions' to pursue common interests, influencing their own governments.[246] Slaughter observed that although state organs interacting with their foreign counterparts 'still represent distinct national or state interests', 'they also recognize common professional identities and substantive experience as judges, regulators, ministers, and legislators'.[247] She argued that transgovernmental networks can play self-regulating functions through the process of socialisation, inducing and compelling their members to behave in accordance with 'network norms', even in resistance against pressures from their national executive branches.[248] Andrea Hamann and Hélène Ruiz Fabri posited that participation in transgovernmental networks help their participants acquire 'a dual loyalty – both to their national constituents as well as to their commitments in respect of solving border-transcending problems', which may cause

[246] RO Keohane and JS Nye, 'Transgovernmental Relations and International Organizations' (1974) 27 *World Politics* 39, 44, and 46–50.
[247] AM Slaughter, *A New World Order* (Princeton University Press 2005) 18.
[248] ibid 195–96.

'an erosion of state consent'.[249] The concept of 'double mandate' introduced in PACE Resolution 1823 seems to reflect these theories. It emphasises that PACE members are under a particular duty to contribute to the effective implementation of international human rights norms with their 'double mandate' – as members of the Assembly and of their respective national parliaments.[250]

By further advancing and refining these observations through distinguishing between the national, transnational (inter-state organ) and international planes, this book proposes the triple identity theory. This theory consists of the following three steps. First, the development of inter-state organ organisations/bodies/networks such as the GANHRI, the PACE and the IPU fosters the dual identity of their members – identity as a state organ and as a member of the transnational community of state organs – leading these state organs to accept inter-state organ norms that are created, interpreted and applied by these organisations/bodies/networks, and whose compliance is promoted within them. Second, owing to their acceptance of inter-state organ norms on human rights, cooperative interactions between these norms and human rights treaties make state organs become involved in and aware of the activities of human rights treaty organs. This leads to the gradual emergence of the triple identities of state organs – an identity as a state organ, an identity as a member of the transnational community of state organs and an identity as an organ serving human rights treaties. Finally, based on these triple identities, state organs make efforts to simultaneously achieve their triple duties – those under national constitutions and laws, those under inter-state organ norms on human rights and those under human rights treaties – albeit with different levels of motivation and dedication. This contributes to the gradual permeation of the separation of powers in a globalised democratic society model into national legal orders, and to the harmonisation between international and national laws on human rights.

To assess the practical value of this theory, comprehensive empirical studies are necessary to explore whether, to what extent and under what specific conditions the theory effectively functions; these explorations are left for future studies. Nevertheless, practices that support the theory are readily observable, not only in relation to NHRIs, whose identities are tightly anchored in transnational and international recognition owing to their unique origin (see section 5.2.3), but also in relation to parliamentarians whose identities were originally hardly transnational or international. For example, at the European level, given PACE Resolution 1516 (2006) and subsequent resolutions, a Romanian PACE member Pantiru Tudor took initiatives to successfully establish the Subcommittee for Monitoring the Enforcement of Judgments of the European Court of Human

[249] A Hamann and H Ruiz Fabri, 'Transnational Networks and Constitutionalism' (2008) 6 *I-CON* 481, 489–90.

[250] PACE Res 1823 (n 141) para 3.

Rights.[251] A Ukrainian PACE member Serhiy Holovaty, who had served as the Chairman of the Committee on Legal Affairs and Human Rights and Vice President of the PACE, submitted a proposal for a legislative amendment to improve parliamentary control over the implementation of ECtHR judgments.[252] Dick Marty, a Swiss PACE member, tabled a motion concerning anti-terrorism sanctions and human rights[253] based on his experience as a member of the PACE Committee on Legal Affairs and Human Rights.[254]

At the universal level, presumably given the interactions between the IPU and UN human rights treaty bodies, the Parliament of Finland began sending members of the Parliamentary Constitutional Committee for the CEDAW's consideration of the state report for Finland. In the CEDAW's consideration of Finland's report in 2008, MP Ms Nauclér explained to the CEDAW the parliamentary efforts for women's rights,[255] and expressed a commitment that she would 'report to Parliament on the proceedings of the Committee and would be attentive to follow-up'.[256] The Public Consultation Committee of the upper house of the Parliament of Ireland (Seanad) submitted a report to the HRC in 2014, independent of the state report, as 'part of its ongoing work to participate in parliamentary oversight of Ireland's constitutional, European and international human rights obligations'.[257] In drafting the submission, the Public Consultation Committee held a series of consultations and webcast public hearings considering the HRC's List of Issues.[258] The report not only contained information that supported the government's position, but also critically noted the deficiencies, underdiscussed problems and tasks for further improvements. Additionally, the National Assembly of the Republic of Korea adopted the Framework Act on General Equality in 2014, which stipulated that the government's reports to the CEDAW must first be submitted to the National Assembly.[259] It also created

[251] 'Subcomisia pentru monitorizarea executarii hotararilor Curtii Europene a Drepurilor Omului' *Parliament of Romania*, http://www.cdep.ro/pls/parlam/structura.co?leg=2008&idl=3&idc=111.

[252] Draft Law No 9489 'On Parliamentary Scrutiny of the Implementation of Decisions of the European Court of Human Rights' (22 November 2011) (Ukraine), http://w1.c1.rada.gov.ua/pls/zweb2/webproc4_1?id=&pf3511=41858. In the interview with Donald and Leach, Holovaty recalled that the motivation for such a proposal was not to lose the delegation's credentials at the Parliamentary Assembly. See A Donald and P Leach, *Parliaments and the European Court of Human Rights* (Oxford University Press 2016) 180.

[253] Marty Dick, Motion 09.3719 déposée au Conseil des Etats, 'Les fondements de notre ordre juridique court-circuités par l'ONU' (12 June 2009) (Switzerland).

[254] See, eg, PACE's Committee on Legal Affairs and Human Rights, Mr. Dick Marty (Rapporteur), 'United Nations Security Council and European Union Blacklists' (2007) PACE Doc 11454.

[255] CEDAW, 41st Session, 841st mtg (9 July 2008) UN Doc CEDAW/C/SR.841, paras 32–34.

[256] ibid para 66.

[257] Seanad Public Consultation Committee, 'Report on Ireland's Compliance with the International Covenant on Civil and Political Rights with Observations and Recommendations to the United Nations Human Rights Committee and to the Irish Government' (2014) para 4.

[258] ibid paras 5.1–5.2 and 7.

[259] 'Emerging Good National Parliamentary Practices and List of Recommendations for Action' *Seminar: Parliamentary Engagement on Human Rights: Identifying Good Practices and New Opportunities for Action* (organised by the IPU with the OHCHR) (Geneva, 24–26 June 2019) 1.

a sub-committee within its Gender Equality Committee to monitor the implementation of the Convention on the Elimination of All Forms of Discrimination against Women.[260]

5.6. CONCLUSION

This chapter has addressed questions posed regarding the nature of state organs' 'duties' under the separation of powers in a globalised democratic society model, and the status of state organs in human rights treaties. It argued that state organs' duties are not equivalent to states' international law obligations, and thus that state organs are not subjects of international law, at least not in the same way as states. Instead, state organs possess or are in the process of acquiring an autonomous status in human rights treaties that is distinct from that of states. This chapter introduced the original concept of 'inter-state organ norms' – autonomous normative orders of, by and for individual state organs and not states (section 5.1), and showed that such norms are emerging for NHRIs (section 5.2), parliaments (section 5.3) and national courts (5.4), respectively, albeit to varying degrees and in varying modes. The autonomous status of state organs and their 'duties' are anchored in the cooperative interactions between inter-state organ norms on human rights and human rights treaties under global legal pluralism (sections 5.5.1–5.5.3). Such cooperative interactions lead state organs to gradually acquire triple identities and duties – not only identities and duties under their respective national laws but also under inter-state organ norms and human rights treaties (section 5.5.4).

In Chapter 3, this book built the separation of powers in a globalised democratic society model based on widely shared principles in national constitutional laws so that the model could be acceptable not only in the eyes of human rights treaties but also in the eyes of national laws. Nevertheless, Chapter 4 only demonstrated that the model is embraced by human rights treaty organs and left the question of 'whether' and 'how' the model will be accepted by national legal orders. This chapter has answered the question of 'how' by showing a possible path for the model to be accepted into national legal systems and practices: the development of inter-state organ norms on human rights and the cooperative interactions between them and human rights treaties under the shared values of globalised democratic societies provide state organs with triple identities and duties. Efforts by state organs to fulfil these duties simultaneously will contribute to the gradual permeation of the separation of powers in a globalised democratic society model into national legal systems and practices. Answering the question of 'whether' and to what extent the model will be accepted by national legal orders remains an issue for future research.

[260] ibid 2.

6

Conclusion

TRADITIONAL INTERNATIONAL LAW has viewed 'states' as unitary and monolithic entities, considering them the sole units of legal observation and regulation. However, the increasing phenomena of 'disaggregation of a state' in the human rights law field, where human rights treaty organs foster a direct relationship with various state organs beyond the executive that has traditionally represented the state on the international plane, casts doubt on the validity of this traditional paradigm from a descriptive perspective. The traditional paradigm is also challenged from a normative perspective, especially in terms of aspirations to enhance the effectiveness and democratic legitimacy of human rights treaty systems. Nevertheless, international law scholarship has not been able to present a new paradigm in a comprehensive manner. Against this background, this book established an original 'separation of powers in a globalised democratic society' model as a candidate for a new paradigm (section 6.1). This model supplements, rather than supplants, the traditional paradigm, making both theoretical and practical contributions to international law scholarship (section 6.2). Although the model is not free from criticism and requires further research (section 6.3), it can serve as a foundation for open discussions and constructive academic engagement on how to establish a new, comprehensive paradigm for understanding and guiding recent human rights law practices, where both actors and norms are pluralised beyond a unitary and monolithic 'state' and international law as norms of, by and for 'states'.

6.1. THE MAIN ARGUMENT OF THE SEPARATION OF POWERS IN A GLOBALISED DEMOCRATIC SOCIETY MODEL

The main argument of the separation of powers in a globalised democratic society model can be summarised as follows.

Given the growing intrusion of human rights treaties and treaty organs into national legal orders, the boundary between international and national sources of legitimacy is becoming increasingly blurred in the human rights law field. Today, we live in 'globalised democratic societies', where democracy is exercised primarily within each national society, but such societies are heavily affected by human rights treaty standards and have become spaces where treaty organs and state organs – national courts, parliaments, administrative organs and NHRIs – closely intersect, regardless of their formal origins.

Therefore, we must seek a new legitimacy standard for globalised democratic societies, one that integrates international and national standards of legitimacy, drawing on the intellectual heritage of national constitutional law scholarship. This book thus relies on the framework of the separation of powers, a widely shared fundamental principle in constitutional democracies across the globe. It posits that authorities and duties are allocated to treaty organs and each type of state organ in accordance with their particular legitimacy assets by virtue of their composition, capacity, decision-making process and function, in light of the 'two-tiered bounded deliberative democracy' theory that guides and embodies globalised democratic societies.

The two-tiered bounded deliberative democracy theory asserts that decisions and measures affecting human rights should be made through deliberation, which should primarily take place within each national society. However, deliberations at the national level should be guided and limited by 'bounds' that have been established through long-term and mature deliberations at the international level. The interplay between the two tiers of deliberation – national and international levels – creates a circular process: the 'bounds' produced through international deliberations set the frameworks and limits for national deliberations, while the outcomes of deliberations within individual national societies contribute to creating new 'bounds' or to modifying the existing ones at the international level.

In globalised democratic societies, each type of state organ bears a duty to take part in national 'bounded' deliberations in their respective ways. National parliaments should be assigned with the primary responsibility for deliberating on matters of general public policy involving human rights where there are 'reasonable disagreements'. In making decisions, they have a duty to ensure the effective representation and inclusive participation of all sectors of society and conduct 'bounded' deliberations. National courts should be assigned the primary responsibility to adjudicate one-off and bilateral disputes between parties while also serving as guardians against the tyranny of the majority. They have the duty not only to ensure independence and fairness in their composition and procedures, but also to engage in 'bounded' deliberations across all three phases: pre-decisional, decisional and post-decisional. Administrative organs should be accorded the primary authority to address technical and complex matters in the application and implementation of parliamentary legislation to individual cases. When making such decisions, they have the duty to conduct thorough investigations and assessments of the technical aspects involved, and engage in 'bounded' deliberations by exercising their statutory discretion through dialogue with affected individuals. NHRIs should retain compositions and procedures that are independent of the government while ensuring pluralism and openness to civil society, and implement two duties: first, enrich national deliberations and ensure they are 'bounded' by bringing inclusive perspectives, including those of minorities and marginalised groups, and information on relevant international human rights law into national deliberations in parliaments, courts and other governmental bodies; and, second, actively provide inputs regarding the broader background and national contexts of the issues at hand to treaty organs, enabling them to assess national deliberations and to supplement those deliberations when necessary.

On their part, human rights treaty organs should exercise the following three duties: first, protect the basic preconditions for the proper functioning of deliberation by adopting protective standards for those rights that directly relate to deliberations; second, respect the outcome of national deliberations as far as the deliberative process works properly, but if a national deliberative process has deficiencies, fill the gaps by conducting intrusive examinations on the substance of the decisions arrived at; and, third, set 'bounds' on national deliberations through the outcomes of long-term and mature deliberations at the international level. The relationship between human rights treaty organs and each type of state organ is regulated based on the principles of 'subsidiarity' and 'principled and continuous dialogue'.

The 'duties' of state organs described above are grounded in the cooperative interactions between 'inter-state organ norms' – an autonomous normative order of, by and for individual state organs and not states – and human rights treaties under global legal pluralism. Such cooperative interactions are guided and promoted by the shared values in globalised democratic societies.

The cooperative interactions between inter-state organ norms and human rights treaties can help transform state organs into organs with triple identities and duties – not only those under national constitutions, but also those within the transnational communities of state organs and those under human rights treaties. As state organs strive to fulfil their triple duties simultaneously, they will facilitate the gradual integration of the separation of powers in a globalised democratic society model into national legal systems and practices, thus promoting harmony between human rights treaties and national laws.

6.2. THEORETICAL AND PRACTICAL CONTRIBUTIONS OF THE SEPARATION OF POWERS IN A GLOBALISED DEMOCRATIC SOCIETY MODEL

The separation of powers in a globalised democratic society model offers three key contributions to theory and practice. First, although the human rights law community has long strived to promote the effectiveness and the democratic legitimacy of human rights treaty systems, these two aims are not easily reconcilable, as effectiveness requires greater intrusion on domestic legal orders, whereas democratic legitimacy demands respect for national decisions (see Chapter 1, section 1.2). This book posits that the duality inherent in subsidiarity, one of the principles regulating the relationship between human rights treaty organs and state organs in the separation of powers in a globalised democratic society, is a key factor in harmonising the effectiveness and democratic legitimacy of human rights treaty systems. On the one hand, the treaty organs' intrusive approach to malfunctioning national decision-making processes, where the state organs fail to fulfil the above-stated duties concerning bounded deliberation, contributes to ensuring effectiveness. On the other hand, their deferential approach towards well-functioning national decision-making processes, where state organs properly fulfil their duties concerning bounded deliberation, promotes democratic legitimacy within the meaning of the two-tiered bounded deliberative democracy. These two approaches of the treaty organs can be harmoniously understood as they represent two sides of the same coin, embodying positive and negative subsidiarity, respectively.

Second, the separation of powers in a globalised democratic society model offers a new paradigm supplementing the traditional paradigm of international law, which is based on the conception of 'states' as unitary and monolithic entities. Indeed, given the blurring of the boundaries between international, transnational and national laws, and between legally binding and non-binding norms, there have been many attempts to restructure the global legal system, involving proposals such as 'global administrative law, 'global constitutionalism/constitutionalisation of international law', 'informal international law-making' and 'global legal pluralism' (see Chapter 1, section 1.2). While sharing with these theories the ambition to restructure the global legal system, the separation of powers in a globalised democratic society model focuses on a narrower and more concrete set of phenomena, actors and fields than these theories; specifically, the disaggregation of the state into its component organs – national courts, parliaments, administrative organs and NHRIs – in human rights law practice. Thus, it succeeds in developing a denser content. Embodied by the two-tiered bounded deliberative democracy theory, the separation of powers in a globalised democratic society model provides concrete duties for each type of state organs and treaty organs, as well as the principles governing the relationship between them in concrete situations. These duties and principles allow for descriptive observation and normative regulation of the various phenomena involved in disaggregation of a state in a holistic and systemic manner, rather than in the more typically fragmented manner of previous efforts.

Third, the model builds on long-standing theoretical debates on the relationship between international and national laws from a new angle, by considering the relationship between actors instead of legal orders as such. This shift in focus is important because laws only produce effect through the actors who interpret and apply them. Previous studies on the relationship between international and national laws generally assumed that international law is interpreted and applied by international judiciary and national laws are interpreted and applied by the respective national courts (see Chapter 1, section 1.1.1). The presented model challenges this assumption and proposes the concept of 'globalised democratic societies' where human rights treaty organs and state organs – not only national courts but also parliaments, administrative organs and NHRIs – closely interact, and concurrently interpret and apply human rights treaties and national laws. By setting out duties for each of these types of state organs and treaty organs and the principles governing their relationship, this model systemically regulates the relationship between international and national laws in the field of human rights, shifting focus from abstract legal orders to concrete actor-centric relationships. In addition, even from the perspective of legal orders, the model introduces a new dimension to the binary structure of international versus national laws by offering the concept of 'inter-state organ norms'. Relying on global legal pluralism, it posits that cooperative interactions between inter-state organ norms and human rights treaties through the activities and jurisprudence of inter-state organ organisations/bodies/networks and human rights treaty organs will contribute to the eventual harmonisation of human rights treaties and national laws by cultivating a 'triple identity' for state organs and their members.

6.3. QUESTIONS AND TASKS FOR FUTURE STUDIES

In addition to the specific questions and tasks highlighted in each chapter, certain broader questions and tasks also remain for future studies. First, one of the most important aspects of the separation of powers in a globalised democratic society model that this book could not fully explore is that, as much as treaty organs scrutinise the decision-making processes of each state organ, state organs should also scrutinise whether treaty organs have properly fulfilled their duties, in the form of principled and continuous dialogue. Future research should explore the avenues through which state organs can exercise such scrutiny, integrating this aspect into the model.

Second, this book has focused on the commonalities among the three human rights treaty systems to construct a single, universal model that applies to them all, and it has considered their differences only when analysing the practices of the treaty organs. However, future studies could examine whether a single, universal model is desirable, or whether different treaty systems require different models, considering the particularities of each treaty system and the national societies included under it. Such an examination may lead to enrichment or modification of the separation of powers in a globalised democratic society model concerning respective human rights treaties.

Third, this book has proposed specific duties for each type of state organs in a uniform manner, focusing on common elements concerning compositions, mandates and functions of the organ across the globe, and without fully considering their varieties. Future studies should explore whether and how the diversity of national systems, including differences between parliamentary or presidential systems, single-chamber or bicameral systems, monist or dualist systems, and different modes of judicial review (for example, having a constitutional court or not), affect the design and operation of the separation of powers in a globalised democratic society model. Moreover, future studies should examine how the model applies to cases in which states lack NHRIs or parliaments established through elections.

Finally, this book has only applied the separation of powers in a globalised democratic society model to the phase of interpretation and application of human rights treaties. Its applicability to other phases of the life cycle of human rights treaties, such as the conclusion of, reservation to and withdrawal from these treaties, remains uncertain. Interestingly, in its advisory opinion OC-26/20 in 2020, the IACtHR held that while Member States have the right of denunciation under Article 78 ACHR, the decision-making process leading to the denunciation of a human rights treaty should fulfil the 'minimum level of democratic quality' including respect for human rights, rule of law, free and fair elections, pluralistic system of political parties and organisations, and separation of powers,[1] and should 'be subject to a pluralistic, public and transparent debate within the States'.[2] Future studies should investigate whether national bounded deliberations are – and should be – required not only in the interpretation and application of human rights treaties but also in their ratification, reservation or denunciation, and how such a requirement could intersect with general international law concerning these matters. In the same vein, the implications of the separation of powers in a globalised democratic society model for the broader institutional and procedural design of human rights treaty organs – including their composition (for example, whether to allow judges of nationality and judges ad hoc) and the modes of election of their judges and members – merit further examination.

[1] *Denunciation of the American Convention on Human Rights and the Charter of the Organization of American States and the Consequences for State Human Rights Obligations*, IACtHR, Series A No 26, Advisory Opinion OC-26/20 (9 November 2020) para 73 (fn 110).

[2] ibid para 64.

Index

www.ingramcontent.com/pod-product-compliance
Ingram Content Group UK Ltd.
Pitfield, Milton Keynes, MK11 3LW, UK
UKHW020801290926
15470UKWH00003B/885

9 781509 984077